1 MONTH OF
FREE
READING

at

www.ForgottenBooks.com

By purchasing this book you are eligible for one month membership to ForgottenBooks.com, giving you unlimited access to our entire collection of over 700,000 titles via our web site and mobile apps.

To claim your free month visit:
www.forgottenbooks.com/free791391

ISBN 978-0-483-60885-6
PIBN 10791391

JOURNAL

OF THE

MASSACHUSETTS ASSOCIATION OF BOARDS OF HEALTH.

THE OFFICIAL JOURNAL OF THE PUBLIC HYGIENISTS OF THE STATE.

SAMUEL H. DURGIN, M. D., - - *Editor.*

CONTENTS:

BOSTON:

THE MASSACHUSETTS ASSOCIATION OF BOARDS OF HEALTH.

VOLUME XIII.   OCTOBER, 1903.   NUMBER 3.

JOURNAL OF THE

MASSACHUSETTS ASSOCIATION OF BOARDS OF HEALTH.

ORGANIZED 1890.

[The Association as a body is not responsible for statements or opinions of any of its members.]

| VOL. XIII. | April, 1903. | No. 1. |

JANUARY QUARTERLY (AND ANNUAL) MEETING

OF THE

Massachusetts Association of Boards of Health.

The quarterly (and annual) meeting of the Massachusetts Association of Boards of Health was held at the Brunswick Hotel, Boston, on Thursday, January 29. Dinner was served at 1 P.M.; and after dinner a business meeting was held under the presidency of Dr. H. P. Walcott, officers for the ensuing year were elected, and papers were read and discussed.

On motion of Dr. Hill the reading of the records of the October meeting was dispensed with.

Mr. E. L. Pilsbury, of Boston, Dr. L. M. Palmer, of South Framingham, and Dr. J. Arthur Gage, of Lowell, were appointed a committee to nominate officers for the coming year.

Members of the Association were elected as follows, upon the recommendation of the Executive Committee: —

FRANK E. WINSLOW, of Chelsea.
CHARLES M. HARGRAVES, of Framingham.
Dr. VICTOR A. REED, of Lawrence.
Dr. JOHN W. PRATT, of Dedham.
ALLEN F. CARPENTER, of Somerville.
EDMUND S. SPARROW, of Somerville.
Dr. A. A. MacKEEN, of Whitman.
GEORGE J. HEBERT, of Palmer. (P. O. Address Three Rivers, Mass.)

Dr. James B. Field, of Lowell, presented his report as Treasurer. It was as follows: —

TREASURER'S REPORT FOR 1902.

Receipts.

Balance from 1901		$1,202.82
Interest on deposits, 2 years	$65.25	
Assessments for 1898, 1899, 1900	4.50	
Assessments for 1901	21.00	
Assessments for 1902	315.00	
Assessments for 1903	10.63	
Total receipts		416.38
		$1,619.20

Expenses.

Printing . . . . , . .	$28.25	
Postage	38.50	
Cigars and dinners for guests	34.25	
Clerical assistance	9.25	
Treasurer's bond	4.00	
Travelling expenses of speaker	20.00	
Plates and typewriting for Diphtheria Committee . . .	44.50	
Purchase of 2,000 old *Journals*	8.00	
Report of meetings	116.30	
Publishing *Journal*	393.90	
Total expenses		$696.95
Balance to 1903		922.25
		$1,619.20

Respectfully submitted,

JAMES B. FIELD,
Treasurer.

Examined and approved as correctly cast and properly vouched for.

J. ARTHUR GAGE,
Auditor.

DR. FIELD.— You will see by this report that the expenses in 1902 were $280 in excess of the receipts. This was due to the fact that the Association was obliged to publish its own journal. Even with an increase of the annual dues to $2, assuming that the membership held the same, there will be a deficiency of $240 next year, unless our Publication Committee is enabled to make some arrangement for publishing the *Journal*. This, I am assured, the Publication Committee is trying earnestly to do.

The report was received, and placed on file.

Dr. Durgin.— Notice was given at the last meeting that a motion would be made at this meeting, in accordance with the By-laws, for an increase of the dues from $1.50 to $2. This becomes necessary principally because we must aid in the publication of the *Journal.* You have seen proof of that from the reading of the Treasurer's Report. I now make this motion that the dues be increased from $1.50 to $2.

The motion was seconded and adopted.

Dr. Durgin.— It might be interesting to say, in connection with this rise in the dues, that, when the Association began eleven years ago, the dues were made $3. They were then gradually reduced until they got down to $1.50. This was made possible by a favorable contract which had been made for the publishing of the *Journal.* The publishers failed up, and threw the *Journal* upon the hands of the committee. The Publishing Committee has done the best it could in getting the work out without using up the treasury too badly. Unfortunately, there have been some of the most expensive numbers published since this failure of the publishers. We expect to make another contract very soon.

The President.— Mr. Pilsbury, is your committee prepared to report?

Mr. Pilsbury.— Mr. President, the committee recommends that the Association elect the board of officers as now constituted, with the exception of one member of the Executive Committee, W. H. Chapin, of Springfield, who is not now a member of the Association. The committee offers in lieu of Dr. Chapin the name of Dr. Herbert C. Emerson. Otherwise, the list will be as it has been during the past year. To save time, the committee will not read the list. I move that the Secretary be delegated to deposit one ballot as representing the sentiment of the Association for the list presented.

The motion was adopted, and the Secretary cast the ballot.

The President.— The Secretary reports that he has cast the ballot that he was authorized to cast, and that the gentlemen named by your Nominating Committee have been duly elected officers of this

Association for the ensuing year.   For my own part in it, gentlemen, I thank you most heartily.

The regular business of the afternoon is, first, a paper on " The Outbreak of Foot-and-mouth Disease in New England," by Dr. D. E. Salmon, of Washington, D.C.   I now have the pleasure of introducing Dr. Salmon.

THE PRESENT OUTBREAK OF FOOT–AND–MOUTH DISEASE IN THE NEW ENGLAND STATES.

BY D. E. SALMON, D.V.M., CHIEF OF THE UNITED STATES BUREAU OF ANIMAL INDUSTRY.

Mr. President, Ladies and Gentlemen,— I must confess that it was with some hesitation that I accepted the invitation to present a paper to this distinguished body.   I did think before I came up here to try to control this outbreak of disease that I knew something about foot-and-mouth disease ; but it has been impressed upon me during the past few weeks that I ought to speak with considerable humility in regard to a subject of this kind.   However, I trust to your consideration as medical men and sanitarians to overlook any deficiencies which may appear in my brief paper.

The unexpected outbreak of foot-and-mouth disease which began in this State about August of last year, and extended to the States of New Hampshire, Vermont, and Rhode Island, has awakened especial interest in this disease, its nature, characteristics, and effects.   This is my reason for consenting to read a short paper before this meeting upon a subject which, at first sight, might appear to be somewhat foreign to its work and purposes.

Foot-and-mouth disease, or epizoötic aphtha, has been known to the veterinarians and agriculturists of Europe since the time when, with advancing medical knowledge, it was possible to discriminate between the different plagues of animals.   It has been more or less constantly present in the countries of Europe, particularly those of the continent, but has only appeared in America a few times.   In 1870 there was a rather extensive outbreak, affecting the New England States and New York.   The type of the disease at that time was mild, and the dissemination of the contagion was quite easily arrested. About 1880 there were two or three lots of cattle and sheep brought to the United States affected with this disease, but there was no extension from the animals originally affected. In 1884 there was a small outbreak at Portland, Me., caused by imported cattle; and the disease spread to a few herds outside of the quarantine station. Owing to the small number of animals affected and the limited area of territory covered by the disease, it was easily controlled by the ordinary measures of quarantine and disinfection.

In general, foot-and-mouth-disease begins with an elevation of temperature amounting to from two to six degrees Fahrenheit, and the formation of vesicles in the mouth, upon the udder and teats, and on the feet. These vesicles are of various sizes, the epidermis being raised by a clear exudate which soon escapes by the rupture of the membrane. The membrane covering the vesicles is torn away by abrasion of the parts, or hangs in shreds, leaving a raw, ulcerated surface which is extremely sensitive. When the vesicles appear in the mouth, there is considerable salivation, the saliva gathering in a white foam about the mouth and attracting the attention of the observer. This is one of the first symptoms, and the salivation may be so abundant as to saturate the hay and floor in front of the affected animal. Affected cattle may also make a peculiar smacking sound with the mouth, which is no doubt due to the soreness of the tongue or adjacent parts. When the vesicles appear about the feet, the animals may be seen to raise and shake the posterior extremities in a manner which indicates the pain that they feel in the affected regions. Large vesicles appear upon the udder and teats, which interfere seriously with milking, and from which secretions issue which may contaminate the milk at the time it is drawn. There is often congestion of the mammary glands, with induration and the formation of abscesses.

The acute stage of the disease is generally terminated within a period of two weeks, after which time convalescence occurs with more or less rapidity, according to the conditions of existence, and the extremes of temperature to which the animals are subjected.

The disease is not one which produces a high fatality. The average loss by death in European countries has been from 2 to

5 per cent. The actual losses of cattle owners are, however, much greater than this. The high fever causes a rapid loss of flesh, which loss is augmented by the fact that, owing to the large vesicles and resulting ulcers in the mouth, the animals are not able to masticate their food. On account of this loss of flesh their value is decreased from 20 to 25 per cent. At the same time the milk secretion almost disappears, and the owner loses all revenue from his animals for from four to six weeks. When the animals have recovered from the acute form of the disease, many of them are found to be more or less injured, some of them having lost the horn from their feet, others having ulcers of the feet which cause chronic lameness, a considerable proportion having abscesses in the udder, which make them worthless for milk production, while numerous others abort and become emaciated and of little value. On the whole, I think, it is probably not far from correct to estimate that in an outbreak such as we now have in Massachusetts the average loss on account of the disease equals 50 per cent. of the value of the cattle affected.

A number of herds have been preserved, which had the disease in a mild form and which had apparently recovered at the time our inspection was made. In about one-third of these the owners have since come to us with the statement that a relapse had occurred with their animals: some were again affected with the formation of vesicles, and most of the others had abscesses in the udders which made them unfit for milk production. At the time these cattle were slaughtered the udders of many of them were so distended with pus that they were ruptured as the animals fell, and discharged vast quantities of this liquid, showing that they had been practically converted into sacs of pus.

Now a few words as to the management of the present outbreak. Some persons more or less acquainted with the history of the disease and the methods of handling it abroad have expressed surprise that I should have adopted such a radical plan as the slaughter of all diseased herds.

The measures which are indicated for controlling a disease of this kind must necessarily vary more or less according to the conditions which are found to exist. Foot-and-mouth disease is one of the most contagious of the diseases of animals, there being no other except rinderpest that equals it. It is therefore extremely difficult to confine the contagion by quarantine. Persons, animals, or even birds, going from infected premises to other places where cattle are kept, carry the contagion, and thus cause the disease to spread with surprising rapidity. There are few cases where the disease has succeeded in disseminating itself to any extent where an outbreak has been arrested by quarantine. An example of this is seen in the recent spread of the disease over the continent of Europe. It has invaded nearly or quite every country on the continent, and has remained for four or five years, notwithstanding the application of quarantine and the ordinary sanitary measures.

The present outbreak in Massachusetts has been one of the most virulent of which I have any knowledge. It has spread with extreme facility, and has affected all of the cattle in the infected herds in a very few days; while the fever has been very high, the loss of flesh extreme, and the after results very unfavorable. At the time of my arrival in this State there were at least 100 herds affected in Massachusetts and a considerable number in both Rhode Island and Vermont. Newly infected herds were being found daily, and the disease was spreading with alarming rapidity. The map which I show you, and which covers Massachusetts, Rhode Island, Connecticut, and the lower part of New Hampshire and Vermont, will give you an idea of the dissemination of the contagion. You see by these pins with red heads the towns that have been affected with the disease. In some cases there are quite a number of herds for each pin: in other cases one pin represents a herd. There were four herds in New Hampshire, at three different places, Hudson, Hancock, and Salem; and then there was an outbreak in the neighborhood of Chester, Vt., farther up in the State than would appear from this exhibit. By far the greater number of cases, however, were in Eastern Massachusetts, as shown by these pins. By the aid of this map you can all, I think, get an idea of the territory that has been affected and of the distribution of the disease.

It was plain that nothing but the most prompt and radical measures would be sufficient to confine the disease to the territory then infected. We could not for a moment contemplate the idea of allowing the disease to spread over the whole State and much less over the whole United States.   In the State of Massachusetts alone there are 300,000 head of cattle which would be affected, at an average loss of something like $15 per head, making, all told, a loss for the State of between four and five millions of dollars, without considering the loss to commerce which would result from the continuance of quarantine restrictions for three or four years, and the losses which would occur by the disease being transmitted to other species of animals, such as sheep and swine.

The presence of the disease has made it necessary to close the port of Boston to export animals and prohibit the shipment of cattle, hides, and various other articles of commerce from Massachusetts to other States.   If the disease should escape from control and spread over this State, the fear that it would cause in other States would lead to a great extension of the quarantine restrictions and heavy losses from interference with commerce.   If the disease should escape from the New England States and spread over the country, affecting all the cattle, the losses would be tremendous, and would constitute a national calamity.   A thousand million dollars would not be too high an estimate.

I have inserted a table which shows the number of herds and animals affected up to the present time and the number which have been slaughtered.   With the slaughtering of the diseased animals the extension of the contagion has been arrested in Vermont, New Hampshire, and Rhode Island, and in all parts of Massachusetts except a small section south of Boston, where newly affected herds are still being found.

State.	Total Affected since Appearance of Disease.		Slaughtered up to Date (Jan. 29, 1903).			Sheep and Goats.
	Herds.	Cattle.	Herds.	Cattle.	Swine.	
Massachusetts	143	2,727	113	2,340	217	47
Vermont	21	335	21	335	54	74
Rhode Island	17	367	4	75	8	—
New Hampshire	4	37	4	37	—	—
Total	185	3,466	142.	2,787	279	121

You will see from this that, unless it should happen that we discover some newly infected district, or it is much more difficult to eradicate the disease in the small territory in which it still lingers than is anticipated, we shall be able to eradicate it at an expense probably not exceeding $250,000 or $300,000.

There remains for us to consider the matter briefly from the public health standpoint. What is the effect of this disease on the consumer of animal products, and what would be the effect of an extension of the disease to all parts of the country?

Fortunately, the disease is only rarely conveyed to the human subject. In all extensive outbreaks, however, more or less cases are reported where the contagion has affected human beings, especially children, and in some cases with fatal results. However, no bad results appear to come from the meat of diseased animals, probably because cooking destroys the contagion; and it is believed the milk is not dangerous if pasteurized.

The disease spreads so rapidly and affects such a large proportion of the cattle that, when uncontrolled, it causes great shortage of the milk supply and suffering on that account. Doubtless, also, there are more or less serious digestive troubles caused by the pus contained in the milk, which reaches this product either from the ulcers on the teats or the abscesses in the udder or by contamination with the discharges from the vagina which are a consequence of abortion. To what extent the contamination of milk with pus and the various microbes which it may contain affects the health of the consumer is a question for the practising physician and the sanitarian to answer.

Under any circumstances, disease among food-producing animals is a serious subject from a sanitary point of view. Any disease accompanied by a high fever, which spreads so rapidly as to affect all the animals of one or more species, making it impossible under certain conditions to obtain meat or milk from unaffected animals, is a matter which must cause grave concern. Every shortage of the food supply must increase the misery and disease of the poorer classes in our large cities; and the sanitarian is therefore interested in maintaining both an abundant supply of food and one which is uncontaminated by disease, whether the specific affection is or is not communicable to the human consumer of animal products.

Gentlemen, I thank you for your attention. [Applause.]

THE PRESIDENT.— Dr. Salmon's very interesting and authoritative paper upon this subject is before you for discussion. Dr. Peters, what have you to say about the matter?

DR. PETERS.— Mr. Chairman and gentlemen, I think that after the interesting paper Dr. Salmon has given us there is very little to say. This outbreak was first called to my attention about November 12; and the first I heard of it was out of Massachusetts, in Rhode Island. I wrote to Dr. Salmon at the time, telling him what I had heard, and that I would investigate matters further, and, if anything more developed on investigation, I would notify him in another letter. A few days after that, about the middle of November, the disease was called to my attention in Dedham; and I telegraphed him at once. After agents of the Bureau of Animal Industry had verified my diagnosis, Dr. Salmon established headquarters here, and has been co-operating with the State authorities and doing all that he possibly could to eradicate the disease since that time.

A good many of you may remember that we had foot-and-mouth disease in this country about thirty years or a little more ago. In 1870 and 1871, I think, there was an outbreak that spread over a large portion of New England. Dr. Abbott gave me a report of the State Board of Health the other day — it was for 1871 — in which there was reference to an article by one of the Dr. Marions, of Allston, in which Dr. Marion speaks of a number of cases occurring in his practice among people who had milk from cows in certain herds in Brighton. It is a very interesting article.

I have heard of very little trouble from foot-and-mouth disease among people during this outbreak. I don't know of any authentic cases from it. I think, perhaps, one reason is that the present State law provides that, where cattle are quarantined as having contagious disease, the owner may be forbidden to sell the milk from the cows, and, wherever a herd was quarantined, the owner was forbidden to sell the milk. The result has been that very little milk — practically none — has reached the market from cattle with foot-and-mouth disease; and hence there seems to have been very little likelihood of cases among humans as the result of this outbreak among cattle.

The law also provides that, where any one has animals quarantined on his premises and is forbidden to sell the product, he must keep the animals at his own expense for ten days. After ten days the owner is entitled to remuneration from the State in a reasonable sum for the expense of maintaining the animals. I have now in the office of the Cattle Bureau claims from owners of cattle for about $5,000 for keeping animals, and there are other claims to come in, that will probably amount to $3,000 or $4,000 more. So the board bill on these animals to the State will be $8,000 or $9,000. Perhaps the owner, having this to console him, has in a measure been compensated for being deprived of the proceeds of the sale of the milk, and possibly that has had something to do with making him careful not to sell milk. Certainly, there seems to have been very little complaint from this outbreak as to its danger to the public health, which of course is the standpoint from which this Association views it. It also has its commercial aspect, the dollars-and-cents point of view, which is very important.

I think, Mr. President, it would be very interesting to hear from Dr. Marion his experience at the time of the other outbreak.

THE PRESIDENT.— It is not always that we can find an offender that committed his offence thirty years ago. When we do find him he is not likely to be as young a man as Dr. Marion.

DR. HORACE E. MARION.— Mr. President and gentlemen, I had, forgotten entirely that I was ever so foolish as to write an article for the Board of Health ; but I do remember distinctly that in 1870 or 1871, which was the first year of my going into practice, I saw a family where I could trace the trouble I was called to treat to nothing else than the foot-and-mouth disease. Not being willing to risk my own observations, I called into council Dr. Arthur H. Nichols, then of Roxbury, now of the city proper ; and, if I wrote anything that was of any worth then, it was in all probability due to Dr. Nichols's pushing me on. This family was affected with an eruption in the mouth, very much like herpes, and herpetic eruption on different parts of the body. They were ailing about two weeks, and gradually got over the disease. I don't remember any special thing about it, except this eruption and tracing it to a diseased herd.

THE PRESIDENT.— If any gentleman present has anything to contribute on this subject, the Association would be very glad to hear it.

DR. BURR.— Mr. President, I cannot help feeling that this State is under great obligation to Dr. Salmon and his bureau, working in connection with the Cattle Bureau of this State, for arresting the outbreak of this disease. There has been a great deal of comment upon the method pursued, but I cannot conceive of any practical way that we could have stopped the spread of this disease into other States excepting by these radical measures that have been taken by Dr. Salmon. We have been fortunate in Boston in having only one herd affected. I don't know why we have been favored so, because we have been right in the midst of it. I rather hoped that Dr. Salmon would tell us something about the after-treatment of these cases; that is, disinfection of the barns and treatment of the grounds around them. There has been talk about quarantining these animals upon the premises. All of us who have had experience in quarantining patients in houses, etc., know how difficult it is to maintain quarantine; and it must be a great deal harder to quarantine upon farms. I know that it was very difficult to keep people away from the small herd that we had in Boston; and I cannot conceive of any way that we could have stopped the spread of the disease — that is, carrying it from one barn to another — except by the measures taken by the United States Bureau of Animal Industry and the Cattle Bureau of Massachusetts.

MR. C.-E. A. WINSLOW.— I should like to ask one or two practical questions, if I may, that I know are of great interest to those living in the infected districts. In the first place, I should like to ask as to the transmissibility of the disease to horses, dogs, and cats; in the second place, as to the incubation period of the disease in animals which are susceptible to it; and, in the third place, as to the length of time for which it is necessary to quarantine animals not susceptible to the disease, but which have been exposed to it, before they can be allowed to go free.

DR. SALMON.— That is a question I cannot answer. There have been a number of people who have isolated different causes for it. As far as I am concerned, I have not had any investigations made in this country, because I did not care to take the chances of spreading the disease. Our people at Washington did desire to make some cultures and inoculations; but I preferred to let them investigate the disease in Europe, where they have more of it.

It is believed that horses take the disease in a mild form. I have never seen any horses affected with it; and there have been none in this outbreak, so far as my information goes. The same is true of dogs and cats. These animals are principally dangerous in carrying the contagion in their fur and hair or on their feet, when going from infected premises to others. I think that small animals, such as cats and dogs, are more dangerous than is generally believed or understood. At one of the places where we killed a herd there were twelve or fifteen cats in the barn; and, in trying to identify these cats, it was found that they represented two or three different farms in the neighborhood. It has seemed that pigeons have had something to do in spreading the disease in this outbreak. The herd at the Concord Reformatory was a herd that was isolated; and there seemed to have been no communication established with outside premises, especially infected ones, except by pigeons. There were a great many pigeons around there, which fed part of the time about the stables in the Reformatory and part of the time at other stables in the neighborhood, where there were infected animals. Flying a short distance, probably half a mile or so, it is quite conceivable that they could carry the contagion as well as a person could who walked that distance. On premises where we are killing off a herd to-day there are probably two or three hundred pigeons which have been flying round the neighborhood, and we have stipulated that those pigeons should all be killed. In that section of the State, as I say, the disease has been kept up somewhat mysteriously. We have not been able to learn how the infection was carried. In some cases it seemed as though it was carried by cats and dogs, and in others it possibly has been carried by pigeons.

The period of incubation is quite short. In some cases it is not over two days, but it may be five or six days. It is always short. Disease comes on very suddenly in a herd. At the Concord Reformatory, for instance, on Saturday they had one case, on Sunday they had eight cases, and on Monday they had some thirty or forty cases, in a herd of 58 animals. That is a fair illustration of the rapidity with which the disease goes through a herd.

Then as to the precautions which should be taken with insusceptible animals. We have endeavored where it was possible to disinfect such animals by washing them with a creoline solution and then keeping them away from infected premises. I think that that can be done readily with most animals.

THE PRESIDENT.— If there is nothing else to be said upon this subject, we will proceed to the next paper of the afternoon, a report by Dr. Hill, of Boston, on " Paratyphoid Fever."

A NOTE ON PARATYPHOID FEVER FROM THE PUBLIC HEALTH STANDPOINT.

BY HIBBERT WINSLOW HILL, M.D., DIRECTOR, BOSTON BOARD OF HEALTH LABORATORY.

One hundred years ago typhoid fever was not recognized as a distinct disease, but, when encountered, as it must often have been, was considered a form of typhus fever. It is a little difficult in these days to understand how typhus fever and typhoid fever were ever confused, although there is a more modern example in the case of certain throat affections. From some work done in the last few years, it would seem that even typhoid fever as commonly diagnosed clinically may be further subdivided.

The old idea of a disease was a condition presenting a certain set of symptoms. If a certain set of symptoms were present, and the physician could give the name by which that particular set of symptoms was commonly known, his diagnosis was made. Now, however, the effort is made to deduce from the symptoms and the history of the patient what the cause of the symptoms is, and, in the case of symptoms pointing to bacterial infection, to determine the exact organism concerned. Thus it is possible to know more exactly what is really the matter with the patient and what is most likely to aid his recovery. From the sanitarian's standpoint the identification of the disease is necessary, that he may judge of the danger to the public health involved and take proper measures regarding it. The name of a disease, therefore, has come to stand for the results of the action of a certain cause rather than merely for a set of symptoms.

Until comparatively recently the diagnosis of typhoid fever has been a clinical matter, notwithstanding the fact that the bacillus of typhoid was known. This was because, although known, the bacillus is difficult to isolate with sufficient rapidity and certainty. The introduction of the Widal reaction furnished a bacteriological method easy of application,— a method which has been very widely adopted. Briefly, this method consists in taking a drop of blood from the ear or finger of the patient and testing it, not for typhoid bacilli, as is often supposed by the general public, but for the presence of a peculiar substance found only in the blood of true typhoid fever patients. The test for this peculiar substance is made by mixing the blood to be tested with a culture of typhoid bacilli, kept for this purpose in the laboratory. The typhoid bacilli, before the addition of the blood, swim freely about in the liquid culture. On adding the blood of a well person or of a sick person not affected by typhoid bacilli, the bacilli are not affected, but continue to swim about freely, as before. But, if the patient be suffering from true typhoid, his blood will contain the peculiar substance already referred to; and this acts at once on the bacilli. Under the action of this substance they move more and more slowly, gathering at the same time into little groups, so that finally one sees only a few motionless masses of bacilli drifting slowly with the current or lying quite still.

Now true typhoid fever yields this peculiar substance capable of acting on true typhoid bacilli in this way. But what is true typhoid fever? True typhoid fever is that disease caused by the true typhoid bacilli. But the practitioner finds cases which give all the symptoms of typhoid fever, running a fairly typical course, in which repeated tests show that the patient's blood has no effect upon the cultures of typhoid bacilli in the laboratory. Clinically, it is a case of typhoid: bacteriologically, it is not. In the last few years such cases have worried every one who has had to do with them.

Briefly stated, the typhoid bacillus is not the only bacillus which can produce the symptoms of typhoid fever. There are other bacilli which affect man very much as the typhoid bacillus does. These are known by different names; but the paratyphoid fever group interests us particularly, because they are very much like the typhoid bacillus in nearly every way, as well as in the similarity of the diseases they produce. But, in spite of this likeness in so many ways, the blood of a patient infected with typhoid bacilli often will not affect cultures of paratyphoid fever organisms; nor will the blood of a paratyphoid fever patient, as a rule, affect cultures of typhoid bacilli. This depends somewhat on the dilution used. In low dilution all of this group tend to be " serum-identical"; *i.e.*, to be affected in the same way by the same blood. Now, since it has been customary to test the blood of suspected patients only with cultures of typhoid bacilli in routine work, the paratyphoid cases sent in to be tested are likely to give negative results. Wherever the blood test has been employed, then, in this limited way, true typhoid fever has been correctly diagnosed; but paratyphoid fever has been set down either as not typhoid at all or as clinical typhoid which refused to give the test reaction. Such merely clinical cases have been usually looked upon with doubt, especially when endeavoring to trace the course and source of an outbreak of typhoidal character.

Paratyphoid fever should be kept in mind by the professional hygienist. By whatever ways the typhoid bacillus may be distributed, by the same ways may the paratyphoid organisms be distributed. If an outbreak of true typhoid occurs, the health officer immediately considers all the possible sources of the bacilli, such as water, milk, foods, direct contact, etc. These same routes of infection must be considered for paratyphoid fever. In all outbreaks both diseases must be sought out. The tracing of outbreaks is really a high class of detective work, on which the safety of the public is often just as dependent as it is upon police detectives for protection in another direction. In guarding water supplies, milk supplies, etc., so far as concerns the principal criminal, the typhoid bacillus, best known and for whose identification there has been a definite test, a less important criminal, having practically the same stamping ground and committing very much the same sort of mischief, should not be overlooked.

SUMMARY.

Besides true typhoid fever there exists another disease very like it, caused by organisms very like the typhoid bacillus, but distinct from it.

These diseases may be distinguished from each other by the fact that each gives a reaction with the bacillus which causes it, and not with the other, if proper dilution be used.

Since both typhoid and paratyphoid fever have very much the same sanitary significance, both should be taken into account in dealing with these diseases against which protection depends on purity of water, milk, and raw foods.

THE PRESIDENT.— Dr. Hill's paper is now before you for discussion.

DR. DURGIN.— Mr. President, on the day of our last meeting, three months ago, there occurred reports of typhoid fever at a house in Columbus Avenue, Boston. Reports came over the telephone to me about eleven o'clock from the City Hospital concerning three or four cases that had been admitted. Suspicion at once rested upon this house and its restaurant in Columbus Avenue. There was something said at that meeting about boards of health barking up the wrong tree, etc., and that the board of health had examined the plumbing in this instance, and taken a sample of milk. I had known of this outbreak, then, about two hours. I made a few remarks concerning the matter at that time, and promised the Association I would report progress, not being able at that time to say more about it than that two experts had been put upon the case, and that they were then at work on it instead of coming to the meeting. In less than two hours after the investigation was begun, the clew was obtained; and in a few hours more the cause of the outbreak was clearly traced to its source. Two sisters were waitresses in a restaurant where the outbreak occurred, and both had typhoid fever. The first case (one of the waitresses) began in the first week in October. She continued to wait on the table until the 15th. She was then in bed until the 19th, when she was sent to the hospital. The other sister nursed the first case until it was sent to hospital, and she also waited on table and washed dishes in the restaurant until she was sent to hospital with typhoid fever on the 29th of October.

On the very day that this came over the telephone to me, Drs. Shea and Burr traced the disease, and had the disinfection performed the same afternoon and everything cleaned up, so far as it wa⁻ possible to do it. I want to say once more that the board of health in question has never in its history looked for typhoid fever by any examination of the drainage or the plumbing; nor has it or any of its officers ever taken a sample of milk on account of typhoid fever. The fact that the drainage is examined where this disease exists has nothing whatever to do with the search for the cause of typhoid fever. There were, as a result of this infection, about 28 cases. They took their meals at this place in Columbus Avenue. Some were medical students, some were students at the Technology, 'and there were other boarders. The celery, which was mentioned to me over the telephone as being a common article used at the table, was considered; but neither this nor any other article of diet appeared as the common source of the trouble. The two waitresses were the undoubted source of the subsequent cases.

The question is asked as to the number of people who boarded at this place. I am not able to state what that was.

Dr. Shea.— Three hundred, doctor.

Dr. Durgin.— About three hundred boarded at the same restaurant.

Mr. C.-E. A. Winslow.— I was extremely interested in Dr. Hill's admirable presentation of the work on paratyphoid fever; and I think it is of especial interest, taken in connection with the paper presented at the last meeting of this Association. The somewhat iconoclastic conclusions of Dr. Chapin have been well illustrated by this recent epidemic in Boston. We at the Institute of Technology have been inclined to feel that the old ideas as to the spread of typhoid fever must be modified under modern conditions in Massachusetts. The spread of typhoid fever by water mainly is a condition that prevails in uncivilized communities, in such communities as Philadelphia and Pittsburg, and, if Dr. Salmon will pardon me, even in Washington. We have got by that here. The typhoid fever death-rate in Massachusetts is in almost every city and town in the State identical with that which occurs in communities having absolutely pure water supplies. We here must look for the source of typhoid fever epidemics mainly in personal infection, as it has been shown in this particular instance,— not in the water supply, not in the milk supply, except in isolated cases, but in the presence of persons carrying the disease.

I think Dr. Hill's paper indicates another point on which we must modify somewhat our preconceived ideas. The exaggerated importance of the agglutination reactions is a third fetich, which must, to a certain extent, follow the plumbing fetich and for us here the water-supply fetich. We have been attaching too much importance to the agglutination reactions as absolute diagnostic tests. They are undoubtedly of very great value, perhaps of greater value than any other single test. Dr. Hill probably remembers the paper presented at Washington by Dr. Bergey, of the University of Pennsylvania, in which he showed that a bacillus isolated from river water gave an almost perfect serum reaction for the Shiga bacillus, the bacillus which has been identified as the cause of some forms of dysentery, whereas it was a bacillus belonging to an entirely different group. By the serum reaction it would have been identified as the Shiga bacillus. So that we must regard these agglutination tests as only one link in the chain of evidence; and it is hardly, perhaps, safe now to define typhoid fever as the disease in which the blood of the patient will give a typical reaction with the typhoid bacillus. If we don't adopt that absolute arbitrary definition, of course it won't be necessary to class these cases as paratyphoid cases. We can call them all typhoid cases, some giving better and some less marked serum reactions. That will avoid the danger of overlooking the atypical cases which Dr. Hill has so well pointed out.

Dr. Hyde.— I just want to ask Dr. Durgin a question. In fact, I have asked him it. I understood him to say that he never looked to the milk supply in outbreaks of typhoid fever. Am I to infer from that, are we all to infer from that, that you do not consider, doctor, that with a milk route, or the milk from a herd of cattle, a person with typhoid may be capable of spreading the disease?

Dr. Durgin.— I understood you to ask me if we look in samples of milk for the typhoid bacilli, and I said no. I want to say, however, in regard to the rest of the question which you now ask that we do most certainly trace in every instance the milk supply to see if there is connected with it any case of typhoid fever, and that I regard milk as one of the common, and one of the most common, agents in the spread of typhoid fever.

Dr. Shea.— We in Boston have to deal with typhoid fever; and, as a rule, it is brought to us, imported from the outside. As health officers, when called to a case of typhoid fever, we never inquire about the water supply. Our first question is the milk; and, as a result of that question, I can recollect, in my experience of the past ten or twelve years, of running down probably a dozen or fifteen outbreaks of typhoid fever. Within three years we had an outbreak of 41 cases in West Roxbury. It was traced to a farm in Needham, and the people with the typhoid fever all obtained their milk from that particular place. When we have typhoid in a neighborhood, the milkman or contractor is under suspicion immediately; and many a day and night the inspectors of our department have travelled over New England, seeking the source of infection, and in the majority of cases with very good results. We find, in a little town or village, a man running a milk farm. His wife or some of the help have been sick with typhoid fever, and the conditions existing there all point with strong suspicion that the typhoid is coming to Boston in the milk from that farm. Again, 60 per cent. of the cases of typhoid fever that we have to deal with in Boston we find are contracted by the people that have been away on their vacations. They have been to the beach or the mountains. Of the other cases, I think it is fair to say that 15 or 20 per cent. can be directly traced to the milk supply.

It is a standing rule that, when a physician or a sanitary inspector is sent to investigate a case of typhoid fever, the question is immediately asked, "Where do you obtain your milk supply?" and if John Jones leaves milk to three or four families in the neighborhood, and there is typhoid in these families, we immediately find out where this milk is coming from, and, as a rule, we find the infection is in the milk.

And another regulation of the department that Mr. Jordan calls to my attention. After a case of typhoid fever is reported, the milkman of the party leaving the milk at the residence or store is immediately notified that "no cans, vessels, or bottles should be carried into or handled by any person living in said premises until the patient has recovered. If any milk is left at the premises it must be poured into a receptacle furnished by the family." I do not know how it is in other cities, but in Boston the milkman is always under suspicion with typhoid fever.

DR. SALMON.— Mr. President, perhaps I ought to say, in justice to Washington, where the water supply is to be more or less suspected as causing typhoid fever, that that is not as much of an indication of the uncivilized character of the inhabitants as it is in some other cities. Gentlemen will recall, I have no doubt, that in Washington we have not the advantage which you have in Massachusetts, of electing the people who legislate for us. We are obliged to accept legislators who are elected from all parts of the United States, some of them from Massachusetts [laughter and applause]; and, while they are a very intelligent and progressive set of gentlemen, they do not always agree with us in our views as to what they should do. We have for quite a number of years felt the necessity of improving our water supply. In fact, when I first secured the establishment of a bacteriological laboratory in Washington, which was one of the first in the country, I had some bacteriological analysis made of the water of the Potomac River, and concluded that the water was very bad for civilized people to drink. I expressed my opinion very freely, and saw that it reached members of Congress, who legislate for us; but they did not take the same view of it, and it has only been recently that we have impressed upon them the fact that their own health, as well as ours, depended upon improving the water supply. Recently we have had an appropriation, which is now being expended; and we hope to have a filtration plant in operation within the next few years at farthest.

MR. COFFEY.— The President has asked me to cite an instance that came under our observation at Worcester within a short time, that goes to prove that milk is a vehicle of contagion in typhoid. I want to say that in October of last year one of the inspectors reported that two cases of typhoid existed on the route of a certain milkman. As is our custom, we immediately looked that milkman up. He lived in an adjoining town, some seven or eight miles away. We found a case of typhoid fever in his immediate family, convalescing. We also found a case of typhoid in a family on an adjoining farm, from which he received part of his supply. We immediately forbade their taking any more milk into the city, and had the cans and bottles thoroughly disinfected. No new cases appeared on that man's route. In all there were eleven cases, all of which dated prior to our discovery of the existence of the typhoid on the farm ; and there were three deaths.

Two years ago we had a similar experience in another town adjoining the city, where we found by visiting the town that the milkman himself was down with the disease, and that on two farms, from which he received most of his supply, there were also cases. In that case we immediately shut off the supply of milk, and had the cans and bottles thoroughly disinfected; and no new cases resulted on that route subsequent to the time we discovered it.

Both of those instances have occurred very recently. One, as I say, was only last October : the other was about, I think, two years ago. Both of them go to prove, it seems to me, very conclusively that milk cannot be left out of account by any health officer in searching for the cause of typhoid fever.

Dr. Denny.— I should like to ask Dr. Hill if there are any cases on record where there have been epidemics of paratyphoid fever or where it is known that the disease spread from one case to another. I should also like to know what the *post-mortem* findings are.

Dr. Hill.— The subject is so new that there is not a very extensive literature as yet, and there are not a great many (70–80) cases on record. For one thing, they have not heretofore been looked for systematically. But the history of the paratyphoid organism, so far as it has been worked out, justifies the conclusion that its history outside the body is very closely that of the typhoid bacillus. The autopsy findings are very varied, but in a general way similar lesions are presented as in true typhoid. The most striking fact is, of course, the absence of the true typhoid bacillus. Some years ago Dr. Councilman described to me a case which persistently refused to give the Widal reaction. It came to autopsy, and presented at the autopsy lesions which would have justified any one in saying casually, "This, of course, is typhoid fever." However, the most careful search failed to reveal any typhoid bacilli anywhere. The very good reason for the absence of the Widal reaction was the fact that the typhoid bacillus was not present.

I should like to say something concerning one remark made by Mr. Winslow, relating to the names "typhoid" and "paratyphoid." It is all a question of definition and nomenclature. I think, however, that we are sufficiently far ahead now not to further confuse names and symptoms. Take tuberculosis, for instance. We now speak of tuberculosis as any form of disease caused by the bacillus tubercle. We do not now have half a dozen different names of supposedly different diseases; but we put all caused by the tubercle bacillus under one name, that of the organism which produces the disease. So I think that in typhoid fever we are perfectly justified in saying that true typhoid, whatever its exact symptoms, is that disease due to the true typhoid organism, and that a disease which is due to a different organism, never mind how closely similar to typhoid fever it may be, should have a different name, and that that other name should refer to the organism which produces it. It does not seem to me that we should go any further than we must in confusing nomenclature and facts. If we do distinguish paratyphoid and typhoid fever by name, yet recognize the fact that they must be very similarly dealt with, we have achieved two things. We escape from the error of believing that the two are distinct because the names are different, yet we do not confuse two things which are somewhat different because the names are the same.

MR. C.-E. A. WINSLOW.— Mr. Chairman, there is just one word more. Dr. Hill appears to have understood me as advocating the classing of diseases caused by different organisms under the same head merely because the symptoms are similar. My point only was that in respect to typhoid fever we are hardly in a position yet to say certainly that there are two distinct organisms or two distinct diseases; and, until we are sure of that, it is dangerous to introduce a confusion of terms.

DR. AGNES C. VIETOR.— Mr. President, I have been very much interested in the discussion on typhoid and paratyphoid fever, particularly because I have, in common with other practitioners, had cases of typhoid fever, clinical typhoid, that did not give the laboratory reaction. In reading a number of articles on this subject, within recent times, I was impressed with the resemblance of the problem to the problem of the streptococcus, on which I did a little work some time ago. To summarize what you are probably all familiar with, the streptococcus is open to question as to its identity and as to its behavior; that is, apparently the same streptococcus will, under differing conditions of culture, give different results, even in regard to the action of the antitoxine developed in the serum. In the study of the varying typhoid reactions, it has occurred to me that perhaps the typhoid bacillus resembles the streptococcus in these laboratory variations, and that the two varieties of paratyphoid bacilli, at present isolated, may be cultural variations of the typhoid bacillus.

THE ACTION OF VAPORIZED FORMALDEHYDE AND VAPORIZED CARBOLIC ACID AS GASEOUS DISINFECTANTS.

BY HIBBERT WINSLOW HILL, M.D., DIRECTOR BOSTON BOARD
OF HEALTH LABORATORY.

Mr. President and Gentlemen,— By the kindness of your Programme Committee, I am allowed to make a brief statement of some recent results we have obtained in the Boston Board of Health Laboratory in testing formalin gas.

The points which are of especial importance are these : —

First, that, if the humidity of the air be low, in the room which is to be disinfected, very much more gas is required than if the humidity be at the saturation point. Formalin gas thus resembles sulphur, and high humidity is important in one case just as it is in the other.

Second, that a given amount of formalin gas, which in air of high humidity kills promptly, would, if placed in an equal quantity of water, be practically inert. For instance, three ounces of formalin in one thousand cubic feet of air saturated with moisture will kill; but it would require from one to three thousand times as much formalin to kill in the same time if it were placed, not in one thousand cubie feet of air, but in one thousand cubic feet of water. Neither of these points is strictly new, but so far they have attracted little attention.

These considerations suggested to the writer that perhaps both of these principles might apply to disinfectants in general, and it was determined to try carbolic acid and other disinfectants on these lines. Carbolic acid solutions require about the same amounts of carbolic acid, in order to be effective, that formalin solutions must contain of formaldehyde to achieve the same results; and it seemed not unlikely that perhaps approximately equal amounts of their vapors might also be equally effective.

A series of experiments was begun. They are very far from completion yet; but we have got so far as to justify the statement that carbolic acid vaporized will kill the diphtheria bacillus in about the same time, and, roughly speaking, in about the same amount as will formaldehyde. Every one knows the disadvantages of formalin as well as its advantages. The use of carbolic acid vapor seems to get rid of the one, while preserving the other. High humidity is necessary in both cases; and the cost of carbolic acid is not greater practically, strength for strength, than that of formaldehyde.

Going somewhat further, we tried bichloride of mercury, which is volatile, and found that at saturation point its vapor also killed, so far as we have gone, somewhat better than formaldehyde. Whether bichloride is a practical thing to use for municipal disinfection we shall have to consider further, but in France it has been used in the form of a spray for some considerable time.

This work is only in the experimental stage as yet, but so far it seems to promise results of considerable advantage in the future.

REPORT OF COMMITTEE ON DIPHTHERIA BACILLI IN WELL PERSONS.

THE PRESIDENT.— Has the Committee on Diphtheria Bacilli in well persons anything to report in the way of a conclusion?

DR. HILL.— Mr. President, this committee has reported already some nine months ago; and our conclusions have been in the hands of all the members for that period of time. I think it is hardly necessary to read them again now, but I will do so if you wish.

THE PRESIDENT.— There is nothing additional to what has been already reported?

DR. HILL.— Nothing additional, no. We consider that we have said about all that we could say in this report.

On motion of Mr. Coffey the report of the committee was accepted, and the committee was discharged from further consideration of the subject.

Adjourned.

JOURNAL OF THE
MASSACHUSETTS ASSOCIATION OF BOARDS OF HEALTH.

ORGANIZED 1890.

[The Association as a body is not responsible for statements or opinions of any of its members.]

| VOL. XIII. | July, 1903. | NO. 2. |

APRIL QUARTERLY MEETING

OF THE

Massachusetts Association of Boards of Health.

The quarterly meeting of the Massachusetts Association of Boards of Health was held at the Hotel Brunswick, April 30, Dr. H. P. Walcott, the president, in the chair. After luncheon the record of the previous meeting was read by the secretary and approved. The following were elected to membership, upon the recommendation of the executive committee: William Berger, Lawrence; Dr. Holbrook, Lowell; Dr. Jackson, Lowell; Dr. Wheatley, North Abington; Dr. Lawrence, Brockton; Dr. J. W. Bartol, Boston.

President Walcott—Is there any other business to be brought before the society at this time? If not, we will proceed to the programme of the afternoon. The first paper is upon "Educational Sanitary Inspection," by Mrs. Richards.

Dr. Hill—If I am not too late, I have a paper here which I should like to read and present for the consideration of the association.

Gentlemen:—The anti-vivisectionists this year made again an attempt to attain legislation delegating to them or to their agents the authority of the State to inspect the animal experimentation of the colleges of this State. While forbidding the State Board of Health to perform other than inoculation experiments, the bill absolutely excluded municipal Boards of Health from any animal experimentation whatever.

The time being too short for the securing of an official expression from this association, a form of protest was drawn up for signature by the individual members of the association, and a second for the official signature of Boards of Health. Most of you doubtless have already seen both of these. About 115 signatures of members were secured, in spite of the difficulty of getting at all the members in the limited time. The Board of Health of every city in the State, except that of North Adams, signed the official protest. The North Adams chairman expressed himself as in favor of the bill and refused to sign the protest. Besides these 32 cities, 19 or 20 towns responded favorably.

The Committee on Probate and Chancery, after a brief hearing, reported leave to withdraw, three of the eleven members dissenting. The dissenters were House members—Messrs. Potter of Worcester, Booth of Springfield and Sleeper of Natick. When the report came up before the House the bill was tabled.

We have good reason to believe that our opponents will appear again next year, and I would suggest, Mr. Chairman, the appointment of a committee, whose business it should be to see that this association and the Boards of Health of the State are properly represented in this and other legislative matters from year to year, as occasion may arise.

The bill and the forms of protest drawn up for use this year are appended:

House bill, No. 87, entitled "An Act Further to Prevent Cruelty to Animals," reads as follows:

Be it enacted by the Senate and House of Representatives in General Court assembled, and by the authority of the same, as follows:

Section 1.   No person shall perform on any animal any experiment of a nature to cause pain to such animal, except subject to the restrictions hereby imposed, namely: .

(a)   Such experiment shall be performed only under the authority of the faculty of a college or university incorporated under the laws of this Commonwealth, and in a building and in a part thereof which has been previously registered with the secretary of the Commonwealth by the person or corporation having control thereof, for the practice of animal experimentation; but nothing herein contained shall be construed to prevent the State Board of Health from making any experiment described in section two hereof.   Such registration shall be made and a certificate thereof issued in such manner as the secretary of the Commonwealth may from time to time by any special or general order direct; provided, that every legally chartered college or university in this Commonwealth shall be entitled to registration under this act.

(b)   The animal, before the beginning and thenceforth during the whole course of such experiment, shall be sufficiently under the influence of a general anæsthetic to prevent the animal from feeling pain.   The substance known as urari or curare shall not, for the purposes of this act, be deemed an anæsthetic.

(c)   Every animal subjected to such experiment, if the pain is likely to continue after the effect of the anæsthetic has ceased, or if any serious injury has been inflicted, shall be killed immediately upon the conclusion of the experiment and while under the influence of the anæsthetic.

Section 2.   The inoculation of or administration of drugs or disease to, any animal for any medical or scientific purpose under the authority of the faculty of any college or university incorporated under the laws of this Commonwealth (or under the authority of the State Board of Health) shall not by itself be deemed an experiment to which the restrictions of this act apply.

Section 3.   The authorized agents of any society for the prevention of cruelty to animals incorporated under the laws of this

Commonwealth shall be permitted to enter any place registered as required by section one hereof, at any time, without previous notice, and to take the name and residence of any person found therein.

Section 4. Any person who performs, or assists in performing, any experiment described in section one hereof, in violation of either of the restrictions thereby imposed, or excludes or assists in excluding any agent described in said section, or, being in such a place, refuses to disclose his true name and residence to any such agent, or violates any other provision of this act, shall be punished by imprisonment in the jail not exceeding one year, or by fine not exceeding three hundred dollars, or by both such fine and imprisonment.

Protest of Members of the Massachusetts Association of Boards of Health Against House Bill No. 87.

To the Committee on Probate and Chancery:

Gentlemen:—

We, the undersigned, members of the Massachusetts Association of Boards of Health, desire to record for your consideration our emphatic personal and individual protests, against the legislation proposed in House bill No 87, as detrimental directly to present methods in actual daily use in the protection of the public health, and indirectly as tending to limit investigations into physiology and pathology which have already placed medicine and so hygienic work, on a sound common-sense basis, and which promise to continue in the future the long record of successful advances shown in the past.

Protests of Boards of Health Against House Bill No. 87.

To the Committee on Probate and Chancery:

Gentlemen:—

The undersigned municipal Boards of Health of the State of Massachusetts desire to protest in their official capacity against House bill No. 87 for the following reasons:

(1) The bill specifically excludes from animal experimentation all persons except those acting under authority from universities, colleges and the State Board of Health. Municipal Boards of Health are therefore excluded.

(2) Well-known statutory requirements are made of Boards of Health in the detection, restriction and prevention of disease. This bill limits the means at the disposal of Boards of Health to these ends, in an arbitrary and retrogressive manner, preventing specifically the following important determinations with many others:

(a) The detection of bubonic plague, glanders (in horses or in human) hydrophobia (in dogs), and other similar tests.

(b) The recognition of tuberculosis of the kidneys, bladder, etc.

(c) The recognition of chronic pleuritic tuberculosis.

(d) The testing of the action of disinfectants on tubercle bacilli, the presence of tubercle bacilli in rooms occupied by consumptive patients, the presence of the tetanus (lockjaw) bacillus in dust, the detection of virulence in diphtheria bacilli.

(e) The testing of methods of treatment such as formaldehyde injections.

(f) The study of the serum reactions in typhoid fever, paratyphoid fever, dynestery, summer diarrhœa, etc., other than with human serum.

(g) The study of bacteriolysins, hemolysins, etc., bearing directly on the treatment and prevention of disease and now supplying steps in advance of great significance.

(h) The study of the action of deleterious substances other than disease, such as the action of gaseous disinfectants, illuminating gas, ptomaines, etc.

(i) The complete identification and study of new or unknown bacteria.

(3) The bill prevents Boards of Health from participating in the advancement of their own work, so far as this is aided by animal experimentation.

(4) As interested officially in and closely related to all study

of health and disease, we protest against the interference which this bill imposes upon the work of the universities and colleges along physiological and pathological lines, from which work the public health has benefited in the past and will benefit in the future.

(5) The bill also gives the power of inspection to untrained agents or associations now existing or that may be formed in the interest of opposition to animal experimentation.

We do not ask for amendment of this bill to include Boards of Health with universities and colleges, or with the State Board of Health in the permission to perform animal experimentation under the inspection provided for. We desire, rather, to protest against any legislation of the proposed character, placing these duly incorporated bodies and these statutory bodies, which are responsible already to the people at large and amenable to the ample laws now existing, under the official inspection of private associations of individuals.

(Signed)

For the Board of Health of ———

(Signature.)   ————.

The President.—You have heard Dr. Hill's paper. It is a matter, of course, to be published in the proceedings of the association. You have also heard his motion that a committee be appointed to represent this association at the State House at future hearings upon this matter, which so closely concerns the necessary work of the Boards of Health. Is it your pleasure that a committee of three be appointed for that purpose?

The motion was put and adopted.

The President—The committee will be announced later. I now have the pleasure of introducing Mrs. Richards.

EDUCATIONAL SANITARY INSPECTION.

BY ELLEN H. RICHARDS.

Mr. President, Ladies and Gentlemen:—The educational effect of legal enactment and enforcement none should know better than health officers. But it is also painfully evident to those in whose hands lies the enforcement of sanitary law that this education has not gone very far or very deep, and that year after year the same sort of work has to be done as if it had never been done before.

The non-intelligent masses rebel against the rules they do not understand, and evade all that they find it safe to ignore. It is like sweeping back the sea with a broom, since each year brings a fresh contingent of ignorance. A respect for the power of the law is inculcated by the enforcement of the ordinance against spitting in public conveyances, but no permanent cure for the evil habit can be expected until the children and young loafers are also reached by the reasons why it is dangerous.

Until both children and parents understand the reason why rubbish in the streets and garbage in the back alleys is not to be tolerated, it will continue to be found there in spite of city ordinances and health officers. There is thus, (a) a waste of effort on the part of the inspector and the court; (b), the immoral effect of evasion of the law, and, (c), a general discouragement which tends toward a low condition of the civic health and civic morals.

It has been our custom to give vote and bath first and educate up to privilege afterward, but we ought to have recognized that the giving is not enough without the education how to use. We have furnished water, gas and pavements, but the personal unit behind all has been somewhat neglected, the school has not done all it ought. We have not had a Mrs. Hunt on the sanitary side to go at the root of the matter, bad air, poor food and squalid surroundings.

The question is, how to provide for such contingencies in the future. If we attempt to do it by private organization, by any sort of social center or civic betterment association, we find that it is rather difficult to gain access to the premises of the ordinary tenant, in order to know what the conditions are which ought to be remedied.

Now, there are two people who can gain this knowledge at the present time, and these are the physician and the district nurse, and the success of instructive district nursing in many places has naturally suggested the extension of that sort of work toward a certain degree of sanitary instruction. The person who can go to the houses with the official badge of an inspector, and on his official rounds, may, instead of leaving irritation and animosity behind him, be welcomed as a friend and a helper; and, if this could be done to a greater degree, I believe some rapid reforms might be effected, and certainly much money might be saved to the city. I think you will all agree that there is a great deal of good work done, but even more is left undone, and that if we could carry our prevention still further in this direction, we should gain a great deal in health and also save money in the end.

The confidence of the family group must be obtained in some way, and then, the officer, instead of having to wink at violations of the ordinances in order to retain their good will, would be considered as their friend. I suppose the officers in every town know that if the law was fully enforced in all cases there would be trouble in almost any community. Now, in order to do a little good, we know you have to overlook a certain amount of evil. We know from experience that when we sometimes try to get a good thing done, we find the health officer is not inclined to do it. We understand, of course, in many cases, why.

In other words, the law can be carried out only when the constituency is sufficiently enlightened as to its value as affecting themselves. The commonest plea for the existence of unsanitary conditions in violation of statute provisions is the ignorance of the masses. But why this continuance of ignorance? We are under obligations to "do away with the inconvenience of ignorance," as John Eliot wrote in devising his Jamaica Plain property for a school.

It is both humane and economical to educate the people for their own good. As a frequent speaker before women's clubs of various kinds, I have become impressed with the eagerness with which the housewife asks how to do this or that which I have suggested, but I have been much more impressed with the ignorance of simple laws of mechanics and physics, which makes all my explanations and suggestions of little or no value. It is too hard a problem, and she sighs and turns away.

Working women are hemmed in by even greater restrictions. They are afraid as well as ignorant. The initiative must come from someone else, and they must use their imitative faculties to follow out directions. We are all influenced, more or less, by the next above us in the social strata, and if we could only get hold of the people through their imitative faculties and through teaching their children, we might be able to make some headway.

If it is of great value to be able to go as a friend and teacher, not with a warrant to arrest, at least, until friendly advice has failed, time must be allowed in which to exercise the tact necessary to get at the people. Hence, an instructive inspector may not be able to make as many visits a day as a mere legal inspector, but each place where the instructive inspection has been given, and well given, will be a center from which other influences will radiate. I suppose it is well understood that the visit of the police officer is known at the end of the street as soon as he enters it; and I venture to say that notice of the presence of the sanitary inspector is sent forward by this mysterious communication which the people have with each other, about as quickly.

This rapid movement of information from house to house has its great advantage in the case of instruction, so that perhaps all of it would not need to be repeated everywhere. In the case of certain alleys, for instance, the law says the owner is responsible. But he is never there, and when the neighbors complain to the health officers they can only report to the owner, I suppose. The tenants may be told to clean up. But it is not the officer's business, I take it, generally, to see that this is done. He goes away. He never comes back—at least, he doesn't for months—to see that his orders are obeyed. The tenants won't clean up, and so the stuff remains in the alley. And more, the receptacles for the garbage, for instance, are not properly looked after. They overrun, and the dogs pull them about; and so the cabbage stalks and the bean shells stay from week to week. And I am sorry to say, in some of the towns of Massachusetts the garbage collectors are not careful, and spill about as much as they put into the carts, and it is nobody's business to see that it is cleaned up. And so, the condition of the alleys is sometimes very trying, to say the least.

Then, this continual moving about of the people, not only in our tenement house district, but in our apartment houses, which come, perhaps, not so often under inspection, is, I am pretty sure, largely due to the fact that the tenants are not instructed in the use of the appliances and something goes wrong. They make complaint to the landlord. He doesn't remedy the trouble directly, and they go away and leave it. The landlord is very apt to put a little superficial coating on, and somebody else comes in, and so things go from bad to worse.

I heard only the other day of a place in a city in Massachusetts where a poor, common tenant had moved out, and the owner living in some distant place, sent a painter in to make some repairs. The painter found the traps entirely stopped up, and all the plumbing fixtures overflowed everywhere. The thing was in such a condition that he said he would not stay in the house. He could not do his work and went away. The inspection of plumbing will accomplish more by teaching occupants what will and what will not go down the drain than by looking for sewer gas.

I don't know that we can entirely blame the foreign population for their ignorance of our methods. They perhaps have just come over on the steamer. They may possibly have been on a train somewhere. And on the steamer or the train they have found that when they throw the material down into the large orifice, it goes into the sea or goes out readily. How should they know when they go into a house that there are traps and small pipes which are liable to fill up? Can we blame them, when we find guests in four-dollar-a-day hotels doing practically the same thing. Ignorance as to what a half-inch pipe will carry, and what will go through a trap, is not confined to the tenement-house district.

How are we going to get at these people? There must be some sort of teaching, somehow, somewhere. It is not at present the inspector's duty to do that, I take it. It is his business only to see that the things are in fair working order, and to complain if they are not. But really, our machinery is pretty complex, and it would be a great piece of wisdom if we could have a little teaching of the various methods of getting the best out of it.

We have, most of us, very little idea of the unequal share of water, for instance, which our people get. We complain of the great unwashed. What opportunity have they to keep themselves or their clothes clean? We say everybody in Boston has 100 gallons of water a day. Well, some people do not; some people have more. And the question of getting water in the tenement-house regions is certainly serious. I always wonder when I go through them that the people can keep anything like as clean as they do.

Of course, we have plenty of public baths which are greatly conducive to public health. But how about the laundries? Where is there a free, open laundry where people can go to keep their clothes and their children's clothes clean? The children wear woolen clothes to school, and of course they don't need washing! Sometimes they are sewed on and stay on all winter. They have no encouragement to wear washable goods, because they have no water and have no chance to have it in the tenement. The landlord says they wouldn't use it if they had it; but isn't it our duty to see that they have an opportunity, at least, to learn how to use it?

The workers in these poorer quarters are ready to testify to the value of teaching the children. I suppose that the health inspector on his rounds is more often confronted with the stolid foreign woman, and sometimes the men, whom it is impossible to move. It is very difficult to make much headway with that sort of person. Very likely she does not understand your language. She has no idea of what you are talking about, and you feel so discouraged, because you begin with the people who are too old—who have been brought up under different conditions. But if you can get at the children, either through settlement work, through the public schools, or in any way that you choose—if you can get at the children and teach them some essential facts, they will have an effect upon the homes.

I am assured by some of the club workers in the poorest quarters of the city that in the last five or six years, since that work was begun, very great improvements have been seen in those neighborhoods. In one street that I know of, a very decided effort was made last year to keep the street clean. The children were got together and taught how to pick up the papers and to keep the things out of the streets. But there were enough careless people to spoil the effect since there was no power of the law behind the effort. I do not mean in any way to say that our present corps could spend the time to do this instructive work. I only mean to say that it ought to be done, and in some way the health officers, who know better, better than anyone else, the needs of a given district, ought to devise some way of doing it.

It has been very well said by a recent writer that modern sanitation must be constructive as well as restrictive. We have heretofore dwelt more on restrictive measures than on constructive ones. The people have now become used to the power of the health department. That power may be turned—I believe the time is ripe—and should be turned to some practical educational use.

At present, I believe, inspection is made once or twice or three times a year. It seems advisable that when a set of premises has been inspected and the returns made out of what is wrong, somebody should go through that street and show the people how to make it right. If the well-to-do people who go to our women's clubs feel themselves helpless over the question of ventilating a room for an afternoon tea, how can we expect these tenement women to understand plumbing and keeping things clean in various ways. So, there should follow with the list of inspection somebody (perhaps a tactful, attractive woman) to tell them how to do the things required. And then should not the inspector go about again and see that it is done? Three visits in one week would have more effect than three visits in a year, as usually made.

When I refer to the moral effect of the non-enforcement of law, I mean that if you tell a person to do a thing—it is just the same with the child—and he knows you will never come to find out whether he has done it, of course it isn't done. That is the trouble with our inspection. Talking until doomsday will accomplish very little compared with actually showing people how things work. An association like this, an organization of boards of health, should first say what they want taught to the people. You konw what it is that is most in need of remedy. Then you might ask certain clubs, hygiene committees and civic leagues to do the work as you have laid it out. Much of the work that is undertaken outside by organizations is begun at the wrong end; and I think most of you in your cities and towns dread to have a health protective association or a committee on hygiene attempt to do anything in the line of sanitary reform, because they are sure to hit upon the wrong thing—the thing that is least necessary. They are sure to think they can do something that you are quietly doing much better, and don't see the thing they might well do.

If you would make up your minds what you want to have, what help you need from outside, you might get women's clubs—they are in every city, and every town—to do some work which would be of great value. In every such club there are a number of women who are ready and anxious to help, but they don't know how to go about it. What you need to do is to take the initiative here.

That is why I was willing to come here to speak to you. You may make out some rules for the schools, as I believe Providence and Brookline have done, and perhaps some of the other boards throughout the state. You may decide what you would like to have posted in the school-room—what you would like to have the children taught as to sanitary matters. Don't leave it to some of us outsiders who will put our fingers in the pie in the wrong way; but decide what you want done, and I will promise you my help in carrying it out. Until you do this, these organizations, in their eagerness to do work will continue to try to help, and it is the blind leading the blind, with the result that both will surely fall into the ditch.

There is only one thing more. Of course, we all understand that this going about among people telling them how they ought to live is believed to be quite un-American. But if we stop to think, we decide that the man who is the freest is the Indian—I mean the people in India under British rule—and that the people of India can do anything they please, except where it touches the European in the matter of crime. That is a sort of protective government. And that is not what we have here in America. It seems to me a true democratic government takes care of the people—that is, the people take care of the people, the more intelligent people taking care of those who are less intelligent. If we are to have this idea carried out in our life, it is the people's duty to see that the people are educated. So it does not seem at all un-American that it has not been done is because no one has heretofore cared to take the trouble. Perhaps we haven't put our finger on just the thing we might best and most effectually do. But somewhere, somehow, I believe that certain instructive inspection—whatever you choose to call it—certain educative phases of the work should go along with the legal phases. And I don't believe that any outside people can do it the right way. I believe it lies with you experienced men on boards of health to lay out this work and to show those of us who want to do the work what we can do to help. (Applause.)

The President—One of the guests of the association this afternoon, fortunately, is Miss von Wagner, of Yonkers, who has had a very useful experience there of some six years in sanitary inspection, and can say very much to us of interest in connection with Mrs. Richards' extremely instructive paper.

INSPECTION OF TENEMENT HOUSES.

BY JOHANNA VON WAGNER.

It is six years since I commenced tenement house work in Yonkers. A few months previously the Health Officer, who alone was not able to deal with the situation, had requested the President of the Civic League, Miss Mary Marshall Butler, to look into the conditions of tenement houses, which were frightful, even worse, I think, than in New York, because in the latter city there was tenement supervision, and Yonkers, being one of the suburbs, had the same conditions on a smaller scale, and no supervision. The members of the Civic League wished to employ a woman because in the work it is the woman who has to be dealt with.

Twenty-five years ago the Chief of the Department of Health in Glasgow realized the need of women inspectors in connection with the Health Department, and ever since that time the work has been done there by women health visitors, as they are called. The larger cities in England have followed the example of Glasgow, and there are several sanitary institutes, where men and women are graduated to do the work of sanitary inspection.

Several years ago, in Chicago, the Board of Health appointed women to inspect factories, sweat-shops and tenement houses, and six years ago, as already stated, Yonkers first took up the systematic, house-to-house inspection, emphasizing the instructive and preventive work, because the qualifications which a nurse has enable her to do better work than an untrained woman. Also my knowledge of several foreign languages aided me in reaching the people and helping them more effectively, and many times my presence was welcomed, and even celebrated, because I could converse with them in their own tongue.

The first days spent in one of the worst parts of Yonkers, realizing the awful conditions and the great amount of work that ought to be done, were very discouraging and hopeless. I hope to be forgiven for wishing to have street, people and myself, wiped out of existence. The large foreign population with their many different customs, the over-crowding, the dirt inside and outside the homes, the lack of privacy and moral sense, a great deal of sickness and consequent poverty—all this was appalling. The Civic League, after being made acquainted with existing conditions, decided to take up the work, relying upon private subscriptions for necessary expenses. It was carried on for three years. At the end of this time both the necessity and benefits of the work were thoroughly proved, and the Board of Health was induced to adopt the office, and after the passing of civil service examinations, the position of woman sanitary inspector of the Board of Health of the City of Yonkers, was established.

This was not accomplished without opposition from the kind of men who objected to having a woman appointed; it was argued that it would be taking away a man's work; the men could do the work better, and many places were not fit for women to enter. Well, I am sorry to say that there are places in existence where men and women should not live, but as long as people live there, I can go there.

Nine other cities have since employed women sanitary inspectors, but the real tenement-house work, I think, was commenced in Yonkers. It is a great privilege to have been able to do it, and to have proved the necessity of it.

The best way to help the people and the only way, is to go to their homes and give them the benefit of our experience and the knowledge derived from scientific research. Our best efforts should be used in teaching the people practical application of preventive medicine, as disease causes so much poverty and wretchedness.

While there has been a decrease in the spread of contagious diseases and infant mortality, the practice of physicians was not interfered with, as a few feared; on the contrary, the finding daily of neglected sick, who had to be placed under medical care, gave additional practice. Also the opposition of landlords, agents and tenants, had to be overcome; landlords and agents will have to learn that it is profitable to keep houses in good condition, as it secures a better class of tenants. Tenants no longer look upon me as an intruder, but are glad that some one is going around looking after their interests. They have no knowledge of the importance of ventilation, pure food, pure water and milk; I think more children die in tenement houses because, of lack of ventilation than of improper food. The Russian and Slavish people nail down their windows in winter and stuff the cracks up with paper and cotton, so as not to have a draft, because there is a baby in the house, or else coal is dear; and they will be of course, overcrowded. They always have boarders. The Italian people are more overcrowded than any other nation; shelves are put in rooms to accommodate the boarders at night, while the Slavish people put their boarders on the floor. Many rooms are without windows, and the odors from bedding, clothes and washings is overpowering, especially on Monday mornings. When women with their hands busy in the washtubs, with their feet rocking the cradles behind them, and steam finding no outlet, condensing on windows and walls—is it any wonder that another baby has died since I was there only a short while ago. It is impossible for the little ones to live.

You cannot scold, you cannot threaten, but can do nothing but sit down and try to prove to them that fresh air is essential, and the baby will not die if given a sponge bath, and kept on milk diet when sick. I have gone three or four days in succession, begging for permission to care for the child, before consent was obtained. Beer, wine and garlic water, which are given for good luck, according to the nationality, had to be discontinued, and after the baby survived the new treatment, the women would say, "Why did we not know this before; a birth and a death every year, undertaker's bills, keep us forever in debt."

The prevention of the spread of contagious diseases had to be taught by enforcing isolation, careful cleaning and fumigation, especially the care of the tuberculosis cases, and prevention of infection to other members of the family or community. The extermination of vermin in all its forms in the homes, such as flies, roaches, bugs, pediculi, which may carry infection, as also the house animals, such as rats, mice, dogs and cats is quite important as I have found dogs and cats showing similar symptoms as a case of diphtheria in the same house.

It is not an easy task to enforce vigilance and cleanliness, and in some instances it is impossible to make dirty people clean. The children, of course, I teach wherever I can; they rather think that I have police power, and the Board of Health being around, is a signal for a general cleaning. The children will take care of the sidewalks and yards, while the mothers clean up the rooms, and the offer to show me where the dirty floors are I have to decline, as in their turn they will be found.

After six years of labor I can appreciate the results I see; while a great deal has to be done, much has been accomplished; greater cleanliness, better plumbing, less overcrowding, fewer carpets on stairs and halls, more light and air in halls and rooms, a greater interest on the part of tenant and landlord, rich and poor alike, has been shown in the housing problem. More workers in the field, both from the Board of Health and charity organizations.

Since I have had the authority of the Board of Health, it has been easier to gain entrance. "Come in; we have been waiting for you all this time," or "I am glad it is a woman this time," are daily remarks. I am expected to help in all sorts of difficulties, from finding work and rooms to baking bread or buying pianos. A request to call again, or to spend Sunday or an evening with them, shows that the visit has been appreciated.

I think there is a great field for social service, and I am thankful to be here today, even if I have not much to say, to tell you that the people are waiting for the help of city officials or for those who know, to bring them the knowledge to better their conditions. They need it very much, and this is the opportunity for boards of health, I think, especially, to enlighten the people as to the best ways and means of having and keeping healthy homes.

The President—The subject is open for discussion.

Dr. H. L. Chase—Mr. President:—I want to say a few words. I suppose that I am responsible for the fact of sanitary inspection being brought up six months ago, when the association was about to meet in Brookline. Dr. Durgin asked me if I knew of any subject that would especially interest our board of health; for it is the custom to consult the board of health of the town in which we are to meet about our program. I told him we were struggling with the sanitary inspection question and would like enlightenment. He said he would find someone to present a paper on that subject, and accordingly invited Dr. Chapin, who gave us an excellent paper, as you all remember. There was not time at that meeting to finish the consideration of the subject. I am very glad, therefore, that Dr. Durgin asked Mrs. Richards to prepare a paper on the same subject for our meeting today. It truly is a most important, living question, what to do with our tenements. Mayor Collins, you know, has just appointed a tenement commission for Boston, and we all of us are dealing with the tenement problem. I am sure we have had food for reflection given us in the paper just read, and in the remarks of the lady who has so ably discussed it. I had great pleasure today in seeing Mrs. von Wagner again. It is the first time I have seen her since the summer of 1898, when one or two members of this association and myself were at the great quarantine camp at Montauk Point soon after Shafter's army returned from Cuba. The Second Massachusetts Infantry encamped at Montauk, and alongside was the regiment of regulars I was associated with for a month—the 22d U. S. Infantry. Mrs. von Wagner spent her summer vacation in the adjoining town, and was the head of a little party of women who every day came over to Gen. Ludlow's brigade, which included the 2d Massachusetts and two other regiments, and brought with them ice and milk and various other things that the sick and exhausted soldiers greatly needed. She and her fellow workers came to me each morning and got the list of men who were specially in need of help, and brought them just the articles they most needed, straightened out their housekeeping arrangements, and did everything in their power for their comfort. We spoke sometimes of sanitary matters, and she told me that Yonkers had just established public baths and was doing some other progressive things. She had then just begun her sanitary inspection work there. It is most fortunate, I think, that Mrs. Richards succeeded in getting Mrs. von Wagner here today to relate her practical experiences with instructive sanitary inspection.

The President—The next paper upon the program is a paper on "The Recent Smallpox Epidemic in Massachusetts," by Dr. Morse.

THE RECENT SMALLPOX EPIDEMIC IN MASSACHU-SETTS.

BY FRANK L. MORSE, M. D.

The presence of an unusual, and, from a medical point of view, an unwarranted number of cases of smallpox during the past two years, in fact, an epidemic of greater severity than has occurred since 1872, has again awakened the physicians of this state and shown to them how incompletely were the inhabitants protected by vaccination from the disease.

If we review the history of smallpox in this state we find that it has been present almost uninterruptedly since the Pilgrims first settled at Plymouth in 1620, for epidemics are reported to have occurred five times between 1631 and 1678, and it is stated that between 700 and 800 died of the disease during the latter year.

In 1702, it is stated that 213, or about 4.4 per cent. of the entire population died of it, and again in 1721 there were 5989 cases in Boston, more than half of the population being ill with the disease, of which number 850, about 14 per cent., died. In 1730, with a population of 15,000, it is estimated that 4000 were ill and 500 died of smallpox. In 1751, an English vessel with smallpox on board was wrecked near Nahant and was the means of spreading the disease again, for there were 7653 cases and 545 deaths, a fatality of 7 per cent. resulting from this infection. It was during this epidemic that practically every person in the city of Boston susceptible to the disease contracted it, for the population at that time was 15,684, and of this number 5998 were protected by a previous attack, 1843 moved away from the town on account of the presence of the disease, and with the exception of 174 all of the other inhabitants contracted the disease. It occurred in the American army in 1776 at Cambridge, and it is stated that there were scarcely enough men free from it to keep guard at the different hospitals.

In 1792, of a population of 20,000 people, 8346 had the disease and 198 died.

Such was the history of smallpox in Massachusetts up to practically the time of the discovery of vaccination, and for a period of nearly 200 years we find that almost all of the inhabitants of the state had passed through an attack of smallpox; but the history of the first 100 years differs much from that of the period remaining before the discovery of vaccination. From 1631, the date of the first epidemic, until 1721, the disease progressed in its natural virulent, unmodified form, sweeping away many of the inhabitants of the colony, as many as 800 in a single year, and leaving the remainder marked by the disease for life. With the epidemic of 1721 we find that the practice of inoculation smallpox was introduced, and from that time until the close of the century the mortality steadily decreased, and since that time we have never seen the disease exist as it did in the early history of the state. The inoculation theory of smallpox is rarely spoken of at the present time, except as a matter of history, but following the year 1721, until vaccination was introduced, it was certainly of as much benefit to the people as vaccination has been in the present era. It was found, if a person was inoculated with smallpox infection, instead of contracting the disease in the natural way, that he passed through a much milder course, and with practically no mortality compared with the disease itself; but, on the other hand, the disease was true smallpox and could be conveyed, even in a most virulent manner, to another not so protected. There was much opposition to this practice when it was first introduced and it required several epidemics to show the inhabitants the value of its introduction, and in 1764 three hospitals were opened for the reception of patients to be treated with inoculation smallpox. On account of the disease spreading from the hospitals to the residents in the neighborhood, the reception of patients was discontinued, and it was not until 1776, when the legislature enacted a law licensing inoculation, that the population as a whole received the full benefit of the practice. The mortality of smallpox per 1000 inhabitants under this method of treatment diminished from 77.3 in the epidemic of 1721 gradually to only 9.9 in that of 1792.

With the introduction of vaccination, we find but few instances of the true character of the disease as it existed in the early history of the state, and although it had become less virulent under the inoculation theory, the history of the disease following vaccination is even more marked. It appears that vaccination was quite generally used after the year 1800 in the state, and the legislature in 1810 passed a law making it obligatory and providing for each town to appoint a suitable person to superintend the vaccination of its inhabitants. This was in force until 1836, when it was repealed. As a result of this legislation we find that while it was in force there were only 37 deaths from the disease in the city of Boston for a period of 26 years, while in the twelve years following, when vaccination was optional instead of obligatory, there were 533 deaths from it.

Beginning with the year 1842, we have complete returns of the deaths from smallpox up to the present time, and we find that in no instance has the disease ever attained the virulence and high fatality which it had in the early history of the state. There are several years in which in the neighborhood of 300 deaths are registered, but these were previous to 1871. During this latter year and in 1872 and 1873 smallpox visited the state to an alarming degree, and in 13 months 5606 cases were reported, with 1029 deaths from 197 cities and towns. That this condition must result when laws passed by the legislature make vaccination optional, rather than compulsory, is to be expected, and following this great epidemic—for it was certainly great for the time—we have seen little of smallpox until the past two years. The people of '71 and '72 evidently learned their lesson well by experience, and in the following years profited by the benefits of vaccination, but a new generation has grown up, uneducated to the ravages of the disease, and new societies have been formed to tell us of the injurious effects of vaccination, and these influences we must hold as partially responsible for the epidemic which we have had with us today. Following the epidemic of 1872-73 there was little smallpox, and in no year have the deaths been over 47, which number occurred in 1881. In 1885, the deaths reached 19 and in 1894 there were 33 in the state, these being the largest years up to 1901. In 1883 a law was enacted requiring local boards of health to report cases of smallpox to the State Board of Health, and since this time the records of smallpox have been particularly complete. For the 18 years ending with 1900 there were 628 cases reported, with 111 deaths, this being a most remarkable showing with the laws so constituted that vaccination was not compulsory, except as a requirement for school children, and even in this instance a loophole existed by which it was possible, for those so disposed, to obtain certificates exempting their children from vaccination. This exception in the law has been made use of in a manner entirely at variance with the meaning of the law, and at the session of the General Court last year legislation was enacted which to a certain degree removed the objectionable feature.

During this period of 18 years there has been no year in which cases have not appeared, but there have been four years when no deaths have been reported. These years were 1886, 1895, 1896 and 1898, and it is to be presumed that as year after year went by and few cases occurred, the inhabitants failed to improve the protection offered by vaccination, and in some of the smaller towns in the interior of the state the law relative to school children had been grossly neglected.

In 1899, 105 cases were reported, the city of Fall River having 37, Boston 29, and Chelsea 27, and among these cases 11 occurred among unvaccinated mill operatives at Fall River, and four among unvaccinated pupils in the public schools, in violation of the laws of the state. Of these 105 cases, 14 died, a fatality of 17.5 per cent. In 1900, 104 cases were reported, Fall River again leading with 37 cases, Lowell with 23, and the town of Westport, to which the infection was brought from Fall River, with 19. The fatality was very small, only three deaths resulting, and it was for this reason that many people in the state doubted its being true smallpox. The disease was also prevalent at this time in the southern and western states and the fatality was even less than in this state. During 1901, the disease continued to increase in the number of cases reported and also in the fatality. A limited outbreak occurred in May and June, during which time 115 cases were reported, most of them occurring in the cities of Boston, Worcester, New Bedford, and Fall River, and the town of Leominster. This was followed by a less number of cases during July and August, but in the latter part of September it recurred with increasing numbers, until 235 cases were reported in November and 274 in December, infecting 62 cities and towns in the state. Seven hundred and seventy-eight cases were reported during the year, of which 514, or nearly 66 per cent., occurred in the city of Boston. Of these cases 101 died, a fatality of 13 per cent.

During the past year the disease has continued to a degree almost comparable with the epidemic of 1872-3, and over 2300 cases have been reported, with 278 deaths, a fatality of 12 per cent. At no time during the past two and a half years has the state been without the infection, and in only seven weeks of this time have no new cases been reported. There was a slight cessation in the number of cases in the latter part of August, and the first of September of the past year, but during the winter the cases increased in numbers and have continued even up to the present time.

The practice of vaccination for the prevention of smallpox, although doubted by only a few, is as powerful and trustworthy as it was 100 years ago; in fact, with our continued studies upon the cases of smallpox occurring in this state for the 14 years, definitely than at any time in the history of the disease. A single table of the cases of the disease occurring in this state alone during the past 14 years ought to convince the most skeptical of the efficacy of vaccination. Accurate records have been kept of the cases of smallpox occurring in this state for the 14 years, 1888-1901, and a table has been made comparing the cases, ages and vaccination of the patients.

	Vaccinated.		Unvaccinated	
	Cases.	Deaths.	Cases.	Deaths.
0—1	1	0	52	15
1—5	19	0	163	18
5—10	16	0	78	4
10—15	29	0	31	0
	65	0	324	37
15—20	49	3	80	11
20—30	190	13	166	31
30—40	144	21	71	22
40—50	89	18	26	7
Over 50	47	5	11	4

From this table we find that of a total of about 1300 cases only 65 appeared among the vaccinated during the first 15 years of life and not a single one died. Among the unvaccinated, however, it is another story, for during the same age period 324 contracted the disease and 37 died at a time of life when conditions for fighting an acute disease are of the highest.

During 1902 we find the conditions just as marked, for of 78 deaths among 979 vaccinated patients, none was among those who had been vaccinated within 20 years. There were 15 deaths among patients vaccinated from 20 to 30 years ago, 23 deaths among those vaccinated 30 to 40 years ago, 15 deaths among those vaccinated 40 to 50 years ago, and 25 deaths among those who had not been vaccinated for a period of over 50 years. The fatality of this group of cases is less than 8 per cent., and over one-half of the deaths occurred in patients vaccinated so many years ago that the protection given them by vaccination had entirely disappeared.

Among 1328 unvaccinated cases during 1902, there were 200 deaths, a fatality of over 15 per cent., and just double that of the vaccinated patients. The cases also occurred outside of the city of Boston to a greater extent than during the previous year, 44 per cent. only occurring in this city.

The remedy for smallpox, as we all know, lies in vaccination, but the methods for carrying it on must be directed by the legislature of the state. In 1810, if you will remember, such laws were enacted and remained in force until 1836, when they were repealed, and it was during this time that the people of the state enjoyed an immunity from the disease, which never existed previous to that time, and we have never been favored with it since. It is true that at times special legislation has been passed, controlling vaccination in incorporated manufactories and among school children, but laws relating to the general public are still wanting. As each year goes by we find appearing before the legislative Committee on Public Health a body of citizens, both men and women, filled to the brim with the alleged injuries of vaccination and clamoring for the repeal of all vaccination laws. They contend that it is a sacrifice of their personal rights, that people who have been vaccinated contract smallpox, and year after year they present statistics which, on their face, would seem to bear out their opinions. Opposed to them are a few of the representative medical men of the state, not asking for any new legislation, but that the present laws be allowed to remain as they are. What is desired is legislation compelling everybody to become vaccinated at an early age, and revaccinated at certain definite periods thereafter. Then, we should enjoy the same privileges which are present in Germany today, where little or no smallpox exists except on the borders of the empire, when all other countries about them have numerous cases of the disease. A concerted effort on the part of the boards of health and medical profession of the whole state would, we believe, bring about the passage of such laws, eradicate the disease from our midst, relieve local boards of health from such work as is connected with an epidemic of smallpox, and save the people of the commonwealth hundreds of thousands of dollars in the future.

When a suspicious case of smallpox appears, two questions arise for immediate answer: First, Is this a case of smallpox? and, second, If it has been so decided, what will be done with the patient? The diagnosis of a case with any eruption whatsoever should be suspected of being smallpox until it is known definitely that it is some other disease. The three important points in making a diagnosis are, first, The presence or absence of a successful vaccination and the length of time which has elapsed since it was performed. Second, The location of the eruption upon the surface of the body; third, The character of the eruption.

With but very few exceptions, if a person has been successfully vaccinated within five years, and has a good scar present, the possibility of smallpox can almost immediately be ruled out. The location of the eruption is usually upon the exposed surfaces of the body, upon the face, the hands and forearms, and to a less extent upon the trunk and lower extremities. An important point of diagnosis is the location of the eruption upon the palms of the hands, soles of the feet or upon the surfaces between the fingers. This condition is almost invariably present to some extent, even in the mildest cases of the disease, and although seen occasionally in chicken pox it occurs usually only when the eruption is very extensive on other parts of the body.

The character of the eruption present indicates that it is in the true skin, and when the papule first appears it has a hard, indurated feeling which increases as it comes towards the surface and then passes, at about the third day, into a vesicle, developing rapidly from that stage into a pustule, sometimes as early as four or five days after the first appearance of the eruption. In the confluent form, as it appears among the unvaccinated, the eruption is so extensive that practically the entire surface of the body is involved, but in the discrete form single eruptions over the whole body may be seen passing from day to day through their usual course.

The constitutional disturbance preceding the appearance of the eruption is almost invariably present, if a true history can be obtained from the patient. It is of value in making a diagnosis, for with the appearance of the eruption the headache and backache disappear and the patient is often heard to say that he is practically well.

The diseases which may be taken for smallpox are chicken pox, measles, typhoid fever, and, strange as it may seem, influenza.

The location of the eruptive in chicken pox is exactly opposite to that of smallpox. It appears upon the covered parts of the body, the chest, back, and abdomen, rather than on the exposed parts, although individual lesions do appear upon the latter surfaces. The constitutional disturbance preceding the appearance of the eruption is usually wanting, and the clear, raised vesicle of chicken pox, involving only the superficial skin, is in marked contrast to the hardened one of smallpox. The cough, coryza, and conjuncivitis of measles are usually sufficient in making a diagnosis; they very rarely appear in smallpox, although the papular eruption of one may resemble the other.

In the early stages of typhoid fever, for the first two or three days, on account of the headache and backache, the two diseases may be confounded, but the almost complete remission of these symptoms with the appearance of the eruption of small-pox would, in an ordinary case, make the diagnosis certain. Cases of smallpox have, however, in this epidemic been sent to hospitals with a diagnosis of typhoid fever. The headache and backache of smallpox and influenza very closely resemble one another, and on account of the usual short duration of the latter, it some-times happens that the former is overlooked, for at about the third day, when the grippe symptoms would be less severe, and at a time when the eruption of smallpox would be appearing, both the attending physician and patient may conclude that the sickness is at an end. Such a condition did occur in the town of Northbridge last winter, and as a result 43 cases of the disease were present, which in the early part of the illness had been called grippe.

The diagnosis of a case having been made certain, the patient should be reported to the board of health as ill with smallpox. In most cities and towns in the state the board assures imme-diate care of the patient and provides for the medical care and nursing. The ideal way to care for a patient is to remove him to a hospital maintained for such cases, or, if none exists, the erection of one, which can usually be accomplished within 24 hours. The house from which the patient is removed should be immediately quarantined, the inmates and those exposed, imme-diately vaccinated and kept under observation for two weeks, to determine if any are to become ill with the disease.

Smallpox at the present time is not prevalent in this Metro-politan district, but, almost daily, cases are reported from the smaller cities and towns in the interior of the state, where vac-cination has not been carried on to the extent which has been accomplished in this district, and during the coming summer and even next winter local boards of health must be on the lookout for the disease at any time. The officials of the local boards of health in the localities where smallpox has prevailed, many of whom are represented here today, are to be praised in the man-agement of the cases as they have appeared in their different

cities and towns and for the almost constant success which has
followed their supervision of the cases. All of you are acquainted with the criticisms which are so frequently and unjustly hurled
at the local boards of health at such a time by those incompetent
to judge, but I believe in every instance the authorities have done
their best under the existing conditions, and in most instances
the disease has been confined to its original limits.

The President—Dr. Morse's paper comes at a most auspicious
time. I suppose you are aware that the question of vaccination
is still at the front at the State House. Strangely enough, in
some quarters it seems to be regarded as an agricultural question. (Laughter.) I think it is really a medical question. I think
we should agree here that it is a medical question and not an
agricultural question.

But the matter is exciting a great deal of interest, as you
know. The medical associations of the state have acted. One
of them, the District Medical Society, or the Norfolk District
Society, went so far as to ask a very prominent member of the
legal profession to represent the interests of medicine at the
State House, and we fortunately have this afternoon as our guest
Mr. Lawrence, the gentleman who was invited to represent the
medical society at the State House. I think it is always interesting to us who are employed in the actual administration of
health questions to know how these questions are viewed from
the outside—especially how they seem to a sharp, witty member
of the legal profession; and I am going to ask Mr. Lawrence
to say a few words to you this afternoon on this subject.

Mr. Lawrence—Mr. President and Gentlemen:—It is somewhat of a surprise to me to be here this afternoon, as I had not
heard anything about it until a short time before 1 o'clock, and I
come, therefore, wholly unprepared. But I imagine that what
you most desire is a knowledge of the proceedings before the
Legislature upon this bill that has been introduced, to know
what the conditions are at the present time, and to know what
action could be taken by boards of health, physicians and others
interested in the matter to secure the passage of this bill.

A bill was introduced before the House this year—House bill 329—which was in the form of an amendment to the revised laws, granting authority to the State Board of Health to manufacture and distribute anti-toxine and vaccine. The manufacture and distribution of antitoxine and vaccine were joined because these two articles were considered of the utmost importance and were both desired. We also felt that it might help us in the passage of the bill. Everybody in the state knows the beneficent results of the state manufacture of anti-toxine during the last eight years, and there is not anybody who would undertake to say that the conditions have not been materially better under the administration of the State Board of Health.

We had several hearings. I was approached by Dr. Gilbert, the chairman of the sub-committee of the Norfolk District Society, who asked me to undertake the matter, and at the time I supposed I was going to have what would be commonly called a cinch. I thought we would be present at the hearing about half a day, or possibly a day, introduce a little evidence, have a few doctors testify, and the thing would come through in great shape. But to my disappointment, we spent three entire days before the committee. We met unusual opposition, not, perhaps, before the committee directly, because, as I remember, there were only three witnesses who appeared for the opposition, one a manufacturer of vaccine in New Hampshire, Dr. Martin, whose testimony was more in our favor than in that of the opposition; the second, a druggist of Boston, who appeared to be very much prejudiced, and who was the first man to make the statements in regard to the outrageous condition of affairs at Bussey Institute under the management of the State Board of Health, his statement being founded entirely on information, he not having visited the Bussey Institute himself; the third man was Mr. Bartlett, a representative of the Pharmaceutical Association, who appeared as the representative of the local opponents of this bill, and who read at that meeting a report of a visit to the State Board of Health, which I have had occasion to denounce in the Transcript as a most scur-

rilous article in relation to this matter. It was untrue in most
respects and grossly exaggerated as to the rest.

The opposition, in the first instance, has come almost entirely
from the large manufacturers of serum and similar articles—
Mulford, Parke Davis and other similar institutions. Mulford had
three representatives present at every hearing at the State House;
Parke Davis had, I believe, the same number; and, while they
produced no one to testify before the committee, everything has
been done that could be done to influence the committee in an
indirect way. The result has been that the committee have considered the matter very carefully. They have been loath, apparently, to come to any decison one way or the other. Their report
was to have been rendered about a month ago. They asked for
an extension of time until some two weeks ago, I believe, and
then they had a further extension and yesterday their time
elapsed.

At the executive session of the committee yesterday, I understand it was decided to divide the bill which we introduced. A
new bill was drafted, which provides that the State Board of
Health shall manufacture and produce anti-toxine for free distribution to the hospitals, charitable institutions, and worthy poor
of the State. They are granted no authority to sell the anti-
toxine, and they are not to distribute it to anybody who is able
to buy it for himself. As to the vaccine, the committee requested
further time to consider the matter, and were granted, I believe,
an extension until next Monday.

While I cannot say positively as to the form of that bill, I have
been led to believe, from information which comes pretty direct,
that the way the bill will be reported will be as a bill attached to
the petition of the Board of Agriculture, in which they make
their report that the State Board of Agriculture is in a position,
and is the proper body, to manufacture vaccine, and that the vaccine should be manufactured at Amherst College. The bill which
is to be introduced, as I understand it, will be a bill for the State
of Massachusetts to manufacture and distribute vaccine lymph—I
cannot say positively whether free or not, although I think it is

to be free—the manufacture to be under the supervision of the Board of Health and to be conducted at the Agricultural College in Amherst. I understand there is one dissenter to this bill in the House and one in the Senate, and I should like to direct your attention for a moment to the result, if the bills are passed as proposed.

To begin with, the bill with relation to anti-toxine provides that it shall be distributed free to the hospitals, charitable institutions and worthy poor. Now, the first thing we run up against is the question as to who are the worthy poor. Who is going to settle that question? The next thing is, after you have decided that certain persons are not worthy poor, and are not entitled to the State anti-toxine, how are they to get it? The State can not sell the anti-toxine to them, because they cannot go into the manufacture of the product in opposition to private manufacturers and put it on the market for sale. They can't give it to them, because they are not the worthy poor. There is nothing left for the people who are not "the worthy poor" but to go and buy the product of the manufacturers on the market. The result is that the State anti-toxine is limited to a very small proportion of the patients who require it, and it doesn't provide the protection to the people which is desired by having the State manufacture the article. It is of just as much importance to the community that the rich man should be able to get his anti-toxine at a moment's notice, and prevent the spread of the disease, as it is that the poor man should get it.

Supposing a man in a small town in the State of Massachusetts is able to pay for anti-toxine. He can't get the State's anti-toxine, because they won't allow him to have it. He may not be able to get the anti-toxine of any private manufacturer, because the druggist in that town may not have a supply on hand, and if he has, it may be an old supply which is worthless. What is the result? The man is obliged to wait until he can get his anti-toxine from some private manufacturer, and in the meantime the most dire results may have occurred.

Now, that is practically a nullification of the effect desired by the passage of this act.   It amounts to nothing, and the restriction as to the distribution of the anti-toxine should be removed. The Board of Health should be given authority to distribute in its discretion anti-toxine to the people of the Commonwealth.   And we assume that the Board of Health would use its own judgment as it has in the past as to who were the proper persons to receive the anti-toxine.

Now as to the vaccine bill.   The first thing that suggests itself to one's mind is the fact that we have two co-ordinate bodies— two State boards—which are liable to come into friction with each other.   We all know the gentlemen of the agricultural board to be most estimable gentlemen, and we all know—certainly this body would know—the calibre of the men constituting the State Board of Health.   But we also know that you can't get two co-ordinate bodies of that kind to regulate the manufacture of any article of that kind without some trouble sooner or later.

It is suggested that the State Board of Health shall have entire supervision of this matter and shall run it to suit themselves, the only limitation being that they shall manufacture the vaccine at Amherst College.   That is the important thing.   The force of the State Board of Health is in Boston—the principal force— not in Amherst.   Amherst is over a hundred miles, two or three hours' ride from Boston.   For a member of the State Board of Health to go from Boston to Amherst, to perform the duties which would be required of him there, to inspect the plant, or anything of that kind, and get back again to Boston, would use up the entire day.   It would make it highly inconvenient and cause endless and entirely unnecessary annoyances.

There is another place where this product can be manufactured, and that is at Bussey Institute, where the anti-toxine is at present manufactured.   Now the advantage of having it close to Boston is patent to everybody right on the surface.   To begin with, Dr. Theobald Smith, who needs certainly no recommendation or qualification by my hands, would be the inspector, you might say, of the institution.   His duties in connection with the anti-toxine plant and with Harvard College would prevent his being an effective supervisor of any plant in Amherst. It would be practically an impossibility, and I doubt if the doctor would undertake it with his other duties, even in the event that additional compensation were offered him for the purpose.

In the next place, you are sending it to a small town, isolated from the scientific centres. Bussey Institute is in close touch with the scientific men of Boston, of all the hospitals in the city of Boston, and the metropolitan district, and with the scientific men of Harvard College, Tufts College and other scientific institutions in the neighborhood of Boston; and I think there is nothing which would illustrate the importance of this fact better than the statement of Dr. Councilman, in regard to his recent discovery, that it was due, not to his efforts alone, but to the united efforts of the scientific men with whom he was in close touch in this immediate vicinity. (Applause.)

I think it will be clear to everybody, also, that so long as the State is to pay for this thing, it should be done in as economical a way as possible; and one of the first principles of economy is the centralization of the work. If you can erect a building for the purpose of manufacturing both anti-toxine and vaccine, you will immediately reduce the running expenses of your institution, of your office force and every expense connected with it. It would be a material saving to the State, and I think that should be taken into consideration in the passage of this bill.

Now, as to the indorsements which have been received from all parts of the State. I have had occasion to communicate with every medical society, practically, so far as I have been able to find them out, in the State; and we have the unanimous indorsement of the bill by the Massachusetts Medical Society, through its board of councillors, and the unanimous indorsement by resolutions from every one of the district medical societies, I believe, which has held a meeting since this matter has been brought to the front. In other words, I have received resolutions from 17 of the 21 district medical societies, unanimously indorsing the bill; and in addition to that, I have the indorsement of the Boston Homeopathic Medical Society; and I am assured by Dr. Southerland that, from his talk with the members of the Surgical and Gynæcological Society, and the members of the Massachusetts Homeopathic Society, that these societies would also be unanimously in favor of these measures. I have resolutions from medical clubs in some portions of the State, and a great many indorsements from leading physicians. I don't see how any bill could have a more thorough medical indorsement than this one. It would be a material saving to the State, and I think that should

In addition to that, I sent out letters to the Boards of Health of Massachusetts. Very likely many of you have received them. I sent out 135 letters, one to every city and town in the State of 3,000 inhabitants and over. Of these 135 cities and towns I have received answers at the present time from 73 or 74, and of that number there is only one dissenting voice, and that is the town of Amherst. Yesterday and the day before I sent out letters to the towns that have not answered my first communication, requesting them to sign the resolutions and return them to me, so that we might, if possible, have a unanimous indorsement of this bill by the Boards of Health of the State.

I have received letters of indorsement from all kinds and conditions of men in the State. I have a letter from Lucius Tuttle, the president of the Boston & Maine Railroad, a man who is in as good a position as anybody to know the benefits of vaccination among a large number of employees. I have received indorsements from steamship companies, whose lines touch the State, and also from large dry goods concerns, leading manufacturers and others, and I don't see how it is possible for any bill touching the public good to be more unanimously indorsed than this bill which is now before the Legislature.

In order to get it passed, as we all desire to have it passed, there must be a fight in the House and Senate. The bill is not in the shape in which we want it now. We hope for an amendment, and it is essential to effect an amendment of that kind that the members of the Legislature should be informed as to what is the proper course to take. There are in the neighborhood of 300 members in the Legislature. Perhaps not over 20 at the outside are doctors, or men who are in a position to judge of the advantages of this bill.' It is, I think, therefore essential that men who are in a position to know about these things should instruct their representatives as to their ideas of what is proper in this matter. And I think, gentlemen, that you can do more good if you will write the representative from your district and inform him that your Board of Health is heartily in favor of this bill and wants him to support it, than by anything else that you can possibly do.

There is nothing, absolutely nothing, which has so much effect on the individual legislator as to be personally interviewed by his friends and acquaintances and shown by them that they are interested in a measure and that they want it to go through for the good of the community and what they consider the best good of the Commonwealth.

Now I would suggest that every member who is here, and every person you can get in contact with, should use his best efforts to come personally, either by letter or otherwise, in contact with legislators from your districts and give them your views as to what is the proper course to take in this matter. And I feel certain from the talk that I have had with individual legislators that there is not a man in the Senate or House who, if he really understands the situation, and realizes the importance of this, and the desirability of the passage of the original bill, would not be in favor of it and support it, or see that the bills, as introduced, went through properly amended, as they should be. (Applause.)

Dr. A. E. Miller of Needham.—Mr. President, I want to ask a question, or rather to make a suggestion. I think we could do a good deal of missionary work. I know I can, and I'd like a copy of the bills just as the gentleman who has just been talking thinks they ought to be, and then I can go to our representative and senator and show them how we would like to have this thing passed. If I had a copy of what the gentleman thinks we ought to have, I could do better missionary work than I otherwise could.

Mr. Lawrence.—I would say for the benefit of the gentlemen present that any person who writes to the document department of the Legislature can have a copy of bill No. 329 sent to him. And it would not be necessary to forward a copy of that bill to your representative if you wrote him that you were interested in House bill No. 329 and the bills which have been substituted for it. I also would like to state that I have some printed copies of the names of the members of the Legislature, and if any member would like them I should be glad to give them to him. I haven't them here, but in my office. This would enable you to see whether there are any members of the Legislature that you know personally.

The President.—Is there anything more to be said upon this subject? If not, Dr. Durgin wishes to introduce a piece of business, and moves that he be given authority to spend $7.50 in the purchase of certain numbers of the publications of this society, in order to complete useful files now in existence. Is it your pleasure to authorize the appropriation?

The association voted unanimously to authorize the appropriation.

Dr. Durgin—I move that this association unanimously indorses House bill 329.

The motion was adopted.

Adjournment.

ERRATUM.

JAMES C. COFFEY,
Exec. Officer, *Worcester* Board of Health.

JOURNAL OF THE
MASSACHUSETTS ASSOCIATION OF BOARDS OF HEALTH.

ORGANIZED 1890.

[The Association as a body is not responsible for statements or opinions of any of its members.]

| VOL. XIII. | October, 1903. | NO. 3. |

THE MASSACHUSETTS ASSOCIATION OF BOARDS OF HEALTH was organized in Boston in March, 1890, with the following objects: the advancement of sanitary science in the Commonwealth of Massachusetts, the promotion of better organization and co-operation in the local Boards of Health, and the uniform enforcement of sanitary laws and regulations.

THE JOURNAL OF THIS ASSOCIATION has, for thirteen years, faithfully reflected the views of the public hygienists of Massachusetts

As the only one of its kind in Massachusetts, the Journal so far has had its own field, which, however, it has not yet fully occupied. To take more complete advantage of the available opportunities, some expansion has been determined upon. The outcome is shown in this, the first, issue in the new form. If the general high level reached in the past can be maintained in the future, the chief object of the new management will be accomplished.

We hope that our readers will be moved to show appreciation of this effort by aiding in the expansion of the subscription list, which is open to non-members, as well as to members, of the Association.

EDITORIALS.
THE MILK SUPPLY OF LARGE CITIES. Mr. H. E.
Atwood, Chief of the Dairy Division of the U. S. Dept. of Agriculture, has recently published a very interesting document relating to the milk supply of the cities of the United States.*

---

*The Milk Supply of Two Hundred Cities and Towns. By H. E. Atwood, C. E., and R. A. Pearson, M. S., Washington. Government Printing Office, 1903.

The salient points shown in this report are the decided progress made in recent years in the matter of improving the milk supply of the people, the adoption of systematic methods of inspecting milk in all large cities, greater cleanliness in milking and the care of milk, and the introduction of glass bottles or jars for the purposes of distribution.

So far as Massachusetts is concerned the evolution of milk legislation has not differed from that of other important questions affecting the life and health of the people. The economic or financial view has too often been allowed to influence legislation, rather than the sanitary or life-saving view. When it was proposed to repeal the existing protective law in regard to water-gas in 1890, Addicksism finally triumphed in Massachusetts as it has since done in Delaware, and as a consequence the deaths from gas poisoning have increased more than ten-fold, as had been predicted. The present milk laws of Massachusetts are protective against fraud, and, economically considered, are excellent statutes, but they do not accomplish the object which is of much greater importance, viz.: a strict supervision of the methods of production, and inspection of all dairy farms regularly and systematically carried out, with a view to securing absolutely cleanly methods of milk production and distribution, including the exclusion of all persons suffering with infectious diseases, either acute or chronic, from all connection with dairy work. The powers of a milk inspector are limited by the boundary lines of his own city or town, and he is therefore compelled to give attention to the quality of the milk as it arrives at its destination. There should be, therefore, some other power or authority conferred by law which would enable an official to visit every dairy farm which contributes to the city milk supply, and to compel producers to adopt such sanitary measures as might be found necessary. This is far more important than the mere analysis of milk for the purpose of detecting commercial frauds. · Unfortunately for Massachusetts, a large part of its present milk supply comes from other States, and radical improvement in the direction we have indicated would necessitate the co-operation of the sanitary authorities in such other States.

City	Population, Census of 1900	Avg. Daily Milk Consump'n Total (GALS.)	Per Cap. (PINTS)	Milk Stores	Milk Wagons	Portion Ship'd by Rail (%)	Herds	Cows	H'ds Insp. Last Year	Dairies Outside City Total	Insp'd Last Y'r	Retail Price Summer (cts.)	Retail Price Winter (cts.)	Milk Standard Slds.	Fats.	Cost of Inspection ($)	Samples Analyzed Last Year
New York City	3,437,202	333,856	.78	12,000	4,000	85	5500	23,200	560	3500	..	6	8	12	3	..	79,657
Chicago	1,698,575	169,465	.80	2,162	2,692	97	30	420	30	4000	11	5–7	6–7	12	3	10,000	19,053
Philadelphia	1,293,697	75,000	.46	1,500	2,000	75	500	5,000	500	2500	..	6	8	12	3.5	9,580	47,118
St. Louis	575,238	26,375	.37	1,987	1,109	..	400	8,000	350	119	..	5–8	5–8	11.5	3	1,850	684
Boston	560,892	82,250	1.17	2,900	506	75	126	739	126	..	..	5–8	5–8	13; 12	3.7; 3	13,000	15,000
Baltimore	508,957	25,000	.39	2,530	525	..	539	3,314	539	1500	220	5–10	5–10	12	3	2,300	32,703
Worcester	118,421	16,500	1.11	400	350	1	340	4,036	316	568	..	5½	5½	Same as Boston	Same as Boston	1,000	1,490
Fall River	104,863	6,000	.46	327	320	..	105	350	105	240	240	5–6	6–7	Same as Boston	Same as Boston	1,250	257
Lowell	94,969	7,700	.65	350	156	4	..	100	..	..	..	5	6	Same as Boston	Same as Boston	2,329	2,972
Cambridge	91,886	9,074	.79	410	156	53	76	234	76	500	..	4–8	5–9	Same as Boston	Same as Boston	1,500	3,367
Lynn	68,513	6,000	.70	350	75	67	60	350	60	800	..	4–7	4–7	Same as Boston	Same as Boston	2,500	..
Lawrence	62,559	6,000	.76	700	200	..	8	130	8	..	..	6	6	Same as Boston	Same as Boston	350	179
New Bedford	62,442	7,000	.90	201	170	87	20	700	20	420	..	6	6	Same as Boston	Same as Boston	1,500	900
Springfield	62,059	4,750	.61	103	133	..	20	130	..	..	..	6	6	Same as Boston	Same as Boston	100	575
Somerville	61,643	7,640	.99	300	185	..	2	62	2	300	..	6	7	Same as Boston	Same as Boston	500	..
Holyoke	45,712	4,373	.77	172	136	..	78	858	78	..	..	5	6	Same as Boston	Same as Boston	500	260
Brockton	40,063	3,200	.64	150	150	..	41	584	41	20	20	6	6	Same as Boston	Same as Boston	100	25

In thirty-five States laws now exist referring to the sale of milk. In several other States and Territories there are also food laws which relate to milk. In twenty-six States there are officials whose duty it is to enforce these laws.

In nearly all of the cities having a population of more than 50,000 there is some supervision of the milk supply, but in the smaller cities and towns such supervision is the exception and not the rule.

In addition to the very full tables which give much information as to the milk supply of cities and the extent of supervision, there are several appendices giving the ordinances of different cities, rules, regulations, and blank forms.

In two or three States and cities the sale of milk produced by cows fed upon ensilage is forbidden, and in commenting upon the fact, the compiler refers to ensilage as "a most excellent dairy feed"—a term with which we cannot fully agree.

From the standpoint of the milk-producer in the neighborhood of large cities, whose hayfields are of limited extent, ensilage appears necessary to supplement a deficiency in fodder for his cows and to enable them to yield an abundant flow of milk, but from the standpoint of the physician, and especially from that of the specialist in the care of infants, the use of fermented foods for the production of milk does not appear to be a settled question. So long as infant mortality continues to play an important part in the death-rate of cities, it would seem proper to advise for the nourishment of children who are fed from the bottle the milk of cows fed upon good hay and grain and such other food as nature has provided.

The introduction of glass jars for the delivery of milk and cream appears to have been quite general in nearly all large cities in recent years.

From the very full tables presented in this valuable report, we have selected the principal items relating to the milk supply of large cities (having over 500,000 in each) and have added those which relate to a number of Massachusetts cities and towns.

The largest per capita consumption of milk appears to be found in northern cities: Elizabeth, N. J., 2 pints per capita; Pueblo,

Col., 1.4 pints; Newton, Mass., 1.25; Hoboken, N. J., 1.21; Mt. Vernon, N. Y., 1.18; Boston, 1.17; Fitchburg, 1.15; Worcester, 1.11; New York City, .78; Chicago, .80. On the other hand, in southern cities the milk consumption is very small: New Orleans, .27; Montgomery, Ala., .14; Atlanta, Ga., .12; and Charleston, S. C., .10.

JULY (1903) QUARTERLY MEETING
OF THE
Massachusetts Association of Boards of Health.

The July meeting of the Massachusetts Association of Boards of Health was held at Gallop's Island, Boston Harbor, on Thursday, July 30. Dinner was served at 1.30 P. M., the members of the Association being the guests of the Boston Board of Health; and after dinner a business meeting was held under the presidency of Dr. H. P. Walcott.

The records of the April meeting were read and approved.

Members were elected as follows, upon the recommendation of the Executive Committee:

J. Arnold Rockwell, M. D., of Cambridge.

Goodwin A. Isenberg, of Cambridge.

Roswell Wetherbee, M. D., of Cambridge.

Charles F. Whiting, of Cambridge.

E. B. Phelps, of the Massachusetts Institute of Technology Sewage Experiment Station.

E. S. Hatch, M. D., of Brighton.

E. C. Newton, of Everett.

George W. S. Dockum, of Everett.

Edward A. McEttrick, of Brookline.

T. J. Daly, M. D., of Lawrence.

R. E. Brown, M. D., of Everett.

William H. Colbert, of Salem.

C. C. Crowley, of Clinton.

THE PRESIDENT—In accordance with the direction of the Association at the last meeting, I will appoint as the Committee upon Legislation Mr. Pilsbury of Boston, Mr. Coffey of Worcester, and Dr. E. L. Fiske of Fitchburg.

Is there any other business to come before the Association at this time? If not, the regular business of the Association is in order. First is a paper upon "A Comparison of Some of the More Common Liquid Disinfectants," by Burt Ransom Rickards, Assistant Bacteriologist of the Boston Board of Health.

A COMPARISON OF SOME OF THE MORE COMMON LIQUID DISINFECTANTS.

BY BURT RANSOM RICKARDS, S. B.

Assistant Bacteriologist, Boston Board of Health Laboratory.

Any one who has had occasion to look over the literature relating to disinfecting solutions cannot help being impressed with the ambiguous and often contradictory statements made by different investigators on this subject. The reason for such a state of affairs lies in the different methods employed in performing the experiments and in the varying resistances of the different organisms used. Too often investigators are content with testing a disinfectant upon one or two different strains or races of the same species of organism, making very general deductions from the results thus obtained. Then again, sufficient care is not always taken to properly express the details of the experiment— for example, a writer using the term "a 1% formalin solution" without defining his use of the term formalin, leaves the reader very much in doubt as to the strength employed, since this term is often loosely used and may mean a 1% *formaldehyde* solution, which is two and one-half times the strength of a 1% solution of *formalin* made by diluting 1 cubic centimetre of a 40% commercial solution with 99 cubic centimetres of water.

Such facts have induced the writer to perform a series of experiments under certain very definite conditions in order that the results might be strictly comparable.

In testing disinfectants, there are three main factors to be considered,—the species of organism exposed, the length of time of exposure, and the strength of the disinfectant. To obtain comparable results on a number of disinfectants, two of these factors must remain constant, the other factor being varied. For the purposes of this paper, the bacillus of diphtheria was chosen as one of the constants, ten different races or strains, isolated from as many different typical cases, being employed to eliminate possible errors due to varying resistances of different races of the same species. The times of exposure were one, five, fifteen and thirty minutes. The strengths of the disinfecting solutions used were one and five per cent., made up by volume, except in the case of formaldehyde.

The following technique* was employed,—glass rods were fitted at one end with tapered cork stoppers, the corks being of such a diameter as to fit the test tubes tightly, and the rods of such length as to reach nearly to the bottoms of the tubes when the corks were in place. After being sterilized by dry heat, these rods were infected by first emulsifying a 24-hour agar growth of diphtheria in the water of condensation in the bottom of the tube and then dipping the end of each rod into this emulsion, finally touching the end of the rod to the side of the tube before withdrawing in order to remove any excess. A properly infected rod should show to the eye little if any film when dried, but should give a good growth on media. By using an emulsion in place of taking the growth directly from the agar, one obtains a much more uniform film of bacteria, and thus does away to a great extent with the previous objection to this method—that discordant results were obtained, due to an uneven distribution of the organisms. After infecting the ends of the rods, they were dried for about three hours in a sterile atmosphere, after which they were inserted into tubes containing the disinfectant for the chosen length of time. At the expiration of the time of exposure, the rods were withdrawn and plunged into tubes containing nutrient broth in order to wash off any traces of disinfectant still clinging to them. They were then rubbed carefully over the surface of agar, the tube being finally closed by tightly inserting the stopper, the lower end of the rod remaining in the water of condensation at the bottom of the tube. Both the broth used for

* Hill's Method, Journ. Amer. Pub. Health, Vol. XXIII.

washing and the agars were incubated at body temperature for ten days and were examined each day to detect any growth. This prolonged period of incubation is necessary in order to give any organisms whose growth has been merely checked, owing to their vitality having been lowered, a chance to recover and develop.

The writer wishes to state that, in his opinion, the slightest deviation in method is apt to vary the results obtained considerably. The method described above is not ideal, but it was rigidly adhered to and gives a good basis for comparison.

As regards the composition of the fluids tested, carbolic acid, solutions "A"* "B," "C," "D" and "F" are all coal tar products. Solution "D" is said to contain about .10% of cresols with a small quantity of carbolic acid. It gives a milky appearance with water. Solution "A" contains about 98% alpha naphthalene sulfonic acid, the remainder being phenol sulfonic acid and a small amount of hydrocarbons. It gives a dark-colored solution on dilution with water. Solutions "B," "C," and "F" are probably composed largely of cresols. They have a milky appearance on dilution.

Solution "G" is a 3 per cent. solution of hydrogen peroxide containing a very small amount of hydrochloric acid to render it stable. The solution, diluted for testing, contained therefore .03% and .15% of H_2O_2

Solution "E" is a clear, watery solution composed largely of chloride of zinc with small amounts of the chlorides of aluminum and iron.

Solution "H" is a clear, watery solution. It is said to be made of saturated solutions of the chlorides of zinc, lead, calcium, aluminum, magnesium, potassium and sodium.

All of the above mentioned solutions were diluted to one and five per cent. by volume. In the case of formaldehyde, a commercial solution was first analyzed, and from the data thus obtained, one and five per cent. solutions were then made up by weight.

Chloride of lime was tested under the conditions given, but as it was impossible to verify the results obtained in time for this paper, they have been omitted purposely.

The percentages given in the tables are based on the number

of infected rods which failed to give growth. For instance, a percentage of ninety means that nine of the ten rods, each of which was infected with a different race or strain of the same species, failed to show a growth even on ten days' incubation, after having been exposed to the disinfectant.

In examining the above tables, it should be borne in mind that the figures given must not be considered absolute, as one might regard a table of logarithms. Repeating the same work, using the same technique, one might obtain for carbolic (1%-1.") a percentage of 100 killed instead of 90, and for formaldehyde (1%-1") a percentage of 10 killed instead of none killed, uncontrollable factors giving such a working error. The relative results, however, remain the same, and carbolic and formaldehyde would still stand in the same relative ratio as regards efficiency.

An examination of Table 1 shows that even a 1% solution of the coal-tar products tested kills the diphtheria bacillus in five minutes. When the strength is increased to five per cent., a much greater efficiency in one minute is obtained. Some of the disinfectants given in Table 2 are omitted in Table 1, their effect in a five per cent. solution not being sufficient to warrant a trial with a one per cent. solution. Certain minor discrepancies are apparent in these tables, an interrogation point being inserted after such discrepancy. These fall within the working error, however. The discrepancy between the one and five per cent. solution of Solution "A" is probably due to the fact that the original crude solution was rather unstable, some of the hydrocarbons precipitating between the time of the two tests.

An interesting fact brought out in Tables 1 and 2 is the relative inefficiency of formaldehyde solution as compared with carbolic acid solution. This is more strikingly illustrated by Table 3 which shows that this is true not only for the diphtheria bacillus but for the typhoid bacillus and staphylococcus pyogenes aureus. The results shown in this table would seem to indicate that the relative efficiency of different disinfectants tested by this method would remain the same no matter what organism they might be tested upon, although the actual time of exposure would of course vary according to the resistance of the particular organism.

TABLE No. 1.

Showing per cent. of Diphtheria Bacilli *killed* by a 1 per cent. Solution (by volume) of Disinfectant.

DISINFECTANT.	TIME OF EXPOSURE.			
	1 minute.	5 minutes.	15 minutes.	30 minutes.
	PER CENT.	PER CENT.	PER CENT.	PER CENT.
Carbolic Acid, pure	90	100	100	100
Carbolic Acid, crude . . .	90	100	100	100
Solution " A "	90	100	100	100
Solution " B "	40	100	100	100
Solution "C"	30	100	100	100
Solution " D "	10	100	. .	. .
Formaldehyde Solution (1 % by weight)	0	0	50	80
Solution " E "	0	10 (?)	0	0

TABLE No. 2.

Showing per cent. of Diphtheria Bacilli *killed* by a 5 per cent. Solution (by volume) of Disinfectant.

DISINFECTANT.	TIME OF EXPOSURE.			
	1 minute.	5 minutes.	15 minutes.	30 minutes.
	PER CENT.	PER CENT.	PER CENT.	PER CENT.
Carbolic Acid, pure	100	100	100	100
Carbolic Acid, crude . . .	90	100	. .	. .
Solution " D "	90	100	100	100
Solution " B "	90	100	100	100
Solution " C "	80	100	100	90 (?)
Solution " A "	90	90	90	100
Solution " F "	10	90	100	100
Formaldehyde Solution (5 % by weight)	10	60	100	100
Solution " G "	0	0	10	40
Solution " E "	0	0	10	10
Solution " H "	0	0	0	40

TABLE No. 3.

A comparison of the efficiency of 5 per cent. Solutions of Carbolic Acid and Formaldehyde on B.diphtheria, B.typhosus, and Staphylococcus pyogenes aureus.

ORGANISM.	Time of Exposure.	Carbolic Acid, 5 per cent. (vol.)	Formaldehyde 5 per cent. (wt.)
B.diphtheriæ	1 minute	100 per cent.	10 per cent.
Sta. py. aureus . . .	5 minutes	100 " "	10 " "
B.typhosus	1 minute	80 " "	0 " "

To summarize: Formaldehyde solution, or formalin, although commonly supposed to be superior to carbolic acid as a liquid disinfectant, is really much inferior in equivalent per centum solutions. This fact is all the more striking when one considers the high efficiency of formaldehyde as a gaseous disinfectant. It is also a most efficient deodorizer.

The coal tar proprietary compounds are, as a rule, very good disinfectants. They are not any better, however, than carbolic acid. Moreover, the composition of the proprietary articles may be varied, and the purchaser be none the wiser. Carbolic acid is preferable in all cases when its odor and properties are not objectionable.

The various colorless solutions put upon the market under fanciful names and advertised as "Chlorides," etc., are, as a rule, of little value as disinfectants, their cost usually increasing in inverse ratio to their efficiency.

THE PRESIDENT—The subject of this interesting paper is now before you for discussion, gentlemen, or for question, as may be.

PROF. CHARLES HARRINGTON—Mr. Chairman, I am very glad to have heard this very interesting paper, for I never have seen any figures demonstrating the true value of proprietary disinfectants when the periods of contact are short. Some four years ago, Dr Pearce and I reported to the Boston Society of Medical Sciences the results of our experiments with twelve proprietary and several other non-proprietary disinfectants, but our time of exposure was much longer, namely, two hours. As test objects we employed diphtheria membrane, cultures of the typhoid bacillus, typhoid stools, and tuberculous sputum. Even with the two-hour exposure, we found that not one of the proprietary preparations could be regarded as useful or reliable. I am much interested to learn that carbolic acid is so much more efficient than dilute solutions of formaldehyde in these short intervals, for our experiments led me to believe otherwise; that is to say, we found that formaldehyde in one per cent. solution was uniformly successful in sterilizing the stools, membranes and sputum, while five per cent. carbolic acid gave indifferent results. To be sure, our experiments were somewhat different in the matter of tech-

nique, which improves as time goes on. I think that all experiments along this line should be encouraged and made public,
because the people at large are induced to buy these expensive
proprietary compounds, which are inefficient and often worse
than useless, when they can get a true disinfectant at a very
small price.

THE PRESIDENT—Is there anything else to be said upon the
subject of this paper? If not, the next paper in order is entitled:
"The Mosquito Nuisance and How to Deal with It," and is by
Mr. Underwood, our old friend.

THE MOSQUITO NUISANCE AND HOW TO DEAL WITH IT.

(With stereopticon views and specimens.)

BY WILLIAM LYMAN UNDERWOOD,

Lecturer at Massachusetts Institute of Technology.

Mr. President and Gentlemen:—Last June the Belmont Board
of Health issued a pamphlet entitled "The Mosquito Nuisance
and How to Deal with It." It was illustrated with photographs
from life. Dr. Durgin, having seen this pamphlet, invited me
to come here this afternoon and talk to you upon this subject.
This is not the first time that this pamphlet has gotten me into
trouble.

Unfortunately for the people of Belmont and the Belmont
Board of Health, and unfortunately for the people in this section,
we have been visited this summer by a most unusual plague of
mosquitoes, something worse than we ever remember having
before,—at least, I never remember anything like it, and it has
gotten more or less of those who have been doing mosquito
work into trouble. I venture to say that if you should ask any
person in Belmont how the mosquitoes were this summer, he
would tell you that they were very much thicker now that we
know how to deal with them than they were when we were in
ignorance, when all we knew was that when we saw a mosquito,
we were to kill it. I suppose that other boards of health who
have been trying to regulate the supply of mosquitoes have had

this same trouble. The supply has been very much larger than the demand.

We should not get discouraged, however, and when we are called up on the telephone and asked, "Why don't you come over to my place and do something about these mosquitoes?" "Are you doing anything? The mosquitoes are around my pond." "Why don't you petrolize here?" "Is there anything being done?" and this, that, and the other, we should keep our tempers any say, "Yes, something is being done, and if it were not for the fact that something were being done the mosquito plague would be ten times worse than it is." We should explain to them that we have had a most unusual summer, that it has been an exceptionally fine one for mosquitoes. In June we had long-continued rains, that formed puddles which afterwards became filled with mosquito "wigglers." Warm weather followed this wet period. You all remember the hot weather in July, and it is responsible for the thousands of mosquitoes that we are now having. Then, later, after the mosquitoes had deposited their eggs in these numerous puddles, and after the hot weather, we had more rain, and that made more puddles, and there were still more mosquitoes to lay their eggs in them. I am sorry to say so, but it seems to me that we are going to have still more mosquitoes during the latter part of this month and August. But we all want to keep right at work just the same.

It seems to me that a good way to deal with the mosquito problem, a good way for those towns that have not the money to put into a vigorous campaign of petrolizing and draining the different pools, is to begin a campaign of education; to get the people interested in the subject; to tell them all about the life history of the mosquito; to explain to them the different points about it, and to get people to work upon their own places themselves. Of course I think it is a very excellent thing, a fine thing, for Boards of Health to take up this work, and I think that every board that is able to do it, ought to do it. They ought to put kerosene upon the puddles and see that it is placed there frequently, at least every two weeks. There is no more reason why money should not be expended in this way than there is that it should not be expended in taking away the garbage, the swill, or the ashes. Boards of Health should go on and drain all the places that they can drain, and do all that they are able to do, but they should also try to have the people informed on the subject of mosquito extermination.

In spite of all that has been written on the subject of mosquitoes, there are still a great many people in ignorance regarding their life history. It is rather strange to hear some people express their views on the subject. There are many popular theories that are all wrong. For instance, one of them is that mosquitoes breed in wet grass. We may go out early in the morning, and see thousands of mosquitoes coming up from the grass. We see them sometimes on our lawns. Some people think that they have bred there, but they have not; they have merely gone into the grass to seek the shelter that it affords from the wind, and they have also been attracted there by the moisture of the dew upon the grass; but they have not bred there. They must have water, actual water, in which to live during their early stages. There is a mosquito, *Culex sollicitans*, the typical Jersey mosquito, or the salt marsh mosquito, that does not require water in its first stage, that is, when it lays its eggs. This mosquito lays its eggs upon dry land, but water must come to them afterwards.

Another popular theory is that mosquitoes must have foul or stagnant water to breed in. This is not so. Mosquitoes will breed in the foulest water, and they will breed in stagnant water; they will also breed in the purest water. They don't necessarily have to have stagnant water in which to lay their eggs.

Another mistaken idea is that the mosquito only bites once, and that is not so at all. Mosquitoes may bite a great many times if they can get the chance to do so,—at least, the females may—the males never bite.

It is also a popular idea that a mosquito's life is a very short one. I am glad to say that a great many mosquitoes' lives are very short. Whenever I can I make the lives of those that I have anything to do with exceptionally short. But a great many mosquitoes' lives are not short. Many thousands of them live over winter, and you will often find them if you look in your cellars. I had occasion to notice this fact very forcibly three or four years ago, when I was making some experiments upon mosquitoes. I had a good stock of larvæ in a glass jar in a refrigerator. One unfortunate day I opened the refrigerator door to get them, and out came the jar and everything with it onto the floor. That was the last of those "wigglers." I had planned many interesting things to do with them when they came to maturity, and I was crestfallen to lose the lot. Then I happened to remember that when I was a youngster, and was obliged to go into the cellar to do my photographic developing, on the dark-room ceiling there were thousands of mosquitoes during the winter; at least, I thought they were mosquitoes. I went over there at once, and found in the cellar, in the same place,— not the same mosquitoes, but others, hundreds of them, and I had no trouble in getting all that I wanted. People don't realize that many mosquitoes live through the winter in a state of hibernation.

The vast majority of mosquitoes never get any human blood for food. In its absence they live upon the blood of birds and frogs and other animals that sometimes frequent the marshes where they are born. In the absence of this food, they live upon the juices of tender aquatic plants.

Some three hundred different kinds of mosquitoes have already been described, and more are being found all the time. We have probably some fifty in this country, and these are divided into nine genera, or groups. I shall speak this afternoon of only two of these, because they are the ones that we have to deal with, —the group known as the *Anopheles*, which are the malarial mosquitoes,—the ones that are capable of conveying the plasmodium which causes malaria, and the *Culex*, the ordinary, everyday mosquito, of which we have thousands, and of which there are some twelve varieties that bother us.

Now if you will kindly close the doors. I am very sorry that we shall have to do this, because it may get a little warm in here, but this is a subject that we are liable to get warm over. I will promise to be just as brief as possible, and if any one feels that he is going to faint and will say the word, we will suspend operations and open the doors and windows.

The life history of the mosquito is divided into four stages. Three of them are in the water, first the egg, then the larva, and then the pupa, the mosquitoes in these last two stages being commonly known as "wigglers." The mosquito seeks some very quiet pool in which to lay its eggs, and there deposits them. The majority of mosquitoes that vex and annoy us are bred near by, very often in our door-yards, or in the door-yard of some nearby neighbor. It is this point that I want to emphasize, and it is this point that the people ought to know, because every person should do all he can to co-operate in this good work of mosquito extermination. They can breed in old tin cans, in pools in the rocks, and in barrels where people keep manure-water to put upon the soil. I have found them in my own yard; I did not know that they were breeding there, but I found them in barrels which had been placed in the garden in which water was kept for the plants. They will breed in catch basins, in the foot tracks of the cows in the pasture, in gutters that don't properly run off the water on our roofs, and in fact in any place that will hold water, no matter how small a quantity, even if only a few ounces, if it is protected from the wind.

These photographs that I am going to show you, with the exception of two or three, which are taken from diagrams, are all photographs of live "wigglers," and live mosquitoes. I will explain them as we go along.

The first picture (exhibiting it by the stereopticon) shows you a typical egg mass of the ordinary, common mosquito, *Culex pungens.* It contains from 200 to 400 eggs, and it floats right on top of the surface of the water. It is very easy to see, and is about a quarter of an inch in length. In the course of a few days the bottoms come off these little eggs, and the little "wigglers" are released into the water. The whole length of time in favorable weather, such weather as we are having today, when it is very warm, is ten days from the time that the eggs are laid until the adult mosquito emerges from the water.

Now you will see how different the eggs of the *Anopheles*

are. (Exhibiting another picture.) These two pictures are diagrams. The *Anopheles* lays only from 40 to 100 eggs, and it
does not lay them in rafts as does the *Culex*. Where it takes
only ten days under favorable conditions for the *Culex* eggs to
hatch into "wigglers" and ultimately into the adult mosquito, it
takes twenty-four days for the *Anopheles*. These periods may
be prolonged into weeks and even months by very cold weather.

The next picture is from life, as the ones that follow will be,
and it shows you a typical mass of mosquito "wigglers." There
are some *Anopheles* there, and some *Culex*, though many more
Culex than *Anopheles*. I shall not stop to show you the difference between the two, because I can show it to you better in the
pictures that are to follow. I have seen "wigglers" actually as
thick as they are here in rain-water barrels and in ditches where
farmers have been draining the land and have allowed the
trenches to clog up. This picture was taken in a little glass
case that I arranged for the purpose. Mosquitoes in this state
very frequently live over winter. Some kinds of "wigglers" can
be literally frozen up without harm. They are frequently found
in the leaves of the pitcher plant during the winter, frozen solidly
in icy balls. Last January I found some active "wigglers" in
pools of water under the ice, although the thermometer had
been for a week about 30 below zero. I will speak of these
again, and tell you more about them.

Now we are looking at an individual *Culex* larva and an individual *Anopheles* larva, and you will see that they are very distinctly different one from the other. Here we have a *Culex*
larva at the top of the water. *Culex* does not stay at the surface
much of the time, but it comes occasionally to the top to
breathe, which it does through its respiratory siphon, or breathing tube. It thrusts this tube up into the surface of the water,
gets a breath of air, and goes down again to feed. The *Anopheles* larva, on the other hand, unless it is frightened, stays at
the surface nearly the entire time. It breeds there, and it feeds
there. It lies, as you see, parallel to the surface of the water.
Its breathing tube is very short; you can hardly see it here at all,
but it is located here in the tail. And here is the head. The

two varieties are distinctly different in every way, as they are through all the phases of their life history. They must have air, or they cannot breathe and cannot live, and that is why it is that kerosene is so deadly to them, because it shuts off the air when they come to the surface to breathe. I will speak of this again later.

After a few days they change from larvæ into pupæ, and this picture shows the third stage. Here we have a *Culex* pupa, and here an *Anopheles* pupa. The pupæ are distinctly different. Although you cannot see the difference in this photograph, still with the naked eye you can see it very easily. I will point out the difference to you in a few minutes in a picture which is to follow. This stage is simply a resting one, the insect doesn't feed at all now. It stays at the surface nearly all the time, breathing through these little trumpet-shaped breathing tubes situated at each side of its thorax or head; there are two now instead of one as before in the larva. It remains quiet until the time comes when it is going to emerge as an adult insect. Finally, it begins to split up the back, and the full-grown insect comes forth just as you will see it in the next three pictures. A mosquito never grows after it comes from the water. We frequently hear it said, "We have some small mosquitoes now that later will be larger," but they won't. A mosquito never grows after it is able to crawl and fly. It is then the size that it is always going to be.

This picture, while it is taken from life, does not represent a normal position, because this insect was inside of a little glass cell that was only about an eighth of an inch wide. The insect, which is a female, is putting its feet up and is pulling itself out on the glass. Really it is upside down. In nature it would be turned round the other way, and would be resting with its feet on the water.

In the next picture you will see that the insect has turned over and is now in its proper position, the position that it would assume in nature. It now has its feet upon the surface of the water and is pulling itself out. Notice its tremendous size. It does not seem possible that it could have come out of that little shell, which you see has been left in the water. This is the critical time in the life history of a mosquito. If the wind should blow enough to ripple the surface on the water, the insect would be upset and would be drowned. So you see it is very important that it should seek some quiet pool where the wind cannot disturb the surface. We won't find mosquitoes in ponds where the surface is free from weeds and where the edges are abrupt; even if it is a pond only the size of this building you would hardly find any mosquitoes in it, because it does not offer any shelter for them. They must have some quiet place, some little pool or some little nook in a big pond where there are weeds or rushes, or something of that kind to keep the wind away. It only requires about seven minutes from the time that the pupa begins to split up the back until the adult mosquito has come out, has dried its wings, and is ready to fly away, and, if it is a female, ready in a short time to deposit two or three hundred more eggs, which mean trouble in future for us.

Here in this picture you see the empty pupa skin. Let us stop for a minute to look at these empty skins, for by them you can often tell whether or not mosquitoes have been breeding in a pool where they are not present when you are looking in it. These skins keep intact for a long while. They float at the surface of the water. We can now see their respiratory siphons, and see the difference in their shapes. These which you will see are quite flary, or trumpet-shaped, are *Anopheles.* These which are long and slender, are *Culex.* They can be easily told by these distinctive features, the difference in the shape and size of their breathing tubes.

This picture shows *Anopheles punctipennis.* This is one of the malarial group that we have very commonly about here. I want to call your attention to its spotted wings, which are very prominent, and also to the fact that this insect has its bill or its proboscis, and its body, all in one straight line. It is a female mosquito. I will call your attention to the antennæ, which are very small. You will see how different are those of the male in the next picture. These mosquitoes, when they alight, don't search round for a favorable place to bite. Generally they come down bill first and get to work at once, and in a few minutes you feel a pricking sensation. That pricking sensation is the result of a definite purpose. When the mosquito bites it injects saliva or poison into our flesh in order that the blood shall become thinner, so that the mosquito won't have to work so hard to pump it out. If it is a malarial mosquito, one of the kind that is able to carry malaria, and it has, at the right time, bitten a person who is ill with malaria, when it injects this poison or saliva into the blood the plasmodium of malaria goes with it. It seems very simple now that we know how it is done, and rather queer that we did not think of it before, because, as you all know, malaria is essentially a disease of the blood. Under a microscope you can see these little plasmodia in the red blood corpuscles. They are drawn into the stomach of the insect, and they eventually get all over the body cavity, and into the salivary glands, where they are thrown out with the saliva into the blood of the next person that is bitten, and there the cycle is completed. It seems all very simple now that we know about it.

The next picture shows you a male of this same species, and now you can see the distinct difference. The antennæ here are very much more prominent. This fellow has moustaches, or whiskers, as it were. The male mosquito is the best chap in the world. He only lives a short time, and then he passes away. He does not bite; all that he does is just to sing and enjoy himself.

The next picture shows you the typical resting position of *Anopheles punctipennis.* *Anopheles maculipennis* does not assume quite such an angle as this one does, but still it assumes very much more of an angle than does the *Culex*, as you will see in the pictures to follow. You will see that this insect's body and its proboscis are all in a straight line, as I have said before.

In this picture you see the ordinary, every-day *Culex pungens.* It is a hump-backed, miserable looking insect, but it is a very annoying one nevertheless. You will notice that the proboscis and the body are at an angle; they are not in a straight line, as they were in *Anopheles.*

The mosquito breathes through numerous little holes on both

sides of its body. In speaking of a mosquito's breathing, I want to tell you of a very good way to rid yourselves of mosquitoes if they trouble you when you sit out on the piazza in the evening. It is by the use of Pyrethrum powder, which is commonly sold in drug stores under the name of Persian Insect Powder, and sometimes under the name of Dalmatian Powder. By burning this powder in the evening you can enjoy comfort on the piazza, where otherwise you would not be able to endure the mosquitoes. The smoke from this powder stops up the little holes through which the mosquitoes breathe, and smothers them. It is an excellent thing to burn in our cellars in the winter when mosquitoes are hibernating there. Pyrethrum smoke has rather a pleasant odor. The powder may be bought for from twenty-five to thirty-five cents a pound, and a little of it goes a long way. The easiest way to start the smoke is to get a live coal out of the kitchen stove, place it on a small shovel and sprinkle a little of the powder on it. It will immediately begin to smoulder, and no mosquitos will stay where this smoke is present. Now and then one may make its appearance; but they won't stay to annoy you. During the tremendous plague that we have just had I have been able to sit out on my piazza in comfort in the evening when burning this powder.

Here we have a male *Culex pungens*, and now again you see the characteristic resting position of this species. You may perhaps be interested to know how I took these photographs, and so I will tell you something of my method. I made a small glass cage, two or three inches square. Here is one in reality. (holding up a small glass box) and it has some live mosquitoes in it. I will show them to you later. I placed the mosquitoes in this little glass cage, and there I photographed them. It was not always easy to make them sit still and look pleasant. They were generally flying around. I had to work pretty quickly, and take a good many snap shots before I got any satisfactory pictures. I well remember one day in the fall I had a particular mosquito I wanted to photograph, I forget what species of *Culex* it was, and it was the most persistently uneasy thing I ever saw in my life. It flew all over the cage and would not keep quiet. So I

went into the house and got some ether, and put a drop or two in
the box, thinking that this would quiet the insect. It worked
nicely, too nicely. The mosquito kicked up its feet and laid on
its back perfectly still. I looked round for half an hour, trying to
find another specimen, then gave it up, came back and found the
mosquito had come to life and was flying round again just as
lively as ever. I now put the restless insect into an ice-cream
freezer. I must have left the mosquito in too long, for when I
removed the cover it was frozen stiff and was again on its back
with feet in air. To make a long story short, this hardy mosquito
thawed out, came to again, and was as busy as ever, and in putting it black into the glass cage, it got caught beneath the cover.
This settled it, for its back was broken.

I had no trouble in making the mosquito which you see in this
picture stay still as long as I wished. You can see it was full of
blood; it had bitten me a few moments before. It stayed perfectly
still for two hours and allowed me to photograph it in every
position.

Now we are looking at *Anopheles maculipennis*, the mosquito
that is known to carry the plasmodium of malaria. It corre-
sponds identically to the one upon which so much work has been
done in Italy. It is commonly said that these mosquitoes bite
only at night, but I know that this is not so. I have been bitten
by them at all times of the day, and a person does not want to
go about feeling sure that he is not going to get bitten during
daylight.

Now we will look at some places where mosquitoes are liable
to breed, also at some places where they are not liable to breed.
You might say this was a place where they would breed, but it is
not. The surface of this water is covered with Lemna, or duck
weed, and it covers the surface so thickly that mosquito larvæ
cannot get through it to breathe. This picture, and the four that
follow, were taken out on the Fresh Pond marshes (you probably
all know where they are; the Fitchburg road goes over them after
it leaves Cambridge). There are some six or seven hundred
acres in this swampy area.

This view shows a place that is favorable for the breeding of mosquitoes. This pool was located in Belmont. I say "was located," for it no longer exists. Two or three years ago, you will remember, I talked to you about the draining of marsh lands, and showed some of these photographs. The Board of Health of Cambridge and the Board of Health of Belmont co-operated, and at an expense of $1,600 we drained off about three feet of water from this very spot. This picture was taken in July, in one of the driest seasons that we had for years. This next picture of the same place was taken in the following December, after a very rainy season. Three feet of water have disappeared. This is what draining did in that locality. We drained and reclaimed about seventy-five acres of land that were under water and unfit for anything but raising mosquitoes. There is still much more work to be done in the lower section of this marsh territory.

This photograph shows you the location as it is today where no draining has been done. This view is right back of the Boston Packing and Provision Company's plant on Concord Avenue. The Fitchburg road goes by on this side. I can remember when I was a boy that a grove of maple trees stood there, and I used to go to this pond to shoot wild ducks. The water has come up there now so that it has killed off the trees; it is full a foot higher than it used to be twenty years ago. This is because the brooks that drain the marshes were not properly taken care of, and because the swampy area is situated in four different municipalities, and what was everybody's business was nobody's business. But this is all going to be changed. During this last session of the Legislature a special act was passed authorizing the cities of Cambridge and Somerville and the towns of Arlington and Belmont to clean out and straighten the channels of Alewife Brook, which drains this territory, and tide gates are to be put in where the brook enters Mystic River. A commission has been appointed to do this work, and by these means we hope to drain off two feet and a half more water from this district.

Here is another picture that shows conditions just as they exist today. You can see this very spot out of the car window as you go out on the Massachusetts Central track. Here is the Fitchburg Railroad, and here are the buildings of the Boston

Packing and Provision Company, and this is Alewife Brook, which often flows one way and then another, and then does not flow at all. Within half a mile of the Fresh Pond marshes, where mosquitoes are breeding by the thousand, there are 1,100 dwelling houses, 100 of them in Belmont, 200 in Arlington, 300 in Somerville, and 500 in Cambridge.

This is the principal work that the Belmont Board of Health has been doing out in our section to regulate the mosquito nuisance. We are getting these marshes cleaned up. In our town we have not had very much money to spend in petrolizing or draining, but we have tried to get individuals interested to do this work upon their own places, and we hope that we are succeeding in a measure.

This is a photograph of a ditching machine. I have not seen this machine in operation, but I have read a good deal about it. It is owned and patented by a man named Mark B. True of Newburyport. He contracts to make ditches with it, and can dig from 40 to 100 yards a day, making a ditch from four to eight inches wide, and from two to three feet deep, as occasion requires, and he charges ten cents a rod for doing the work. This is an excellent machine to use when draining marshy land, because it can do quick work. It makes narrow ditches, straight up and down, ditches that can be easily taken care of. It is very important after these ditches are made that they should be kept cleared out, because if they stop up they are worse than no ditches at all, for then they offer very favorable places for Anopheles to breed in.

Here is a ditch in Belmont, on a farmer's land. It was dug to drain his celery patch, and he let the water accumulate, and did not take pains to see that it was kept clear. Thousands of mosquitoes, of *Anopheles*, were breeding in this ditch all unknown to him. That is an excellent place to use petroleum or kerosene, and a very few ounces of it will suffice, all that is necessary to use is an ounce to fifteen square feet. A very few ounces placed on this ditch would do away with all the mosquitoes there. Of course it is very important that it should be renewed at intervals of about two weeks.

Now I am going to show you the effect of kerosene upon

mosquito wigglers. We hear a good many laughable comments about mosquitoes living on oil, and what oil does to mosquitoes, and all that. There is a good deal of fun made of it, but it is a very practical thing if used in the right way. This picture will show you the way it works. Here is the film of kerosene, up above this point, and this is all water below. Of course this is very much more oil than you would get by applying an ounce to fifteen square feet. Here are the larvæ of *Culex* coming up and trying to breathe. You see this one thrusting its tube up into the kerosene, trying to get air, and you see these two are going down to the bottom. They are ready to give up the fight. At once, or generally within a few seconds, when it gets the end of its breathing tube stopped up with kerosene, the wiggler frantically grasps its respiratory siphon with its mandibles, and vainly tries to pull off the oil. It is a most pleasant thing to watch, I can assure you, and I think that even the Society for the Prevention of Cruelty to Animals would stand by and say not a word if they saw these experiments being made. (Applause). They struggle, and they gasp, and within a few minutes go down to the bottom to die. Anyone can make this experiment for himself. He can get a few "wigglers," put them in a tumbler, put a few drops of kerosene on the water and see what happens. He can see whether or not this method of dealing with the mosquito nuisance is efficient.

There may be some places that we don't want to put kerosene upon. There may also be places that we don't want to drain. I have a lily pond that I constructed on my place some ten years ago, before we knew very much about mosquitoes, except that there were such troublesome things in the world. I dug this pond in a meadow in order to drain the land to get all the water in one place, and I planted lilies and put a lot of gold fish in the pond. When I became a member of the Board of Health, and it came to be known that mosquitoes were responsible for malaria, I thought I would have to do away with this pond, for it seemed to be an ideal place for mosquitoes to breed in. I did not want to treat it with kerosene, for I thought the oil would kill the gold fish. I went down to the pond to look for mosquito "wigglers," and was much surprised, when, after a careful search, I could not find any. It seemed rather queer that there were no larvæ in the pond, for within twenty feet of it was a slow-running brook, and here, in and about the numerous patches of weeds that were growing in the water, I found a great many "wigglers," both *Culex* and *Anopheles*. Why were there none in the pond where the conditions were so favorable for them? I suspected that the gold fish had something to do with it, so I caught two of them and placed them in a glass tank, and in the water I put some mosquito larvæ. Within five minutes I had the pleasure of seeing these two fish that you are looking at on the screen (they were not more than three inches long) eat ninety-eight "wigglers" in four minutes. This settled the question for me. My pond was not touched and I have never been troubled with mosquitoes from it. The brook was easily fixed; it was simply a question of keeping it clear of the weeds that offered a shelter for the mosquitoes in their early stages.

A great many people don't know that gold fish will live naturally in many of our ponds hereabout, especially in small ponds, where the water is shallow and warm. This pond of mine has only an average depth of about two feet, and it freezes almost to the bottom every winter, and yet the fish multiply in it. There are other fish that do this same thing. Our friend Dr. Abbott, once told us, I remember, that when he was a boy there was a certain rain-water barrel that he was interested in, where an old hornpout used to swim around, and he observed that during the evening this hornpout would come up to the surface and with cavernous mouth would take in thousands of mosquito "wigglers."

The "top minnow," the roach, the sunfish or "pumpkin seed" all play an important part in reducing the numbers of mosquito "wigglers." Besides the fishes, there are other "foes of the water" that prey upon the mosquito larvæ. Many of the predatory water bugs feed upon them.

In this connection a brief description of a newly discovered mosquito, to which has been given the name *Eucorethra underwoodi*, should be of interest, since it has been found that their larvæ devour the wigglers of other mosquitoes, and unlike other mosquitoes, the adult female insect does not bite. As the proboscis of this insect is so formed that it cannot puncture the skin, it should not perhaps be called a true mosquito, though it has been classed as one, since it belongs to the family Culicidæ.

The larvæ of this insect were found by the author on January 27, 1903, in the Maine woods in the eastern section of Penobscot County, and were discovered in a spring of water from which a crew of lumbermen were getting their water supply. A few days later, other larvæ of the same species were found in a similar spring about eight miles distant, though in this case, as the spring was not in use, its surface was covered with a coating of ice about an inch thick. The temperature of the water at the bottom (it was about two feet deep) was 42° F.

At first sight this larva would be taken for an *Anopheles* of extraordinary size, as it is of the same general shape, and when the water was cleared of ice, it lay just beneath and parallel to the surface, breathing through a short respiratory siphon, as is characteristic of the larvæ of *Anopheles*. In this spring a barrel had been sunk and in the fifty gallons, or thereabouts, of water which it contained there were twenty-five larvæ. They were all of about the same size—12 to 14 mm. long—and almost black in color. All were secured and taken into camp for further investigation.

Close observation of the larvæ showed that besides being much larger (12-14 mm. long instead of 5-7 mm.) they differed in many other particulars from the larvæ of *Anopheles*. In proportion to the rest of its body, its head is larger than the head of *Anopheles*. It does not turn its head upside down when feeding as does *Anopheles*. Its mandibles are strikingly large and powerful, and are prominently toothed. It lacks the frontal tufts or brushes which are conspicuously present in *Anopheles*, and its antennæ, which extend directly forward parallel with the sides of the head, are much longer and more slender, and are tipped each with three hairs of equal size. The thorax is broadly elliptical and is much wider in comparison with its abdominal segments than is the thorax of *Anopheles*. The sides of the thorax and the abdominal segments bear fan-shaped tufts of hairs, not plumosed as in

Anopheles. The tufts on the last segments, both dorsal and ventral, are more profuse in *Eucorethra* than in *Anopheles*, especially the ventral tuft which in *Eucorethra* occupies nearly the whole segment. Only two anal papillæ are present, while *Anopheles* has four.

A few days before the author returned to Boston several larvæ died, and three changed to pupæ. The pupa resembled that of *Culex* rather than of *Anopheles*, and its respiratory siphons are of the same shape as those of *Culex*. When stretched out at full length, the pupa measures ten mm.

On reaching home, the new wigglers, eighteen in number, were put into a quart jar which was placed near a window where it would receive the sunlight for two hours each morning. The temperature of the water now averaged about 70° F. and with this change the larvæ developed a new trait—they began to eat each other up. The act was witnessed on several occasions. The larva would grasp its adversary just forward of the respiratory siphon with its powerful mouth parts, and working the tail in first it would gradually swallow its victim, shaking it now and then as a terrier would shake a rat.

After losing many of the insects in this way, those that remained were separated, and each individual was placed in a small bottle by itself. Eventually, I succeeded in rearing a number of males and females. The pupal stage of this insect varies from five days and nine hours to six days and ten hours. The adult resembles *Anopheles* in having maculated or spotted wings, but is much larger and measures eleven millimeters in length. Its mouth parts, however, are not adapted for biting. A full description of the imago is soon to be recorded by Mr. D. W. Coquillett, of the National Museum, by whom the name above mentioned was given.

During a visit to Maine in June, a large number of larvæ of *Eucorethra* were taken from the spring where the barrel had been sunk. It was noticeable that larvæ of other kinds of mosquitoes were absent, although the adults were very numerous in the immediate vicinity.

The absence of other mosquito larvæ was accounted for when

later it was discovered that the larvæ of *Eucorethra* fed upon the larvæ of other mosquitoes, eating them apparently with great relish. On several occasions fourteen *Eucorethra* larvæ ate, during the night, sixty *Culex* larvæ out of the seventy that had been placed in the water with them. When eating the larvæ of mosquitoes smaller than themselves, the victim is caught, shaken violently a few times, and swallowed in a few seconds, in very much the same way that a pickerel would catch and swallow a smaller fish.

As yet no experiments have been made to see if this new species will devour the larvæ of *Anopheles* as readily as they will those of *Culex*. Whether or not this species will thrive in the climate of southern New England is as yet uncertain, but experiments are now being carried on to determine this point.

Although myriads of mosquitoes are destroyed by the natural enemies which have been mentioned, man should be the most destructive foe of these insects. There is no doubt that the mosquito pest may be very largely abated by the employment of scientific methods for causing its destruction in the early stages of its development.

While it is the duty of boards of health to recognize mosquitoes as active agencies for the dissemination of certain diseases and to take such measures as are possible for their extermination, the work can never be effectively done until the people of each community are fully informed in regard to the life history of the mosquito so that all may co-operate intelligently to secure its destruction.

I would like to pass round a bottle containing the larvæ of this new mosquito. Before I pass it round, I will pour into it a lot of Culex "wigglers." If you will look closely you will probably see, as it passes from hand to hand, this new mosquito engaged in the work of destroying these "wigglers." You can see the difference in size between the two. Most of the *Eucorethra* larvæ are down at the bottom just at present, but in a few minutes you may see them reach out and catch the ordinary "wigglers," and eat them up.

(Members gathered around Mr. Underwood as he displayed his specimens, and examined them critically.)

Program of Next Meeting—Summer Diarrhea,—*Hastings*, Metropolitan Water Supply,—*Walcott*. At Clinton, Mass., Oct. 22, 1903.

ABSTRACTS, REVIEWS, NOTES AND NEWS.

FOURTH OF JULY CASUALTY LIST—The Journal of the American Medical Association, published August 29th, 1903, the results of an investigation showing that 466 persons were killed and 3,983 persons injured by accidents due to explosives used in celebrating the Fourth of July in the current year. Of the deaths, 406 were due to the terrible disease of tetanus (lock-jaw). Of the injuries, loss of sight constituted 10 cases, loss of one eye, 75; loss of legs, arms or hands, 54; loss of fingers, 174; and other injuries 3,670. The blank cartridge provided 363 tetanus cases and 1,309 cases other than tetanus. These figures were obtained from the newspapers of the country. The deplorable suffering and death here recorded occurred in spite of the very general warnings and urgent advice given to the public this year by the medical and lay press, as well as by various city authorities. Boards of Health are urged to co-operate in doing away with this annual holocaust by the careful collection and publication of the data relating to deaths from tetanus, especially those from explosives. It is worth noting that only ninety-five deaths from tetanus after vaccination have been collected from all medical literature. (MacFarland, Journ. Medical Research, VII., 1902.)

THE QUESTION OF TETANUS BACILLI IN BLANK CARTRIDGES—The lay press has of late informed the public of the alleged discovery of tetanus bacilli in blank cartridges by the bacteriologist of Newark, N. J. It now appears, according to the Journal of the American Medical Association, that the bacteriologists' report was based on examinations of cartridges made without inoculation tests in animals. There is good reason, therefore, to consider his findings not proven, especially in view of the fact that other investigators, working with animals in different places and at different times, have uniformly failed to find tetanus bacilli in such cartridges. Two of these investigators report finding bacilli which, in the absence of animal experiments, might have been mistaken for tetanus bacilli. It still remains probable therefore, that tetanus following blank cartridge wounds is due to the character of the wound and infection of the wound with extraneous dirt, rather than to the infection of the cartridge itself with tetanus bacilli.

NEW VACCINATION LAWS IN FRANCE—In February, 1903, there went into effect in France a law holding parents and guardians personally responsible for the vaccination and re-vaccination of children in their first, eleventh, and twenty-first years. Bovine vaccine matter, prepared under the supervision of the government, is prescribed—to be transferred directly from the heifer to the arm when possible, or used in the form of a glycerinized pulp.

The laxity regarding vaccination in France heretofore has therefore now been replaced by rigid requirements similar to those which have made smallpox almost unknown to the next-door neighbor, Germany. Evidently, France has at last learnt wisdom by experience.—Abstract from Boston Medical and Surgical Journal, October, 1903.

COMPULSORY VACCINATION CONSTITUTIONAL IN MASSACHUSETTS—In April, 1903, in the case of Commonwealth v. Pear, the Massachusetts Supreme Judicial Court handed down an opinion, holding the statute authorizing compulsory vaccination constitutional. The case grew out of the refusal of the defendant to submit to vaccination at the hands of the Cambridge Board of Health, the Board having complied with the statute in all particulars in the making and carrying out of an order for the vaccination and re-vaccination of all persons under their jurisdiction not successfully vaccinated since March 1st, 1897.—(Condensed from the Review and Record & Banker and Tradesman, of April 18th, 1903, where the opinion is given in full.)

THE BOSTON ASSOCIATION FOR THE RELIEF AND CONTROL OF TUBERCULOSIS, recently organized in Boston, has for its object the teaching of the public, through lectures and circulars, and particularly through district nurses sent into the homes of tuberculous patients, concerning the communicability and the prevention of tuberculosis. Boards of Health welcome these efforts, since such work covers certain fields which they cannot so well do. Particulars can be obtained from the Secretary, Harold K. Estabrook, Room 47, 43 Hawkins St., Boston.

GENERAL HEALTH OF THE STATE—From advance sheets of the Annual Report of the State Board of Health for the year 1902, we learn that the death-rate of the State for that year was the lowest ever recorded in the history of the State, namely, 16.17 per 1,000 in an estimated population of 2,937,600, that of the two previous years, 1900 and 1901, having been respectively 18.2 and 16.8 per 1,000. A very decided fall in the mortality from consumption and from other infectious diseases appears to have been one of the chief causes of this unusually low death-rate.

The Massachusetts Institute of Technology has recently established a laboratory for the study of sewage disposal under the directorship of Professor William T. Sedgwick. The laboratory is situated at 786 Albany Street, Boston, opposite the South Department of the City Hospital, on the line of Boston's largest main sewer. The opportunity for the study of the sewage of a city of the first rank is believed to be unique. Some interesting work on the bacterial contents of Hospital sewage is, we believe, in contemplation. A full description of the laboratory is given in The Technology Review, July, 1903.

Mr. C. E. A. Winslow, of the Massachuetts Institute of Technology, has contributed to "Science" (July 29, 1903), a review of the statistical arguments for and against vaccination, concluding that the protection afforded by vaccination is absolutely proved by the evidence examined. No one who has had practical experience with smallpox asks for statistical evidence in its favor, but to the laity only evidence of this character can usually be made available. ·

For the treatment of fresh wounds of such a nature as to make requisite specific provision against the later development of tetanus, Calmette has recently advised dusting with dried tetanus antitoxin. This, done within a few hours of the injury, is an almost perfect safeguard. MacFarland has recently repeated Calmette's experiments and confirmed his results.

The vaccine plant of the Massachusetts State Board of Health is under construction at the Bussey Institute, Forest Hills, Boston. Dr. Theobald Smith, who is in charge, has recently returned from a trip to Europe, which included visits to the chief vaccine establishments in the old world.

Professor Loeffler of Greifswald has reported to the German government that a protective serum against foot and mouth disease is now available for cattle, and advises the immunization of all cattle brought into the market with the serum.—(Am. Med., Sept. 26, 1903.)

The New York Board of Health has ceased to produce diphtheria antitoxin or vaccine for sale. It will hereafter supply only the City of New York. Such supplies will of course be free as heretofore.

Hingham

Charles H. Marble. 1
J. Winthrop Spooner, M. D. 2

Hyde Park

Willard S. Everett, M. D. 2
Edwin C. Farwell.
William W. Scott. 2
Charles F. Stack, M. D. 1

Hanover

A. L. McMillan, M. D.

Jamaica Plain

Theobald Smith, M. D. 5*

Lancaster

Chester C. Beckley, M. D. 2
Allen G. Butterick. 2
Albert E. Harriman, M. D. 1

Lincoln

Stephen H. Blodgett, M. D. 2

Lexington

George O. Whitney.

Lawrence

William Berger.
Charles E. Birtwell, M. D.
A. D. V. Bourget. 1
T. J. Daly, M. D.
George S. Fuller, D. V. S.
F. W. Kennedy, M. D. 2
John A. Magee, M. D.
Victor A. Reed, M. D.
George W. Smith. 6
J. F. Winchester, M. D. 8

Leominster

C. E. Bigelow, M. D. 1
Fredson N. Grey. 2
H. N. Spring. 2, 6.
A. L. Whitney.

Lowell

James B. Field, M. D.
J. Arthur Gage, M. D.
Thomas F. Harrington, M. D.
Guy Holbrook, M. D. 1
William B. Jackson, M. D. 2
H. H. Knapp. 6
W. P. Lawler, M. D.
J. N. Marston, M. D.
Thomas B. Smith, M. D. 5

Lynn

R. E. Hillard. 2
W. E. Holbrook, M. D. 2
W. R. Woodfall, M. D. 1

Melrose

John Timlin, M. D. 2

Melrose Highlands

Clarence P. Holden, M. D.
Paul H. Provandie, M. D. 1

Milton

A. W. Draper, V. M. D. 2
Charles R. Gilchrist, M. D. 1
W. C. Kite, M. D.
Jacob S. Lincoln. 2
Samuel D. Parker.

Marshfield

C. W. Stodder, M. D. 2

Needham

A. E. Miller, M. D.
A. M. Miller, M. D.

New Bedford

J. T. Bullard, M. D. 2
E. H. Gammons.
W. G. Kirschbaum. 1
L. H. Richardson. 7
Manuel V. Sylvia, M. D. 2, 9

Newport, R. I.

Joseph W. Sampson.

Norwood

E. C. Norton, M. D.
Lyman F. Bigelow, M. D. 1

Newton

John C. Brimblecom
W. F. Harbach. 2
Arthur Hudson. 5, 11.
A. Stanton Hudson, M. D.
Harry A. Stone. 3, 6
E. R. Utley, M. D. 10

New York, N. Y.

Col. W. F. Morse.

No. Brookfield

T. J. Garrigan, M. D.

No. Abington

F. G. Wheatley, M. D.

No. Andover

Charles P. Morrill, M. D.

Palmer

J. P. Schneider, M. D. 1

Plymouth

W. G. Brown, M. D.

Providence, R. I.

Ernest F. Badger.
C. V. Chapin, M. D. 12
F. P. Gorham.
Gardner T. Swarts, M. D. 13*

Rockland

J. C. Batchelder, M. D.
Gilman Osgood, M. D.

Salem

C. A. Ahearne, M. D.
G. Arthur Bodwell. 2
Wm. H. Colbert.
Joseph A. Fitzgerald. 1
W. H. Gove.
Raymond L. Newcomb. 3, 4
A. N. Sargent, M. D.
Benj. R. Symonds, M. D. 2

Somerville

A. C. Aldrich. 2
Robert Burns.
Allen F. Carpenter. 1
W. H. Hitchings, V. S.
F. L. Lowell, M. D.
A. E. Merrill, M. D.
A. R. Perry, M. D.
Edmund F. Sparrow. 2

So. Framingham

L. M. Palmer, M. D.

Springfield

A. L. Brown, M. D. 2
T. J. Collins. 1
H. C. Emerson, M. D. 3, 5
James Kimball. 6
B. D. Pierce, M. D.
J. C. Rausehousen.
S. J. Russell, M. D. 10

Southbridge

Humphrey C. Moynihan. 1

Three Rivers

Geo. J. Hebert. 2
S. O. Miller, M. D.

Taunton

Charles H. Macomber. 2
Edward J. Shannahan, M. D. 2
Henry H. Wilcox. 7

West Newton

Francis G. Curtis, M. D. 1
Geo. H. Ellis.

Waltham

H. D. Chadwick, M. D.
C. J. McCormick, M. D.
Marshall J. Mosher. 1
Charles A. Willis, M. D.

Watertown

Sumner Coolidge, M. D.
Vivian Daniel, M. D. 2
Julian A. Mead, M. D.

Waverley

L. B. Clark, M. D.

Westboro

C. S. Henry. 2
Charles S. Knight, M. D. 2

Weston

F. T. Hyde, M. D. 2
F. W. Jackson, M. D.
S. Sanford Orr, M. D.

Whitman

C. E. Lovell, M. D. 2
A. A. MacKeen, M. D. 1

Winchendon

F. W. Russell, M. D. 1

Winthrop

A. B. Dorman, M. D.
H. J. Soule, M. D.

Woburn

George Buchanan. 2
Dennis S. Doherty 2
William H. Kelliher, M. D. 1

Worcester

F. H. Baker, M. D. 5
Geo. W. Batchelder. 2
W. T. Clark, M. D. 1, 10
James C. Coffey. 2
May S. Holmes, M. D.
Prof. L. P. Kinnicut.
W. W. McKibben, M. D.
L. F. Woodward, M. D.

Minneapolis, Minn.

F. F. Wesbrook, M. D.
(Honorary Member)

JOURNAL OF THE
MASSACHUSETTS ASSOCIATION OF BOARDS OF HEALTH.

ORGANIZED 1890.

[The Association as a body is not responsible for statements or opinions of any of its members.]

VOL. XIII.	November, 1903.	NO. 4.

THE MASSACHUSETTS ASSOCIATION OF BOARDS OF HEALTH was organized in Boston, March, 1890, with the following objects; the advancement of Sanitary Science, the promotion of better organization and co-operation amongst local Boards of Health and the uniform enforcement of sanitary laws and regulations.

THE JOURNAL OF THIS ASSOCIATION has, for thirteen years, faithfully reflected the views of the public hygienists of Massachusetts. As the only one of its kind in Massachusetts, the Journal has had its own field, which, however, it has not yet fully occupied. With the October issue of this year, 1903, a policy of expansion was adopted. The subscription list showed an immediate and most gratifying increase, so that this, the second, issue has a total circulation three hundred per cent. of that of the July issue.

In order that the Journal may appear within the next month after each quarterly meeting of the Association, the date of publication changes with this issue and hereafter will be FEBRUARY, MAY, AUGUST *and* NOVEMBER *of each year.*

THE JOURNAL will contain the papers read at the meetings of the Association, verbatim reports of the discussions, Editorials, Abstracts, Reviews and hygienic notes of professional interest. Subscription rates $1.00 per year.

All communications concerning the ASSOCIATION should be addressed to the Secretary of the Association, JAMES C. COFFEY, CITY HALL, WORCESTER, MASS.

All bills not relating to the Journal, and MEMBERSHIP DUES ($2.00 per year) should be sent to the Treasurer of the Association, DR. JAMES B. FIELD, 329 WESTFORD ST., LOWELL, MASS.

All communications concerning the JOURNAL, copy, proof, sub-scriptions, advertisements, etc., should be addressed to the Managing Editor, DR. H. W. HILL, 607 SUDBURY BLDG., BOSTON, MASS.

We regret the misprinting, in an editorial of our last issue, of the name of the author of the Report on Milk Supplies, therein reviewed, which should have read Mr. H. E. Alvord.

EDITORIALS.

THE ETIOLOGY OF DYSENTERY.—Since the introduction of modern bacteriological methods, the infectious diseases which exert their deleterious effect upon the mucous membranes, more particularly those of the digestive tract, have presented unusual difficulties to the bacteriologist. Among them, dysentery, until recently, has been an unsolved problem. The amœbic form, a disease of warm climates chiefly, has been recognized for some years and each year brings additional evidence that certain amœbæ have true pathogenic power. The suspicion that there were also forms of the disease due to bacteria was very strong, but it was not until 1898 that a bacillus was isolated by Shiga in Japan, which bids fair to meet all the conditions necessary to make it accepted as a genuine etiological factor in dysentery.

The bacillus of Shiga has many characters in common with the typhoid bacillus, but it is readily distinguished from the latter by absence of certain morphological and bio-chemical characters, such as motility and action on mannite.

Though it has not the power to produce disease in animals fed with cultures, it is quite virulent when injected, either under the skin or into a vein. Its pathological power resides in a powerful toxin which is probably liberated during the disintegration of the bacilli in the body. Animals, being thus immune to natural infection by the mouth, are not likely to transmit the bacilli to man excepting as accidental carriers. This view is supported by the fact that since its discovery the Shiga bacillus has not been found in animals.

Flexner has found the same bacillus associated with dysentery both in the Philippine Islands and in our own country. Strong and others have also isolated this organism from cases in our eastern possessions. Vedder and Duval, W. H. Park and others have extended and amplified the work of Shiga and of Flexner, and quite recently, through their efforts, the same or very closely related bacilli have been found in cholera infantum and other intestinal affections of young children. During these researches, the subject has been somewhat complicated by the discovery of varieties or well-defined races of bacilli associated with dysenteric diseases. Two groups have been temporarily formed, differentiated by certain delicate bio-chemical tests and by agglutination with specific blood sera. It would seem as if there existed a series of races of the same species, some more highly adapted and specialized than others. Shiga's original bacillus evidently stands at the head, followed by less pathogenic forms which grow more vigorously in cultures, act on mannite and produce indol. This bacillus, or group of bacilli, resembles the typhoid bacillus, as stated above, in that it does not produce resistant spores, and is destroyed in fluids at 60° C. In nature drying and sunlight quickly make it inert. It is furthermore easily destroyed by ordinary disinfectants, and the same general rules apply to the disinfection of the stools in this disease as in typhoid fever.

The modes of dissemination of dysentery bacilli are similar to those of typhoid bacilli. In addition to the direct transmission of bacilli from the patient to those in his immediate environment through the stools, the infection may enter wells, springs and larger water supplies, and it may be carried in the milk. In this way it may reach a larger circle of patients and form more distant centres of infection.

The dissemination may also be effected by mild and chronic or relapsing cases against whom the suspicion of harboring dysentery bacilli may not exist at the time. The disease may, in this way, be imported into a community from outside and establish itself before attention is directed to it. Since the disease is most frequent in the summer months, flies may become active distributors in uncleanly surroundings.

In the presence of this infection in any community it should be borne in mind that a predisposition may be created by disorders of digestion and catarrhal conditions of the intestinal tract. During the progress of the disease, the blood acquires agglutinative properties, but these are not so constant or so pronounced as in typhoid fever, presumably owing to the local character of the disease. The absence of agglutinins, therefore, in the later stages, of the disease, does not necessarily imply that it is not dysentery. In epidemics, however, agglutination serves a most useful purpose in enabling us to recognize the nature of the disease and the kind of bacilli involved.

Both Shiga and Flexner have been experimenting with a serum prepared by injecting dysentery bacilli into horses. Shiga claims that his serum fulfils scientific requirements, but we shall have to wait for the results of tests made by Prof. Flexner and his co-workers before raising our expectations to what may possibly prove too high a level.

It is obvious that many minor problems have been raised by the extensive researches on bacillary dysentery, though the main question of etiology may be considered solved. One of the more important of these is the probable existence of varieties of different degrees of virulence and toxicity, the milder ones appearing in sporadic cases and possibly in the summer diarrhœas of infants, the highly virulent ones in well-defined epidemics affecting adults as well.

Public health authorities should be promptly notified of such outbreaks for further investigation, since these can be made satisfactorily only in the early stages of the disease.

THE CANTEEN. The so-called Canteen system was first authorized by the War Department in the year 1889, and during the next two years it gradually supplanted the old system of sutlers' and post-traders' stores throughout the Army. The authorization was given in the following terms:

"1st. Canteens may be established at military posts, where there are no post-traders, for supplying the troops at moderate prices with such articles as may be deemed necessary for their use, entertainment, and comfort; also for affording them the requisite facilities for gymnastic exercises, billiards and other proper games. The commanding officer may set apart for the purpose of the Canteen any suitable rooms that can be spared, such rooms whenever practicable to be in the same building with the library or reading-rooms.

"2d. The sale or use of ardent spirits in Canteens is strictly prohibited, but the Commanding officer is authorized to permit wines and light beer to be sold therein, by the drink, on week-days, and in a room used for no other purpose, whenever he is satisfied that the giving to the men the opportunity of obtaining such beverages within the post limits has the effect of preventing them from resorting for strong intoxicants to places without such limits, and tends to promote temperance and discipline among them. The practice of what is known as 'treating' should be discouraged under all circumstances.

"3d. Gambling or playing any game for money or other thing of value is forbidden."

Subsequent order dated May 13, 1890, provides that

"The practice of what is known as 'treating' must not be permitted."

After the abolition of post-traders, the Canteen became also a coöperative store and supplied the officers and men with the necessaries and luxuries which the government does not provide, and as such exercised also a very important economic function.

The establishment of the Canteen system, in the light of evidence now in the possession of the War Department, proved to be the most efficient prophylactic measure for the diminution of vice and drunkenness among the troops, and its abolition by an act of Congress, approved February 2, 1901, on purely sentimental grounds, must be deeply deplored by all interested in the prevention of physical and moral diseases.

The whole question seems to have been discussed on the one side from a theoretical or sentimental standpoint, and on the other side from a study of statistical evidence and practical experience before and after the period of Canteen existence: on the one side, by those who believe that the temperance question can be treated in the abstract and on the basis of absolute prohibition, and on the other side by those who find that rational temperance among the troops can be secured only by a careful consideration of the enforced limitations of life, environment and general needs of the soldier, especially in camp-life, where discontent and unrest is most likely to occur.

The official records and published reports of the War Department will show that in comparing the seven-year period before with the six-year period after the establishment of the Canteen, the average annual number of admissions to the sick report for alcoholism was reduced by 23.6 per cent. In 1890 there were seventeen army posts at which the admission rate for alcoholism exceeded ten per cent. of the garrison strength. In 1891, the number of such posts had decreased to eleven, and in the following years diminished at the following rates: 10, 7, 4, 5, 2, 2.

As a single instance, in 1889 the post of Willet's Point had an admission rate of 222.97 per thousand strength. For 1890, during which year the Canteen was established at that post, the rate fell to 157.50, and in 1891 was further reduced to 70.46.

The gravity of the cases of alcoholism was also reduced through the influence of the Canteen,—the rate for cases of delirium tremens for the period 1892–1897, showing a diminution of 31.3 per cent. as compared with the seven-year period before the Canteen was established.

For the same periods, also, the rates for insanity were reduced by 31.7 per cent., and the number of days of service lost to the Government from this cause were reduced by 40.9 per cent.

For the year ending June 30, 1898, the profits of the post exchanges in operation throughout the army amounted to a total of $323,661.51; which sum was returned to the men and expended to improve their food, to purchase reading matter and gymnasium and athletic equipment, and in other ways make their lot more comfortable and the military service more attractive. The effect of this betterment of conditions was at once shown in a remarkable decrease in the rate of desertions; the percentage of these being 9.18 for the period of 1885–1891, and but 4.53 for the period 1892–1897. This reduction in desertions was practically progressive as post exchanges were established throughout the Army,

—the rate of desertions for the two years prior to the war with Spain being scarcely one-fourth as great as the rate for three years immediately preceding the introduction of the Canteen system into the Army. As each United States soldier costs the Government $1,014.66 annually, this decrease in desertions meant for those years a money saving to the Government of more than two million dollars.

The number of soldiers depositing savings with the Army paymasters for the period of 1892–1897, as compared with the average for the pre-Canteen period 1885–1891, increased by 13.3 per cent., —a deposit by the soldier being practically a bond for the good behavior of the latter and his continuance in the service.

The establishment of the Canteen was also followed by an extraordinary diminution in the number of convictions by court martial for drunkenness,—the pre-Canteen period mentioned having an annual average of 372.5 such convictions, while the annual average for the same cause after the Canteen system was established was but 160.6. The year before the Canteen was established, the convictions by court martial for drunkenness numbered 423; in 1894, the third year after the system had been generally established throughout the Army, they had fallen to but 120.

Brig.- General Frederick Funston, U.S.A., Commanding General Department of the Colorado, reports the number of trials by court martial for 1902, the next year after the abolishment of the Canteen system, as 194, and, compared with the previous year, the percentage of average enlisted strength had nearly doubled.

He also gives the per cent. of average enlisted strength deserting in his department as increasing from 3.20 in 1899 to 11.00 in 1902. and writes as follows:

"It is therefore plain that there has been a deplorable increase of offenses in general and of desertions in particular. In my opinion there are two principal causes for this state of affairs: First, resentment to unaccustomed limitations and restrictions felt by men returning from field service to the monotony and routine work of garrison life; second, the abolition of the Canteen feature of the post exchange.

"Since this action was taken, saloons of the lowest type have been established just outside the boundaries of the various reservations; their proprietors are, in almost every case, unprincipled scoundrels, who leave nothing undone to debauch the soldiers and obtain their money. Gambling is universal in these dives, and they are frequented by dissolute women. The soldier whose desire for a drink would ordinarily be satisfied by a few glasses of beer in the canteen of the post exchange goes to one of these resorts and does well if he escapes before he has spent or gambled away all his money, overstayed his leave, or engaged in a altercation. In short the recent legislation of Congress on this question, so far as this department is concerned, has had no effect except to lower the discipline of the army, ruin scores of good soldiers, and fill the pockets of a lot of saloon keepers, gamblers and prostitutes."

The Honorable Secretary of War, Mr. Elisha Root, and the Rt. Rev. Archbishop of Ireland, in their testimony before the Senate Committee on Military Affairs, Dec. 14, 1900, also favored the Canteen system and deplored the legislation which deprived the soldier of a restraining influence and left him exposed to the "horrible and demoralizing and damning surroundings that cluster around the outside of the camps."

In a word, Drunkenness, Desertion, Courts-Martial, Insanity, Venereal Diseases and their correlative vices, were all greatly diminished during the ten-year period of the Canteen and Post Exchange system, and they all have increased since the system was abolished.

That the Canteen, as formerly operated, was a positive element for good, was attested by 95 per cent. of the more than six hundred officers of the Army who have made reports concerning its influence to the Secretary of War. Its misguided opponents could merely oppose theory to facts, and sentiment to statistics. Backed by political prestige, theory and sentiment have temporarily succeeded in destroying an institution whose influence was wholly beneficial, much to the sorrow of those who have the true interests of the soldier at heart, and who must treat human nature as it exists in the Army, rather than attempt the attainment of impossible ideals.

OCTOBER (1903) QUARTERLY MEETING

OF THE

Massachusetts Association of Boards of Health.

The quarterly meeting of the Massachusetts Association of Boards of Health was held at Bigelow Hall, Clinton, October 22, 1903.

After a visit to the Reservoir and Dam of the Metropolitan Water Works, followed by the usual Association dinner, Dr. H. P. Walcott, President, being obliged to return to Boston on an early train, Dr. Samuel W. Abbott, Vice-President, presided.

Members were elected as follows, upon recommendation of the Executive Committee:

Dr. C. W. McClearn, of Malden;
Mr. Joseph T. Wilson, of Nahant;
Dr. E. H. Mackay, of Clinton;
Mr. Dennis J. Hern, of Boston;
Dr. John L. Hildreth, of Cambridge;
Dr. F. H. Burnett, of Brockton;
Dr. Joseph G. E. Page, of Southbridge;
Mr. W. H. Brock, of Athol.

THE CHAIRMAN. Dr. Walcott has, I am sorry to say, unfortunately been called away, and the paper which is upon the programme to his name, upon "The Metropolitan Water Supply," will be read by Dr. Morse.

DR. MORSE. Mr. Chairman and Members of the Association: I hoped it would be our mutual good fortune to hear Dr. Walcott deliver this paper himself, but unfortunately the duties of his office in carrying on the work which you have seen a part of to-day have necessitated his going to Boston at an early hour. His address is as follows:

THE METROPOLITAN WATER SUPPLY.

BY HENRY P. WALCOTT, M.D.,

Member Metropolitan Water Commission.

In 1890 it had become quite evident that the city of Boston and the cities and towns adjacent thereto had reached the safe capacity of the existing sources of domestic water supply.

The State Board of Health had on several occasions called the attention of the Legislature to the necessity of some concerted action on the part of the municipalities in the vicinity of Boston for the purpose of securing a better and larger water supply.

The Legislature of the year 1893 authorized and directed the State Board of Health to investigate, consider and report upon the question of a water supply for the city of Boston and its suburbs within a radius of ten miles from the State House, and for such other cities and towns as in its opinion should be included in connection therewith.

The board presented its report to the Legislature early in the year 1895. The recommendations of that report were promptly adopted without substantial changes. A commission of three members was created to carry out the work, and within six months from the time when the board's report was first presented, the operations had begun; and you have to-day seen the great dam more than half completed, which to the world at large seems the most serious portion of the undertaking. It is indeed the most conspicuous single feature, and such it will always remain, but some other portions of the work have called in play equal if not greater engineering capacities, and have involved greater expenditures of money.

The first requirement of a water supply is a pure source. The south branch of the Nashua River drains a watershed at the dam of 118 square miles. This territory is sparsely inhabited, and is not the seat of any great manufacturing industries which would tend to seriously pollute the river. The manufactories are few in number, are not likely to increase, and the wastes from them can be easily cared for without injury to the purity of the stream.

A very large sum of money—several millions of dollars—has

been spent in a thorough preparation of the reservoir above the dam. This reservoir has a water surface of 6.56 square miles, is over eight miles long, and at its greatest width two miles broad. The land required for it contained six large mills, eight school-houses, four churches, and about three hundred and sixty dwelling-houses occupied by upwards of seventeen hundred people.

The buildings, vegetation, and surface soil are all to be removed. The soil has been removed from about two-thirds of the area, and at the end of this year the cleared surface will be about four-fifths of the whloe. The result of all this work will be a cleaner reservoir than exists anywhere else in the world. In no case within my knowledge has so complete a stripping of the surface been made Through the lower portion of the valley, soon to be flooded, ran the tracks of the Mass. Central R.R. for the distance of 6.56 miles. A relocation of the road has been made, so that it now crosses the Nashua River just below the dam and skirts the northern margin of the water basin. The relocation of the road required works of considerable magnitude, a tunnel 1063 feet long on the easterly side of the Nashua River, a viaduct 917 feet long across the valley of the river, with a height above its bed of 132 feet, and a rock cut having a maximum depth of 60 feet on the westerly side of the river.

Quite as important as the dam, and of even greater engineering interest, is the great north dike which shuts out the waters of the reservoir from Coachlace pond and the Nashua River below Clinton. The dike is two miles long, has a maximum height of 65 feet, and a maximum width of 1930 feet. It covers 143 acres and contains 5,500,000 cubic yards of earth.

From below the dam the water of the reservoir is carried by a conduit twelve miles long to the Sudbury basin. This conduit consists of two miles of tunnel, seven miles of covered masonry construction, and three miles of open channel. From the Sudbury reservoir another conduit 13.4 miles long has been built to Auburndale in the Metropolitan district. These conduits have capacities respectively of 300,000,000 gallons and 350,000,000 gallons.

In the Metropolitan district itself additional storage reservoirs have been constructed, new pumping stations erected, additional pipe lines laid, and various local water systems assumed and paid for.

The cost of the whole scheme will be $40,000,000, and the residents of the Metropolitan district will have an abundant supply of good water for many years, at an expense to the individual water-taker not greater than that hitherto paid for waters of doubtful quality and insufficient in quantity.

But this great reservoir here is only the beginning of a water system which settles forever the question of a water supply for eastern Massachusetts. Beyond the Nashua is the Ware River, easily brought down here by works of no greater magnitude than those I have described to you. Beyond the Ware are the waters of the Swift River, and further west beyond the Connecticut are available the waters of the Deerfield. All these can be brought to the Metropolitan district by gravity, and they all must pass through this dam at Clinton.

The benefits of this great water supply are not limited to the city of Boston and the Metropolitan district; but the right of the city of Worcester and of the towns of Clinton, Sterling, Boylston, West Boylston, Lancaster, Holden, Rutland, Princeton, Paxton and Leicester to take water from this supply are by the act of 1895 jealously guarded. It is well on every account, both for financial and sanitary considerations, that sources of domestic water supply should be thus concentrated. The precautions which are now considered necessary for the protection of a water supply are inconsistent with the presence of a considerable population upon the watershed and with the existence of any large manufacturing industries upon the streams. This territory is fortunately for us not provided with a rich soil, nor does it now offer many opportunities for manufactories. And what is true of this water basin is also true of the Ware River, of the Swift River, and of the Deerfield. The water diverted from these streams would indeed have been of value as a source of power to the mills lower down the stream. But this power can be paid for, and as a matter of fact, whenever it has been interfered with the courts have seen to it that a most generous compensation has been rendered to the parties who have suffered a damage.

Another procedure on the part of the water board has caused an apparent loss to the district, and that is the reforesting of the open lands.

The board controls an area about the basin fully equal to the basin itself. This seemed to be essential in order to adequately guard the water from pollution. It was quite evident that any of the operations of farming or grazing would create conditions dangerous to the water supply. There was one use, however, of this large area wholly consistent with perfect security for the waters of ten reservoirs, and that was the creation of a forest here. This is already well under way. Several hundred thousand young trees have been planted or are ready in nurseries in condition to be transplanted when places have been made ready for them. The plantations when well grown will have a tendency to protect the snow and ice deposited in the shade from quick thawing, and will thus produce a moderate and long-sustained flow into the small streams which run down to the basin.

Moreover, in another generation these trees will have reached a size when they can be profitably marketed, and if the successive cuttings are properly arranged, the State can exhibit here an experiment which no private person has undertaken or is likely to undertake, at any rate on so large a scale.

All the conditions of this experiment will be publicly known; the actual cost will be a matter of public record, so that our successors will have before their eyes an object lesson of great value.

The concentration of the sources of water supply also gives opportunity for a better sanitary oversight than the smaller supply ever receives, because the large district can afford to employ a permanent and well-paid force of experts, and the small district cannot do so. The arrangements of the Metropolitan water board make it possible to know all the recognized cases of communicable diarrhœal diseases in the watershed, and it has apparently been thus far possible to escape the very obvious dangers of fœcal pollution by the thousands of laborers employed within the water basins, or upon the construction of the water ways leading down to the Metropolitan district.

THE CHAIRMAN. Gentlemen, you have heard Dr. Walcott's

paper, and we should be glad to have any discussion now upon it, or any questions will be in order.

Before proceeding any further, I would like to speak of one or two things that have been mentioned to me on the way up here, and several times before. The first is an erroneous impression that this water is to be filtered at some time or other. That is not so. There is to be no filtration. It would be an enormously expensive thing to filter the water of this basin, and it is not necessary. I may say in regard to the entire water supply of Boston for the last fifty years, since 1847 or 1848, when the Cochituate was first introduced, that I do not think that any epidemic of disease or illness has ever been traceable to it, not even when the most polluted supply in the State was a part of the city of Boston's supply, that is, for East Boston, Chelsea, Somerville and Everett —I mean the Mystic, which has been abandoned for several years; and that was one of the worst supplies in the State. There was not even any epidemic of disease traceable to that, that I can recollect. Now, the same is true of the Cochituate, the same is true of the Sudbury, and in the future I have no doubt it will be true of this much purer supply than either of the other three, the new Nashua River, or Wachusett supply. I simply mention this because there has been an erroneous idea that this water is to be filtered. The question came up in the original plan of bringing down the water of the Merrimac River into Boston and filtering it, but that would be far more expensive than this, and a very polluted supply, as everyone knows.

Dr. H. W. Hill. Mr. Chairman, I would like to ask the question as to how long the water is supposed to be in storage before it is used, and what the effect of the storage will be on the color of the water and its purity?

The Chairman. I cannot say so much about that as some of the experts might. It will take a year or two to fill the basin. But I think it is true that in very large and deep basins like this there is a considerable amount of purification which goes on, and also a brightening of the color, that is, a more transparent color.

Dr. Jackson, of Lowell. Mr. Chairman, I would like to ask if any trouble is to be apprehended from the growth of algae in the water?

THE CHAIRMAN. That has been practically avoided, I think, by the enormous amount of work that has been done in stripping the basin of soil down to a very great depth. We know this fact, that in all deep waters, both artificial and natural, the water grows cold as the depth increases. If you strip the soil off the banks down to say twenty-five feet or more, you get down to a depth where the water is cool; the water is always cool in the lowest depths of very deep ponds. The Board has made several experiments on the waters of deep ponds, in the Jamaica Pond and in the Lower Mystic Pond, which are, each of them, about eighty feet deep, showing that the lower you go the cooler the water. Even in the hottest months, July and August, you never get at a depth below forty feet a temperature much above forty degrees, it is almost down to the freezing point, and at that point, there is practically no production of algae.

THE CHAIRMAN. There is a note here which I will read, from Dr. Hill, who, I am very glad to hear, is taking up the work of this Association, as you well know, in the publication of its Journal, now in its thirteenth year of publication, and we hope now it will be on a better footing than heretofore:

"It is requested that members will send at once to the Managing Editor all corrections in their names, addresses or titles indicating their positions in relation to their Boards of Health, at an early date.

"It is intended to record in the Journal such items of interest as may be sent to the editor by secretaries or members of Boards of Health throughout the State, and each Board is requested to consider itself appointed as a correspondent of the Journal for this purpose. The items might be, for instance, notes on changes in the personnel of the Boards, or of heads of departments, notes on legal cases out of the ordinary, outbreaks of infectious diseases, new regulations adopted by the Boards—in brief, such news as may show the progress of hygienic matters in this Commonwealth, and tend to aid in achieving the objects for which the Association was formed—the advancement of sanitary science, the coöperation of Boards of Health, and the uniform enforcement of sanitary regulations."

If there is no further discussion upon the paper, I will call upon Dr. Hastings for his paper on "Notes on the Etiology and Treatment of the Summer Diarrhœas in Infants."

THE ETIOLOGY AND TREATMENT OF THE SUMMER DIARRHŒA IN INFANTS.

BY ROBERT W. HASTINGS, M. D.,
Resident Physician of the Boston Floating Hospital.

Mr. President and Fellow-Members of this Association.

I suppose that of the many subjects which have in recent years interested students of public hygiene, none has been more strongly emphasized than the preservation of the lives of little children. Analysis of the statistics of births and deaths everywhere shows a most startling death-rate among infants under two years old. I need not quote the figures to you, for they are too well known. A further study reveals the proof that one of the chief causes of this high infant mortality is in the great number of cases of indigestion occurring during the hot months and classed collectively as "summer diarrhœa." Children's diseases itself has been one of the last branches of medicine to receive careful scientific study. Hence the leading authorities are not yet agreed how these troubles should be classified. Practically, however, for many years physicians and health authorities everywhere have recognized the danger to infants which finds its expression in the popular anxiety to "get the baby through his second summer."

The next step in the study of the figures reveals the fact, long recognized clinically, that nursing babies with healthy mothers are singularly free from these dangers. It is desirable, therefore, that mothers should nurse their babies. But the conditions of modern life interfere, and to-day often forbid this most efficient prophylactic treatment of the condition we are considering. Not least important in this prohibition is the fact that so many mothers must work to attend to the many cares of a large family, or it may be to secure support for themselves and children.

The investigator is, therefore, confronted by the fact that a host of bottle-fed infants die every summer. Search for a cause leads in many directions. First and foremost and still probably most important is the milk supply. I wish very much that I could impress upon you my own belief of the vast importance of having pure, clean, fresh milk. It is a subject well worth the whole time of a meeting of this Association. For, until the local Boards of Health wake up to the importance of strict attention to the milk supply, with such practical regulations of the farmers as shall secure pure milk, it matters little how much is done at the other end of the line. But I must not enlarge upon this point here. I may say in passing, however, that I know from actual tests, day after day, that it is possible to have milk delivered to the consumer so free from contamination that there are less than fifty bacteria per cubic centimeter, instead of the three to five millions often found in commercial samples.

The same line of investigation has taught and is teaching care and cleanliness in the handling of the milk and in the serving of it to the babies. Here, again, the best modern thought advocates giving the infant pure, clean, uncooked milk food, in place of the pasteurized food which may often contain toxins and whose constituents *may* be seriously damaged by the heat. Moreover, Dr. Rotch and his followers in Boston advise the removal from the milk of the tough curd, which is apparently designed to stimulate a calf's gastric mucous membrane and enable it to digest grass, and use for infants whey-cream mixtures. Here, again, I can bear personal testimony to the success of this form of food and to the practicability of it, even with poor mothers.

But it has been all the time recognized in this research that a more definite cause must be determined. Nowadays in medicine we always look for bacterial causes. The term dysentery is one used more or less loosely to indicate a bloody, slimy diarrhœa. In the far East it is a definite disease with a high mortality. In 1875 amœbæ were found in the stools of certain cases of tropical dysentery. Since that time very many forms of bacteria have been isolated from similar cases and successively considered to be the cause. But in 1898 a Japanese named Shiga demonstrated a bacillus constantly present in the discharges and in the inflamed mucous membrane of certain types of the disease and *not* present in healthy subjects, or in those suffering with other diseases.   He tested it by agglutination after the fashion of the Widal test for typhoid, and later produced from horses a serum which, acting somewhat as does the diphtheria antitoxic serum, has very greatly reduced the death rate from dysentery in Japan.   Since then the germ has been isolated by Flexner in Manilla and in the United States, and by various other observations in other parts of the world.

Just what led Dr. Simon Flexner, who is in charge of the investigations made by the Rockefellar Institute for Medical Research, to associate *Bacillus dysenteriae* (Shiga) with the summer diarrhœa of infants I do not know; but one of the first questions which this great Institute has set itself to solve is this one: Is the *Bacillus dysenteriae* (Shiga) the cause of this disease so fatal to our American babies?

In the summer of 1902 studies were made at the Thomas Wilson Sanitarium by Duval and Bassett.   Success crowned their efforts. Forty-two out of fifty-three sick babies were proven to be infected with this germ, by finding it in the stools.   But it might be that this was peculiar to Baltimore, from which city most of the patients of that hospital are drawn.   Hence it was decided that this last summer a more exhaustive study should be made.

One of these points for study was the Boston Floating Hospital, of which I am the resident physician, and Arthur I. Kendall was assigned to work with us.   Through the very great courtesy of Drs. Durgin and Hill, he had the full facilities of the laboratory of the Boston Board of Health at his disposal, and was able to study most exhaustively the cases selected.   These were, for the most part, patients showing blood and mucus in the stools.   This was partly because it is extraordinarily difficult to find them in the other cases.   By this I mean, that a man may need to "fish" five hundred, six hundred, or even seven hundred colonies before he finds the one which will give him the cultural peculiarities of this bacterium.   Another reason was that we desired him to check up the cases to whom we gave the antitoxin serum, and he had no time to investigate the milder cases.   Of this serum treatment I will speak later.

The peculiarities of the *Bacillus dysenteriae* (Shiga) I need not give you in detail. That is a portion of the subject which it is more satisfactory to read for one's self than to hear read.

Dejecta containing blood and mucus were saved for Kendall. A loop of the mucus least contaminated with feces was suspended in sterile water and a high dilution thus established. Agar plates were made in the usual way and the colonies studied to determine their cultural peculiarities. Among other tests of identity required were these—that the bacilli should not coagulate milk, nor produce gas from glucose-agar and that they should agglutinate with immune serum.

Thirty-five cases were thus studied with us this summer. In two no organism was obtained. In three tuberculous infections were demonstrated. One was a Proctitis, a dejection of almost pure mucus being followed by a normal dejection, and one was a Typhoid. This last is interesting because of a negative Widal reaction while in the hospital and a positive reaction after the child had been discharged well, when Kendall insisted that the germs were typhoid bacilli. This leaves twenty-eight cases by which it was proven this summer that in and about Boston the form of summer diarrhœa which we call Ileo-colitis and which is characterized post-mortem by much thickened intestinal walls, with prominent, injected, sometimes ulcerated follicles and a coating of thick glairy mucus, is accompanied by *Bacillus dysenteriae* (Shiga). Since this bacillus has been proven capable of producing these lesions in animals, it follows that probably it is *an* ætiological factor, perhaps *the* ætiological factor, in this disease.

How it enters the system is as yet not finally determined. It may be a normal inhabitant of the intestine which conditions as yet unknown may permit to increase rapidly and to produce toxic results. It is present in the dejecta in the same way as typhoid bacilli are present in the dejecta of Typhoid Fever patients. Moreover, a test similar to the Widal test, using the blood of the infected patient and a pure culture of this bacillus, gives in many cases the agglutination reaction. Here, then, may be the scientific explanation for the success of the prophylactic dietetic, mechanical, medicinal and hygienic treatment which we have adopted on the Boston Floating Hospital.

We have a large barge, much like a Nantasket boat, on which years ago as many as fourteen hundred people have been towed down the harbor to Downer's Landing. It is fitted up with three enclosed wards containing fifty beds and two open wards, one for tubercular patients and one—the entire upper deck—for day patients. The fifty-six beds were full all the time; the out-patients varied with the heat of the morning from twenty-five to seventy-five.

Our prophylaxis embraced "Typhoid Precautions," *i. e.*, screens everywhere against flies, elbow sleeves for doctors and nurses, frequent cleansing of hands and arms in an antiseptic solution, prompt removal and destruction or disinfection of all contaminated clothing or bedding, sterile food, in sterile bottles, through sterile nipples, direct to the babies,—but the milk not ever heated above 100° F.

Dietetic treatment meant the use of Albumin Water, Barley Water or Rice Water at first; later, Whey, Whey-and-Cream, or Modified Milks of graduated strengths, oftentimes peptonized. Finally, a digestive power was attained so that a food of good strength easily prepared by the mother at home was well taken.

Medicinal treatment included usually Brandy, often Strychnine, sometimes Bismuth, or what we have found most efficient, Tannalbrin. By the courtesy of Dr. Flexner we were furnished with a supply of the serum produced under his supervision. It came to us in sterile tubes, much like antitoxin syringes and which were in fact used in just that way. Ten c.c. was given at a dose, usually repeated, sometimes daily, for several days. No unfavorable results were at any time noted. The favorable results expected were a fall in pulse and temperature and a decrease in the number of stools. As we made use of all other forms of treatment just the same, it is not possible to say exactly what the value of the serum is. It was apparently not *very* efficient. Temperature and pulse did, however, often fall shortly after its administration, and several desperate cases to whom it was given, recovered. Another year, a more concentrated form will be available and may be more efficient. Should the results be similar to those which follow the use of the serum in Japan, it will be strong confirmation that the *B. dysenteriae* (shiga) is *the* cause of these troubles.

Mechanically we made much use of colon irrigations, giving two or three quarts through a large, soft, rubber catheter, inserted twelve or fourteen inches and with a fall of not over eighteen inches. Normal salt solution or a weak solution of Bicarbonate of Soda served best, with resort to a solution of Creoline, one drachm to two quarts, if blood was present in the stools.

Most important, however, from our point of view, was the hygienic treatment. By this I mean the abundant presence of pure, fresh sea air. Everywhere it surrounded the sick babies and uniformly its benefits were noted. Those who came merely to spend the day, speedily quieted as it blew over them in their open upper deck ward. Very often babies who came with a history of frequent loose watery movements went home without having a single dejection during the seven hours they were with us; and the fifty odd little ones who were with us all the time and for whom chiefly the sixteen doctors and thirty-two nurses labored always had plenty of fresh air. One large ward had a breeze always blowing gently through it. Two smaller wards had fresh air taken to them by our "atmospheric plant," which takes fresh air, freezes the moisture out of it, warms it to 70° F. and delivers it in abundance over the heads of the infants. This last is a peculiarity of this institution and means that in the dog-days of July and August, these little patients have the clear, fresh, bracing air of October. You need to feel it and breathe it to know its delight and value.

Investigations of these peculiar bacteria demand special laboratory facilities and trained observers. As the years go by such will be more and more easily available to each of you. But the lines of treatment which I have thus briefly outlined to you and in whose employ the Boston Floating Hospital has attained well recognized success, are every one of them available to each of you —typhoid precautions, clean, fresh food, the medicinal and mechanical treatment of which you individually approve and the pressence of an abundance of cool, pure, fresh air.

THE CHAIRMAN. Is there any discussion upon this paper?

DR. HARRINGTON. Mr. Chairman, I cannot agree with the reader that it would be a simple matter to distribute milk containing only fifty bacteria per cubic centimeter, for it would be exceedingly difficult to get milk containing so small a number, even at the stable, under the best of conditions, for the first part of a milking contains myriads of bacteria, and even the strippings often show upwards of five hundred to the cubic centimeter. The reason why milk as delivered contains so many bacteria to the cubic centimeter is that the public very stupidly insists on having what it considers to be fresh milk. The milk of a large city is received in the city in the early morning, after the milk carts have distributed to the houses and the shops their supply for the day. If a milkman should go to his customer and say, "I can give you your milk at eleven o'clock," the customer would probably decline to receive it at that hour. He wants it "fresh"; he wants it delivered earlies; he wants it delivered at five or six o'clock. Therefore, the milkman has to take his milk home and store it in his stable in order that it can be delivered in the early morning, and during that time the bacterial development is enormous. If we could educate the public to take their milk as soon as it gets into the city, and not to insist upon its being delivered before daylight, I think we would have a very much better supply in every household.

THE CHAIRMAN. We would be glad to hear from any others. The business of this meeting has proceeded in a somewhat irregular way, as we did not have the reading of the records, but they can be read now.

On motion, the reading of the minutes of the July meeting was dispensed with.

Adjourned.

The next meeting is the ANNUAL MEETING, to be held in Boston on the last Thursday in January (Jan. 28), 1904.

THE AMERICAN PUBLIC HEALTH ASSOCIATION MEETING.

The annual meeting was held in Washington, D. C., October 26–30, 1903, with headquarters at the New Willard. The officers for this meeting were: President, Dr. Walter Wyman, Surgeon-General, U. S. Public Health and Marine Hospital Service, Washington, D. C.; first vice-president, Dr. C. P. Wilkinson, New Orleans, La.; second vice-president, Dr. John L. Leal, Paterson, N. J.; secretary, Dr. C. O. Probst, Columbus, O.; treasurer, Dr. F. W. Wright, New Haven, Conn.

The first day was devoted as usual to the meetings of the Laboratory Section. In the evening an informal dinner was held by the Section, to which were invited all the members of the Association. Fifty-nine guests attended, Dr. H. L. Russell, chairman of the Section, presiding. After the dinner, the room was thrown open to the public, and Drs. Salmon and Sternberg were called upon to speak. The chairman's formal address followed, and then reports were received in regular session from Drs. Ravenel, De Schweinitz, and Carroll.

From Tuesday to Friday, inclusive, the Association held sessions daily, for reading of papers, reports of committees and discussions, in addition to which were provided an address of welcome from the Hon. H. B. MacFarland, President of the Board of Commissioners of the District of Columbia, receptions by the citizens of Washington, by the President of the United States, and by the Hon. John B. Henderson and Mrs. Henderson, and an excursion to Mount Vernon, tendered by the citizens of Washington.

The new officers elected for the next meeting are: President, Dr. Carlos J. Finlay, Havana, Cuba; first vice-president, Dr. Jesus Monjaras, City of Mexico.; second vice-president, Dr. Wm. C. Woodward, of Washington, D. C.; the secretary, Dr. Probst, holds over, and the treasurer, Dr. Wright, was re-elected. The elective members of the executive committee for two years are: Dr. A. H. Doty, Staten Island, N. Y.; Dr. John L. Leal, Paterson, N. J.; and Prof. F. C. Robinson, Brunswick, Maine.

The next meeting will be held in Havana, December, 1904.

THE COMMITTEE ON VITAL STATISTICS reported that effective coöperation had been instituted between that Association, the Conference of State Boards of Health, the American Medical Association, the United States Census Bureau, and the United States Public Health and Marine Hospital Service for the improvement of the vital statistics of this country. Among the objects sought are the extension of adequate methods of registration, the use of uniform and comparable tables and rates in bulletins and reports, and the improvement of the international classification of causes of death. A pamphlet on "Statistical Treatment of Causes of Death" has been issued by the United States Census Bureau, requests for which should be addressed to Mr. W. A. King, Chief Statistician for Vital Statistics, Census Bureau.

It has special reference to the difficulties encountered in compiling deaths returned from several causes, and asks for the cooperation of the profession in framing a thoroughly satisfactory method of procedure in such cases.

W. A. King, Bureau of the Census.

STATISTICS OF GARBAGE DISPOSAL for the larger American cities presented by C. E. A. Winslow and P. Hansen showed that in about a third of the communities considered garbage is dumped on land or in water, in one-third it is fed to stock or used as fertilizer, and in the remainder it is treated by some scientific process (cremation in 27 cities, reduction in 19). Feeding to stock is especially common in New England. The authors compare the cost of cremation and reduction in a number of communities and conclude that the economic advantages are fairly well balanced. Reduction they do not consider thoroughly satisfactory from a sanitary standpoint, and they suggest as did the Committee of the Public Health Association on the disposal of Garbage and Refuse in 1897 that the cremation of mixed refuse in furnaces of the English pattern would probably prove the most efficient and economical method of all.

Laboratory Section. The new officers are: Chairman, Dr. Veranus A. Moore. Ithaca, N. Y.; vice-chairman, Dr. W. H. Park, New York City; secretary, Dr. John S. Fulton, Baltimore, Md.; recorder, Dr. H. D. Pease, Albany, N. Y.; councillors, Dr. John A. Amyot, Toronto, Can.; Dr. Octaviano Fabela, Mexico City, Mex.; Dr. Charles Harrington, Boston, Mass.; Dr. H. L. Russell, Madison, Wis.; Dr. F. F. Wesbrook, Minneapolis, Minn.

Committees of the Laboratory Section were appointed as follows:

Standard Methods of Water Analysis: Fuller, Clark, Ellms, Jordan, Russell, Weston, Whipple.

Diagnostic procedures: Wesbrook, Denny, Fabela, Gorham, Hill.

Significance of *B. coli* in public water supplies: Prescott, Bissell, Gage, Horton, Stone.

B. tuberculosis [in man and animals: Ravenel, De Schweinitz, Pearson, Smith (Theobald).

Action of formaldehyde as a disinfectant: Hill, Fulton, Horton, Park, Snodgrass.

Antitoxic and immunizing sera: Pease, Kinyoun, MacFarland, Park, Smith (Theobald).

Relation of protozoa to disease: Stiles, Beyer, Carroll, Wilson (L. B.).

Varieties and action of anaerobic bacteria in sewage: Amyot, Kinnicutt, Winslow.

Standard methods for the identification of bacterial species: Welch, Hill, Kendall.

(In each committee, the chairman's name comes first, the other members' names alphabetically.)

Subjoined are abstracts of some of the papers read by the members of the Section. Not all who presented papers prepared such abstracts; in two or three cases the abstracts prepared stated the problem attacked only, failing to give the conclusions reached.

A BACTERIAL STANDARD FOR MUNICIPAL MILK SUPPLY. (*by G. W. Goler, M.D., and F. R. Eilinger, Ph.D.*). The following table shows the result of nearly four years' work in an attempt to maintain a bacterial standard of cleanliness for the milk supply of the city of Rochester, N. Y.:

	1900.	1901.	1902.	1903.
Monthly averages bacteria per c.c.	796,468	275,327	215,917	209,552
Total number of samples	319	287	531	329
Number containing over 5,000,000	33(10%)	28(19%)	26(6%)	13(4%)
Number containing over 100,000	50(15%)	82(28%)	185(34%)	89(33%)

AN EMERGENCY CULTURE MEDIUM FOR DIPHTHERIA DIAGNOSIS (*by Wm. G. Bissell, M.D.*).

Not infrequently laboratories will run short of their amount of Loeffler's Blood Serum. The following mixture can be prepared inside of three hours and answers as a good substitute: 2 parts whole eggs, thoroughly beaten up, and 1 part of 3% Dextrose Bouillon. After being solidified this medium can be autoclaved at six pounds pressure.

THE TERMINATION OF QUARANTINE IN DIPHTHERIA (*by T. W. Salmon, M.D.*).

Evidence was presented to show the relative efficiency of release by one, by two, and by three negative cultures, and the value of throat tests alone as compared with testing both throat and nose.

THE EFFECT OF LEMON JUICE IN LEMONADE UPON TYPHOID BACILLI (*by Wm. G. Bissell, M.D.*).

The investigation was prompted by a newspaper statement purporting to come from a board of health in one of the leading American cities, that lemon juice in lemonade would render typhoid polluted water safe for drinking purposes. Three different methods of testing were tried. First, by infecting water with typhoid bacilli and adding lemon juice. Second, by infecting glass rods with typhoid bacilli and placing them in lemonade. Third, by infecting silk threads and placing them in the lemonade. Culture tests with the first method were faulty. The conclusions drawn are: First, that lemonade cannot be depended upon in this role. Second, that this method of sterilizing typhoid polluted water should be discouraged.

A CRITICAL STUDY OF THE METHODS IN CURRENT USE FOR THE DETERMINATION OF FREE AND ALBUMINOID AMMONIA IN SEWAGE (*by Earle B. Phelps, S.B.*).

The work presented is the first part of a study which will eventually cover the whole field of sewage analysis. It aims to show what accuracy may be expected from the various processes now employed in sewage analysis, and what modifications, if any, will make them more applicable to the problems of sewage disposal.

A DANGEROUS FOOD PRESERVATIVE (*by Charles Harrington, M.D.*).

Sodium sulphite is used very extensively as a food preservative, and, more particularly, for its effect on the color of chopped meat (Hamburg steak) and certain canned vegetables (asparagus and corn). The assertion made in 1896 by Kionka that it is a dangerous admixture has been combated by a number of experimenters and reaffirmed by Kionka and Schulz. Dogs fed on meat containing 0.20% of the salt were found by them to present extensive lesions in almost every organ, while others fed in the same way by Lebbin and Kallmann showed nothing abnormal.

In the writer's experiment, five cats were fed for five months on beef containing 0.20% and a sixth one with untreated beef. All six began at once to gain in weight, but at about the ninth week all but the control began to lose and they continued to do so up to the twentieth week, when all were killed. The organs of the control were normal. The chief lesion observed in the others was a parenchymatous degeneration of the kidneys. Each of the five presented cloudy swelling and marked fatty degeneration of the renal epithelium. Acute interstitial nephritis was present in one case.

REPORT OF THE COMMITTEE ON THE SIGNIFICANCE OF B: COLI IN WATER SUPPLIES (*by S. C. Prescott, S.B., Chairman*).

In order to present a statement of the opinion of the committee individually and as a whole, as probably representing the generally accepted views of sanitary bacteriologists as to the significance of *B. coli.* in water, the following questions were sent to each member.

The answers appended, except as otherwise stated, were practically as given below.

1. In view of the fact that numerous investigators have found *B. coli* in nature where it could not be directly traced to sewage or fecal pollution, do you believe that the colon test of water is as safe an index of pollution as it was formerly regarded to be? Yes.

2. Are you of the opinion that the number of colon bacilli rather than their presence should be used as a criterion of recent sewage pollution? Yes.

3. In order to pronounce a water sewage-polluted, would you

require as evidence that *B. coli* was present in a majority of one cubic centimeter samples? Yes, in general.

4. Are you in favor of recommending that the examination of large samples for *B. coli*, 100-1000 c.c. be discouraged? Four members say *Yes* in reply, one says *No*.

5. In case of a strong presumptive test, what confirmation tests would you require to make certain that the organisms present were *B. coli?* Full set of distinctive cultural tests.

6. In view of the probable presence of streptococci in polluted waters do you think it desirable that they be isolated as well as *B. coli* to confirm suspicious evidence of pollution offered by *B. coli?* Two would not recommend this; one thinks it would be advantageous occasionally, but not practicable because of increase in routine work; one believes it should be done when possible, for the sake of securing additional data, and for its general confirmation of the colon tests; and one is indefinite.

A SIMPLE METHOD FOR THE ROUTINE DETECTION OF COLON BACILLI IN WATER (*by Wm. Royal Stokes, M.D.*).

The work of Theobald Smith has shown that the colon bacillus ferments lactose with the production of from thirty to fifty per cent. of gas, that the medium is acidulated, and that the proportion of gas is usually that of one part of carbon dioxide to two of hydrogen. Jordan studied a large number of bacteria isolated from various rivers, and did not find any fermentative bacteria which carried out all of the phenomena in the lactose fermentation tube which is characteristic of the colon bacillus. The writer also isolated a moderate number of fermentative bacteria from the Baltimore water supply, and failed to find any fermentative bacteria exactly resembling the colon bacillus in lactose bouillon in the fermentation tube.

In addition to the above characteristics of the colon bacillus in lactose bouillon this organism causes a characteristic color reaction when neutral red is added to the solution in the proportion of ten ccs. of a 0.5% solution to one litre. This has been partly described by Irons and others, but they use the test in an ordinary test tube.

When used in the fermentation tube the open bulb remains **a** port wine odor and the closed bulb a light canary yellow, often showing fluorescence. The curved stem joining the closed and open bulbs shows an abrupt contrast of the colors usually in the middle of the curve. The members of the proteus and cloacae group usually turn both bulbs yellow, but not always.

The method recommended is to inoculate a fermentation tube containing 1% lactose neutral red in the routine examination of water. If the percentage and amount of gas, the acidity, and the typical yellow-red contrast reaction all occur the organism can be considered as *B. coli communis.* This is a much short ermethod than isolation in pure culture, which takes from five to seven days, and will also make it much easier to carry out quantitative experiments These four distinct characteristics would seem to be sufficient to identify the colon bacillus in simple routine work.

A DETAILED STUDY OF THE COLON BACILLUS (*by Wm. G. Bissell, M.D.*).

After consulting with many laboratory workers it was decided to inaugurate an investigation along the following lines:

First Division. To ascertain what constitutes a colon bacillus.

The results demonstrate that the amount of gas produced, the production of Indol, and putrefactive odors, are not constant factors with even true *B. coli;* that many of the lactic acid organisms bear a close resemblance to colon bacilli; and that it is not safe to depend upon presumptive tests alone in determining the presence of colon bacilli in water.

Second Division. The amount of water advisable to test in arriving at an indication of pollution. One hundred and four samples of water coming from the Niagara River at points respectively twelve and twenty-two miles below the points where the sewage of over 400,000 people is received. Different amounts of each sample were examined and the comparative frequency of the presence of colon bacilli determined.

A summary of the results demonstrates that colon bacilli were present in 52% of the samples when 1 cc. was the amount examined at the twelve mile distancea nd in but 34% when 1 cc. was the amount examined at the twenty-two mile distance. Both sides of the river are used for farming purposes. Many samples were collected during heavy rain falls. A recapitulation tends to demonstrate:

(a) That colon bacilli were not found in all 1 cc. amounts of the sample.

(b) That there was a decrease in the number of colon bacilli, the greater the distance down the stream.

(c) That the heavy rains did not seem to increase the number of colon bacilli, although the land was used for farming purposes.

Third Division. A test was made as to the longevity of colon bacilli in natural water. Excrement from the horse, cow, and from human beings, were placed respectively in each of three wells. A test was made of each well at different periods. The results tend to demonstrate that colon bacilli can live in well waters at least one hundred and ninety days and that the human variety seems to have a greater resistance than that from other sources.

Fourth Division. Tests were made to determine the degree of frequency with which colon bacilli could be found in waters known to be polluted with sewage. The results obtained tend to demonstrate that not all 1 cc. amounts of such samples show the presence of the organisms. The writer believes that many organisms have been mistaken for the colon bacilli in water-work.

Fifth Division. Tests were made to ascertain the degree of frequency with which colon bacilli can be found in water not presumably polluted. This work was necessarily confined to well water. Results tend to demonstrate that there are many wells, the waters of which do not contain colon bacilli even though large quantities are examined.

ISOLATION OF *B. COLI COMMUNIS* FROM THE ALIMENTARY TRACT OF FISH (*by George A. Johnson*).

It has been shown that the colon bacillus is taken up by fish, and the results of the experiment described indicate that it multiplies rapidly in the intestinal tract of the same. It has been shown that a search of a large number of fish caught in an unpolluted water failed to reveal the presence of this organism in the intestinal tract. It would seem possible, therefore, that fish, having taken up the colon bacillus from a polluted water, might migrate to a water of comparative purity where they would naturally discharge the greatly increased number of these organisms.

Whether the finding of the colon bacillus deposited in a water in this manner would depreciate the value of the colon test in the examination of a public water supply is a question. It would certainly appear that if the colon bacillus can be thus easily transferred from one water to another, the transportation of the typhoid bacillus may be considered quite as likely. At least the above results may explain the apparent phenomenon frequently noted where *B. coli communis* is found in comparatively large numbers in waters apparently open to but remote chances for fecal contamination.

BACTERIA OF SPECIFIC TYPES AS AN INDEX OF POL-LUTION. (*by H. W. Clark and Stephen DeM. Gage*).

The principal types of bacteria used as indices of pollution are the colon type, sporogenes type, sewage streptococcus type, and occasionally the two so-called paracolon types, *i. e.*, the aerogenes or enteriditis Gaertner type and the chologenes type. The colon type is the most numerous of these in normal sewage and is accordingly of the most value as a specific indication of pollution. Bacteria of the colon type can be detected in ordinary city sewage in dilutions of one-ten-thousandth to one hundred-thousandth. i The presumptive test as applied to the colon type, reacting as t does with some fifty-eight well described species of bacteria, covers too broad a field unless followed by confirmatory tests.

Tests for *B. coli* at the Lawrence Expt. Station have agreed well with results obtained by chemical analyses and by inspection of the sources of the samples.

Surface waters having the greatest relative population on their watershed have shown bacteria of the colon type more frequently than others with less population. Ground waters on the other hand unless grossly polluted never show bacteria of colon type.

Samples of shellfish from sources polluted and unpolluted have almost invariably shown the presence of *B. coli* in the polluted samples and their entire absence in the non-polluted samples.

Examinations for *B. coli* in different volumes of water show that tests in both one and one hundred cubic centimeters should be made, the tests in the larger volumes being confirmatory of the tests in the smaller volumes. In cases where a considerable number of samples are taken from the same source, tests in the larger volumes usually give more information day by day as to the quality of the water than do the tests in one cubic centimeter.

Epidemics of typhoid fever coincident with the finding of *B. coli* in normally pure waters, *i. e.*, in waters known to be safe under ordinary conditions, but becoming dangerous by the accidental entrance of polluted water, have occurred within the observations of the writers, where, although the entrance of this pollution was known, the danger was not indicated by chemical tests or by an increase in the numbers of bacteria beyond the usual limits of variation for waters of this class.

Comparative tests for the relative viability of *B. typhosus* and *B. coli* show that there is a very great similarity between the length of life of the two germs under a great variety of condition.

REPORT OF COMMITTEE ON BACILLUS TUBERCULOSIS IN MAN AND ANIMALS (*by Mazyck P. Ravenel, M.D., Chairman,*

In summing up the available evidence, we feel that there is strong ground for believing in the genetic unity as well as the inter-transmissibility of the human and bovine races of the tubercle bacillus. We consider that it has been positively proven that a certain proportion of persons, chiefly young children, meet their death through infection with the bovine tubercle bacillus, but the knowledge at hand does not enable us at present to define the extent of this danger.

ABSTRACTS, REVIEWS, NOTES AND NEWS.

Boards of Health are asked to send to the Managing Editor notes of not more than one hundred and fifty words relating to new regulations passed, legal cases prosecuted, outbreaks of infection, unusual problems encountered, or other matters, the publication of which may further the attainment of the objects of the Association.

STATISTICS OF TUBERCULOSIS IN WORCESTER.—Mr. James C. Coffey, Executive Officer of the Worcester Board of

Health, has investigated statistically the tuberculosis *status* in Worcester. The following is abstracted from his paper:

A desire to learn as nearly as possible the exact number of deaths from pulmonary and laryngeal tuberculosis which occur in Worcester has led to an investigation of the mortality records of the city for the five years beginning with 1898 and ending with 1902. It was also desired to ascertain the particular localities, if any, which are most affected by this disease, together with its distribution among the various nationalities which make up the population of Worcester. The result is given below. The middle year is taken as the basis for calculation. It has also the advantage of being the census year, which gives us the exact population.

All deaths from tuberculosis in which the lungs or throat were involved are included. This embraces general and miliary tuberculosis, as well as pulmonary and laryngeal cases. The deaths of non-residents which took place at the two State hospitals for the insane are not included. The State Board of Health does not credit deaths in those institutions to Worcester, but to the city or town from which commitment is made.

While the number of deaths from tuberculosis in Worcester is far too numerous, it will be noticed that the figures compare favorably with those of a number of cities whose rates are given.

It is lower, too, than the general average for the entire state. This is particularly gratifying when it is considered that everything involving lungs and throat, including general and miliary tuberculosis, as stated above, are included in these figures.

It is not certain that the figures of the other places given cover anything but phthisis.

The following table shows the number and percentage of deaths of all nationalities in Worcester compared with the population and percentage of population:

American of American parentage	38,337	32.37	226	21.9
Irish of Irish parentage	11,620	9.81	166	16.1
American of Irish parentage	15,819	13.35	245	23.76
Total of Irish parentage	27,439	23.17	411	39.86

Swedes of Swedish parentage.. 7,542	6.36	69	6.69
American of Swedish parentage 4,200	3.54	22	2.13
Total of Swedish parentage....11,742	9.91	91	8.82
Finlanders of Finnish parentage 1,143	.96	18	1.74
Total of Swedish, Finnish, Norwegian and Danish parentage 13,438	11.34	124	12.02
French Canadian of Canadian parentage 5,204	4.39	56	5.43
American of Canadian parentage................... 4,848	4.09	55	5.33
Total of Canadian parentage..10,152	8.48	111	10.76

MORTALITY RATE OF TUBERCULOSIS IN AMERICAN CITIES.

State of Massachusetts..............................	17.68
Boston	23.
Worcester	17.40
Fall River	18.94
Springfield	16.56
Lowell	19.5
Cambridge	20.2
Haverhill...	17.54
New York...	22.99
Philadelphia	21.8
Washington	27.8
Cleveland	11.9
Jersey City.......................................	22.4
Rochester	15.28
Syracuse	17 36
Newark	26.
Chicago	14.8

Mortality per 10,000 of population of some foreign cities and countries, taken from Massachusetts Medical Society year book:

1894.............Austria	37.3
1897.............Hamburg	20.1
1897.............Prussia	21.8
1897.............Bavaria	30.
1897.............Saxony	19.8
1897.............Baden...........................	25.5
———.............Paris (last report)...............	42.4

MODERN CREMATION.—Cremation of the dead in its present form dates back about a quarter of a century. The first crematory was inaugurated in 1876, in Milan, Italy; the second, also in Italy, at Lodi, in 1877; the next in Gotha, Germany, in 1878, and the next in London (Woking) in 1885. The United States possessed a crematory as early as 1876, at Washington, Pa., but this was discontinued. There are now twenty-five crematories in the United States and twenty-seven in Italy.

There were 18,388 persons cremated in the United States up to the end of the year 1902; 5,777 in Germany; 3,323 in England; 855 in Sweden; 48,456 in Paris; and 4,504 in Italy. The increasing demand for this method of disposing of the dead is shown by a comparison of the decade ending 1902 with the preceding years. Thus, in the United States the percentage of bodies cremated during this decade to the number cremated in the previous years was 88.2; in Germany, 78.9; in England, 89.1; in Sweden, 73.2; and in Paris, 75.5.

The largest number of cremations, averaging over five thousand per annum, is shown by the crematory erected at Pere la Chaise, Paris, in 1887. These include cremations of the bodies of private individuals, unclaimed bodies in the hospitals, foetuses, etc. Paris sets a good example to other municipalities in this disposal of the pauper dead.

From a sanitary standpoint, cremation is endorsed by all sanitarians and by all philosophers in all civilized nations. But there have been many obstacles retarding the movement—the force of custom, sentiment of a more than usually unthinking kind, religious scruples and legal objections, because of the destruction of evidence in cases of poisoning, etc. Anyone who has looked upon the gruesome condition of a corpse buried for a time long enough to ensure partial decomposition must surely be convinced that the sentimental arguments are all for cremation, which accomplishes in a cleanly, even aesthetic fashion, in a few hours, what the grave takes years to do in a manner so repulsive that the name has become a synonym for all that is most dreaded and loathsome. As for the force of custom, time alone is necessary for its change. The legal objections are easily met by care in the selection of cases for cremation.
                                                            J. MacConnell.

(EDITOR'S NOTE: We are able to make the following statement on very high Roman Catholic authority:

"In May, 1886, by the decree of one of the Roman congregations, approved by the Holy See, the practice of cremation was condemned, not on the ground that it was contrary to the principles of the Christian religion, but on other grounds, not stated in the decree. The theologians, in interpreting this decree and in divining the reasons on which it was based, say that these are: First, that cremation is a pagan and not a Christian custom; second, that in view of the resurrection of the body, cremation does not seem to be so reverential a mode of disposing of the dead as burial in the earth; third, that it seems abhorrent to the feelings of the relatives of the deceased to hasten the dissolution of the body by any artificial means.")

ANIMAL EXPERIMENTS.—The Right Reverend Monseigneur J. S. Vaughn, one of the most prominent prelates of the Roman Catholic Church in Great Britain, has recently communicated to the *Humane Review*, an English periodical, his views regarding "vivisection" thus:

"Here is, let us say, an ordinary, good-natured and able physician, whom we will call Dr. X. His whole aim and object is to diminish pain and to allay suffering. It is not in his power to destroy it, therefore he directs his efforts to alleviate it. He knows that men are by far the most sensitive of sufferers. He knows that they are subject to certain painful diseases. He has good reason to think that a certain treatment would bring great relief, and perhaps even produce a cure. But his reasoning may be defective, and he cannot ascertain with any degree of certainty whether his opinion be well founded unless and until he can test his theories by actual experiment. That is to say, he must actually apply the remedies.

It is essential that he should make the experiment on a living organism of some kind. But on whom? Well, there are but two classes of creatures to choose from. He must make it either on a human being or else on a beast; either, let us say, on a sick child or on a rabbit. The antivivisectionist objects to all experiments on animals, and in effect answers, "The experiment must be made on the sick child, not on the rabbit!" And this is why we call the antivivisectionist cruel. We, on the contrary, hold that the experiment should be made on the rabbit or other beast, and not on the unfortunate sick child. Yet on this account we are called cruel. Our reason for maintaining this view is, first, because the beast is less sensitive to pain. Secondly, because the loss of life, should the experiment prove abortive, is of far less consequence. Thirdly, because the child is our own very flesh and blood, and a member of our great human family, and has immeasurably greater claims on our pity. Fourthly, because God has given man dominion over the beasts of the field."

(Jour. Am. Med. Assn., Sept. 26, '03.)

HISTORY OF TUBERCULOSIS WORK AT SARANAC LAKE.—Dr. Edward L. Trudeau delivered in Philadelphia, Oct. 24, '03, an address under the auspices of the Henry Phipps Institute for the Study, Treatment and Prevention of Tuberculosis, giving an account of the origin, early struggles, and present successful standing of the well-known sanitarium work with which his name is identified. The following excerpts from the published article *(Med. News, Oct. 24, '03)* are of peculiar interest:

"Of the fifteen hundred cases under consideration, (consumptive patients at Saranac Lake) which have been discharged from two to seventeen years, 434 could not be traced, leaving 1,066 which have been traced. Of these, 46.7 are still living; of these 31% are known to be well at present, in 6.5% the disease is still arrested, 4% have relapsed, 5.2% are chronic invalids, and 53.3% are dead. As to the influence of the stage of the disease on the permanency of the results obtained, he (Dr. Lawrason Brown, the compiler of the statistics) found 66% of the 258 incipient cases discharged well at present. Of the 563 advanced cases, 28.6% are well, and of the far advanced cases 2.5% only remain cured."

"Over the doors of the wards and hospitals for consumptives, twenty-five years ago, might have been written these words: 'All hope abandon ye that enter here;' while to-day, in the light of the new knowledge, we may justly place at the entrance of the modern sanitarium the more hopeful inscription, 'Cure sometimes, relieve often, comfort always.' "

" . . . the researches of Koch, Behring, Maragliano, and Neufeld, abroad, and of DeSchweinitz, McFadyean, Pearson and Gilliland and myself in this country, have already brought forward evidence that a marked degree of artificial immunity against tuberculosis can be produced in animals, and the success already obtained in this direction seems sufficient to justify the hope that prevention may some day find a most efficient ally in the discovery of some safe method of immunization applicable to man."

TYPHOID FEVER ATTRIBUTED TO INFECTED ICE. From the St. Lawrence State Hospital, Ogdensburg, N. Y., Drs. Hutchings and Wheeler report (*Am. Journ. Med. Sci., Oct.*, '03) thirty-nine cases of typhoid fever in October and November, 1902, which they traced, by exclusion, to ice cut from the St. Lawrence River in February, seven months before. Their bacteriological examinations resulted in finding three colonies of colon bacilli and one of typhoid bacilli in plates made from the ice, although it appears that but five colonies altogether were examined in detail.

The possibility, but also the extreme improbability, of typhoid infection through natural ice was pointed out in a report on ice, made by the Boston Board of Health in 1901, in which the work of Park, and of Sedgwick and Winslow, was largely drawn on. The rarity of typhoid infection through any ice, and the apparently unfavorable conditions for the infection of this particular ice, the development of the first cases only six days after the first use of the suspected ice, together with the practically unique achievement of recovering the typhoid bacilli from the ice, seven months old, after what was apparently a very brief examination, make this report of Drs. Hutchings and Wheeler a very striking one. It is to be regretted that their evidence is not reported in more exhaustive detail.

The writers were unable to find any similar case on record. The only case at all approaching this one is quoted by Harrington (*Practical Hygiene*, p. 376) from the *Revue d'Hygiene*, April, 1898, in which eight army officers, drinking wine containing ice cut from an infected source, contracted typhoid fever after the usual incubation period. *H. W. Hill.*

SODIUM SULPH–HYDRATE (Na S H), in the form of a 25% aqueous solution, makes an excellent depilatory for guinea-pigs, rabbits, etc., when, for experimental purposes, an area of the skin is to be laid bare. Rubbed into the hair with a glass rod, it is better for the purpose than a razor, especially since it makes sure that scoring of the skin shall not occur.

THE BOSTON ASSOCIATION FOR THE RELIEF AND CONTROL OF TUBERCULOSIS held its first annual meeting at 264 Boylston Street, Boston, November 17, '03, Dr. Edward O. Otis, the President, in the chair. Reports were received from the Secretary, the Treasurer and the Committees on Relief and Control, on Hospitals and Sanitoria, and on Education. The officers and council were all re-elected. The campaign for this season is now fairly under way.

SOCIETIES AND COMMISSIONS FOR INVESTIGATING THE TUBERCULOSIS PROBLEM, and efforts at meeting the requirements discovered thereby, are multiplying rapidly. The Canadian Association for the Prevention of Consumption and Other Forms of Tuberculosis, has encouraged the formation of local societies in affiliation with it, so that there have been established the Montreal League, the Ontario Association, and other similar bodies. The Cuban League against Tuberculosis has a central committee in Havana and a local committee in each of the six provinces of the island. In Ohio, a state-wide movement has been begun by the Ohio Society for the Prevention of Tuberculosis. In Maryland, Rhode Island, Minnesota, Wisconsin, New Jersey and Vermont, State commissions exist, appointed to inform the respective State governments of the necessities of the case. In California two societies, one lay and one medical, are coöperating together. In Cambridge, New Haven, Binghampton, Chicago, Philadelphia, New York and Boston, various forms of association against tuberculosis are established or are about to be established. (*Abst. from Paul Kennaday, Charities, Oct. 3, '03.*) It is pleasant to contemplate so much activity directed against this greatest scourge of the day. If all concerned will only remember that too many cooks spoil the broth, and that coördination is the great essential to the success of sub-divided labors, great advances towards the abolition of consumption may be expected within the next few years.

CONSUMPTION: A CURABLE AND PREVENTABLE DISEASE. By Lawrence F. Flick, M.D. pp. 295. Price, $1.00. David McKay, Philadelphia.

This excellent treatise is designed to tell the exact truth to the layman, and gives the chief facts in a logical, easy fashion, impressive from its simplicity and directness.   Even to those who are familiar with every aspect of the question, this presentation, giving the broad non-technical view, will prove of value for its suggestiveness and as supplying ready-made ammunition for the discussion of consumption with the laity.

Hardly any book of this character could be written to which no exception might be taken, but the teaching of this book is in general thoroughly sound and reasonable, without any tendency to extremism, affording just the sort of information which one must wish that all members of the community possessed.

Some of the most important chapters are: The Relation between Consumption and Tuberculosis: Is Consumption Inherited?; Predisposition to Consumption—with separate chapters on the predisposing causes, Disease, Dissipation, Want, Overwork, Alcohol; How Tuberculosis is Spread by Contact with the Consumptive— with separate chapters on different factors; The Curability of Consumption; The Treatment of Consumption; Should Consumptives Marry? etc., etc.   Registration, and disinfection of the patient's immediate surroundings after death or removal, are advocated as peculiarly the duty of Boards of Health.

A CONSIDERATION OF THE PROBABLE AVENUES OF ENTRANCE to the body of the infective agents of the infectious diseases makes clear the prominence which the evidence available gives to the mouth as a port of entry, particularly in typhoid fever, diphtheria, small-pox, influenza, measles, chicken-pox, pneumonia, tuberculosis and scarlet fever.

Dr. Samuel A. Hopkins (*Internat. Dent. J., Aug.,* '03) gives the results of experiments made to determine the relative infectiveness of mouths kept clean and of mouths allowed to remain dirty and uncared for.   As yet incomplete, these investigations go to show that the pneumonia bacillus, at least, was readily displaced from the mouth by suitable treatment.   He concludes as follows:

"It is well known that croupous pneumonia frequently follows other diseases.   It is one of the most dreaded sequelæ of measles, whooping-cough, and typhoid fever, and appears to develop sometimes from a severe cold. . . .

"Many physicians recognize in a degree the importance of cleansing the mouth, . . . yet it is true that comparatively few physicians or nurses have learned to look upon cleanliness of the mouth as an important factor in preventing complicating diseases.

"If, however, the experiments presented have not been wrongly interpreted, the pneumonia germ is one of the easiest to destroy, and mouth cleanliness will go far to reduce the disease to a minimum."

PREVENTIVE MEDICINE AND NATURAL SELECTION. The sanitarian, by enforcing artificial hygienic safeguards, aids to some extent the survival of the weak, and so incurs the accusation sometimes made, of contributing to race degeneration by the preservation of undesirable elements which would be eliminated in the absence of hygienic measures, by the weeding-out processes of disease.

Dr. C. V. Chapin discusses this question (*Journ. Am. Social Sci. Assn.*, 1903) at some length, concluding that natural selection, left alone, is working for the ultimate good of the race, that public health measures are in some respects antagonistic to it, but that the preservation of life accomplished in the immediate present should not be sacrificed for the, at best, hypothetical advantage, only to be realized, if at all, in the far distant future, which untrammeled nature might otherwise provide. It is pointed out also that, so far at least as the communicable diseases are concerned, there is no evidence that the feeble, the poorly nourished, and the constitutionally defective are in fact particularly more susceptible than are the more desirable elements, although doubtless less resistant after infection. He believes that these diseases form a less important factor in maintaining race stamina than is often supposed, and that attempts at their suppression can be logically supported by philosophic considerations.

INDIRECT TRANSMISSION OF WHOOPING-COUGH.— Dr. John Lovett Morse recently sent letters to number of physicians of experience to elicit their beliefs on the transmissibility of whooping-cough otherwise than directly from patient to prospective patient. He sums up as follows: "It seems hardly possible to draw any very positive conclusions from these replies, except that very little is known as to the indirect contagiousness

of whooping-cough.   The cases reported, although very few, seem
to justify the presumption that whooping-cough may be carried
by third persons or by clothing and other articles. . . . However,
it must be very seldom that whooping-cough is carried in this
way. (*Bos. Med. & Surg. J.*, Oct. 1, '03.)

ELECTIVE INSTRUCTION IN THE INFECTIOUS DIS-
EASES is given annually to classes of medical students at the
Municipal Hospital in Philadelphia.   Only one case of infection
amongst the students has occurred in four years—one of them
who succeeded in evading the strict vaccination requirements
contracting small-pox.   Dr. Benjamin Lee of the Pennsylvania
State Board of Health has recently urged that these courses be
made compulsory. (*Am. Med., Sept.,* '03.)

For many years medical students in Boston have been encouraged by the Chairman of the Board of Health, Dr. S. H. Durgin, to
see infectious diseases in the various hospitals which have been
under his control.   Could such bedside clinics be attended not
only by students, but by physicians and health officers throughout
the State, these diseases, especially small-pox, would become
better known and more easy of diagnosis, to the advantage of
preventive measures and of the public health.

ACUTE RHEUMATISM.—Walker and Ryffel, working under
the auspices of the Scientific Gifts Committee of the British Medical Association report (*Brit. Med. Journ., Sept.* 19, '03) the constant association with acute rheumatism of a particular streptococcus, first demonstrated by Triboulet, which they call Micro-
coccus rheumaticus.   The belief has been held for a number of
years that acute rheumatism is in reality a form of septicæmia,
and the bacteriological evidence seems now to establish this.
Walker and Ryffel also found that the tissues of a rabbit inoculated
with this organism yielded formic acid, and that they could obtain
the same acid from culture of the organism.   They suggest a relationship between the disease and the presence of the formic acid.

The Committee on Hygiene of the Board of Education of Philadelphia has approved a plan for the medical inspection of all schools
and pupils. (*Am. Med.,* Oct. 31, '03.)

ANTHRAX IN THE HUMAN IN LYNN. Several cases of anthrax occurring near Salem and Lynn, Mass., were reported to the Essex South District Medical Society two years ago. The disease has appeared at intervals since then, four cases having been treated at the Lynn Hospital in the last three months. These were all men—morocco workers, one employed in a Peabody factory, the remaining three in one factory in Lynn.

Each of these cases has shown, one to three days before entering the hospital, a small itching pimple, and fever. The local lesion appeared as a dry black crust, $\frac{1}{2}$ to $1\frac{1}{2}$ inches in diameter, on the margin of which were several small blebs or pustules. The amount of œdema varied, one case showing almost none, another very little, another, with the pustule on the side of the neck, showing œdema from jaw to shoulder, while the fourth case, with the lesion on the flexor surface of the fore-arm, presented enormous swelling of the whole limb from fingers to trunk.

In all of these cases, smears from the lesions showed the characteristic bacilli, and in the last two, positive cultures were also obtained.

Three cases were treated by immediate excision of the pustule and a wide margin of the adjacent skin. One of these cases has recovered, one died on the fourth day, and one is now (Nov. 12) convalescent. The fourth case refused operation. The pustule was on his cheek, and there was some involvement of the neighboring glands. He recovered under free injections of pure carboli acid beneath the skin, application of mercuric chloride as a dry powder, and dressings of gauze, wet in 1 to 5000 mercuric chloride solution. *Herbert W. Newhall, M. D., Lynn.*

In Washington, D. C., Oct. 21, met the executive Committee of the Associated Charities Committee on the prevention of tuberculosis. Amongst the leaders are Surgeon-General Walter Wyman, General George M. Sternberg, Drs. Hickling, Kingsman, and Woodward, and Mr. Smith (*Am. Med., Oct.* 31, '03).

The cost of Typhoid Fever to the British Government during the Boer war is estimated as not less than £4,000,000 (over $19,-000,000). This estimate is based on the occurrence of 31,018 cases, each of which is considered as if it occurred in the most cheaply trained infantry soldier.   Of this total, 6,172 died; 15,120 were invalided home; 9,726 convalesced in South Africa.   (*Bos. Med. & Surg. J., Nov. 5, '03.*)

MEDICAL ATTENDANCE REQUIRED FOR MINORS.— The Court of Appeals of New York has handed down a decision confirming the findings of the lower trial court, imposing a sentence in 1901 upon a White Plains (N. Y.) Dowieite, of $500, or five hundred days imprisonment, for criminal neglect in failing to provide medical attendance for his adopted daughter, sixteen months old, who died from pneumonia.   The conviction was secured under the penal code which states that "a person who omits without lawful excuse to perform a duty by law imposed upon him, to furnish food, clothing, shelter, or medical attendiance to a minor, is guilty, etc."

District Attorney J. Addison Brown, of Westchester County, in commenting on this decision, stated that so far as he knew, this is the first occasion where the higher courts in this country have made the law certain, although this has been done in England. He says: "The decision is of the highest importance and means absolutely that the faith curists and others of the same sort must obey the law compelling them to call in regular physicians. in the event of dangerous illness or minors in their families.   The fact that they have called in "readers" of their churches, layers-on-of-hands and others will not shield them from the law."

(*Abs. Bos. Med. & Surg. J. Oct. 22, '03.*)

A Commission to investigate Dysentery in South Africa, appointed by the British Secretary of State for War in August, 1900, has recently reported.   Thefollowing conclusions are of interest:

1.   South African dysentery is not caused by amebae.

2.   The causal agent confines itself to the intestines and is not found in the organs.

3.   No specific organism was found to which could be attributed the dysenteries encountered. (*Bos. Med. & Surg. J., Nov. 5, '03.*)

These conclusions are striking when compared with the very definite results obtained from investigations of dysentery in the

Far East, the Philippines, etc., where both amebic dysentery and bacillary dysentery, the latter due to the organism of Shiga, have been demonstrated.

NEW JERSEY SANITARY ASSOCIATION. Founded in 1874, this association will hold its twenty-ninth annual meeting, Dec. 4th and 5th, at Lakewood, N. J. The topics on the program include: Sanitary Inspection; Medical Supervision of Schools; Garbage Disposal; Civil Sanitary Societies; The Present Attitude of Sanitary Science; The attitude towards Sanitary Science, of —Education,—the National Government,—the Law and the Courts,—the Press; Sewage Disposal in New Jersey; Isolation; Mosquito Parasites; Laboratory Investigations.

Amongst the speakers will be: Dr. H. M. Herbert; Dr. Henry Mitchell; Dr. G. R. Dickenson; Dr. Joseph Tomlinson; Dr. William S. Disbrow; Dr. W. B. Johnson; M. N. Baker, C.E., George P. Ollcott, C.E., W. H. Lowe, D.V.S., Dr. John L. Leal, M.D., Rev. Alfred Roeder; Prof. Austin Scott; Surgeon-General Walter Wyman, Hon. John A. Blair; Hon. George Wurts; Rudolph Hering, C. E.,George M. Fuller, C. E., Allen Hazen, C.E., J. J. Cross, C. E., C. C. Vermule, C. E., J. Waldo Smith, C. E., Dr. A. Clark Hunt; Dr. George McLaughlin; Dr. Charles Wardell Stiles; Prof. John B. Smith; Dr. R. B. Fitz Randolph; Dr. J. J. Kinyoun; Dr. F. B. Kilmer. Dr. John L. Leal is the president.

MANUAL OF HEALTH LAWS OF MASSACHUSETTS. This manual contains, in addition to the statutes relating to public health which appear in the new edition of Revised Laws of 1902, all of the decisions of the Supreme Court relative to these statutes which have been made previous to July, 1903. It also contains all of the health legislation of 1902 and 1903, together with other matters pertaining to public health, which will make it a convenient handbook for all health officials, as well as for medical examiners, physicians and persons engaged in the sale of food products.

A portion of the same manual, containing the laws of the State relative to the sale of food and drugs, will also be issued in a separate form, for the use of persons engaged in the sale of food produstc.

The present edition will be completed and ready for distribution during the month of November of the present year (1903).

COLON BACILLI ON HANDS. At the meeting of the Boston Society of Medical Sciences on Nov. 17, C. E. A. Winslow of the Massachusetts Institute of Technology reported an examination of the hands of school children and students and servants of the Institute for the colon bacillus, the organism being found present in from 5 to 10% of the cases examined. Since the typhoid bacillus would take the place of the colon bacillus in the case of persons suffering from typhoid fever, it is easy to understand how that disease spreads through the community from person to person becoming, under uncleanly conditions, almost a contagious disease.

A NEW JOURNAL, *The Journal of Infectious Diseases*, founded by the Memorial Institute for Infectious Diseases, recently established in Chicago by Mr. and Mrs. Harold F. McCormick, is to appear January 1st, 1904, under the editorship of Ludwig Hektoen and Edwin O. Jordan, in conjunction with Frank Billings, F. G. Novy and W. T. Sedgwick. It will be devoted to original investigations dealing with the general phenomena, causation, and prevention of infectious diseases. Prompt publication is to be insured by issuance of numbers as fast as material accumulates instead of at regular intervals. The subscription price will be $5.00 per volume.

TO AUTOCLAVE SERUM successfully at fifteen pounds' pressure, it is only necessary to make sure that the serum goes into the autoclave hot, either fresh from the Koch coagulator, or out of the free-steam sterilizer. According to Wesbrook, serum can even be coagulated successfully in that form of autoclave which is heated directly by a flame underneath it, by letting the steam escape freely at first, as from an ordinary Arnold sterilizer, until coagulation is complete. Shutting the outlets then and raising the pressure to the desired point provides for sterilizing. When, however, an autoclave supplied with steam from a boiler at a pressure considerably above fifteen pounds is used, this method becomes very difficult, if not impossible.

SANITARY ENGINEERING.

Robert Spurr Weston.

REPORT OF AMERICAN WATER WORKS ASSOCIATION. George W. Fuller describes in detail the construction and operation of the new water purification plant at Little Falls, N. J. The filter plant is designed to treat daily 30,000,000 gallons of colored and slightly polluted water for the supply of Paterson, Passaic, Bayonne and part of Jersey City. The water after treatment with sulphate of alumina is passed through a coagulating basin and thence through rapid filters. The entire plant is built of concrete reinforced with steel. The sand in the filters is agitated, during washing, by air currents, instead of by the mechanical rakes used in many other places. The numbers of bacteria per c.c. in the filtered water average less than 75 for the first year of operation, which indicates excellent hygienic efficiency. The filters cost about $15,000 per million gallons per diem capacity.

J. J. Deery describes the patent sewage disposal plant in operation at Reading, Pa. This plant, as is well known, comprises two sets of sewage beds, the primary beds being so placed above the secondary beds that the effluent of the former rains upon the latter. No results showing quantities of sewage treated or cost of operation were given. The effluent is said to be of good quality.

MANCHESTER, ENGLAND, SEWAGE DISPOSAL.—Annual report of the Rivers Department for the year ending March, 1903. At Manchester chemical precipitation works were put into operation in the spring of 1894. Acting upon the conclusions of the well-known Manchester Experiments, the plant is being changed over to treat the sewage in septic tanks followed by bacteria beds. At present, on the average, about 40% of the dry weather flow, or 10.3% of the whole volume of sewage, is treated daily by the bacteria beds. Both the septic tank and chemical precipitation effluents are applied to the beds, and experiments with these effluents, applied to bacteria beds of various constitutions, are described in the report, which also gives results of experiments to determine the degree of absorption of dissolved oxygen by sewage effluents, and to determine the practicability of producing illuminating gas from septic sludge.

CHARLES RIVER DAM REPORT, 1903. A movement to build a dam across the Charles River so as to form a waterpark in the center of the Metropolitan District, similar to that in Hamburg, has been on foot since 1859, and the report of the present Commission is a fitting climax to the labors of various previous commissions. Mr John R. Freeman, as chief engineer, was instructed to thoroughly sift the conflicting evidence concerning the desirability of such a dam. Mr. Freeman's report and the accompanying reports of Prof. Crosby, the geologist; Prof. Theobald Smith, the pathologist; Dr. Field, the biologist; Mr. Clark, the chemist; and Mr. Goodnough, the sanitary engineer, should be read by everyone interested in questions pertaining to public health, as many long-cherished but fallacious theories are overthrown.

The commission recommends a dam to keep out the tide and thereby form a fresh water basin, all sewage now entering the river to be diverted through marginal conduits discharging below the dam. The investigations of the engineer and the biologist completely overthrow the long-maintained opinion that the harbor channels are maintained by tidal scour, showing that the velocities at the bottom of the channel are too low to erode the same. The harbor deposits are found to be of ancient origin. No appreciable shoaling has occurred since 1835; on the contrary, the bottom of the harbor seems to sink at the rate of about one foot in one hundred years. While at the surface the velocity of the ebb tide is greater than that of the flood, at the bottom, where erosion would take place, the contrary is true.

The preservation of the commercial interests involved is to be provided for by a lock in the dam.

The fear lest the temperature of the air in summer be increased if the sea water be shut out is shown to be groundless, by most elaborate meteorological data collected at points from Boston Light to Waltham. The air temperatures were found to be practically uniform over the whole area, except at points near the surface of the water.

Prof. Theobald Smith concludes that the basin would not tend to favor any increase of malaria, provided present mosquito breeding places are properly dealt with. On the contrary, improvement might be expected. The present pollution of the Charles River seems to be due in the main to the discharge of Stony Brook. Mr. Clark states that the basin filled with still fresh water would be in better condition than the present tidal basin filled with brackish water, as salt water tends to precipitate the sewage. This view is confirmed by Mr. Goodnough and Prof. Field, the latter showing that the vertical circulation in the river would be greater if the salt water were excluded.

SEWAGE DISPOSAL AT FITCHBURG.—The City Council has adopted an order for the construction of new sewage disposal beds. The cost is estimated at $445,012.

A NEW SEWAGE DISPOSAL PLANT IS TO BE BUILT AT AMES, IOWA, consisting of a septic tank containing 56,500 gallons, the effluent of which is to be disposed of upon two filter beds of sand, each containing about 0.2 acre. The cost of the system. including about 8,500 feet of sewer, will be about $25,000.

THE JOURNAL OF THE MASSACHUSETTS
ASSOCIATION OF BOARDS OF HEALTH ✍

Established 1890.

THE OFFICIAL JOURNAL OF THE MASSACHUSETTS ASSOCIATION OF BOARDS OF HEALTH is a quarterly publication, containing the papers read at the meetings of the Association, together with verbatim reports of the discussions following them, and other information of hygienic interest. Publication months hereafter (November, 1903): February, May, August, November.

Subscription rates, $1.00 per year.

Non-receipt of the Journal should be called to the attention of the Managing Editor promptly.

All communications concerning the Association should be addressed to the Secretary, **James C. Coffey, City Hall, Worcester, Mass.**

All communications regarding the Journal, subscriptions, etc., should be addressed to the Managing Editor, **Dr. H. W. Hill, 607 Sudbury Building, Boston, Mass.**

JOURNAL OF THE
MASSACHUSETTS ASSOCIATION OF
BOARDS OF HEALTH.

ORGANIZED 1890.

[The Association as a body is not responsible for statements or opinions of any of its members.]

| VOL. XIV. | February, 1904. | NO. 1. |

THE MASSACHUSETTS ASSOCIATION OF BOARDS OF HEALTH was organized in Boston, March, 1890, with the following objects: the advancement of sanitary science; the promotion of better organization and co-operation among local boards of health, and the uniform enforcement of sanitary laws and regulations.

THE JOURNAL OF THIS ASSOCIATION has for thirteen years faithfully reflected the views of the public hygienists of Massachusetts. As the only one of its kind in Massachusetts, the Journal has had its own field, which, however, it has not yet fully occupied. With the October issue of the year 1903, a policy of expansion was adopted. The subscription list showed an immediate and most gratifying increase, so that this, the third issue has a total circulation of over 1,100 copies.

In order that the Journal may appear within the next month after each quarterly meeting of the Association, the date of publication will be FEBRUARY, MAY, AUGUST *and* NOVEMBER *of each year.*

THE JOURNAL will contain the papers read at the meetings of the Association, verbatim reports of the discussions, editorials, abstracts, reviews and hygienic notes of professional interest. Subscription rates, $1.00 per year. Reprints furnished at cost price.

All communications concerning the ASSOCIATION should be addressed to the Secretary of the Association, JAMES C. COFFEY, CITY HALL, WORCESTER, MASS.

All bills not relating to the Journal, and MEMBERSHIP DUES ($2.00 per year) should be sent to the Treasurer of the Association, DR. JAMES B. FIELD, 329 WESTFORD ST., LOWELL, MASS.

*All communications concerning the JOURNAL, copy, proof, sub-
scriptions, advertisements, etc., should be addressed to the Managing
Editor, DR. H. W. HILL, 607 SUDBURY BLDG., BOSTON,
MASS.*

EDITORIALS.

THE PHYSIOLOGIST, BAYLISS, *vs.* COLERIDGE, THE ANTIVIVISECTIONIST.

A suit for damages for libel. Judgment for the plaintiff in £2000.

The circumstances of this case should be of interest to all those concerned in the advancement of medical knowledge.

They may be summarized briefly as follows: Two young Swedish women, of good education and social position, had been visiting various laboratories and attending lectures in courses on physiology, apparently with the purpose of securing evidence to be used in propaganda against animal experimentation. During the winter of 1902-1903 they visited London, and in February, 1903, at one of a course of lectures in physiology at University College, they claimed to have witnessed experiments that were conducted with great cruelty and in violation of the law. They were at this lecture—as they had been at others—not as genuine students of physiology, but as seekers after evidence in their crusade against animal experimentation of any kind. They were well educated, and might be supposed to be honest. It would be natural therefore to believe that they could see and understand what went on within a few feet of them, and would take great pains to truthfully report what they saw. They testified that they saw no tube connection made for purposes of artificial respiration; that the animal being experimented upon made many purposive movements, indicating a conscious struggling; that they smelled no anesthetic, and believed that none was given; that cries, whines and barks had been heard, and that the animal had made a shrinking movement, as of fear, at the first approach of the operator.

As against this professedly close and accurate observation, it was proved in Court, before the Lord Chief Justice of England:

(1) that artificial respiration was carried on all the time the animal was on the table in front of them; (2) that the animal was profoundly anesthetized,—one and a half grains of morphia had been injected before it had been brought into the room (a very large dose), and that six ounces of the "A. C. E." mixture (alcohol, chloroform and ether) had been used during the operation; (3) that this particular dog was affected with chorea, and that the movements seen were choreic—not purposive—in character; (4) that tracheotomy had been performed, and it was impossible therefore that any cries, whines or barks could have been heard; (5) that the shrinking movement of fear testified to could not have occurred for the above reasons.

The ladies, relying upon their own powers of observation, made a statement of what they claimed to have seen to Mr. Stephen Coleridge, Honorary Secretary of the Antivivisection Society (of England), a lawyer and a member of the English Bar. This gentleman, as he testified, accepted their statement without any attempt at verification, although he knew that giving publicity to it would be likely to be followed by prosecution. Apparently, however, the search for evidence to support the agitation has grown so desperate that this opponent of animal experimentation was ready, even anxious to use this testimony, and did so, amid great enthusiasm, at the annual meeting of the Antivivisection Society, early in May, 1903.

The prosecution for libel followed promptly, with the substantial verdict against the defendant, already mentioned, of nearly $10,000.

That a lawyer, trained in the weighing of evidence and with a knowledge of the necessary responsibility accompanying specific assertions of cruelty, should have taken no step to verify his supposed facts, seems inexplicable. The defendant gave as his reason that he knew they would be denied, and during cross-examination went so far as to say that he still believed the women to have testified to the truth; this after their statements had all been denied under oath!

Here is the condition of mind we have found much nearer home. The opponents of animal experimentation deny its usefulness, in the face of overwhelming evidence to the contrary. Evidence that to them is not such, for they do not believe it when it is stated, and take no pains to verify it by actual observation. It may perhaps be fortunate, after all, that such attempts at verification are not made by such people, if their interpretation of the facts seen by them is to be as false as it was in this instance.

It has not yet happened that specific allegations of cruelty have been made in Massachusetts. Of general assertions there have been many, all of the same character, and repeated year after year. Perhaps such a disastrous failure as that of Mr. Coleridge, in the exploitation of an unsubstantiated calumny, may prove a salutary warning even to the most violent opponents of physiological research and teaching. That simple limitation is not what they desire, but absolute prohibition is becoming more and more evident from year to year.

If the unhampered advance of medical knowledge is to go on, ever watchful care must be taken that methods like those illustrated in this trial are not successful.

Poetic justice sometimes is seen, even in this workaday twentieth century. Dr. Bayliss, on receipt of the money from Mr. Coleridge, turned it over to the laboratory fund for devotion to the furtherance of physiological research!

MR. COLERIDGE IN A NEW ROLE (*Brit. Med. Jour.*, Jan. 2, 1904).—It is not always that one who has suffered bitter defeat as the climax of enthusiastic effort possesses sufficient manliness to give his successful opponents even the most niggardly modicum of respect or credit for decency. Mr. Stephen Coleridge, Honorary Secretary of the Antivivisection Society of England, has gone further than this. Since paying his fine for damages in the case of Bayliss *vs.* Coleridge, he has come to the defense of his late opponents against the unscrupulous attacks of the Secretary of another anti-society, the "National Canine Defense Society." This Secretary published recently a circular containing the usual wild, general statements and emotional appeals, which forms the stock in trade of those agitators who lack sufficient honesty to tell the truth, and sufficient courage to make specific charges which might be met in court.

Mr. Coleridge took up these charges in detail, refuting them seriatim, and wound up with a much-needed admonition to the author of the circular, pointing out that exaggeration, innuendo and falsehood are not the methods by which success is attained or the respect of decent people secured.

We give below some of these statements and Mr. Coleridge's reply:

Secretary of the "National Canine Defense Society":

"Thousands of dogs are tortured annually by licensed experimenters."

Secretary of the Anti-vivisection Society:

"If every animal experimented on in 1902 (under the various licenses) were a dog, the total would not come to thousands.

"The total number of experiments performed in 1902 was 14,906, 12,776 of which were without anesthetics.

"The number 14,906 does not give the number of dogs used, for each experiment may include any number of dogs."

"The 12,776 experiments without anesthetics were inoculations or similar simple experiments.

"The [figure 14,906 included all the animals used, frogs, guinea pig, cats, etc., the animals used are not without limit, but less than the actual number returned."

Mr. Coleridge further states that the circular contains "grossly false and misleading statements." He denounces "the false statements of anti-vivisectionists," and rebukes them for "methods which must bring disaster to any movement that employs them, and justly alienate the sympathies of all honorable people."

This is a striking statement, coming from a leader in the anti-vivisection movement, against the whole policy of those whose protestations, training and associations would lead the uninitiated to believe them highly honorable, scrupulously truthful and entirely trustworthy.

THE EFFICIENCY OF PUBLIC PROPHYLAXIS AGAINST TUBERCULOSIS.—Dr. Thomas J. Mays, in a recent article in the *New York and Philadelphia Medical Journal*, attempts to question the efficacy of registration and disinfection as a means of preventing consumption.   He presents a great mass of statistics which are analyzed and compared in various ways.   He admits that there has been a greater decrease of phthisis in what he terms prevention localities than in non-prevention localities, and that this by itself might be regarded as proof of the efficacy of the methods in question.   But he attempts to show that in prevention localities there has been a more than counterbalancing increase of pneumonia, and that while the latter disease has increased in non-prevention localities, the increase is not nearly so marked.   While he does not definitely so state, he apparently intends his readers to infer that physicians in their returns of death have of late years erroneously reported deaths from consumption as due to pneumonia. This substitution of pneumonia for tuberculosis he seems to believe is the cause of the comparatively greater increase of pneumonia in localities where the attempt is made to restrict tuberculosis than in localities where such attempt is not made.   Asserting this interchange of terms, the author infers that the apparent decrease of consumption which he says is greater in his prevention areas, is not real, and that there is, therefore, no sufficient evidence that registration and disinfection are successful in controlling this disease.

That there should have been a progressive error during the last decade or so, in the diagnosis of these two diseases is incredible.   The only other hypothesis is that physicians have falsely substituted one term for the other and have done so to a greater extent in prevention localities than in the non-prevention.

That such substitution is occasionally made to cheat the insurance companies no one doubts, but it can scarcely be often enough to affect the ratios.   That physicians should deliberately substitute pneumonia for consumption in their returns of death, for the purpose of deceiving the health department, could only be due to the fear that some grievous burden would be laid upon the family. After the death of the patient about the only trouble that could be made for the family by the health department would be dis-infection, and it is absurd to suppose that fear of this would lead physicians to falsify returns. It will be noticed, too, that in some of the cities referred to as illustrating the pseudo-increase of pneumonia, disinfection after consumption is not compulsory. Thus in 1902, in Baltimore it was practiced after only 76 of the 1,159 deaths from pulmonary tuberculosis. Most of those who are familiar with the subject differ entirely from Dr. Mays, and have no doubt that there has been a very real increase in pneumonia mortality during the last few years. Much of this is due to influenza, but whether all of the increase is due to this cause is not certain. Dr. Mays admits that influenza in the early nineties did increase the amount of pneumonia, but claims that its influence is no longer felt. This, however, is not the fact, for the death returns from Boston, New York, Philadelphia, Baltimore and many other cities show that influenza has prevailed very extensively during the last few years, though indeed rather less in 1902 than formerly. And certainly, the medical practitioners in these cities know that the cases of this disease have been very numerous. We can be very sure that pneumonia has really increased, and that some of this increase has been due to influenza. There is little likelihood that there has been any but a slight transference of consumption to pneumonia. And there can be no doubt that the alleged decrease of pulmonary tuberculosis is real.

In the article referred to, localities which have "agitated" the subjects of notification and disinfection are placed in the same category with those in which these methods are actually practiced. How the mere agitation of those subjects has anything to do with the case is difficult to see. Doubtless discussion of the nature of tuberculosis and the methods of prevention has done something to cause physicians and patients to recommend and adopt reasonable, and more or less effectual methods of restricting infection. Such discussion has been very general and it would be difficult to find a city of considerable size in which these subjects have not been pretty well agitated. All this is very different from the adoption of the official restrictive measures of notification and disinfection. If the value of these methods is to be questioned, only those places should be considered in which they are actually in force. It is indeed difficult to understand Dr. Mays' selection of prevention and non-prevention localities. Thus, he includes among the former Chicago, where scarcely any cases are reported, Philadelphia, where a notification ordinance was recently adopted, but where no attempt is made to enforce it, andwhere disinfection is entirely voluntary, and Cleveland, Hartford and New Haven, where neither reports of cases nor disinfection was required, at least as late as 1902. Baltimore and the District of Columbia are contrasted as prevention and non-prevention localities, but in neither city are registration or disinfection compulsory. Thus, in the District of Columbiaa, prevention area, for the year ending June 30, 1902, disinfection was practiced after 92 out of 721 deaths, and in Baltimore, a prevention area, in 1902, after only 76 out of 1,159 deaths. The same contrast is made between New Jersey and Rhode Island, but as a matter of fact the methods in question have not been adopted in any of the principal cities of the former state so that New Jersey is no more a prevention state than Rhode Island, It is true that in the prevention localities of Boston, Worcester and Louisville notification is required, but in Boston it dates only from 1901, in Worcester from 1902, and in Louisville from 1903, far too recently to have had any effect whatever. In order to make good the argument, it should have been shown first that a large number of deaths which a few years ago would have been truly reported as consumption, are now erroneously reported as pneumonia. For this there is no evidence whatever. For the second part of the argument, it is necessary to sharply contrast prevention with non-prevention areas. This has not been done, but Dr. Mays apparently arranges the cities of the country into two groups to fit his argument, instead of basing his argument on the facts as they really are. As his premises are thus seen to be faulty, his discussion of the official methods for restricting consumption now in vogue affords no demonstration whatever of their value or worthlessness. The only cities in which compulsory registration and disinfection have been enforced for a sufficient length of time to make their experience of any value, are New York City and Buffalo. In both of these cities the restrictive measures have been fairly well carried out, for nearly ten years.

At first thought it might be considered useful to compare the rate of decrease of consumption in these two cities with the rate of decrease in those in which restrictive measures have not been promoted by official action. But if the charts in Dr. Mays' article be examined, it will be seen that the death rate from consumption has for a long period varied much in different cities. A part of this difference may in some cities be due to defective registration, but much of it is certainly dependent upon the varying distribution of population, according to sex, age, race, nationality, occupation, etc. Thus the Federal Census of 1890 shows that in New York City the death rate from consumption varied from 646 per 100,000 among those born of Irish mothers, to 98 among those of Polish and Russian parentage, while the rate for the colored population was 774. In properly comparing the death rates in different cities, the errors due to variations in the composition of the population must be corrected. Unless this is done, such comparison is puerile and valueless. Another method of examining this question is to compare the death rate in the cities enforcing notification and disinfection before and after the adoption of these measures. An examination of the New York and Buffalo charts, as shown in Dr. Mays' article, indicates that in these cities consumption has not decreased any more rapidly since the adoption of these methods than before. In fact, in New York (Manhattan and the Bronx) the decrease has been less. Thus, while the rate per 100,000 living was 392 in the six years ending May 31, 1890, for the five years, 1891–1895, it was 291, showing a decrease of 101. During the next five years, during which the notification of the disease was well carried out, it was 255, giving a decrease of 46 (much less a decrease than in the preceding period), while in the three years, 1901–1903, the decrease was only 14 per 100,000 less. We must not, however, be led by this to conclude that registration and disinfection as carried out in New York are harmful, or even worthless. It is rash to draw conclusions from crude death rates, particularly when for other reasons such conclusions seem unlikely to be correct. Too many things may alter the death rate from a given disease during a period of years, to warrant attributing the change to any one factor, unless good reasons therefor can be shown. The registration of cases of consumption, and the instruction of the patient which should follow, are such rational measures, and if properly managed, are accompanied by so little friction, that they should not be abandoned, or their efficacy even seriously questioned because the death rate from this disease in the few cities in which these measures have been tried does not show results that are plainly favorable. We should persist in the experiment of restricting this disease until more data are available, or at least until the data at hand have been more carefully studied. Certainly, Dr. Mays' presentation of the subject has thrown no light upon it.

THE TYPHOID FEVER EPIDEMIC AT BUTLER, PA.— Butler, a rapidly growing manufacturing city, with a population of about 18,000, is at present recovering from the effects of the most serious municipal epidemic on record, about one person in thirteen having had the disease.

The epidemic was investigated by George A. Soper, Ph.D.* who traced the epidemic to the local water-supply.

"Owing to the failure of a dam, the water had been drawn since last August from Connoquenessing Creek at a point where it was obviously polluted. The supply had been filtered until October 20th by filters designed primarily to perfect the appearance of the water only. On that date the filters were shut down until a pipe connection could be made between some new pumps and the basin for filtered water."

The filters were out of service from October 20th to 31st. The epidemic broke out November 2d, and was continued into the new year, largely, it is believed, through secondary infection. By the third week in November the situation became alarming, and on November 29th the citizens held a mass meeting, organized

---

Engineering News, Dec. 24, 1903.

relief work, and took the control of the sanitary situation into their own hands.

The work was overwhelming, and on December 16th an appeal was made for outside help. Contributions of money and, on the part of physicians and nurses, of services were made. Hospitals were improvised, and the committee also undertook the executive and statistical work, which the local Board of Health did not perform with any degree of reliability. The Board of Health held a few impotent meetings, as evidenced by the fact that on December 17th their records showed only about 15 per cent. of the then existing cases. The physicians at Butler were never compelled to report their cases. Why should they, when they were so busy? (!) It is stated that no warning notices were posted while the filters were out of service. This should have been the minimum precaution.

About the first of December the State Board of Health came on the scene and assumed responsibility for the sanitary control of the city. After investigation, the Board took such measures as would tend to prevent secondary infection; it distributed the customary disinfectants, not patented disinfectants as has been reported, and instructed the people in their use. It worked in accord with the relief committee.

The epidemic is a stern and severe arraignment of the wealthy state of Pennsylvania, her legislature, her people and her boards of health. Vital statistics are there none worthy of the name; neither is there any adequate sanitary supervision of the water-supplies of the state. For twenty years Secretary Lee has urged the Legislature to make more liberal appropriations for the work of the State Board of Health, but even such epidemics as those which have occurred in Plymouth and Philadelphia, and are occurring in other places to-day, evidently have not awakened the public or the governmental mind.

The following table, showing the number of deaths by typhoid fever per 100,000 population in some of the principal Massachusetts and Pennsylvania cities, is an illustration of what may be accomplished by skill and a moderate expenditure of money, backed by intelligent public sentiment:

AVERAGE TYPHOID FEVER DEATH RATES.

(1898, 1899 and 1900,—Fuller.)

Pennsylvania.		Massachusetts.	
City.	Death Rate.	City.	Death Rate.
Pittsburg	108	Boston	30
Allegheny	86	New Bedford . . .	30.
Johnstown	83	Springfield	26
York	83	Lawrence	25
Chester	64	Taunton	25
Lancaster	59	Brockton	24
Philadelphia	54	Chelsea	24
MacKeesport	53	Salem	23
Reading	50	Fitchburg	21
Allentown	49	Lowell	21
Harrisburg	41	Lynn	20
Altoona	33	Newton	20
Wilkesbarre	29	Cambridge	18
Erie	28	Worcester	18
Scranton	23	Fall River	15

Many other cities in the United States stand the same chance of an outbreak of this disease as did Butler. In many other cities the typhoid deathrate is culpably high. Because such conditions can be readily remedied, it is wasteful—yes, even criminal—for them not to do so.

JANUARY (1904) AND ANNUAL MEETING

OF THE

Massachusetts Association of Boards of Health.

The quarterly (and annual) meeting of the Massachusetts Association of Boards of Health was held at the Brunswick Hotel, Boston, Wednesday, Jan. 27, 1904. The First Vice-President, Dr. Samuel H. Durgin presided in the absence of the President, Dr. H. P. Walcott.

Mr. Edwin L. Pilsbury, of Boston, Dr. H. C. Emerson ,of Springfield and Dr. Frank A. Woods, of Holyoke, were appointed a committee to nominate officers for the ensuing year.

THE CHAIRMAN: While the nominating Committee is doing its work, we will listen to the Treasurer's report for the past year.

DR. FIELD: Mr. Chairman, in presenting any Treasurer's report for this Association, the members ought to understand that the financial welfare of the Association is intimately bound up with the financial welfare of the JOURNAL. When the JOURNAL is nearly self-sustaining, it is in a prosperous condition, the Association can easily get along on a $2.00 due, sometimes on a $1.50 due. When the JOURNAL is not self-sustaining, and has to call on the Association almost wholly for its support, we would soon get into a condition of bankruptcy. That condition of affairs held for a part of 1902 and the first part of 1903; we were paying out more for the JOURNAL than we were getting in. But owing to the wisdom of our publishing committee the JOURNAL, I understand, is now in a very excellent condition, and so consequently the Association is once more prospering and taking in more money than it spends.

TREASURER'S REPORT FOR 1903.

RECEIPTS.

Balance from 1902	$922.25
Interest	34.45
Annual assessments	433.00
	$1,389.70

EXPENSES.

Clerical assistance	$21.40
Printing	27.55
Postage	40.00
Toward publishing JOURNAL	184.43
Five sets first volume JOURNAL	7.50
Cigars	24.08
Illustrating paper	10.00
Dinner for guest	1.50
Treasurer's bonds	4.00
	$320.46
Balance to 1904	$1,069.24
	$1,389.70

Of this balance $945.39 is drawing interest in a Savings Bank.

Respectfully submitted,

JAMES B. FIELD, *Treasurer.*

Examined and approved as correctly cast and properly vouched for.

J. ARTHUR GAGE, *Auditor*

(On motion of Mr. Coffey the report was accepted and placed on file.)

THE CHAIRMAN: Is the Committee on Nominations ready to report? If not, incidental business is now in order. If there is no other incidental business, I would say in regard to the JOURNAL of the Association, especially after what our Treasurer has stated, that a new contract has been made for the publishing of the JOURNAL. I am happy to say that the last contract was well put, that the JOURNAL is in a better condition to-day than ever before and everybody seems well pleased with it, and that the outlook is better than ever before.

I wanted also to say that there must be very few in the Association who will remember to have seen a copy of the Constitution and By-Laws. There was such a publication, but it would be difficult to find one to-day. I wanted to suggest that the Secretary be authorized to publish 1,000 or 2,000 copies for distribution among the present members. It will be useful for the members to look at occasionally, especially as alterations have taken place since anybody has seen a copy. Is there any motion?

(On motion of Dr. Miller, of Needham, the Secretary was authorized to print and publish 1,500 copies of the Constitution and By-Laws.)

THE CHAIRMAN: Is the Committee on Nominations ready to report?

THE ELECTION OF OFFICERS.

MR. PILSBURY: Mr. Chairman, the Committee on Nominations submits the following list of nominees:

For President, H. P. Walcott, M.D., of Cambridge.
For Vice-President (First), S. H. Durgin, M.D., of Boston.
For Vice-President (Second), S. W. Abbott, M.D., of Newton.
For Secretary, James C. Coffey, of Worcester.
For Treasurer, James B. Field, M.D., of Lowell.
For Executive Committee (for two years), G. L. Tobey, M.D., of Clinton; W. H. Gove, of Salem; C. A. Hicks, M.D., of Fall River; George H. Ellis, of West Newton; C. V. Chapin, M.D., of Providence.

THE CHAIRMAN: Gentlemen, you hear the report of the Nominating Committee. What is your pleasure?

MR. PILSBURY: Mr. President, unless the Constitution requires election by ballot, I move that the Secretary be authorized to deposit one ballot representing the sentiment of the Association, thus saving time, there being but one nominee for each office.

THE CHAIRMAN: In the absence of a Constitution and By-Laws the Chair rules that you are safe.

(The motion was adopted, and the Secretary cast one ballot thus electing the nominees of the committee.)

Is there any other incidental business?

There is a protest from a member of the Association, Dr. Hill, against proposed legislation on vivisection. It is in the hands of Mr. Rickards, who is present, and who will read it and also will explain other matters in its connection.

MR. RICKARDS: Mr. Chairman, notwithstanding the remonstrance that was made last year by this Association to the bill before the House at that time, preventing animal experimentation, the anti-vivisectionists in putting in a bill this year have absolutely forbidden either municipal laboratories or laboratories connected with hospitals making any experiments upon animals. For this reason, the following remonstrance has been drawn up:

To the Committee on Probate and Chancery.

GENTLEMEN: .

The following resolutions relating to House Bill No. 174 are submitted for your consideration:

Resolved, That the Massachusetts Association of Boards of Health assembed at its regular annual meeting in Boston, Jan. 27th, 1904, desires to protest and does hereby protest against the restrictions imposed in Section 1 and 2 of House Bill No. 174 upon the scientific work in animal experimentation of the Universities, Colleges and the State Board of Health of this Commonwealth. This Association recognizes the advances in the knowledge of disease, its cure and its prevention, secured by the free and unhampered investigations conducted by such bodies. The public health has profited in the past and will profit in the future by the results of such work, and the Association believes that the restrictions imposed are unnecessary, retrogressive and harmful.

Resolved, That this Association further protests against Sections 1 and 2 of the same bill, since these Sections taken together do not merely place restrictions upon animal experiments, but absolutely preclude municipal Boards of Health from making any animal experiments whatever. Well-known statutory duties are laid upon municipal Boards of Health in the detection and prevention of infectious diseases. Such exclusion from animal experimentation would deprive Boards of Health of an invaluable means for carrying out their statutory obligations.

Resolved, That this Association call to the attention of the Committee on Probate and Chancery a similar protest, made last year against a bill, identical in the Sections referred to with the bill under consideration; which protest was signed by the Boards of Health of 32 cities and about 19 towns of this State.

Resolved, That copies of this protest be forwarded for signature to the Boards of Health of this State and that those members present at the annual meeting be given the opportunity to sign a copy; said signed copies to be forwarded to the Committee on Probate and Chancery as the official expression of the views of the public hygienists of the State.

The Board of Health of

officially endorses the above protest.

For the Board of Health (Sign.)

Title

It is requested that each member present sign this protest; also that the Association as a whole vote upon it, and that a representative of each Board—not each representative of a Board but a representative of each Board— take a copy and have it officially signed by his Board. Copies of the protest will be passed round. After being signed they should be forwarded to Mr. Pilsbury, of the Board of Health of Boston.

THE CHAIRMAN: Gentlemen, you have heard the protest as read by Mr. Rickards. What is your pleasure? I would like to say that this is a most serious matter with Boards of Health which carry on necessary experimentation with animals. I hope the Boards of Health of the State will do as nobly this year as they did last. Any motion to be made?

DR. WORCESTER: I move that this protest be sent to the Committee on Probate and Chancery, with the expression of this Board attached.

THE CHAIRMAN: The question is asked whether this body will endorse the protest.

DR. WORCESTER: I move that this body endorse the protest. (The motion was seconded.)

THE CHAIRMAN: It is moved and seconded that this Association approve of this protest. Anything to be said?

PROF. SEDGWICK: Mr. President, just one word. In addition to the signatures to this important protest, I trust that all members of Boards of Health, and especially those remote from Boston, will take pains to see their local representatives, and make sure that these representatives are informed in regard to the matter and, as far as is legitimate and proper, are influenced to vote in the right direction. That is quite as important, in my judgment, as entering this protest; although that should certainly be done also.

(The motion was adopted unanimously.)

DR. MILLER: Mr. President, I would like to ask if the gentleman, or you can tell us when this subject will come up before the committee for hearing, and what committee it will come before at the State House. I think a good many of us would like to be there. There is a set of annual, chronic kickers, that come up there as regular as clock work. I think it will be interesting to see them; I have done so several times. There is a certain class of men and women that are born in a negative condition, and are prepared to oppose anything. I believe it will be well for us to know just when the hearing will occur and what committee it will be before.

THE CHAIRMAN: Has Mr. Rickards any information which he can give upon this subject?

MR. RICKARDS: Mr. Chairman, it is before the Committee on Probate and Chancery. The bill is House Bill No. 174. The date of the hearing has not yet been set. Usually it comes up in the latter part of March or the first of April. The calendar is watched very closely, and when it does come up we will notify you.

(NOTE.—The Legislature has since set the date of the first hearing on Wednesday, March 2d, at 10.30 A.M.)

THE CHAIRMAN: Have you copies of this to distribute, Mr. Rickards?

MR. RICKARDS: I have copies of the resolution, yes, sir. Mr. Pilsbury I believe has the copy for members' signatures, and also copies to be passed round for the official signatures of the Boards of Health.

THE CHAIRMAN: Mr. Pilsbury always attends to his duty, and I think he will in this case. Is there anything else to come before the Association under incidental business? If not, we will listen to the paper by Prof. Theobald Smith on: "Some of the ways in which infection is disseminated."

SOME OF THE WAYS IN WHICH INFECTION IS DISSEMINATED.

BY PROF. THEOBALD SMITH,
Pathologist, Mass. State Board of Health.

It has been said somewhere that the chief function of the local boards of health is to abate nuisances, but I believe that their work is much more important than this. I think that perhaps one of the most important of their functions is to prevent the circulation, as it were, of disease germs and to keep them confined to the immediate environment of the patient, where they are most readily destroyed by suitable disinfectants.

When our honored Chairman asked me about a week ago to speak upon some subject at this meeting it seemed to me that I could do nothing better than to speak upon this perennially interesting subject of the transmission of infection, because it is essentially the function of the machinery of public health, not to drive out the disease germs after they once have entered the body, for that is the business of the physician, but to see that they do not pass from one patient to another. This passage of disease germs is so complex, it is so interwoven with all the details of our family and civic life and with traveling and commerce, and our point of view gradually changes with the discovery of new facts that even to-day the precise determination of the sources of infection in many epidemics cannot be made and investigation frequently ends in mere conjectures. We cannot therefore give too much attention to the details of transmission for the more circumspect our information the more accurate our conclusions. It is essential that we should know the disease germ which produces a given disease before we can trace its progress from one patient to another, and you know definitely that in case of the most important of the diseases, those that give civilized society the greatest trouble,—the eruptive diseases,—practically nothing is known of the micro-organisms which cause them. It is true that we know something of the micro-organisms of smallpox, and of scarlatina, but our knowledge of those organisms is still in its infancy. We know practically nothing of their life history, and we are unable at present to follow their entry and exit from the body, as is possible with the pathogenic bacteria.

We are apt to lose sight of the fact that it is a biological necessity for disease germs to be transmitted, and that the entire mechanism of infection is directed towards this necessity of being eliminated or set free to invade another host. When micro-organisms enter an animal or a human body that is susceptible, they find there a soil that is favorable to them, and they begin to multiply. But as they go on multiplying, a time comes when the forces of the body turn against them, when, as we now say, a number of anti-bodies are formed—anti-toxines agglutinins, bactericidal and other, unknown, substances—which begin to interfere with, to suppress and to destroy the bacteria. Hence, after a certain stage of the disease, the soil becomes unfavorable, the bacteria must be eliminated and attack another individual, in order that their own life may be preserved. As a result of this necessity in all infectious diseases, micro-organisms have succeeded in developing a perfectly definite, either simple or complicated way of getting out of the body. In the eruptive diseases perhaps the greatest success has attended their efforts. The infection is presumably drawn into the respiratory passages. After a variable period of incubation and fever depending on the germ, they are distributed over the whole body through the blood and appear in the skin, whence they are shed with the crusts in small pox, the desquamating scales in measles and scarlatina. I might continue to illustrate this process of elimination but it is already well-known, and I simply call attention here to a phenomenon which is a necessary stage in the life history of pathogenic organisms and not merely accidental. It is the one stage demanding the greatest attention from the public health officers and the sanitarian.

The infection, as it leaves the body is in a latent stage and it must be carried passively in some vehicle or medium, living or dead, to reach the next host or victim. The air is, among all the media, the one which has received the earliest and greatest recognition. Being an element of great power, though itself unseen, and transporting visible vapors, smoke and particles of dirt and invisible odors through long distances, it naturally impressed peoples in the infancy of science and the medical art as the one vehicle which was responsible for the mysterious dissemination of plagues. But even to day the air is still regarded as a most important aid to the germs of the eruptive diseases, where the shedding of particles of skin from the body in these various diseases, their transmission through the air, and their inhalation into another body, completes the cycle for those particular organisms. We also know that in tuberculosis transmission of the bacilli through the air is perhaps the most important mode. In the early days of our knowledge of tubercle bacilli the dry sputum, ground up into dust and carried in the air, was considered the chief factor in transmission, but a few years ago Fluegge, the associate of Koch for many years in hygiene, suggested another theory, which he has since demonstrated by exhaustive experiments that a more important vehicle perhaps, than the dry dust are the infinitesimal particles of moist sputum which are cast from the mouth during speech, especially during the formation

of certain letters which cause a sudden expulsive outward movement of the air, and during coughing and sneezing. These minute
particles have been found suspended in the air for half an hour
after they have been emitted. In the case of tuberculosis it is
supposed that this danger of infection exists within a zone of
about three feet in circumference of the patient since these particles appear to be transmitted in all directions. In tuberculosis,
then, the air, not only in carrying the dry particles, but also in
holding in suspension the moist particles, forms the chief vehicle
of contagion. The moist particles are the more infectious for
in drying, a great many tubercle bacilli lose their life.*

The air, also, served a purpose in the earlier days of bacteriology
in the minds of health officers in carrying typhoid, dysentery
and diphtheria. although to-day we do not look upon the air as a
vehicle of any importance in these maladies. It is not more
than eight or nine years ago that these were supposed to be communicated largely in sewer air. We can hardly appreciate that
fact to-day for knowledge is absorbed and diffused so rapidly.
I remember talking in 1895 to a prominent health official of one
of our neighboring States on the subject of diphtheria. At that
time anti-toxine had just been introduced. Evidence had already
been accumulating that convalescents might carry infection and
that diphtheria was transmitted chiefly by direct contact, or at
any rate only in close proximity to the patient. But this prominent health official clung, as all did at that time, to the theory
that sewer gas must be the chief agent in spreading diphtheria.
The only thing that puzzled him was that he just had an epidemic
in a schoolhouse in the country where there was no sewerage
system under investigation, and he began to think about the possibility that there might be other means of contagion. Most of
us, perhaps, remember that at that time, or shortly before, the
plumbing was always overhauled in a house where typhoid and
dysentery occurred. Now I think very few would pay any attention to the plumbing whatever, excepting to see that there were
no open privies on the place.

---

*The theory which press dispatches are ascribing to Prof. Behring, that all tuberculosis infec-
tion is introduced by way of the digestion tract, does not in my opinion have any supporting evidence. Although the possibility of a pulmonary tuberculosis originating from a focus in the
mesenteric glands or the liver is conceded, yet the traces of such a passage must as a rule be in
evidence.

Malaria was also carried by the air in the theories of the past, and this is true in one sense only now we have personified the infection in malaria in the mosquito. The insect simply uses the air in carrying the virus from one individual to another.

With the perfecting of bacteriological methods and the more detailed study of pathogenic bacteria, the air was gradually robbed of some of its functions as vehicle of disease germs and in its place came the food and drink. This vehicle has assumed very great importance in the life of civilized communities to-day in which so little of the food consumed is raised by the consumers. Millions of people in our large cities are fed with food coming from far and near, and a most interesting feat would be the tracing of the sources of the food which appears upon our table on any one day. This great drainage area of our food supply naturally enough signifies many opportunities for our food to act as a vehicle for infection before it reaches us.

Fortunately the cooking of our food enables us to escape all infections coming from unknown, uncontrollable sources. But we still consume certain things raw and it is the raw food and drink which is largely responsible for the endemic scourges of our civilization, typhoid. dysentery, the diarrhœal diseases, cholera and in a few cases tuberculosis. The vehicles are largely drinking water, milk and oysters.

So much has been said in the daily press and medical publications of water as a disseminator of certain intestinal diseases, that I can pass that by to-day. We have had within the last year such marvellous demonstrations of the carrying power of water with reference to typhoid bacilli in different parts of the country that they are all fresh in our minds. It is a strange fact that these large epidemics are associated with progress in public hygiene and sanitation because they mean a large common water supply, and they could not occur without the existence of such a supply; they are in fact the result of sanitary progress in so far as sanitation has just gone half way. We still continue to throw our typhoid-laden sewage into water courses, and then we take our water from them to again contract typhoid fever. The public has acknowledged the necessity for pure water, but it has

not yet torn itself away from the filthy habit of polluting its
rivers whence the water is taken, or else it has not taken suitable
means of purifying its supply from polluted sources.   We have
here an instance of the fact that going half way towards a well-
defined goal and then halting is actual retrogression.

Milk is another vehicle of infection, and inasmuch as Dr. Harrington will speak upon this subject I shall pass it by.   However,
I cannot refrain from making the remark that it is an anomaly
for civilized people, who know so much about the dangers of
miscellaneous dirt as we do, to continue to drink raw milk from
unknown sources, when we consider that it is such a favorable
nidus for the multiplication of bacteria, and that it may contain
infection at any time.   I believe that raw milk as a beverege
ten years hence will be a matter of the past.

In considering the minute details of the elimination and transmission of disease germs, it is of the utmost importance to recognize definitely the true sources of infection.   These, it will be
answered are, of course, the diseased body which is a kind of
producer of infectious organisms.   This is true as far as it goes,
but it is not the entire truth.   In recent years our information
has brought to light the fact that important sources of infection
have been overlooked.   These sources are the individual affected
with a very mild type of disease, the convalescent or recovered
case, and the perfectly well person who may act as carrier.

The individual affected with a mild type of some infectious
disease is producer and carrier combined.   Such cases are the
most trying.   They are probably responsible for more infection
than all the severe cases that the physician has to deal with.   It
is the so-called ambulatory cases of typhoid, dysentery, smallpox, measles, and so on, which are responsible for most of the
dissemination of these diseases.   At present the Widal or agglutination test is of much service in detecting doubtful cases of
typhoid.

The next class of cases might be called the carriers chiefly.
It has been discovered within the last five or six years that the
bacteria which produce certain diseases linger in the body for some
time after recovery; they do not at once disappear.   This is espe-

cially true with the intestinal diseases. When all symptoms of disease have subsided, patients may still harbor bacteria and shed them. This we know is true of diphtheria, because generally two, or possibly three weeks after the disease is over diphtheria bacilli can be detected in cultures. We know that typhoid carriers are often convalescents who have not yet rid themselves of the bacteria. This subject is now creating considerable attention, especially in Europe.

The Institute for Infectious Diseases in Berlin is making exhaustive observations upon the sources of infection in typhoid with special reference to recovered cases and well persons caring for the sick. I was told while there last summer of the infection of a woman with typhoid by her husband six months after his recovery therefrom. The bacilli were being eliminated in the urine.

The last sources of infection I shall speak of are carriers exclusively. They are healthy persons, who have not had the disease, but who have been associated with cases of it. In the case of diphtheria a committee of the Association has worked out that phase of the question very well and it was found from extensive statistics of throat cultures that perhaps one per cent. of persons carry diphtheria bacilli in their throats. In the case of typhoid it has been found that nurses or other persons concerned in the care of typhoid fever patients may have the bacilli in their intestines, as shown by the delicate methods of bacteriology. In the time of the German epidemic some years ago, cholera spirilla were found in the intestines or in the stools of the boatmen who were travelling up and down the streams of Germany, and who were probably responsible for the distribution of the cholera bacilli in a peculiar way, namely, up stream, or against the current. In all these cases, the infection is intestinal in origin and communicated in food and drink.

In regard to the eruptive diseases, we know very little concerning the persistence of these microbes, or their multiplication in the body after recovery, but I think the general consensus of opinion among health officers would be that there is no such thing as indefinitely persisting infection in the eruptive diseases, that after a certain time the patient may be considered absolutely free from infection, and that if there is any infection traced to his case after proper quarantine it is attributable more to his clothing or to his environment than to himself.

When we consider these producers and these carriers of infection more closely, we can understand certain facts that it otherwise would be difficult to appreciate.   One of them is that it is always dangerous to drink polluted water, for the reason that the fæces of even healthy persons, or persons who have had a mild attack of typhoid, may have passed into any stream or river and pollute it.   The argument that there is no typhoid on the watershed is absolutely of no value to-day; the danger is potentially as great, because there may be cases that nobody knows of.

In the next place, all large gatherings of people are likely to develop typhoid sooner or later.   This was clearly demonstrated during the war with Spain in 1898, where nearly all the camps in our country became infected with typhoid fever soon after the soldiers came together.   The unsanitary way of living, the crowding together, and certain other agencies that I shall speak of later on were conducive to the distribution of typhoid, probably from the carriers,—those who were well and who brought the germs into the camp, or those who had just recovered and were still shedding them.   In a similar manner all large collections of human beings, when unsanitary living must be resorted to are likely to contract some form of intestinal infection.

With a better knowledge of the possibility that human beings may carry certain diseases and yet be well, the importance of what has been known in the past as fomites carrying disease has somewhat declined.   It is true that there is always danger in the environment of a tuberculous patient, or, possibly, in that of a typhoid fever patient whose stools have not been properly taken care of; but I think that with our better knowledge of disease carriers during convalescence and even during health, much of the disease that we have hitherto credited to fomites, to clothing, and so on, must be ascribed to these carriers themselves. The length of time during which bacteria live in our environment is a matter of great uncertainty as it depends upon various conditions. If micro-organisms are abundantly encrusted with pus, or blood, or sputum, they will live a much longer time in the dried state than if they are not, for these substances form a protecting envelope. No one can tell exactly how long disease germs may live in our environment. Hence the continued necessity for thorough disinfection. This disinfection must not, however, make us indifferent toward the possibility that the environment may be reinfected by the various carriers cited above.

There is one other class of transmitters of whose agency our knowledge dates back only about twelve or thirteen years. They belong to the class of insects, and to lower forms that are closely related to the insects, namely, the large group of the Arachnids. We are all familiar with the action of mosquitoes in carrying yellow fever and in carrying malaria. These are two diseases that must be carried by these parasites. In other words, there is no other vehicle of transmission. Not only are they carriers but they are producers as well, for the parasites taken from the blood by them are multiplied many times in their bodies. The life cycle of the micro-organism that produces malaria is very complex, for it undergoes considerable development in the body of these small insects as secondary hosts before the infection is ripe to be introduced into the body of another individual. In animal diseases we have learned to know a number of such necessary transmitters. In the case of Texas fever, or hemoglobinuria, in cattle, a malarial disease found all over the world, a skin parasite which stands close to the insects and which is popularly known as the cattle tick carries the micro-organism of this disease, and it cannot be carried in any other way. There is a disease of the blood among domestic animals in Africa, which is carried only by a certain fly (Glossina morsitans) which, resembles the house fly very closely, but which bites or stings. Where this fly is absent the disease which it carries is also absent. This affection, which is due to a little protozoon in the blood, presents such serious obstacles to agriculture that it is almost impossible to bring cattle, and horses, and other domestic animals, into the country to improve agriculture, because of this disease which is carried by these flies.

There is one very important fact which has been brought out in the study of these diseases that are carried by insects and in no other way. After the disease is over the parasite does not leave the body; in fact, it remains indefinitely, but in very small numbers in the body of the immune individual. In our own state much of the malaria that has prevailed in recent years is probably carried hither in the blood of people who have lived in malarious districts ever since their birth, as in parts of Italy. They come to this country, live in crowded labor camps, and give the mosquitoes a chance to carry the parasites in them to the neighboring population. The same is true of the malarial diseases of animals. If we import a cow from North Carolina, South Carolina, or any State still farther South, and bring it into any of our herds in Massachusetts, say, in mid summer, it is probable that at the end of October nearly all of our animals will be dead. The cow brings in her blood the bovine malarial parasite; although perfectly well herself she carries on her body the cattle tick, which transmits the blood parasite from her own blood and inoculates it into the animals in the North. The Southern cow is immune, but the Northern cows are very susceptible, and ninety per cent. of them die when they are infected. The same story may be told of the African blood parasite which is transmitted by the fly. It was found by the discoverer, Bruce, some seven or eight years ago that the game in Africa which he shot contained this parasite. The game was perfectly well, at least it showed no signs of the disease. The fly, drawing the blood from the game which carried the parasite lights upon the domestic animals brought in from Europe and introduces the parasite. The domestic animals, not being immune, being, in fact very susceptible, die.

It should be emphasized that these mosquitoes, flies and ticks, are the only transmitters of their respective diseases; that there is a definite, complex relationship between the human being or the animal, the tick or the mosquito and the blood parasite, in virtue of which the latter needs both the insect and the human or large animal in order to complete its life cycle.

There are a number of other parasites which come up for consideration in our climate as possible carriers and transmitters of disease. For example, the bedbug is quite a universal blood parasite, and is probably found in a great many houses in our country. Those of you who travel on certain steamboats in summer and fall will encounter specimens. In view of the discoveries of the transmission of disease by insects, experiments were made by Nuttall, by letting bedbugs bite animals, chiefly mice, that were infected with various disease germs, but in all cases the transmission proved negative; that is to say, the animals were not infected by the bite of bedbugs after the latter had drawn blood from diseased animals. The flea is another insect upon which suspicion has fallen, but it plays an unimportant role in this country. Occasionally the dog flea is said to attack man, but with us it is a comparatively rare occasion. In countries like India the flea is a common human parasite, and the transmission of the plague from rats to man has been ascribed to it by certain French students of the plague in that country. The rat flea belongs to a wholly different family from that of the human flea, and there are grave objections against accepting the theory that the flea of the rat can transmit plague from rat to man. The probabilities are that the natives are bitten by various insects, that they scratch these wounds, and that by scratching they open a portal for the entry of the plague bacillus, which enters successfully the smallest wound. The native domiciles in India are said to be very primitive. The floors are of earth, and the people walk barefooted. It is easy to conceive that slight injuries may result to the feet, and that the scratching due to the bite of insects may lead to infection; but the flea itself probably is not the transmitter. Occasionally it may occur that by killing an animal upon the skin the bacteria which are contained in that animal are set free when the animal is crushed, and then being in close proximity to the wound produced by that or some other animal they could get in. It is only in such a way, as Nuttall points out, that fleas or bedbugs may carry infection.

There is still one other insect under suspicion to come into consideration, and that is the house fly. I can only say a few words upon this insect, although it is the most important. The house fly does not bite, as you know, but it is a voracious devourer of all kinds of filth. The fly lays its eggs chiefly in horse manure, and at about the end of a week the young have become adult, so that wherever manure of animals is concentrated, flies will breed plentifully. It is well known that flies will pass from filth, like fæces, to food in close proximity, and it has been demonstrated by actual experiment that flies which have been feeding upon fæces from cases of typhoid fever thrown into open privy vaults contain the typhoid fever bacillus. These bacilli may pass through the body of the fly. The discharges of the fly may be dropped upon food, more particularly into milk, wherein they may multiply on a warm day. The milk may then become the source of infection for new cases. The fly may also carry infection on its body and feet. In 1902 an epidemic which was prevalent in Chicago assumed unusual proportions in certain districts, and after a very thorough investigation of all the possible causes that might lead to the dissemination of the typhoid fever bacillus, Dr. Alice Hamilton, who was then working in the laboratory of the Memorial Institute for Infectious Diseases, came to the conclusion that flies were the disseminators. She was able to cultivate typhoid bacilli from flies which had been caught in the infected locality. The sanitary conditions were such that flies were able to get at the virus, because a number of the houses were not connected with the sewers, and still had open privies, into which the stools were thrown.

It seems to me that the fly is the one insect next to the mosquito in this climate to which we should direct our attention. Being a ubiquitous insect, and eating all sorts of things, it is possible that the fly may transmit all forms of intestinal disease that are due to bacteria—typhoid fever, dysentery, the various forms of diarrhœa, and cholera. I should also call attention to the fact that flies will eat sputum, and tubercle bacilli have been known to be carried in the body of the fly from one portion of a hospital to the other. It is very important that houses harboring certain infectious diseases should be thoroughly screened, and that especially the food should be protected in such a way that flies which have had access to filth cannot contaminate it.

In the house fly the earlier theory of the transmission of certain intestinal infections through the air becomes to a certain extent rehabilitated. It is only by the insertion of new links of evidence from time to time that our information becomes more precise, and therefore more effective. It makes a great difference whether infection is carried by insects or by infinitesimal particles floating in the air. The former can be guarded against more or less effectively, the latter not.

THE CHAIRMAN: Dr. Smith's paper is open for discussion. Are there any remarks to be made upon Dr. Smith's paper? Before proceeding to the next paper, we will take up the election to membership of the following list of candidates, which have been approved by the Executive Committee:

Dr. H. Carlton Smith, Chemist, of Brookline.
Dr. E. A. Hubbard, of Ashby.
Herbert A. Tilden, of Cohasset.
Dr. Nelson M. Wood, of Charlestown.
Dr. John T. Cahill, of Lawrence.
Dr. D. B. Sullivan, of Bondsville.
Abbott W. Packard, of Brockton.
Dr. C. A. Cheever, of Mattapan.

(On motion of Mr. Ellis the gentlemen named were elected members of the Association.)

The next paper on the program is upon "The Source, Effect and Prevention of Dirty Milk," by Prof. Charles Harrington.

SOURCES, EFFECTS AND PREVENTION OF DIRTY MILK.

BY CHARLES HARRINGTON, M.D.

Inspector of Milk and Vinegar of the Boston Board of Health.

In bringing this subject to your attention, I am conscious that I have no new facts to present; but the sanitary importance of a clean milk-supply is so great, and so much can be accomplished in the saving of infant life if we can but arouse the interest of the people and of the local boards of health in the matter, that I may be excused if I bring together, for the purpose of discussion, some well-known facts and offer some suggestions for bettering present conditions.

Massachusetts is fortunate in the possession of an almost perfect law for the suppression of milk adulteration, but it was not until 1883, when its general enforcement was intrusted to the State Board of Health, that its provisions were much respected by those who sought profit in water. It was the vigorous action of the body that led the local authorities, one by one, to pay a decent regard to the rights of the consumer, until now the matter of fraudulent manipulation is fairly well in hand, though it requires constant watchfulness to keep it so. Thus far, the supervision of the milk dealer has been more in the nature of police than of sanitary administration, but the time has come for recognizing more thoroughly the true sanitary side. It was, and is, no easy matter to restrain ordinary adulteration; it will be far more difficult to bring about a marked diminution in the amount of accidental deterioration, because among other things it will involve a large measure of popular education in a subject in which, strange to say, the public is not especially interested. But the case is far from hopeless, and I believe that we can succeed, although the fruits of our labors may be slow in growth.

When we speak of dirty milk we mean milk which, largely by reason of the admission of preventable dirt, but equally, or even more, in consequence of improper methods of cooling, handling and storage, contains excessive numbers of bacteria.

The preventable dirt gains access in various ways. It is derived chiefly from the body of the cow, and consists largely of hairs and particles of excrement. A single hair may contribute hundreds and thousands of bacteria to the milking-pail, and the number of hairs which may be dislodged from the parts immediately above the pail during the process of milking, through the necessary manipulation of the udder and the contact of the peson of the milker, is very great. In the same way, and through switching of the tail, particles of excrement laden with bacteria fall in a constant shower into the pail. It has been calculated that, under ordinary conditions of handling and storage, the presence of about a twelfth of a grain of such dirt per quart will cause each cubic centimeter of the milk to yield nearly three and a half millions of bacteria by the time it is delivered to the customer, and Backhaus has reckoned the amount of cow-dung that the population of Berlin consumes daily with its milk at about 300 pounds. Professors Russell, Freeman and others have shown by interesting experiments the yield of bacteria which may be expected during the milking of an ordinarily dirty cow. Thus Russell caused a cow to be milked in the open air, with a gelatine plate exposed for one minute near the pail, and found that in that period no less than 3,250 bacteria must have gained access to the milk; and Freeman collected on a plate of 3.5 inches diameter, similarly exposed for two minutes, no less than 1,800, which means that, in the course of a minute, more than 6,000 dropped on an area equal to that of a ten-inch pail.

Next we have to consider the person and clothing of the milker. His hands, hair, beard and clothes are ordinarily more or less rich in dirt and bacteria, and these he contributes liberally while performing his office.

Of very great importance too, in the bacterial content of milk, is the condition of the milking-pails and other vessels. A milking-pail cleansed in the ordinary way is very different bacteriologically from one which has been properly sterilized. Professor Russell has shown that, under similar conditions of milking, a cubic centimeter of milk drawn into a sterile pail yielded 165 bacteria, while the same volume taken from another which was cleaned in the ordinary way yielded 4,265.

Much dirt and many bacteria are derived also from the dusty air of the cow-stable, especially when dry hay is thrown to the cows just before milking.

But it is not alone from external sources that the bacteria of milk are derived, for myriads exist in the ducts of the teats even under the best of conditions, for when the operation of milking is concluded there is sufficient milk left in the teats to supply nutrient material and favor multiplication of the bacteria that may enter the external orifices during the interval that elapses before the next milking, by which time, under the favoring condition of the body temperature, they increase enormously and are ready to be washed out in the fore-milk. The ducts may be so richly supplied that each jet of milk, even to the last of the strippings, may yield the organisms in great numbers. In case of mammitis, or garget, which is the most common disease of cows, and which may exist without showing any marked evidence of its presence, the number of bacteria per cubic centimeter of milk may be very great. The fact that the onset of the disease is often very insidious and that the milk may show no gross evidence of its existence makes the exclusion of infected milk from the market a matter of very decided difficulty.

Thus far I have dealt with the milk up to the end of the milking process, when under ordinary conditions it is richly endowed with dirt and bacteria. It is a most excellent breeding-ground, and the temperature is favorable for rapid multiplication. If the temperature is not lowered at once, we must expect the inevitable consequence, which is rapid deterioration; but with rapid cooling to below 45° F. the bacteria will not increase materially and may even diminish in number. Indeed, rapid cooling is of even greater importance than cleanliness, for an ordinarily dirty milk, if rapidly cooled, will show better keeping qualities than clean milk not so treated. But it is not enough that it be quickly cooled; it should be kept at as low a temperature as possible from the time it is drawn until it is consumed, for a marked rise in temperature induces bacterial multiplication, which, as Park has shown, may attain almost inconceivable proportions. Thus, he took a specimen containing 3,000 bacteria per cubic centimeter and divided it into five parts, which he kept at different temperatures for 24 hours. That kept below 50° showed no increase; at 60° it went from 3,000 to 180,000; at 68°, from 3,000 to 450,000; at 86°, to 1,400,000,000, and at 94° to no less than 25,000,000,000. Another specimen, kept at 90° for 8 hours, went from 92,000 to 6,800,000, and a third from 2,600,000 to 124,000,000.

It is, of course, quite impossible to market milk containing no bacteria whatever. They are ubiquitous and will gain access in some numbers, but their numbers are dependent upon the conditions at the dairy and during transportation and storage, and especially upon temperature and age.

Next, let us consider the consequences of using bacterially contaminated milk. The enormous loss of infant life during the warmer months has long been regarded as in the natural order of things, but it is only within comparatively recent years that statistics have shown that it is the bottle-fed and not the breast-fed infant that makes up the great bulk of the mortality from diarrhœal diseases, which, in reality, are in most cases nothing more nor less than food poisoning, due either to the bacteria consumed with milk or to toxic substances elaborated before ingestion. If due to the latter, it would appear that these substances are destroyed by exposure to temperatures of about 170° F.

Professor Conn has given a list of about 200 different species of bacteria which he has isolated from milk, but the vast majority of these are probably without sanitary significance. Of the comparatively small number which are known to cause deleterious changes, Professor Russell asserts that six species are almost invariably present. According to English, French, German and American investigators, the latter including Bergey, Reed and Ward, and Stokes, market milk is very commonly infected with streptococci, which organisms are the chief exciting cause of garget, and are believed to be that of much disease among infants and even among adults. Local outbreaks of acute gastric catarrh and of violent diarrhœa with severe abdominal pain have been known to occur among the customers of individual dairies, where investigation has revealed garget in the cows and streptococci in abundance in the milk.

Another source of bacterial infection not hereinbefore mentioned has lately been pointed out, with its consequences, by English observers; namely, the road dust of cities and towns. About five years ago Dr. E. W. Hope produced interesting figures, showing that at Liverpool, during 20 years, the highest death rates from diarrhœal diseases had gone hand in hand with the driest summer weather, and the lowest rates with the wettest weather. The 14 dry summers showed an average rate of death from these diseases about 50 per cent higher than that of the six average wet summers. In the *Journal of Hygiene* for July, 1903, Richards asserts that the infection of food poisoning takes place usually in the home, and that urban conditions are hazardous chiefly from the amount of pollution in the yards and roads; and he advocates, as one important practical preventive measure, the prevention of dust by copious watering of the roads.

In the August, 1903 number of *Public Health* are two papers of interest in this connection. Dr. Arthur Newsholme, the leading M. O. H. in England, states that he is of opinion that frequent summer rains, although the total precipitation be not great, are one of the most effectual means of keeping down the diarrhœal death-rate. He attributes the relative immunity from diarrhœa at Brighton in 1902 to this influence, and advocates thorough wetting of streets in time of dry weather, and the removal of the mud thus formed. In his opinion rainfall is more important than temperature in relation to epidemic diarrhœa. Dr. Herbert Peck, M. O. H. for Chesterfield, ascribes the low diarrhœal death-rate in his district in 1902 to the same cause, and, like Newsholme, believes that the amount of rain is of far less importance than its frequency.

Fortunately, it is during only a portion of the year that polluted milk plays its great part in the causation of fatal diarrhœal disease. In the course of an extensive investigation of the effects of dirty milk conducted by Drs. Park and Holt and reported in the *Medical News* of December 5, 1903, it appeared that during cool weather neither the mortality nor the health of the infants observed was appreciably affected by the kind of milk or by the number of bacteria which it contained; but during hot weather, when the resistance of the children was lowered, the kind of milk taken influenced both the amount of illness and the death-rate. The infants fed on raw milk did much less well in summer than those whose milk was heated. The species of bacteria found were very numerous, but none of 139 which were isolated in pure culture caused any ill-effects in very young kittens.

I have not dealt with the danger to which Professor Smith alluded, the danger of transmitting some of our common infectious diseases, such as typhoid fever, scarlet fever, diphtheria, etc., which comes from contact of the milk with persons who are either convalescing from or sick with these diseases, or who have been engaged in the care of those who are sick; nor with the danger of infection of milk through polluted water, with which milk vessels are cleansed, because I have considered merely the question of what we call dirty milk.

Most of the measures necessary for the prevention of dirty milk are so obvious as to need no more than passing mention. The cow-stables should be clean, well-drained and well-ventilated, the cows should be given the same measure of care as is bestowed upon the ordinary driving horse, and yet how many of what are known as gentlemen-farmers look to the grooming of the cows which supply their families with milk, while the horses which they drive must shine like mirrors; even if the cows are groomed and kept as clean as possible, the parts in the vicinity of the udder should be at least dampened before milking; the milker should not be permitted to perform his office with dirty hands and in his bacteria-laden, ordinary working clothes, but should clean himself and don a special suit of clean linen overalls; the milking-pails and other vessels should be not simply clean: they should be sterile; in all cases the first part of the fore-milk, with its abundance of bacteria, should be rejected, as should the entire yield of an animal known to be suffering with garget; the milk should be removed at once to a separate, clean milk-room, where it should be strained and cooled to below 50° without delay. During transportation it should be kept as cool as possible, and on arrival at its place of sale and delivery it should be subjected to as little manipulation as possible, for every process through which it is put increases the possibility of bacterial contamination. Finally, after delivery in the home, it should be protected from dust and dirt and from the influence of ordinary warmth.

But is it possible to have these measures generally observed? Certainly not, at present, any more than it would be possible to insure that every man seen in the streets shall have clean hands and wear clean linen; but great improvement is possible and is worth trying for. How can this be brought about? The first answer that suggests itself is: by education—education of the producer, of the middleman, of the public generally. But education by the ordinary methods will be, I believe, perfectly barren of results. In the first place, the general public is indifferent; it thinks it cares, but it does not; it knows the value of fresh milk, but obstinately insists upon the delivery of to-day's milk early to-morrow morning rather than to-day during the forenoon; it prefers glass jars, filled in the horse-stable from the large cans and kept over night in a perhaps not over clean refrigerator, to its own clean utensils, which could be filled at the door; it will not pay a fraction of a cent more per quart for that which is raised under sanitary conditions than for that from the foulest surroundings. Unfortunately, the medical profession is to a large extent somewhat apathetic, or sometimes even worse. Within a month, I have heard a practitioner of some eminence characterize as "damned cranks" those who are interested in promoting clean milk. His children, he said, had grown up all right on good old-fashioned milkman's milk, and this agitation made him sick!

If the public is indifferent and cannot be educated, what will be the attitude of the producer toward an education from which he can see no direct benefit, but only increased trouble and expense? He is a human being and in the main a pretty sensible one, but he does not dwell in Altruria. Can we expect him to employ extra help in order to secure perfect cleanliness; to improve the ventilation and drainage of his barns; to remove his cow-manure daily to a place apart; to sterilize his pails with steam; to buy ice for rapid cooling, and to take other precautions merely to send to market a clean milk, for which neither the middleman nor the consumer will pay a cent per can more than his slovenly neighbor receives? Will he feel repaid by the reflection that perhaps, in the tenements where his milk goes, there is less sickness among the offspring of a foreign-born population in which he takes no interest?

Then how can the public, the producer and the dealer be educated in the importance of clean milk? In the first place, let us simplify the question by eliminating the general public, which does not care and must be saved in spite of itself. Let us deal with the producer who is beyond the town and city and with the retailer who is within. Something can be done with these two classes, both of whom, when they learn that it is to their financial benefit to do so, will take hold of the matter.

A few years ago, the Board of Health of Boston established certain sanitary regulations applying to the premises of peddlers and of shop-keepers dealing in milk. These were wise, and, although in some instances they seemed to work some hardship, they were necessary. So far as improving local conditions is concerned, they have accomplished much, but not all that is expected, for it is difficult to look after some 3,000 shops, many of which have a tendency to laxness after a license is secured. Revoking licenses on the ground of unsanitary conditions is a wholesome practice which educates by example.

But if it is not an easy task to manage 3,000 dealers, how, it may be asked, can one hope to regulate the 5,000 or more dairies which supply them? I confess that I can see but one method and that is by coercive education through the establishment of bacterial standards and the giving of periodical certificates through the agency of a milk commission. A maximum limit of 500,000 bacteria would certainly be reasonable so far as the producer is concerned, though it sounds high when considered from the stand-point of the consumer. But if the producer will take the necessary precautions to exclude dirt, so that his milk shall yield no more than that number on arrival, it is more than likely that the bacterial content will fall far short of it. If his milk is returned once or twice because of its filthy nature, his education takes a sudden rise, and soon he will find that dirty milk is a poor crop and that it cannot compete with clean. If he takes extra care, let him be rewarded; let him apply for a certificate from a milk commission that his milk is clean and wholesome, and let him use it in promoting his business. If he persists in neglecting to provide clean milk, let him keep his milk for his own purposes and as a warning to his neighbors. The middlemen, peddlers and shop-keepers can be looked after, punished, and rewarded after the same manner, and after a time the milk trade will be composed of two classes: namely, those whose milk contains a minimum number, say 10,000, of bacteria per cubic centimeter, and may, therefore, display a milk commission's certificate that they deal in clean milk, and those whose supply falls within the regulations, but is not clean enough to be certified—then it will be that the public will have to choose between the two, and if the clean man does not profit much, he shall not suffer at all.

THE CHAIRMAN: Dr. Harrington's paper is now open for discussion, and I see a large number of members who look as if they wish to speak on the question.

MR. BROCK, Athol: Mr. Chairman, I want to ask one question. Of course we are all interested in the practical end of this, and we want to know whether the suggested means of bringing pressure to bear on the milkman is a thing that public sentiment will back up. I understood the speaker to say that the suggested standard would be 500,000 bacteria to a cubic centimeter. Now how does that compare with the good old-fashioned milkman's milk that we heard about?

PROF. HARRINGTON: I think it would compare very favorably with some of the "good old-fashioned milkmen's milk," and not very well with others. Of course, different dairies produce milk of different degrees of cleanliness. It all depends upon the care exercised, the rapidity of cooling, and the care with which the milk is handled afterwards. I don't think that we can say that 500,000 would be an unreasonable standard. It is the one which was adopted in New York, where it worked well.

In Rochester a standard of 100,000 was adopted, and they have had some success in diminishing the percentage of very dirty milk. But my point is that, if we adopt any reasonable standard, such as 500,000, in enforcing that standard we will get a very much smaller number, because if a man is going to take pains to keep his milk clean, so that the number of bacteria will fall below 500,000, the chances are that he is going to reduce it very much below that figure.

MR. BROCK, Athol: What number of bacteria will the ordinary milk that comes in Boston carry, as it is delivered?

PROF. HARRINGTON: I don't know of any recent accounts. As I remember some work done under Professor Sedgwick's eye some years ago, it ranged pretty well in the millions.

THE CHAIRMAN: Perhaps Professor Sedgwick can give us something interesting on this question.

PROF. SEDGWICK: Mr. President and fellow-members, I have been extremely interested in Dr. Harrington's paper, for I doubt if there is any subject to-day more important to the public health, than this question of a reform of the milk supply.

I should differ from Dr. Harrington in one little point. I do believe that the public is beginning to wake up on this subject. He is a little bit pessimistic, and thinks that they don't care. Well, that is true in a large way, no doubt, but I think we are beginning to make some impression on the citadel of ignorance and carelessness in this direction; the attack is coming from trained nurses; it is coming from the physician; it is coming from the sanitarians, and it is coming from the milkmen themselves, who have been some of the most wide-awake in this matter. There are in this community some very progressive milk men, some of whom are in this room at the moment, who have been studying this question and looking into it from various points of view, and I believe that a good deal of progress can be made on the lines that Dr. Harrington has suggested.

In another respect I should differ slightly from Dr. Harrington. He speaks hopelessly of getting the public ever to pay more for milk than they now pay—and I don't wonder he feels so. When we see any talk of an increased cost of milk to anybody—producer, middleman, consumer, or anyone—some of the newspapers simply go wild on the subject, and talk as if a conspiracy was being made to cheat everybody on earth. This is an unfortunate point of view. I have come to the conclusion that there is no hope for the milk industry until we do get people to pay more for milk. I have been working at this matter now for some fifteen years, and I think that my first paper on the subject was read to this Association considerably more than ten years ago. The trouble is we are still in a primitive state in the milk industry.

We are going along just as our ancestors did, expecting to get for six, seven, eight cents a quart the benefit of all the latest conveniences and improvements. Now, that is very unreasonable. We are asking of the milk man many reforms. We are asking him, for instance, to wash his hands before he milks, a thing that never occurred to him in the old days. We suggest that it might be well for him to wet the cow's udder to keep the germs from dropping in. We suggest a uniform. We suggest a lot of things—more ice, cleaner cans, cleaner water. Now, I submit gentlemen, that from the standpoint of the milk producer, it is not fair to expect him to do all these things and get no more money for his milk.

I myself propose, from this time on, in season and out of season, to give lectures whenever I get a chance upon the subject of *ten-cent certified milk.* If I am willing to pay ten cents for a cigar (as I am, and more than ten generally), then I think I ought to be willing to pay ten cents for a quart of decent, clean milk for my family. If any man is willing to pay ten cents for a bottle of beer, or any woman is willing to pay ten cents for a glass of soda or candy, or for some little thing to decorate the table or the house, then I think I ought to be willing as I am, to pay ten cents a quart for milk; and I have issued orders in my house that no milk is to come in regularly that costs less than ten cents a quart. I know that this is advanced ground, and that you will shake your heads and say, "You cannot do it. It is no use. A few dudes may do it, but you will never affect the public generally." But I believe that we shall. I believe that through the influence of the trained nurses, and the physicians, and the public education which we are going to bring to bear on people in the next twenty-five years, people will gradually find, and agree with us, that it is just as nasty to drink nasty milk as it is nasty water, or anything of that kind. We have got to make it understood that dirty milk is nasty milk, and that people ought not to use it, and that it is an anachronism, and an inconsistency to pay ten cents for this, that and the other thing, and then quibble over the two or three cents required between clean and dirty milk. Of course at first this will only effect a limited number of people, but it will lead to the establishment of model dairies, and model dairies will have their influence over dairies that are not model dairies, and little by little, ten, twenty, thirty, fifty years from now, the milk supply will be cleaned up, as water supplies are gradually getting cleaned up.

Still, when all is said and done, I agree with Professor Smith that we have got to pasteurize milk. Cooked milk is the only *safe* milk, and always will remain the only *safe* milk, for the use of mankind. It will be very slow to come, I dare say, but it interests me quite greatly to know that it is coming a good deal faster than it was. I believe that pauteurizers are being put in by milkmen themselves; they are being put in by philanthropic people in various big cities, to save human life. Little by little the idea is spreading that *raw milk* is apt to be—it is not always, but it is apt to be, *dangerous milk*. And in all sanitary matters I have come to the conclusion that we have got to hold the standard up pretty near the ideal. We don't want a drinking water that is slightly contaminated, or that *may be* contaminated but very likely is not. We don't want a milk that *may be* contaminated with infectious diseases, but very likely is not. There is no middle ground in question of diseases and death, and sooner or later we have got to come up to the ideal.

I did not mean to speak so long, Mr. President, because there are practical men here, men dealing with the milk of this city, who can tell us just what the bacteria are when the milk comes in, and just what the practical problems and real difficulties are as they see them, and I should very much prefer to hear from them.

MR WHITING: Mr. President, being one of the milk contractors of Boston, I am naturally very much interested in this subject, have listened with intense interest to Professor Harrington and also to the last speaker. I agree with Professor Sedgwick that the first thing to do is to get a better price for milk in Boston. I think when that is done there is not much trouble in getting cleaner milk for this market. We cannot very well, with existing prices, go back to the producers and insist upon a cleaner condition of things about the farm. We are told at once they are doing already more than they can afford, and I don't know but that it is true. I will say, however, that a great deal has been done in the past two or three years, and a great deal is expected to be done in the next two or three, in the way of getting cleaner milk for this market, and reducing the bacteria. As Professor Harrington said, it is necessary to have the milk thoroughly cooled in order to keep down the bacteria, and that is what we are insisting upon. For the last three years we have put out circulars among our producers saying that we would not accept milk that was not cooled with ice, and we have accomplished a great deal on these lines. We shall insist this coming summer upon taking no dairies that do not use ice in cooling their milk. We know very well from past experience that that is the only way to get a good article of milk into the market, something that will keep the required time. If you gentlemen, or anybody else, can tell us how to get more per quart for milk in this market, we shall be glad to hear from you. If there are enough people, like Professor Sedgwick, who are willing to pay ten cents a quart, they can get milk, I think, just about as they want it.

Mr. Hood: Mr. Chairman and gentlemen, I have been very much interested in the papers read and the discussion this afternoon. A short time ago I noticed some milk which was being served on a table in a large hotel, that seemed to be loaded with bacteria. I noticed it by the peculiar flavor of the milk. There was a large dairy connected with the hotel, and a little later I visited it and found they had engaged the best talent they could secure, to have everything in perfect sanitary condition. They had granolithic floors in the stables, with sanitary base, cement wainscotting on the walls back of the cows, the stable was kept very clean, and they even had a man there during the night so that the floors should be kept perfectly clean. The cows were cleaned thoroughly, and the udders were wiped with a moist cloth before the men began milking; the utensils were sterilized; but by investigating still further, the cause of the bacteria in the milk was easily discovered. The milk was not quickly cooled after milking.

That endorses very strongly the statement that has been made here to-day: that cooling immediately after milking is of great importance. From the commercial standpoint, it is even more important than having everything clean about the stable. To get the best results, we must have everything clean, and then we must have immediate cooling of the milk.

The average farmer and milk dealer wish to do what they are paid for, and as little more as is absolutely necessary. The producer is getting for his milk about $\frac{1}{4}$ of a cent per quart more than he did a few years ago, while the consumer is paying but very little, if any, more than he did a few years ago. That reduction in the margin is bringing hardship upon nearly all the dealers. The smaller dealers and those who cannot do business on the reduced margin are going out of business. Many of the small dealers have already gone out. It is because they cannot pay from one-half cent to one cent per quart more than they did a few years ago and serve their customers at the same price. It is difficult for any of the dealers to do so.

If the standard for cleanliness of milk is to be raised, possibly it can be done along the line of certified milk, reference to which has already been made. We know what the standard for solids in milk is to-day, but what is the standard for its cleanliness? If the Board of Health established some standard for cleanliness, I am very sure all progressive companies will be pleased to come under such regulation. We can then sell milk as certified milk, and such milk will be subject to inspection for cleanliness, as well as for solids. Something can be done almost immediately to fill the demand for clean milk, which already is being furnished by some of the producers. We must be in a position to pay those producers a higher price for their milk. We must pay them considerably more money, and in paying them more we must sell the milk in the city at a higher price than the ordinary milk. That will bring about two prices, as well as two qualities, of milk and it may be best in starting this method that any dealer who may wish shall carry the two grades of milk; one as certified milk, so labeled, and subject to inspection for bacteria and solids, and the milk not labeled certified milk should be the same milk as is carried at the present time, and subject to present inspection.

I am pleased to hear to-day that there are some men who advocate that higher prices should be paid for milk. The producers do not get enough to give us the article we want, and the consumer ought to understand the value of a superior article.

A few years ago, at the time when nearly all food products were advancing in the market, some of the Boston newspapers had a great deal to say about the price of milk. They greatly damaged the business by advocating no rise in the price of milk. We feel sometimes like saying to some people we will supply them with milk free for their family use, house-to-house delivery, if they will pay a fair price for making the delivery. This would especially apply to many family customers who wish to buy their milk at three and one-half cents per pint; and certainly we believe that deliveries cannot be made for less than about that price per parcel.

There are many large users of milk in Boston whom we should expect to demand the highest quality of milk at a fair price, but it is found they want a fair quality of milk at the lowest price. We all want the best and safest milk for use in our homes, and we must co-operate in any movement to raise the standard.

DR. MILLER: Mr. President, I understood the reader of the last paper to favor a commission. Now, I have just two suggestions to make. I am not in favor of two grades of milk; I am in favor of having pure milk. It strikes me that if we had a State commission, whose business it was to examine milk, suppose some user of milk fancies that the milk he is getting is not pure, a member of that State commission might be called there to examine it. I think it would do a great deal of good to have a State commission and let us have pure milk, and pure milk only. If a poor man is not able to buy milk that is worth ten cents, he had better buy half the quantity. He had better buy a pint and have it pure, than to buy a quart that is impure; and he can weaken it with water. That is one remedy I would suggest. Then here is another suggestion. In the city you have plenty of machinery to enforce any law against adulterated milk, but in the country towns they don't have that. The remedy in the country, where the milk is produced, will be, first, education. We have got to educate the people, and that education will have to be done through two sources, aside from this milk inspection I have spoken of; one is the family physician, and the other is the teacher. The mass of people think that the doctor and the teacher know a little more than the rest of the people, and they have more influence. Now, if this organization could send out circulars on this point to the physicians, every physician in the commonwealth, and to all the teachers in the commonwealth, we would do more toward educating the people on this subject of pure milk than in any other way.

THE CHAIRMAN: Gentlemen, I think there can be no question but that these educational measures are very serviceable; but they are slow. It is very well to pay more for your milk; I think we should; but you will never find the farmer sending ten-cent milk in here until he is told that he must, until he is told that his poor milk will not be sold in Boston. A few years ago the Boston Board started this question, wrote some regulations, proceeded to put them in force. We wanted the whole State with us and we came into this Association for that purpose. We invited the milk contractors of Boston to come in here with us. They came heartily, stood up and talked like men, business men; they were with us in the proposition for clean milk. It was found that the other boards of health of the State were not quite as fortunate in some respects as the Boston Board, owing to some differences in relationship between themselves and the milk inspectors. This Association had a committee on legislation, and that committee under request went before a legislative committee, and tried to help the rest of the Boards of Health to get a uniform law. We did not exactly get kicked out, but we came away defeated. The Boston Board alone went ahead with its regulation. It has, as has been said, done some good.

The Boston Board is about to take another step, and we would like very much to have the other Boards of the State with us. In union there is strength. While the other Boards of the State may not have comfortable official relations with the milk inspectors of their cities and towns, they can do this. They have just as much authority to regulate the sale of milk in their town or city as the Boston Board has. We propose to fix some standards. We propose to have the bacterial count reasonably low, and we propose to have the temperature held down to a reasonable degree, as has been indicated here by Dr. Harrington. It can be done. It only needs a will and a union of forces. We are ready to lead off. We hope, through what has been said here to-day, that there will be a general feeling that this is a necessity. It is time that we took another step. It is time that we had cleaner milk. It is very well to sterilize the milk, of course, but why should we encourage laziness and carelessness in the producer and retailer by taking milk in a dirty condition? Let us make them do better work and pay them for it, and then, if we want to sterilize the milk by boiling, let us do it.

I hope that this meeting will bear the fruit that is looked for. I hope we will all have regulations, and will enforce them, against dirty milk.

DR. WORCESTER: Mr. Chairman, if it is in order, I should like to move that the President appoint a committee of three, or five, to draw up a bill to be presented to the present Legislature in this matter, covering the lines of Dr. Harrington's scheme. I think it is an absolute necessity. I have lived in the country as well as in the city, and country milk is just as dirty as city milk. We may get it a little fresher in the country, but it is not as well cared for as it is in the city. The milk as brought here is pretty well iced—has to be, in order to be accepted by our milk dealers in the city. I think it is just as important, if not more so, for the country as for the city, that something of this kind should be done, and have thought so for a good many years, and I am very glad that this has come up now.

THE CHAIRMAN: Perhaps Dr. Worcester does not understand precisely how the law stands. Every Board of Health in this Commonwealth has authority to make a regulation, and enforce it, against dirty milk. The only thing that you would need to do with the Legislature is to secure a better union between the

Boards of Health of the several cities and towns and the milk inspectors of those cities and towns.

DR. WORCESTER: Mr. Chairman, I understand that Boards of Health have absolute power in these matters, and the only thing for them is to feel that they have. If there was a public statute to a certain effect, with a State commission to look after the milk supply especially, I think something more could be done. Then they would feel that they could go ahead better. I know it is the same in respect to the spitting nuisance and a number of other things in the past. The Boards have, under the General Statutes, power in all nuisances, and if they merely say bad milk is a nuisance, they can abate it.

THE CHAIRMAN: If you will secure a law to place every inspector of milk under the kindly care of the Board of Health, and let it stand by him, the difficulty will take care of itself very quickly.

DR. WORCESTER: Mr. Chairman, I will move that such a Bill be brought before the Legislature.

MR. COFFEY: Mr. Chairman, some four or five years ago an attempt was made, as the Chairman has stated, to get a uniform law passed, by which Boards of Health might have the right to appoint the inspectors of milk. That bill was before the Legislature, and I believe met the opposition of the farmers of the State, and was defeated. Now, as far as I know, there are but three or four cities in the State that have control over the inspectors of milk. Boston has it in its charter. Lynn has a special act. Springfield, I believe, has also a special act. The city of Lowell, by an arrangement made with the City Council, has control over the inspector of milk. Those are the only cities, so far as I know, in the State, that have anything whatever to do with the inspection or licensing of milk dealers or peddlers. I know at Worcester we have absolutely nothing whatever to do with the milk, except what might be given us under the General Statutes, which allow Boards of Health to make rules and regulations governing anything that may affect the public health.

With an inspector of milk appointed by the Mayor and confirmed by the Board of Aldermen, who has not any interest in the milk question other than simply licensing and making tests, looking to see whether the milk is adulterated or not, the Boards of Health of course are situated so that they cannot very well interfere with the inspector, who holds a political appointment from the Mayor. He has no interest in the subject from a sanitary standpoint. His thought and his action does not run in that direction. That is only natural. He is not trained to look at it from that point of view.

I remember when this subject was up some five or six years ago in this meeting, and I think it was at the annual meeting, a member here from North Adams discussed the subject and was very radical in his utterances on the question of the purity of the milk supply. He pledged himself here that in his own town of North Adams he would see that the milk law was strictly enforced, and that milkmen would be obliged to comply with the terms of the rules as laid down by the Board of Health of that town. At that meeting there were some representatives of the farming interests. After the meeting was over I heard them express, in very decided terms, what they thought of that man from North Adams, and with it they implied that when they got at him he would no longer be a member of the Board of Health of that town. I subsequently was interested enough to inquire if that threat was carried into execution, and I found that it was; that the member who expressed himself so radically at the meeting here five years ago, when his term expired as a member of the Board of Health of North Adams, was not reappointed.

It may be that, as Professor Sedgwick has said, and also as Professor Harrington has said, a change has taken place in the opinions of the milk producers, as well as the middlemen, who send the milk to the consumers. That may be; I have not any means of either proving or disproving it. I certainly know that four or five years ago the feeling among the farmers was not at all favorable to giving Boards of Health the control of the milk business. Lynn at that time, I remember, made some rather radical rules, and stirred up the entire farming interests.

The Lynn Board of Health has control of the licensing of milk peddlers. It is my opinion that until you can get a law passed by which Boards of Health will have the right to license the peddlers, and in that way have some control over them, you cannot do much toward improving your milk supply. The State Board of Health has certain powers now about the adulteration of milk; it might be given additional powers, so that it might examine and look into the dairies. If that was done, then probably your milk supply would improve. But my own experience has been that some of the milk that came from the farms was in very bad condition.

It was only about six weeks ago that I had occasion to go to an adjoining town to the city of Worcester to look up typhoid fever. We have a practice in Worcester that when we get one or two cases of typhoid fever on any milkman's route, we look him up. The inspector reported to me two cases on the route of one of the milkmen who supplied milk to Worcester, and I drove out to the adjoining town where his home was, and I found a very dirty condition of affairs. It was a dirty, slack, run-down-at-the-heels place. The farmer was dirty and unkempt, and his wife was as bad, and the whole place had a look of poverty. I found his son down with typhoid in the house, and his driver had been sent to the hospital, also with typhoid; no precautions whatever had been taken toward caring for those in a sanitary way, or toward keeping that milk supply pure. I had to take arbitrary means. I simply told them that unless they did what I wanted them to do, I should publish in the papers of Worcester the fact that there was typhoid in their house, and also the dirty condition of the place, and ruin their business; that I did not want to do that, and if they would carry out the orders that I was there to give, I wouldn't interfere with their business. They adopted my views. The milk supply was moved, with all the utensils, to another farm, where it was clean, to be cared for. But that only shows how careless and how ignorant and how dirty some of the farms are from which the supply of milk goes out to the various cities and towns of the State.

PROF. THEOBALD SMITH: Mr. President, when this question of the milk supply came up in this Association some five or six years ago, the agitation against tuberculosis was uppermost, and everything appeared to revolve about the tubercle bacilli in the milk. Cleanliness was entirely subordinated to it, although I urged the fact that there were half a dozen other diseases, that were fully as important from a sanitary standpoint, that might be disseminated in milk. At that time I felt that the tubercle bacilli in the milk had very little to do with tuberculosis, and I felt very lukewarm in the whole matter; but it seems to me now that we have come to the position that dirty milk is likely to contain a variety of disease germs; we have attained the right standpoint from which to begin our agitation over again. I think also that the problem of the pasteurization of milk should not be lost sight of, and I have no doubt that it will become in the future one of the most important safeguards. In order to put this matter into motion, I move that a committee of three be appointed by the Chair to consider the whole question of the sanitary bearing of milk, and to report to this Association at some later meeting, because there are so many questions involved, among which the price and food value of milk are of considerable importance.

DR. MILLER: Mr. President, I heartily second that motion.

THE CHAIRMAN: It is moved and seconded that the Chair appoint a committee of three to take the question of milk sanitation up and report to the Association at a subsequent meeting.
(The motion was adopted.)

THE CHAIRMAN: The Chair will take time to appoint this committee and will call on Professor Harrington to close the discussion.

PROF. HARRINGTON: Mr. President, it may be, as Professor Sedgwick has said, that I am somewhat pessimistic in regard to public interest in this matter of clean milk; but if I am, it is because I have been preaching clean milk for a number of years, and certainly Professor Sedgwick has been preaching it most eloquently for the last fifteen years, and yet I fail to see that the public shows any particular interest. To be sure, Professor Sedgwick is willing to pay ten cents, and probably most of us are; but the general public is *not* willing to pay ten cents. I know of a number of milkmen in this city who have tried to put out pasteurized milk at ten cents a quart. They got as clean milk as they could; they put in a lot of expensive apparatus; they pasteurized their milk and charged ten cents a quart, and that is all they could do; they could charge it, but they could not get it, and they have gone out of business. We cannot interest the public in paying ten cents. Men may be willing to pay ten and fifteen and more for their cigars and their beer, but only a very small minority are willing to pay ten for their milk. Two weeks ago I was at a meeting held on this very subject, by the County of Albany Medical Society. I heard there that there is one model dairy, a few miles out from Albany. The cows are well looked after; the milk is examined periodically at the Bender Institute. The number of bacteria in it is very much under 10,000, I think about 4,500. The owner charges ten cents per quart, and has succeeded in getting a trade of forty quarts per day in the whole city of Albany, and that is all. I think that I am less pessimistic on the whole than Professor Sedgwick is. I say, let us take hold of this thing; I believe we are going to accomplish something, and we are going to accomplish it pretty soon. It is going to be a matter of slow growth to attain perfection; but I don't believe, as Professor Sedgwick does, that it is going to take fifty years. He is satisfied if in fifty years we have made some progress. Well, some of us will not be here in fifty years, but I expect to see a good deal of progress within five years. When Boards of Health take this matter up and do the thing in earnest, as will be done in Boston, I expect to see good progress in less than five years—and very marked progress, you will find. I think that in this whole matter we certainly shall have the cordial co-operation of the milk contractors. It is for their interest to have clean milk. If they can induce the farmer to send them clean milk, they will have less milk souring on their hands. If the consumer will pay ten cents a quart, they can afford to give the farmer more for his product.

In the matter of commissions, spoken of by Dr. Miller, I think that the only possible way of running a milk commission is for men who are interested to take hold and form an organization which will not be political, raise whatever funds are necessary, employ a veterinarian, a chemist, perhaps a physician, and a bacteriologist, and make periodical examinations of milk. When milk falls within certain limits of bacterial impurity, say 10,000 per cubic centimeter, which is the standard set in Philadelphia, let the commission give the milkman a certificate. As long as the milkman lives up to that standard, let him keep his certificate; as soon as his milk falls off, let his certificate be taken away.

DR. NORTON, Norwood: Mr. Chairman, I want to add just a word in view of Dr. Harrington's remarks. He seems to think that there are no people that pay ten cents a quart for milk. I want to say that in an adjoining town, in Westwood, there is a first-class dairy. I do not recall the owner's name; but at any rate it is there, and I have visited it. That man's milk is sold in Dedham and Jamaica Plain—those are two places—at ten cents a quart, and he sells all he can produce. I just add these remarks to make Dr. Harrington more hopeful.

PROF. HARRINGTON: Jamaica Plain is a center of great intelligence. It is willing to pay ten cents a quart.

THE CHAIRMAN: The Chair would announce as the committee Prof. Theobald Smith, Prof. Charles Harrington and Prof. William T. Sedgwick.

PROF SEDGWICK: Mr. President, I am quite likely to be out of the city a good deal for the next two or three months, and besides, it seems to me desirable that the committee should be somewhat differently constituted. I should like to withdraw my name.. My objection is that you have got three professors on the committee. Professors are all very well in their place, but it seems to me three of them are a little too many.

THE CHAIRMAN: Two out of the three appointed are begging off. The Chair will make up this committee and notify later.

If there is no other business to come before the meeting, a motion to adjourn will be in order.

MR. COFFEY: I move we adjourn.

(The motion prevailed, and the Association adjourned.)

The next meeting will be held on the last Thursday in April (April 28), 1904.

ABSTRACTS, REVIEWS, NOTES AND NEWS.

Boards of Health are asked to send to the Managing Editor notes of not more than one hundred and fifty words relating to new regulations passed, legal cases prosecuted, outbreaks of infection, unusual problems encountered, or other matters the publication of which may further the attainment of the objects of the Association.

References are indicated by numbers. See list at end of column.

THE PRESENT PRICE OF DIPHTHERIA ANTITOXIN.— The advance in price widely heralded of late seems to have a real basis in fact.

Hitherto two grades of antitoxin have been on the market, the cheaper grade being the more dilute, so that 3,000 units of the cheaper grade occupied more actual bulk, and was to that extent less desirable than 3,000 units of the other. There is little question that unit for unit the cheaper grade is just as effective as the dearer.

The cheaper grade has now been withdrawn from the market entirely. This leaves the poor man compelled to buy the dearer grade or go without. It is true that this dearer grade is not now so dear as it was when the cheaper grade was also available, but it remains dearer than the cheaper grade was when it could be obtained. Thus 3,000 units (dilute) used to cost about $4.50; now 3,000 units (concentrated) costs $5.00. The mere decrease in bulk of the latter over the former is not worth the difference.

When it is known that the discount to the retailer offered by antitoxin manufacturers has been 25 per cent.; that the discount to wholesalers has been 33⅓ per cent.; that the Chicago Board of Health is said to have received a discount of 62 per cent., and that the Massachusetts State Board of Health has made for $7,500 what private manufacturers at market rates would sell for $80,000, it will easily be seen that the antitoxin manufacturers are not exactly trembling on the point of bankruptcy as yet. (See 14.)

MILK IN INFANT FEEDING.—Drs. W. H. Park and Emmet Holt summarize their paper on this subject in the *Medical News* of Dec. 5, 1903, as follows:

The observations here recorded were made upon the groups of infants for periods of about three months only, and the conclusions drawn relate especially to the more immediate effects of the milk.

1. During cold weather neither the mortality nor the health of the infants observed in the investigation was appreciably affected by the kind of milk or by the number of bacteria which it contained. The different grades of milk varied much less in the amount of bacterial contamination in winter than in summer, the store milk averaging only about 750,000 bacteria per c.c.

2. During hot weather, when the resistance of the children was lowered, the kind of milk taken influenced both the amount of illness and the mortality; those who took condensed milk and cheap store milk did the worst, and those who received breast milk, pure bottled milk and modified milk did the best. The effect of bacterial contamination was very marked when the milk was taken without previous heating; but, unless the contamination was very excessive, only slight when heating was employed shortly before feeding.

3. The number of bacteria which may accumulate before milk becomes noticeably harmful to the average infant in summer differs with the nature of the bacteria present, the age of the milk, and the temperature at which it has been kept. When milk is taken raw, the fewer the bacteria present the better are the results. Of the usual varieties, over 1,000,000 bacteria per c.c. are certainly deleterious to the average infant. However, many infants take such milk without apparently harmful results. Heat

above 170° F. (77° C.) not only destroys most of the bacteria present, but, apparently, some of their poisonous products. No harm from the bacteria previously existing in recently heated milk was noticed in these observations unless they had amounted to many millions, but in such numbers they were decidedly deleterious.

4. When milk of average quality was fed sterilized and raw, those infants who received milk previously heated did, on the average, much better in warm weather than those who received it raw. The difference was so quickly manifest and so marked that there could be no mistaking the meaning of the results. The bacterial content of the milk used in the test was somewhat less than in the average milk of the city.

5. No special varieties of bacteria were found in unheated milk which seemed to have any special importance in relation to the summer diarrhœa of children. The number of varieties was very great, and the kinds of bacteria differed according to the locality from which the milk came. None of the 139 varieties selected as most distinct among those obtained, injured very young kittens when fed in pure cultures. A few cases of acute indigestion were seen immediately following the use of Pasteurized milk more than thirty-six hours old. Samples of such milk were found to contain more than 100,000,000 bacteria per c.c., mostly spore-bearing varieties. The deleterious effects, though striking, were not serious nor lasting. At the present time there is in New York City, no general sale from stores of "Pasteurized" or "sterilized" milk, so that it is here very rare for such milk to be used thirty-six hours after heating.

6. After the first twelve months of life, infants are less and less affected by the bacteria in milk derived from healthy cattle. According to these observations, when the milk had been kept cool the bacteria did not appear to injure the children over three years of age, at any season of the year, unless in very great excess.

7. Since a large part of the tenement population must purchase its milk from small dealers, at a low price, everything possible should be done by Health Boards to improve the character of the general milk-supply of cities by enforcing proper legal re-

strictions regarding its transportation, delivery and sale. Suffi
cient improvements in this respect are entirely feasible in every
large city to secure to all a milk which will be wholesome after
heating. The general practice of heating milk which has now
become a custom among the tenement population of New York
is undoubtedly a large factor in the lessened infant mortality
during the hot months.

8. Of the methods of feeding now in vogue, that by milk from
central distributing stations unquestionably possesses the most
advantages, in that it secures some constant oversight of the
child; and since it furnishes the food in such a form that it leaves
the mother least to do, it gives her the smallest opportunity of
going wrong. This method of feeding is one which deserves
to be much more extensively employed, and might, in the absence of private philanthropy, wisely be undertaken by municipalities and continued for the four months from May 15 to September 15.

9. The use, for infants, of milk delivered in sealed bottles,
should be encouraged whenever this is possible, and its advantages duly explained. Only the purest milk should be taken
raw, especially in summer.

10. Since what is needed most is intelligent care, all possible
means should be employed to educate mothers and those caring
for infants in proper methods of doing this. This, it is believed,
can most effectively be done by the visits of properly qualified
trained nurses or women physicians to the homes, supplemented
by the use of printed directions.

11. Bad surroundings, though contributing to bad results
in feeding are not the chief factor. It is not, therefore, merely
by better housing of the poor in large cities that we will see a
great reduction in infant mortality.

12. The observations indicate that close percentage modification of milk, although desirable in difficult cases, is not necessary
to obtain excellent results with the great majority of infants,
and that a certain adjustment of a healthy infant to its food is
usually soon secured.

13.   While it is true that even in the tenements the results with the best bottle-feeding are nearly as good as average breast-feeding, it is also true that most of the bottle-feeding is at present very badly done, so that as a rule the immense superiority of breast-feeding obtains.   This should, therefore, be encouraged by every means, and not discontinued without good and sufficient reasons.   The time and money required for artificial feeding, if expended by the tenement mother to secure better food and more rest for herself, would often enable her to continue nursing, with advantage to her child.

14.   The injurious effects of table food to infants under a year old, and of fruits to all infants and young children in cities, in hot weather, should be much more generally appreciated.

CAISSON DISEASE.—Experiments by MacLeod and Hill, London City Hospital Laboratory, show that the fatal effects of decompression usually result from the setting free in the blood of gases with which the blood had become saturated during compression, thus permitting "air embolism." Very slow decompression obviates this by permitting the gradual escape of the gases in amounts too small to form definite bubbles. Besides air embolism, oxygen poisoning and excessive loss of body heat, the latter due to the increased conductivity of air when compressed, lower the vitality of the body. According to Dr. Frank Roth, air embolism has been noticed in men working in the Cleveland crib. Dr. W. T. Howard of Cleveland has observed air bubbles in the brain and cord in fatal cases. (1.)

RECENT LEGISLATION.   (3.)

Toy Pistols.—South Carolina (ch. 79, 1903) prohibits the sale of any toy pistol in which caps or cartridges are used, or of any caps or cartridges therefor, under a penalty of $100, or imprisonment for thirty days.

Hydrophobia.—Texas (ch. 125, 1903) appropriates $5,000 for a Pasteur Department at Austin, under the control of the State Lunatic Asylum.

TOBACCO.—Utah (ch. 135, 1903) makes it a misdemeanor for any one under eighteen to have in their possession any form of tobacco or opium or other narcotic.

INFECTIOUS DISEASE HOSPITALS.—Utah (ch. 36, 1903) provides that no infectious disease hospital shall be located within twenty rods of any public highway, or within quarter of a mile of any open running water used for domestic purposes as a public water-supply.

TYPHOID FEVER.—Utah (ch. 81, 1903) makes the omission to disinfect the excreta of a typhoid patient a misdemeanor. Also . it is a misdemeanor on the physician's part to fail to instruct the attendants how to disinfect the feces. He must also satisfy himself that his instructions are carried out.

SCHOOLS.—Pennsylvania (ch. 132, 1903) requires the disinfection of schoolhouses at intervals of not more than two weeks. The system adopted in each place must receive the approval of the local Board of Health, or if there be no such board, of the State Board of Health.

North Carolina (ch. 690, 1903) excludes from school children in families where other members are suffering from certain infectious diseases, and excludes them also for two weeks after the death, recovery or removal of the patient. Mumps and the itch are added to the infectious list.

VACCINATION.—Oklahoma (ch. 2, 1903) appropriates $2,500 for the manufacture and free distribution of vaccine in the territory by the Oklahoma Agricultural Experiment Station at Stillwater.

South Dakota (ch. 223, 1903) prohibits any board, physician, or person from compelling vaccination by physical force. No child successfully vaccinated within five years shall be prevented from school attendance.

Minnesota (ch. 299, 1903) permits school attendance in the absence of vaccination, except during epidemics of smallpox, and even then a physician's certificate of physical unfitness exempts the child from vaccination.

TUBERCULOSIS.—Minnesota (ch. 316, 1903) provides a State sanitarium for consumptives.

New Mexico (ch. 17, 1903) exempts from taxation for six years all sanitarium property, the construction of which is begun within a year of the passage of the act, if not less than $100,000 is expended on it within two years of such passage.

New York (ch. 638, 1903) provides that the consent of a town must be obtained before the establishment within it of any sanitarium of any description for consumptives.

POISONOUS ADVERTISING SAMPLES.—Both New York (ch. 494, 1903) and North Dakota (ch. 81, 1903) forbid the distribution of free samples of drugs, medicines, etc., about streets, premises, etc., in a manner such that children may get at them.

LEGAL DECISIONS.

VACCINATION OF PUBLIC SCHOOL CHILDREN. — In the case of Viemeister of New York City, who sought to compel the admission of his child to school without vaccination, on the ground that the statute requiring vaccination before admission was unconstitutional, the Appellate Division of the New York Supreme Court upheld the statute, declaring it constitutional, since it operates equally on every person who is or may desire to become a pupil in the public schools, and affords equal protection to all. (4.)

It will be remembered that a similar decision was reached recently in Massachusetts (this JOURNAL, October, 1903).

CHRISTIAN SCIENCE AND MEDICAL ATTENDANCE. — Under a clause of the Act for the Prevention of Cruelty to Children, which makes it a misdemeanor to willfully neglect a child in a manner likely to cause unnecessary suffering or injury to its health, Lord Russell, Lord Chief Justice of England, on appeal, upheld (1899) a conviction for manslaughter in a faith-healing case where death had resulted. In Canada the Ontario Court of Appeals has decided recently, in a Christian Science case, that medical attendance is a "necessary," the failure to provide which for children under sixteen years constitutes a misdemeanor; where death follows, it is manslaughter. (Abs. 9.)

A recent ruling similar to the above, in New York State, was commented on in our last issue. In contrast to this, the Supreme Court of Ohio is reported as recently acquitting the parents of the charge of manslaughter, consequent on the death of their child under Christian Science treatment. (10.)

Judge Cleaveland of New Haven recently refused to appoint an Eddyite as guardian to a nine-year-old child, as the result of some questions asked as to the proposed conduct of the prospective guardian in the case of serious illness of the child. (8.)

TYPHOID FEVER NOT FROM GARBAGE.—A man recently brought suit against the city of Philadelphia, alleging that members of his family had contracted typhoid fever from foul gases arising from garbage. Expert testimony was adduced in defense, showing that typhoid fever is not introduced by breathing impure air. The man lost his suit. (5.)

It is curious to note from time to time how obstinately the exploded ideas concerning the relation of bad odors and specific diseases persist in the lay—sometimes, alas, also in the medical —mind.

BRIBING THE PUBLIC TO PROTECT ITSELF.—The City Council of the French community of Rouen has passed an ordinance which not only bestows $2.00 on the first person reporting a new case of typhoid fever, but further offers $4.00 to the infected family thus "betrayed" if they will agree to follow the directions of the Board of Health.

Two members of the City Council only voted against this ordinance. Both of these were physicians. (14.)

This legislation certainly deserves to be compared with that of Utah, quoted in another column, which provides penalties for the physician who fails to give prophylactic instruction in typhoid fever, and for the householder who fails to carry out such instructions when received.

THE EYES OF SCHOOL CHILDREN.—At the last annual meeting of the American Medical Association, the following resolution was passed by the House of Representatives, at the suggestion of the Ophthalmologic Section:

Resolved, That it is advised by the American Medical Association that measures be taken by the various school authorities and boards of education, boards of health, and, if possible, state legislators, to secure the examination of the eyes and ears of all school children in this country, with a view to the suitable treatment, for the relief of ophthalmologic and otologic imperfections. (12.)

.. PROPER SUPPORT OF THE WEIGHT OF THE CLOTHING IN CHILDREN.—Dr. Joel E. Goldthwait recommends that the clothing of children, too often suspended, through the waist, from the outer part of the shoulder, should be suspended from the inner part of the shoulder, next the neck. He advises narrow-backed, high-necked, full-fronted waists, with bands attached, fastened in front to a broad waist belt, passing over the shoulders near the neck, crossing each other in the middle of the back, the back ends attached to the waist belt at the sides over the hips. At this point, and not, as is usual, at the front, the stocking suspenders should be attached.

For summer wear, a skeleton waist, consisting alone of the bands described, connected across the back of the neck by another band, to prevent slipping, is recommended. Further suggestions are also made, for special cases. He adds that while these simple apparatuses will not serve universally for the prevention and treatment of round shoulders in children, they are of real value in many cases. (11.)

SCHOOL AND SPINAL CURVATURES.—Schulthess denies that the school is the only or even the principal cause of lateral curvature and round shoulders, on the ground that many of such cases are seen well advanced before the school age. He says that certain curvatures are especially favored by school occupations, the position in writing giving to the spine of a child who is naturally disposed to yield toward the left the opportunity to assume this position and to maintain it for long periods. Curves whose beginnings were indicated before the commencement of school life are accentuated. Sitting, the lack of exercise, etc., further abnormal development, but the school is not entitled to all of the blame. In prophylaxis he recommends short hours, regular gymnastic exercise, hourly pauses, proper illumination, suitable furniture, perpendicular writing and frequent physical examination of the children. Decidedly deformed children should be put in special classes. (Abs. 11.)

THE UNCONSCIOUS DEAF.—E. Felix (*La Semaine Medicale*, April 1, 1903) tabulates examinations of 1,050 adults under fifty years of age, and 1,038 children under twelve. Two hundred and ninety adults had hearing defective from disease, twenty-two of these only being aware of the defect. Among the children, 327 were affected, only twelve of these knowingly so. Prophylaxis in infectious diseases and the medical examination of the ears of school children are urged. (Abs. 6.)

TRAINED NURSES FOR PUBLIC SCHOOL SERVICE and for visiting contagious disease cases have been employed by the New York Board of Health since June, 1903.

Municipal district nursing, under the control of a Board of Health, is a departure which promises well under favorable circumstances. As adjuncts to the Medical Inspection of Schools the nurses visit at home the children excluded for minor affections, trachoma, pediculosis, ringworm, eczema, etc., and instruct the mothers as to treatment. (8.)

GONORRHEA IN INFANTS.—From experience in the Babies' Hospital of New York, Reuel B. Kimball concludes that gonorrhea prevails widely amongst infants and children, especially in institutions where many children live together. It takes the forms of ophthalmia, vulvo-vaginitis, and pyæmia. Careful physical and microscopical examination and complete isolation are necessary to its eradication and exclusion from hospitals where infants are cared for. Health authorities, he thinks, should include gonorrhea amongst the acute infectious diseases of children. (8.)

PROPHYLACTIC DISINFECTION OF NOSE AND THROAT FOR MEASLES AND SCARLET FEVER.—Egart (Zeit. f. Hyg. u. Infek., 1903, p. 196) urges the value of sprays and inhalations for the noses and throats of children in hospitals or institutions, as preventing the development of these diseases in exposed persons and in lessening the severity of the disease when contracted. The earliest localization of the infective agents seems to be in the upper respiratory tract, and the author offers statistics to show the effectiveness of his methods. He advises lime water with an equal part of water, 3 per cent. boric acid solution, .05 per cent. tri-chlorid of iron, and 3 per cent sodium chlorid solution, using "all four solutions alternately for five minutes twice daily." (5.)

FALSE VACCINATION SCARS.—In a late issue of *Medical Talk for the Home*, an organ said to be maintained by the Peruna Company, there occurs an article advocating the use of nitric acid to form scars on the arms of children, which scars, the writer says, pass as vaccination marks. The writer tells physicians not to say or certify that vaccination has been performed in such cases, but merely to show the scar to inquirers and let the scar deceive them. He would not wish them to lie about it though. (12.)

The morality which recommends acting a lie is not superior to that which recommends straight lying, and acting a lie which one has not the courage to tell, is the meanest form of lying.

Boards of Health will do well to watch for nitric acid scars on the arms of the unfortunate offspring of the disciples of this writer, and should make an example of the first responsible person caught thus fraudulently evading the statutes.

TYPHOID FEVER FROM A NATIONAL STANDPOINT.—Dr. John S. Fulton, in discussing the general subject of typhoid fever, reiterates and emphasizes, from careful statistics, the principle that typhoid fever is a rural rather than an urban disease. He attributes this to the greater carelessness regarding typhoid excreta in country districts. He thinks that the physician recognizes only 60 per cent. of the total cases, and that although the lack of laboratory facilities for diagnosis accounts for some of these failures, the general lack of realization of the ubiquity and perennial activity of the disease is more at fault.   (13.)

DETECTION OF TYPHOID BACILLI IN WATER.—The recorded cases of successful isolation of undoubted typhoid bacilli from water supplies are few in number. Loesener (Arb. a. d. kais. Gesund., 1895, p. 207) isolated them from the laboratory tap water of the Hygienic Institute at Berlin. Remlinger and Schneider (Ann. de l'Inst. Pasteur, 1897, p. 55) asserted the ubiquity of, and isolated frequently what they considered to be this organism, but their results are doubtful. Hankin (Cent. f. Bakt., 1899, p. 554) found typhoid bacilli-like organisms in India. Kuebler and Neufeld (Zeit. f. Hyg., 1899, p. 133) report finding typhoid bacilli in a shallow well, the absence of colon bacilli suggesting that the well has been infected through urine rather than through feces. Genersich (Cent. f. Bakt., 1900, p. 241) isolated eleven cultures from suspected cisterns. Sischer and Flatau (Ibid., 1901, p. 329) apparently obtained undoubted typhoid organisms from a well at Rellingen.   Sion and Negel (Ibid., 1902, p. 480) found para-typhoid bacilli in water.   (5.)

In this country Wesbrook isolated typhoid bacilli from the water supply of Minneapolis by passing the water through a Pasteur-Chamberland filter and testing the material filtered out. (Minn. State Board of Health Reports, 95-98.)

The disappearance of the bacilli from infected water supplies before investigations are set on foot, due to the non-survival of these organisms in water, is usually given as the explanation for the infrequency of their isolation.

TYPHOID FEVER IN LOWELL, MASS.—The city water consists of artesian well water, pumped to the city reservoir to secure pressure.   The manufacturing companies have a reservoir of their own, thirty feet higher than the city reservoir. The pipes from the two reservoirs intersect, a flap valve, kept closed usually by the greater pressure of the corporation supply, separating the two streams. In case the corporation reservoir were lowered by excessive draft, the flap valves would open under the city pressure and the corporation pipes thus would be replenished.

On July 18, 1903, a large fire reduced the corporation supply to the point where the flap valves opened as designed, but when later the corporation reservoir was being refilled by pumping, the flap valves, which were supposed to close under the increasing corporation pressure, remained open long enough (seven hours) to permit 500,000 gallons of Merrimac River water (at the time, very strongly polluted with Lowell sewage), or about one-twelfth the average daily supply, to enter the city service pipes. About August 1, or fourteen days later, typhoid cases began to take to bed. A total of 136 cases was reported in August, 38 in September. Between July 20 and August 1 many cases of enteritis and gastroenteritis occurred, many of which recovered. On July 29, the first bacterial examination of the city water after the admission of the Merrimac River showed only the usual low bacterial content, but *B. coli* was present (in 100 c.c.) in two samples. On July 31st no *B. coli* were found in four 1,000 c.c. samples tested. In this epidemic the incubation period of the first cases was fourteen days (to going to bed). The maximum number going to bed in any one day was seventeen, on August the 12th, twenty-five days after the accident, and fourteen days from the only finding of *B. coli* in the city supply. The mains were flushed on July 29th, just after the collection of the polluted samples. · The worst of the outbreak was over by August 22d, after which comparatively few cases occurred, a certain number of which were doubtless direct case-to-case infections. (1.)

TYPHOID FEVER IN SPRINGFIELD FROM SPRINGS.— A number of cases of typhoid fever in Springfield recently were traced to the use of contaminated springs, the water from which was bought by citizens and used in preference to the city supply, because the latter, although sanitarily good, possessed an objectionable color. The State Board of Health, on analysis, condemned seven springs, five of which were in the Springfield Park System. The owners of several other springs were warned that their springs were not up to the standard.

WILLIAMSTOWN TYPHOID FEVER.—Dr. George A. Soper, the sanitary engineer who investigated the Ithaca (N. Y.) epidemic for the New York State Board of Health, reports that the Williamstown epidemic resulted from infected cream eaten with breakfast food. A can of this cream was placed in a vat of infected water to cool, and became accidentally contaminated therefrom.

TUBERCULOSIS AND THE HOME.—Dr. Wm. Osler, at the Phipps Institute, Philadelphia, Dec. 3, 1903, gave the second of the series of addresses now being conducted there on this subject. Among the essentials in combating the disease the speaker included educational campaigns, compulsory notification, increased power for Boards of Health, permitting the cleaning out of notoriously bad unsanitary localities, and the compelling of good buildings to replace these. Osler states that 98 per cent of all cases must, after all, be treated at home, that the medical practitioner is here the "man behind the gun," and that early recognition and immediate masterful treatment are the main points for him. (2.)

PROTOZOA IN SCARLET FEVER.—Dr. F. B. Mallory, at a meeting of the Boston Society of the Medical Sciences, Dec. 15, 1903, demonstrated, in the skin of four fatal scarlet fever cases, bodies not unlike, but much larger than, the well-known organism of malaria. Dr. Mallory, while expressing his personal belief that these bodies are protozoa, and that they are the cause of scarlet fever, made it clear that he did not assert the establishment of these beliefs by complete proof.

PNEUMONIA IN NEW YORK.—Dr. Thomas Darlington, the new Health Commissioner, acting with his recently appointed honorary advisers, Dr. Lederle, former Health Commissioner, and

Dr. Chandler, has begun a crusade of cleaning public buildings, schoolhouses and sidewalks, preventing spitting, and enforcing heating and ventilation of street cars, in order to check the outbreak of pneumonia, the deaths from which reached 899 in the last five weeks of 1903, as against 586 for the corresponding period of 1902. (14.)

INDIANA HEALTH OFFICERS' SCHOOL.—The Indiana Legislature of 1903 authorized the State Board of Health to require a certain sanitary training of the health officers, and the holding of a school for them. There are 516 such officers. Two schools annually are held—one for county and city health officers; one for town officers. Practical prevention of disease is considered. The first division of the school was held in June, 1903, the other in December. (2.)

A LEAGUE AGAINST MOSQUITOES.—Under the auspices of Governor Murphy, of New Jersey, a national association was organized in December, 1903, with delegates from several states and from the Department of Entomology at Washington, to formulate plans for the extermination of the mosquito. (3.)

PLAGUE PROPHYLAXIS IN INDIA ABANDONED.— It is reported that the opposition of the natives to all measures taken against the plague by isolation, segregation, and inoculation has at last led the English Government in India to give up attempts to reduce the mortality by these methods, since the Government found that it was undermining its own power amongst the ignorant and bigoted peoples, over 2,000,000 of whom have died of the disease within the last few years. Commerce also has suffered greatly. (3.)

It is not only in India that ignorance and bigotry sometimes reduce almost to despair those who attempt to combat infectious disease. With Ithaca, Butler and Philadelphia in mind, and recalling also the recent smallpox flurry throughout most of this country, we cannot yet hold ourselves wholly superior to our lesser brethren of the older race.

DUNBAR'S ANTITOXIC SERUM FOR HAY FEVER.—
A. W. MacCoy tested Dunbar's serum in fifteen cases, his observations relating to periodic attacks, and extending over July,
August and September, 1903, with admirable results. The
serum was applied with a pipette to the eyes and to the nasal
mucous membrane. (7.)

THE "HOLY GHOST AND US" SOCIETY was in strict
quarantine in Maine recently, on account of the number of smallpox cases in its membership. Their religious beliefs preclude
medical measures, and they disseminated the disease widely in
that region. (5.)

NEW ORLEANS PASTEUR INSTITUTE.—It is reported
that the Pasteur treatment for Rabies is to be established in a new
department of the Charity Hospital in New Orleans.

THE CLEANSING POWER OF SOAP.—H. W. Hillyer
(*Journal Am. Chem. Soc.*, XXV, p. 511) reviews at considerable
length the reasons heretofore advanced as to why soap cleanses.
He considers such theories as "the alkali set free by the hydro-
lysis of the soap acts on the fat to remove it by a process of saponi-
fication" and refutes this and other less common ideas by logic,
by experiment or by both, and finally concludes that the cleansing power is "largely or entirely to be explained by the power
which it has of emulsifying oily substances; of wetting and pene-
trating into oily textures; and of lubricating texture and impurities so that they may be removed easily. It is thought that all
of these properties may be explained by taking into account the
low cohesion of the soap solution and their strong attraction,
adhesion or affinity to oily matter, which together cause the
low surface-tension between soap solution and oil."

The same author suggests "A Method of Grading Soaps as to
their Detergent Power," (*Journal Am. Chem. Soc.*, XXV, p.
1206) based on his conclusions as given above.—*B. R. Rickards.*

(In the Nov. issue of the same journal F. G. Donnan says he
published methods and conclusions similar to these in 1899.)

THE VALUE OF TESTING CHEMICAL SUPPLIES.—
Every Board of Health should realize the importance of having

such substances as chloride of lime, formalin, peppermint, etc., tested chemically before buying in bulk. The value of such a procedure is very evident. If a dealer understands that the goods he sells are to be subjected to chemical analysis and are likely to be rejected if they do not prove to be pure and up to the proper standard in strength, he invariably ships the very best, leaving the poorer grades to be disposed of to those Boards that make no test.—*B. R. Rickards.*

References.

Journal American Medical Association.

1. Dec. 19, 1903.	8. Nov. 28, 1903.
3. Dec. 12, 1903.	13. Jan. 9, 1904.
5. Dec. 5, 1903.	14. Jan. 23, 1904.

American Medical.

2. Dec. 19, 1903.	12. Jan. 9, 1904.

Boston Medical and Surgical Journal.

    4. Dec. 17, 1903.
    6. Dec. 5, 1903.
   10. Nov. 26, 1903.

New York Medical Journal.

    7. Nov. 21, 1903.

British Lancet.

    9. Nov. 21, 1903.

American Journal Orth. Surgery.

   11. August, 1903.

SANITARY ENGINEERING NOTES.

ROBERT SPURR WESTON, M.A.

DIARRHŒA AND POLLUTED WATER.—While many epidemics of typhoid, such as the recent unpardonable case at Butler, have been caused directly by a polluted water-supply, a wide spread epidemic of diarrhœa due to this cause is extremely rare, if not unprecedented. J. C. Thresh describes an epidemic in Chelmsford, Eng., which began suddenly July 25, 1903, and ended as abruptly on August 25. During one month there were 1,400 cases among persons of all ages and classes and both sexes, of whom fourteen—thirteen of whom were young children—died. The town water, which was from an unimpeachable well, was stored in an open reservoir, so placed in the ground that it was subject to surface pollution, especially during and after heavy rains. On July 22, two days prior to the outbreak, a storm occurred, washing into the reservoir the manured surface of a nearby garden plot. No cases occurred outside of the region supplied by this water. Results indicate that more care should be taken in the design and care of open reservoirs. In this country covered reservoirs for ground water are always to be desired, on account of growths of algæ, which are almost sure to occur in open reservoirs.

EXTENSION OF THE LAWRENCE FILTER PLANT.—The plans for the new city filter have been completed, and it is said that work will probably be started this year.

PROPOSED SANITARY LEGISLATION IN NEW YORK STATE.— Senator Stuart of Ithaca, N. Y., has just presented a bill in the New York Legislature which provides for a State Sewerage and Water Commission of three members, to be appointed by the Governor for five years each, and each to receive a salary of $8,000 a year. One of the board would be a competent hydraulic engineer, and one a competent sanitary engineer and bacteriologist. The bill would appropriate $15,000 a year for permanent subordinates, and would allow something for the temporary employment of engineers, chemists, etc., provided the total annual expenditure did not exceed $75,000.

Among other things, the Commission would be required, like the Massachusetts State Board of Health, to pass upon all plans for water-supply and sewerage systems; it would have sanitary control of the water-supplies of the state, with semijudicial powers, and it would be required to investigate all typhoid fever epidemics, and after investigation, if necessary, compel any city or town to change its water-supply or sewerage system to suit the ideas of the Commission.

The *Engineering News*, in an editorial (Jan. 28, 1904), states that "the intimate relation between the usual work of the state boards of health and that of the proposed commission is strongly in favor of reorganizing the former and increasing its powers," rather than increasing the number of commissions. This opinion is borne out by the history of the defunct State Sewerage Commission of Connecticut, and "the returns now being secured in New Jersey for the $20,000 a year which is being paid as salaries to the members of two sewerage commissions."

Some of us believe that if the State Board of Health of New York were enlarged so as to consist of two physicians, one hydraulic engineer, one sanitary expert and one lawyer, all compensated for their actual services, and that if this augmented board were given some of the power which the Stewart Bill would give the new commission, and ample means to engage the best obtainable sanitary experts and health officers, it would take a rank worthy of New York, and consistent with the excellence of sanitary conditions which should be expected of such a prosperous state.

THE FOURTH REPORT OF THE ROYAL COMMISSION ON SEWAGE DISPOSAL.—This report treats of the question of shellfish contaminated by sewage. It is a progress report only, and the commissioners admit their inability to define the conditions of pollution and their own lack of power to remedy them. It is stated that the appearance of the contaminated shell fish does not differ from that of the healthy ones, nor is bacteriology at present of great service in these cases. It is proposed to establish what is called "A Sanitary Coast Guard Service," to gradually eliminate the sources of pollution by insisting upon proper sewage disposal methods.

PURIFICATION OF HIGHLY COLORED TROPICAL WATERS (Chadwick and Blount, Proc. Institute C. E., December, 1903).— This paper treats of the purification of waters from Mauritius, Uganda and the West Indies. These waters, so loaded with vegetable matter that they are unfit to drink, are changed by thorough aeration into drinking waters of excellent quality.

CHEMICAL PURIFICATION OF DRINKING WATER.—In Europe at the present time much attention is being given to the so-called chemical purification of water; that is, purification by means of ozone, chlorine, bromine, etc. It is undeniably true that water can be purified with these methods. The chief objection to them is that as yet they are ill adapted to large supplies. Their chief use at present has been for military purposes. The plant established at Wiesbaden for the purification of water by means of ozone has been abandoned (Arch. f. Hyg., Hyg. Rundschau, and Central b. f. Bakteriologie, Abt. I, Bd. XXXIV, No. 6). Some recent investigations show that some of the processes are much less efficient than was first supposed.

TYPHOID FEVER IN AMERICAN CITIES.—Reports of typhoid epidemics appear in the press with alarming frequency. Following the epidemics at Ithaca and Butler, comes the report that in Pittsburg between December 1st and 26th there were 496 cases of typhoid. In December, 1902, there were 108 cases. On January 4th of this year it was reported that there were about 100 cases at Kittaning (population 3,902 in 1900), a town located on the Allegheny River above Pittsburg. Philadelphia reported 131 cases for the week ending December 26th, and at present severe epidemics are in course at Columbus, O., and Leadville, Col. The bad social economy of allowing these preventable epidemics to exist should be realized by every municipality.

AIR IN HOUSE OF COMMONS (W. Atkinson Butterfield, *J. of Hygiene*, 3 (4), 1903, 486–497). The author made a number of analyses of the air in the Debating Chamber of the House of Commons during 1902-03. The following were the results obtained:

	Volumes Carbon Dioxide in 10,000 Volumes of Air.		
	Max.	Min.	Mean.
Air supplied to the Chamber,	3.74	3.14	3.37
Air at breathing level in the body of the Chamber,	5.23	3.35	4.59
Outgoing air from about 6 inches below the ceiling of the Chamber,	5.60	4.82	5.27

TYPHOID FEVER EPIDEMICS. — George A. Soper (Engineering News, Dec. 24, 1903, also Jan. 21, 1904), has compiled the leading typhoid epidemics, of which the following is a brief summary:

Date.	Place.	Populations.	Cases.	Deaths.
1879.	Caterham, Eng.,	5,800	352	21
1885.	Plymouth, Pa.,	8,000	1,104	114
1889–90.	Lowell Mass.,	77,696	858	65
1890–91.	Lowell, Mass.,		1,997	152
1889–90.	Lawrence, Mass.,	44,654	693	53
1890–91.	Lawrence, Mass.,		1,099	84
1893.	Worthing, Eng.,	16,606	1,411	168
1893–94.	Grand Forks, N. Dak.,	6,000	1,245	96
1897.	Maidstone, Eng.,	33,820	1,928	150
1903.	Ithaca, N. Y.,	13,000	1,300	78
1903.	Butler, Pa.,*	18,000	1,270*	56*

*To Dec. 17, 1903.

Officers and Men.

1862–63.	U. S. Army,	460,000	29,666	7,092
1898.	U. S. Army,	107,973	20,738	1,570
British Army, Bloemfontein, 2½ months,		230,000	60,000 (circ.)	8,000

While the most of the above are directly traceable to impure water, it is still to be noted in many cases, especially where typhoid fever has occurred in armies, that much of the disease was caused by secondary infection.

It should also be noted that if the typhoid excreta had been disinfected the degree of the epidemics would have been greatly reduced. Physicians cannot be urged too strongly to be sure that all typhoid excreta are disinfected; disinfection should be performed regardless of the sanitary engineering precautions which a state, city or town may have instituted. Typhoid is a contagious disease.

REDUCTION OF NITRATES BY SEWAGE AT BELFAST, IRELAND. — E. A. Letts, R. F. Blake and J. S. Totton. (Brit. Association

Advancement of Science, Southport, 1903.   *Journ. Soc. Chem. Industry*, 1903, p. 1206.)

The discharge of untreated sewage at Belfast causes enormous growths of green seaweed (Ulva latissima) which washes ashore and putrifies.   The growth is caused by the nitrogenous fertilizing constituents of the sewage.   Experiments with potassium nitrate and septic tank effluent, showed that the nitrate is decomposed, free nitrogen and sometimes nitric oxide being evolved.   The oxygen in the nitrate appears either wholly or partly as carbon dioxide.

The production of free nitrogen in contact beds is probably due to the fact that when the beds are in contact with air they become charged with nitrates and then when the sewage is introduced the latter are decomposed.   The decomposition of the nitrates is caused by certain micro-organisms and not by enzymic or chemical action, as sterilized effluents were found to have no effect on the nitrates.

Experiments with *B. coli communis* and *B. lactis ærogenes* which in pure broth cultures caused the production of hydrogen, showed that in nitrated broth *B. coli communis* liberates nitrogen from the nitrates.   It should be stated for comparison that when a water containing nitrate is seeded with algæ, growth occurs and nitrogen is evolved.

SANITARY SECTION OF THE BOSTON SOCIETY OF CIVIL ENGINEERS. —The first meeting and dinner of the Sanitary Section of the Boston Society of Civil Engineers was held at Hotel Nottingham, February 3.   The topic discussed by the meeting was the septic tank.   F. A. Barbour of Boston opened the discussion, and was followed by G. A. Carpenter of Pawtucket, George Bolling of Brockton, X. H. Goodnough and H. W. Clark from the State Board of Health, L. P. Kinnicutt and H. W. Eddy of Worcester, C. E. A. Winslow of the M. I. T., and F. H. Snow of Boston. The discussion was very able, and very broad in its scope.   (See *Engineering News*, Feb. 11, 1904.)

The new Sanitary Section has been formed under the auspices of the Boston Soc. C. E., for the purpose of bringing together those—not necessarily health officers or engineers—who are in any way interested in the design, construction or operation of sewage and garbage disposal plants, the cleaning of cities, and, in general, the employment of the sanitary acts other than, those strictly medical.

Meetings are to be held quarterly. The next meeting will discuss the general topic of the "Care of Sewers." All persons interested are asked to join this Section. The annual dues are five dollars. Application blanks may be procured from the Clerk, W. S. Johnson, Assistant Engineer, Massachusetts State Board of Health, State House, Boston.

JOURNAL OF THE
MASSACHUSETTS ASSOCIATION OF BOARDS OF HEALTH.

ORGANIZED 1890.

[The Association as a body is not responsible for statements or opinions of any of its members.]

| VOL. XIV. | May, 1904. | NO. 2. |

THE MASSACHUSETTS ASSOCIATION OF BOARDS OF HEALTH was organized in Boston, March, 1890, with the following objects: the advancement of sanitary science; the promotion of better organization and co-operation among local boards of health, and the uniform enforcement of sanitary laws and regulations.

THE JOURNAL OF THIS ASSOCIATION has for fourteen years faithfully reflected the views of the public hygienists of Massachusetts. As the only one of its kind in Massachusetts, the Journal has had its own field, which, however, it has not yet fully occupied. With the October issue of the year 1903, a policy of expansion was adopted. The subscription list showed an immediate and most gratifying increase, so that this, the fourth issue has a total circulation of over 1,200 copies.

In order that the Journal may appear within the next month after each quarterly meeting of the Association, the dates of publication will be FEBRUARY, MAY, AUGUST *and* NOVEMBER *of each year.*

THE JOURNAL will contain the papers read at the meetings of the Association, verbatim reports of the discussions, editorials, abstracts, reviews and hygienic notes of professional interest. Subscription rates, $1.00 per year. Reprints furnished at cost price.

All communications concerning the ASSOCIATION should be addressed to the Secretary of the Association, JAMES C. COFFEY, CITY HALL, WORCESTER, MASS.

All bills not relating to the Journal, and MEMBERSHIP DUES ($2.00 per year), should be sent to the Treasurer of the Association, DR. JAMES B. FIELD, 329 WESTFORD ST., LOWELL, MASS.

All communications concerning the JOURNAL, copy, proof, sub-scriptions, advertisements, etc., should be addressed to the Managing Editor, DR. H. W. HILL, 607 SUDBURY BLDG., BOSTON, MASS.

EDITORIALS.

THE UNITED STATES SOCIETY FOR THE STUDY OF TUBERCULOSIS.

The appointment of a committee, composed of Drs. Trudeau, Biggs, Welch, Sternberg, Flick, Osler, and Jacobs, to draw up a Constitution and By-Laws for the new "United States Society for the Study of Tuberculosis," by a meeting of those interested in the tuberculosis problem, held in Philadelphia on March 28th, is the final outcome of a struggle which has been going on for over a year between the various interests in that field of endeavor.

At the meeting of the American Congress Tuberculosis held in New York city in the spring of 1902, the President of the Congress, Dr. Henry Holton, and some of his prominent associates, became deeply impressed with the fact that the interests of the crusade against tuberculosis would best be served by an entire reorganization of the Congress. This they attempted to bring about by the election of an entirely new list of officers, which was accomplished in a perfectly proper and legal manner. Dr. Daniel Lewis, Health Commissioner, was induced to accept the presidency of the Congress and Dr. George Brown of Atlanta, Ga., was chosen Secretary. After the adjournment of the Congress the former Secretary, Mr. Clark Bell, refused to be governed by the action of the Congress in electing new officers, declining to recognize their appointment, and soon after claiming that the real officers were elected after the adjournment by a so-called "Executive Committee," the formation of which and the authority for which is shrouded in mystery.

The officers regularly elected by the Congress applied for and received articles of incorporation as officers of the American

Congress on Tuberculosis, and became thereby the only organization entitled to the use of that name. Notwithstanding this, however, the mysteriously created "Executive Committee" and its appointees continued to use that name, and in addition settled upon St. Louis in the summer of 1904 as the time of their meeting, which was the place, and practically the time decided upon by the regular officers of the incorporated Congress for the holding of its meeting.

Not wishing to enter into an open conflict with the organization so mysteriously created, the officers of the incorporated Congress decided at a meeting held on May 7th, 1903, to eliminate one element of confusion by postponing the time and changing the place of meeting to April, 1905, and Washington, D. C. They were also influenced in making this decision by the fact that the International Congress on Tuberculosis was planning to meet in Paris in 1904, and they did not desire their meeting to conflict with it. At the same meeting the officers appointed a committee of some of the leading scientific workers in the profession to direct the more scientific work of the Congress, and they further decided to invite all the medical organizations whose members were eligible for membership in the American Medical Association to send delegates to the Congress.

At the Washington meeting of the American Public Health Association in October of last year, members of the staff of the Henry Phipps Institute endeavored to enlist support for the organization of a new national tuberculosis society for the express purpose of inviting the International Congress on Tuberculosis to hold a meeting in this country in 1905, it being stated that acceptance of the invitation was already assured. The supporters of this movement were entirely opposed to union or affiliation with any existing American anti-tuberculosis organization. Much to their surprise it was soon announced that the Paris meeting of the International Congress had been postponed until 1905 on the plea of not desiring to conflict with the meeting of the so-called "Clark Bell Congress" in St. Louis.

To the difficult task of endeavoring to bring order out of this chaos, a physician, Dr. Knopf, whose name has for several years been a prominent one in anti-tuberculosis literature, directed his efforts by sending an open letter to some of the weekly medical journals in which he outlined the situation, and commented freely on what he considered to be the deficiencies in the lists of prominent supporters of some of the existing organizations. He also issued a call for "all interested" to meet in Baltimore on January 29th. While "all interested" may not have been present, there were indications that, had circumstances permitted, several distinct national organizations would have been projected before the end of the meeting.

The most decided effort to produce harmony was the submission of an offer of the American Congress on Tuberculosis through its President, Dr. Daniel Lewis, to permit a committee, of some of the persons present at this meeting, to assume charge of the affairs of their organization and do with it what seemed best for the general interests involved. Towards this end Dr. Lewis stated that the Congress had changed its corporate name to American Anti-Tuberculosis League at the suggestion of one of the prominent supporters of the Phipps Institute plan.

From the tone of the discussion it became apparent to all that nothing could be settled at that meeting, and under the masterful direction of Dr. Welch the meeting finally voted to submit the whole question to a Committee to be appointed by the Chairman, and to be bound by its decision.

The members of this Committee, which included Drs. Biggs, Osler, Trudeau, Theobald Smith, Bowditch, Knopf, Jacobs, Bracken, Flick, and Ravenel, met subsequently in New York, and after some discussion it was generally understood that a large majority of the Committee were favorable to the plan of accepting the offer of the President of the Anti-Tuberculosis League made at the Baltimore meeting. It was considered wise, however, before settling the matter definitely, to enlarge the membership of the Committee, and to hold another meeting.

Advantage of this change was taken by those supporting the

Phipps Institute movement, who had from the first vigorously opposed affiliation with any existing organization, by inviting the Committee to hold their next meeting in Philadelphia on the date previously set for the presentation of a paper by Dr. Maragliano before the Phipps Institute.

The enlargement of the Committee naturally increased the Philadelphia representation upon it, and the holding of the meeting in that city insured the entire attendance of that representation while lessening the attendance from distant points, so that by actual count fifty per cent. of the persons present resided in Philadelphia or vicinity. With the assistance of a few ardent supporters from outside of their district, the Philadelphians were manifestly in control of the meeting, and it was seen beforehand that it would be useless to attempt to follow the plan of recommending affiliation with the Anti-Tuberculosis League, which had been deemed the wisest course by a majority of the Committee as originally constituted.

The struggle attending the birth of the Society, and the experience and results obtained from the Tuberculosis Exhibition and series of lectures held in Baltimore, have shown conclusively the need of an organization which will bring to the immediate attention of the profession as a whole and to the general public the essential truths concerning the nature, dissemination, prevention and treatment of the great plague.

That the United States Society for the Study of Tuberculosis will be a well conducted, thoroughly scientific and valuable organization no one questions for an instant. We hope that it will not confine itself to the scientific and more detailed clinical study of the tuberculosis problem, but will, as well, conduct a campaign of education for the benefit of the mass of the medical profession and the public, which was the aim and object of the American Anti-Tuberculosis League.

UNIFORM STANDARDS IN PUBLIC HEALTH ADMINISTRATION.

An excellent editorial on this subject in the *Journal of the American Medical Association* calls attention to the very vary-

ing practice in the large cities regarding the reporting of infectious diseases, the placarding of houses, and the extent of isolation required. The editorial urges that some understanding
should be reached resulting in uniformity of procedure, and
recommends that the American Medical Association should take
up the consideration of the subject.

The ASSOCIATION which this JOURNAL represents was
founded to promote uniformity of precedure amongst the local
Boards of Health of this State, and it is therefore fully in sympathy with the general principles advocated by our contem-
porary. Of five or six different procedures only one can be the
best. To find this best and to adopt it should be the aim of all
interested in hygienic administration. The recommendation that
this subject should be taken up by the American Medical Association involves, however, an unintentional but none the less
poignant reflection, perhaps not altogether undeserved, on the
hygienic associations of this country. It is reform from within,
and not under compulsion from without, that is the best and
most sincere, as well as the most creditable and encouraging.
In hygienic matters the reforms should be initiated and carried
out by the hygienists themselves. The American Public Health
Association, the Conference of State Boards of Health and the
local State hygienic societies constitute bodies not only the best
informed on these subjects but the most likely to have weight
with the public hygienists generally. The American Medical
Association, representing the medical profession as a whole, is
entitled to, and does, carry great weight, but the hygienic associations represent specialists in hygiene who have evolved, many
of them from the medical profession, and it is no more proper
that the American Medical Association should recommend procedures to the public hygienists than that the American Medical
Association should recommend procedures to their own ophthal-
mological section or to their section of pathology and bacteriology.

The fact that official public hygienists have been slow in securing national or even State uniformity in many details furnishes,

perhaps, some excuse for an appeal elsewhere. The fact that such an appeal has been made should be a sufficient spur to us in this at present rather neglected line.

MEDICAL INSPECTION OF SCHOOLS.

American Medicine, Feb. 27, '04, contains this item in the column on "Foreign News and Notes":

"MEDICAL SCHOOL INSPECTION ABROAD.—An exchange says: The foreign custom, universal in France and Germany, of insisting upon each child entering school, and at regular intervals thereafter submitting to a medical examination, is an example worthy of emulation in vaunted up-to-date communities. The question of vaccination and the control of contagious epidemic are the only occasions when medical intervention is usual in the schools in this country. Abroad it is customary to appoint school physicians, whose duty it is to examine twice a year all the pupils with reference to the senses, the spinal column, the development of the limbs, and to make recommendations for their special instruction on account of stuttering, etc. Not their least important work is the quarterly or in some cities semi-monthly sanitary inspection of school rooms and buildings. It is one of the duties of teachers to call the attention of the school physician to any pupils whose state of health during the interval since the previous visit creates suspicion. The physician can, however, in case of sick pupils, only notify the parents formally of the child's condition, their treatment being left entirely in the hands of the family physician. It is proposed by the French medical fraternity to have the school physician's duties extended to an inspection of the condition of the dwellings of sick school children, and also to give advice concerning the architecture of schools and the division of school hours."

The medical inspections thus vaunted are at most semi-monthly. It is interesting to compare this item, written recently, with the following paragraphs from a paper by Dr. E. M. Greene, Philadelphia Medical Journal, Feb. 16, 1901.

"The first city in this country, or abroad, to establish a system of daily medical inspection in all the public schools was Boston. Since then similar methods of inspection have been adopted in New York City, Chicago, and in most of the large cities, as well as in many of the smaller towns. Within a few years we may expect to see some method of medical inspection in general used throughout the country. The important questions are how comprehensive and searching an inspection is desirable, or practicable, and how to organize and conduct the work in the most efficient manner.

Medical inspection of schools, both public and parochial, was begun in Boston in the fall of 1894, and was secured only as the result of 4 years of persistent effort on the part of the efficient and progressive chairman of the Boston Board of Health, Dr. Samuel H. Durgin. The immediate occasion which made his appeals successful was the unusual prevalence of diphtheria in Boston during the year 1894.

The system of inspection is under the control of the Board of Health. The School Committee co-operates cordially in the work, by giving permission for inspectors to enter the school buildings and examine pupils, and by directing teachers to watch for cases of illness and to bring them to the notice of the inspectors."

TYPHOID FEVER EPIDEMIC AT COLUMBUS, O.

Mr. R. Winthrop Pratt, Engineer of the Ohio State Board of Health, has very kindly furnished us with the following notes of the recent epidemic in Columbus:

In the early part of the present year there occurred at Columbus a typhoid fever epidemic of considerable proportions. Out of the city's population of about 140,000, there were 1606 cases and 162 deaths during the months of January, February and March. The typhoid fever death rate previous to this time had never been as great as that of many other cities. This fact led many of the citizens, including several physicians, to believe that the water supply was quite safe, although sources of pollution were known to exist.

WATER SUPPLY.—Columbus is supplied with water from the following sources: 1st. The Scioto River; 2nd. Filter Gallery on the bank of the Scioto River. 3rd. Alum Creek, and 4th, wells driven along the bank of Alum Creek.

At the "West Side Pumping Station" water is pumped from the first two sources and supplied to the central or business part of the city as well as to the western and northern portions. About 11,000,000 gallons per day are supplied by this pumping station and the proportion drawn from the river direct depends upon the quantity available from the filter gallery. The latter is used when possible but is never able to furnish enough water for any considerable time so that the raw river water is almost always being pumped into the mains in greater or less amount.

Just previous to the epidemic 3,000,000 to 4,000,000 gallons per day, out of the 11,000,000 pumped at the West Side Station, was raw river water.

At the "East Side Pumping Station" water from Alum Creek or from driven wells near by, depending upon the quantity available from the latter, is supplied to the eastern portion of the city. The quantity from this source is perhaps 75 per cent. of that furnished by the West Side Station.

The approximate dividing line between the districts supplied by the East Side and the West Side pumping stations is shown on the map.

DISTRIBUTION OF CASES. Almost without exception the typhoid fever cases occurred among the residents of the district supplied with Scioto River water or among the business men, who, though residing outside of this district, were supplied with Scioto River water at their offices. This fact proved that the water supply was the cause of the trouble and also showed that the Scioto River rather than Alum Creek was infected.

SOURCES OF POLLUTION OF THE SCIOTO RIVER. The watershed of the Scioto River above Columbus covers an area of 1070 square miles and consists principally of farm land, although several communities, acting as serious sources of pollution to the river water, are located upon it.

Within 65 miles of Columbus, 27 towns and four institutions exist upon the river or its tributaries, representing a population of about 43,000, while the sewers of six of the towns and three of the institutions discharge directly into the river or its tributaries, representing a population of about 30,000.

CAUSE. Although there are many places which might have infected the river water with typhoid bacilli, investigation has shown that by far the most probable cause of the epidemic was the State Hospital for Insane, one of the institutions mentioned, located within the city limits of Columbus.

The sewerage system at this hospital is rather unusual. The domestic sewage from the institution, which is occupied by some

1600 people, is collected in an 8-inch or 10-inch cast iron sewer laid within a 36-inch storm water sewer. A short distance away from the institution buildings the sanitary sewer leaves the storm sewer and connects with the city's sewerage system; but the storm sewer discharges into Dry Run, which is a small intermittent stream entering the Scioto River about a mile above the water works intake.

Shortly after the epidemic broke out an inspection showed that connections between the sanitary sewer and laterals, coming from various parts of the institution, were made in at least two cases by simply discharging the laterals into the big storm sewer and constructing a bulkhead immediately below the point of discharge, through which bulkhead the open end of the main sanitary sewer projected. Under these conditions, with every storm, the water collected by the storm sewer carried the accumulated filth from behind these bulkheads into Dry Run and thence to the river. Moreover one of the bulkheads was found to be broken, permitting some of the sewage to flow continuously into Dry Run. It was necessary to take twenty-two and a half tons of putrefying sludge out of the storm water sewer in order to clean it.

Twelve cases of typhoid fever had occurred at the institution one year previous to the epidemic, since which time there were no reported cases until January 3rd, 1904. The case reported on this date was soon followed by seven more, two of which died.

Typhoid fever had occurred to a greater or less extent at Kenton, the Girls Industrial Home, near Delaware, and at Arlington, all having sewers discharging into the river or its tributaries, and possibly at the Stone Quarries, a small settlement of unsanitary character 3 miles above the intake of the Columbus water works.

There is no doubt that the Insane Hospital discharged the greatest amount of sewage into the river with the exception of the cities of Kenton and Marion. Therefore, considering this as well as the proximity of the institution to the water works intake (one and one-half miles following Dry Run and the river), the extremely low stage of the river at this time, and the fact that there was typhoid fever at the institution at least ten days previous to the beginning of the rapid increase in the cases in Columbus, it seems fair to conclude that the principal factor in causing the epidemic, if not the sole cause, was the State Hospital.

MONTHLY RECORD OF CASES.

Month.	Cases Reported.	Deaths.	Annual Death Rate per 100,000
December, 1903	40	4	34
January, 1904	725	35	300
February, "	798	94	805
March, "	83	33	283

In April the reported number of cases and deaths were both much decreased.

DAILY RECORD OF CASES.

	Jan.	Feb.	Mar.		Jan.	Feb.	Mar.
1	1	138	9	17	2	19	2
2	0	52	4	18	24	25	2
3	0	29	1	19	48	22	1
4	1	28	4	20	24	27	0
5	8	26	5	21	44	4	4
6	3	48	3	22	35	21	0
7	3	16	7	23	41	8	0
8	7	74	2	24	16	15	0
9	4	34	1	25	43	19	2
10	1	26	3	26	25	14	4
11	5	19	5	27	48	5	0
12	9	15	2	28	35	2	2
13	26	36	1	29	47	4	2
14	34	12	2	30	81	.	2
15	43	36	2	31	23	.	.1
16	47	13	4				

APRIL QUARTERLY MEETING

OF THE

Massachusetts Association of Boards of Health.

The quarterly meeting of the Association was held at the Brunswick Hotel, Boylston Street, Thursday, April 28th, 1904, the luncheon beginning at 1 P. M. Dr. H. P. Walcott presided.

THE CHAIRMAN: The Association will come to order. We will listen to the records of the last meeting.

(Records read by the Secretary, Mr. James B. Coffey.)

THE CHAIRMAN: Is there any change to be made in the record as read? If not, it will stand as the record of the last meeting of this Association. The Executive Committee, in accordance with your by-laws, report to the Association, with the recommendation that they be elected, the names of the following gentlemen:

George B. Robbins, Boston.
John A. Morgan, M. D., Hyde Park.
Stephen DeM. Gage, Lawrence.
William C. Doherty, Lowell.
Leonard Huntress, M. D., Lowell.
Joseph S. Hart, M. D., Lincoln.
Martin T. Field, Salem.
Caleb A. Page, Somerville.
Wesley R. Lee, M. D., Somerville.
Edward B. Hodskins, M. D., Springfield.
D. P. Cilley, M. D., Westboro.

THE CHAIRMAN: It is moved that these gentlemen be elected members of this Association. If that be your pleasure, you will signify it by saying aye.

THE CHAIRMAN: These gentlemen are duly elected members of the Association. Is there any incidental business to come before the Association at this time? If not, we will proceed to the regular programme of the afternoon. The first item is a paper on "Sanitary Dangers of Certain Occupations," by C. E. A. Winslow. I have the pleasure of presenting to the Association Mr. Winslow.

THE SANITARY DANGERS OF CERTAIN OCCUPATIONS.

BY C. E. A. WINSLOW, M. SC.

Mass. Inst. of Technology.

Sanitary authorities exist to protect the citizen against dangers which in his individual capacity he is unable to avoid. First, water supply, milk supply and food supply, must be safeguarded, since the life of every citizen depends upon these necessities. Second, the insidious spread of contagious diseases must be checked, since unrecognized cases of diphtheria or of small-pox menace the safety of all with whom they may come in contact. These two vehicles of disease, infected food and infected persons, threaten every individual in the community and rightly challenge the most ardent efforts of the sanitary engineer and the public hygienist. Of the less general dangers which affect only certain classes of individuals none can, I think, be more important than those connected with trades and occupations. The force of economic necessity too often makes it impossible for the factory operative to escape from the unsanitary conditions which surround him. He is helpless unless the State, or that matured public opinion of which the State is the expression, shall come to his aid. Therefore he has a special claim upon the consideration of such an association as our own.

Thanks to the admirable statistics collected by the Registrar-General of Great Britain, we have a pretty precise idea of the extent to which health may be affected by various trades and occupations. Dr. Tatham's figures, for example, show that the general death rate of Plumbers, Painters and Glaziers, and of Cotton and Linen manufacturers, is nearly twice, that of Potters, Earthenware manufacturers and File-makers is more than three times, that which obtains in the professional and agricultural classes. Unfortunately American vital statistics, both State and National, are so inaccurate and so incomplete that comparable data for this country are wanting. Such figures as we possess indicate the same startling discrepancies; and Dr. C. F. W. Doehring in the Bulletin of the U. S. Department of Labor for January, 1903, cites statistics for our own State according to which the average life of factory workers in Massachusetts is only 36.3 years against 65.3 for farmers.

The cause of excessive mortality varies widely in different occupations. Most prominent perhaps are those trades liable to accidents in the operation of machinery. English regulations class under four heads the mechanisms which prove most often dangerous, (a) Prime movers, (b) Mill-gearing and belts, (c) Machines for manufacturing purposes, (d) Hoists and other lifting tackle. Mules, looms, circular saws, planing machines and power presses all add their quota of victims. The manufacture of explosives should be placed under this head, with certain electrical processes in which the liberation of charges of high voltage may be the result of careless handling.

Of far greater importance, although less dramatically impressed upon the public mind, are the harmful effects of those occupations in which the worker is subjected to the breathing of excessive quantities of dust. The increase of tuberculosis and other pulmonary disorders due to this cause is unquestionably the gravest feature in the hygiene of occupations. Dust in various trades differs widely in character, but from the fine metallic particles produced in needle-making to the fragments of stone inhaled by quarrymen and the fine fibrous material which fills the air of a carding-room, all in varying degrees produce their bad effects. Dr. Doehring in the paper above cited gives a list of 38 injurious varieties of dust, and in Dr. Thomas Oliver's classic work on "Dangerous Trades," it is shown that in 19 different dusty industries the death rate from tuberculosis and other diseases of the respiratory system is more than twice that of the agricultural class. The rate among agriculturists being taken as 100, that of Potters and Earthenware manufacture is 453, that of Cutlers 407, that of File-makers 373, that of Glass-makers 335, etc. Less serious but yet appreciable is the danger from metallic dust to Miners, Iron and Steel workers, Gun-smiths and Needle-grinders—from stone dust to Masons, Stone-cutters and Cement-makers—from fibrous dust to Shoddy-makers, Rope-makers, Rag-pickers, Cotton and Woolen mill operatives, Carpet-makers, Flax and Hemp carders, and opera-tives in horsehair factories—from wood dust to Coopers and Carpenters—from flour dust to Millers, Bakers and Confec-tioners.

Next to dust, excessive temperature and moisture probably contribute most to make certain industries unhealthful. The effect of such conditions upon the general resistance of the or-ganism and particularly upon the vaso-motor system of heat regulation is well understood; and Laundry workers, Glass-blowers, Iron and Steel workers and the operatives in wet spin-ning rooms pay a heavy tribute of deaths from tuberculosis and other pulmonary disorders in which these form a predisposing cause.

Another important series of industrial disorders are the intox-ications due to the introduction into the system of certain metal-lic poisons. Plumbism is the familiar example of this class. If deaths from lead poisoning among all occupied males be taken as one, the comparative mortality in England is, among Lead workers, 211; among File-makers, 75; among Plumbers, 21; among Painters and Glaziers, 18; among Potters, 17; among Glass-makers, 12, while Copper-workers, Coach-makers, Gasfitters, Locksmiths, Calico printers, Enamellers, Solderers, Type founders and others suffer to a lesser degree. Mercury poisoning occurs among the makers of thermometers and other physical instruments, the makers of incandescent electric light bulbs and other electrical supplies, and in certain more restricted industries. Cases of arsenical poisoning, though becoming year-ly more and more rare, are not entirely abolished. Copper and zinc poisoning are not unknown; and chromium sometimes affects workmen in bichromate works and those who use dyes containing this metal.

Still another group of diseases are caused by the fumes of various non-metallic chemical substances. Carbon bisulphide as used in certain processes for treating india rubber and gutta-percha produces severe hysteria and exhaustion. Strong acids and alkalies sometimes overcome the workmen engaged in their manufacture. Benzine, as used in cleansing, and certain other commercial spirits, more rarely cause toxic effects. Here, too, we may mention the manufacture of fertilizer, rendering, bone-boiling, tanning and other industries accompanied by the production of noxious odors of decomposition which slowly undermine the general vitality.

Finally, as a last class of occupation diseases, there are certain bacterial maladies which under unusual conditions may be transmitted by trade materials. Cases of typhoid infection among laundry workers are so common as to warrant their inclusion under this head. Anthrax affecting wool-sorters and the handlers of hides is a typical case in point; and those vocations which bring men much in contact with the lower animals lead, though rarely, to infection with glanders, foot-and-mouth disease and other disorders.

In looking over this list of the dangers to operatives from accident, from dust, from heat and humidity, from metallic poisons, from noxious fumes and from infectious diseases, it seems obvious that most of them are preventable and thus legitimately within the field of sanitary science. The fencing of machinery, with proper regulations as to its operation—the removal of dust by special ventilation and the substitution of processes in which no excessive amount of it is formed—the regulation of humidity and temperature, the government of lead and other chemical factories by such rules as shall prevent the ingestion of poisonous substances, are all practical preventive measures. The problems, however, are various and complex, and each industry requires detailed study and specific treatment. So in England, the country which first took the lead in factory legislation, we find a maze of statutes under the general heading of Mines and Factory Acts, which have gradually grown up year by year to meet the exigencies of individual cases. Beginning in 1802 with an act for preserving the "health and morals" of apprentices in cotton mills, various statutes provided for general sanitary conditions, and in 1883 a bill for the government of white lead works recognized the principle of special regulations for particular trades, a principle extended by the Act of 1891, so that such rules can be drawn up by the Factory Inspectorate for any industry certified as dangerous by the Secretary of State. A similar development has taken place in Germany, where factories must receive authorization dependent on compliance with elaborate rules as to general ventilation, removal of dust and fumes, temperature, lighting, proper rooms for meals, lavatories. and cloak rooms, water-supply, protection from accidents, and exclusion of women and children from dangerous and exhausting processes. The special trades for which regulations have been drawn up in England and Germany are shown in the appended table, taken from Oliver.

INDUSTRIES FOR WHICH SPECIAL RULES HAVE BEEN ENACTED.

ENGLAND.

1 Bichromate works
2 Bottling of aerated water
3 Brass and alloy mixing and casting
4 Bricks, glazing of, by lead
5 Chemical works
6 Earthenware and china
7 Enameling of iron plates
8 Electric accumulator works
9 Explosive works in which dinitro-benzole is used
10 Flax spinning and weaving
11 Lead (red and orange) works
12 Lead (white) works
13 Lead (yellow) works
14 Lead smelting works
15 Lead, yellow chromate of
16 Lucifer match factories
17 Paint and color works, and extraction of arsenic
18 Skins and hides, sorting
19 Tinning and enameling of metal ware
20 Tinning and enameling of iron hollow ware
21 Transfers (lithographic) for decoration of china, etc.
22 Vulcanizing of india rubber
23 Wool sorting
24 Wool combing

GERMANY.

1 Basic slag works
2 Bichromate works
3 Brick works
4 Brushmaking works and horsehair spinning
5 Cigar factories
6 Chicory works
7 Electric accumulator works
8 Glassworks
9 Hackling and preparing rooms in textile factories
10 Lead, color and acetate of lead works
11 Letterpress printing works
12 Lucifer match works
13 Sugar refineries
14 Vulcanizing of india rubber
15 Wire-drawing mills

Less elaborate systems of factory legislation are in force in France, Austria, Belgium, Holland, Sweden, Switzerland and other European countries. It is, however, significant to note that the two nations which have advanced farthest along this path are the two leading commercial powers of the Old World, and that one of them at least owes its ever increasing pre-eminence to the general application of the broad scientific principles of economy of force upon which such legislation is founded.

Turning to the United States we find the regulation of dangerous trades in a primitive and undeveloped state. We lack even statistical information as to the extent of occupation diseases; we wholly lack scientific study of existing factory conditions. In our State of Massachusetts there is indeed a Department of Inspection of Factories and Public Buildings under the Chief of the District Police, but the officials of this department, however able and efficient, cannot properly solve such complex problems as those of factory sanitation without special expert assistance. Chapters 104 and 106 of the Revised Laws, under which for the most part they work, contain several admirable general principles. It is provided, for example, in Section 51, Chapter 106, that "a factory in which five or more persons are employed shall, while work is carried on, be so ventilated that the air shall not become so impure as to be injurious to the health of the persons employed therein, and so that all gases, vapors, dust or other impurities injurious to health, which are generated in the course of the manufacturing process or handicraft carried on therein shall, so far as practicable, be rendered harmless." This is good so far as it goes. It does not apply, however, to small factories or to workshops where men only are employed. It gives no power to deal with such special evils as lead or arsenic poisoning. Even with respect to ventilation general provisions are useless unless applied in the form of such detailed and specific regulations as can be drawn up only by expert sanitary authorities.

The backwardness of factory legislation in this country is no doubt in part due to the fact that we have never had the gross evils which elsewhere become so patent as to demand drastic measures for their redress. Evils exist, however, and though less obvious than those which caused Sir John Simon to speak of "the canker of industrial disease" gnawing at the root of England's national strength, it is high time that we gave them some attention. From the figures in the Census of 1900 I find that there were 127,000 persons in Massachusetts engaged in trades shown by investigation in other countries to be more or less prejudicial to health, including 38,642 foundry and machine shop workers, 26,211 house and sign painters, 17,696 brick and stone masons, and 8112 plumbers and gas and steam fitters. In the more intensely dangerous trades we find 2395 cutlers, 289 emery wheel workers, 89 file makers, 264 grinders of kaolin and other earths, 270 operatives in needle and pin factories, 758 persons engaged in the making of pottery, terra cotta and fire-clay products, and 449 workers in shoddy mills. Judging from analogy it seems probable that the unregulated conduct of these industries and certain others is causing a constant drain upon the health of the community; and in spite of the absence of good vital statistics or scientific factory inspection specific instances every now and then attract our notice. The spread of the disease, Anthrax, in Lynn from a morocco worker who had handled infected hides, was noted in the newspapers only a few weeks ago. The death rate from consumption in Massachusetts according to the United States Census of 1900 was 2.5 among all males, 3.7 among marble and stone cutters and 4.1 among masons; and Dr. T. J. Dion of the Quincy Board of Health writes me that the excessive prevalence of tuberculosis among the stone cutters in that city is a well known fact. In Chester is a factory of which Dr. C. J. Shepardson, a leading local physician, says, "We have a mill in town where quartz or silex is reduced to sandpaper, etc., which has been responsible for a great many deaths. Not much work is done there, however, and I think the force of employees is kept so low that the law as it now exists is not applicable to the place."

At East Douglas is an axe factory, in relation to which Dr.

Titus P. Holbrook allows me to quote the following statement: "I have been in practice in East Douglas since 1863 with the exception of some thirteen years following 1872. I have seen quite a number of cases of so-called grinders' consumption. I have examined one case post mortem. I found the smaller bronchial tubes thoroughly filled with the grindstone grit; the lung in the lower part looked like and felt like the liver after cooking. The symptoms are excessive dyspnœa on slight exertion, dry cough and great prostration. The grinders are from the Polanders and Finns for the past dozen years. The disease takes hold of them more frequently, and is more rapidly fatal than among the grinders of former years and of other nationalities. When I came here 40 years ago I found the victims among the Yankees who had ground some 20 years before. Those would grind 18 or 20 years before having to give up work. The French Canadians were then grinding. They could work 12 to 16 years. They became frightened off, and the Swedes took up the work. They would get the disease in 8 or 10 years. Now the Finns and Polanders are at it, and they last only 3 to 5 years, and the disease is more common among them."

It is not surprising to find on an examination of Massachusetts Registration Reports that while the death rate from consumption for the period 1881-99 was 2.5 for the whole State, it was 3.4 for the town of Douglas.

Nearer home I visited within a month a twine mill not five miles from where we are gathered at this moment. I wish I could take you through that factory and show you the dry spinning room with its clear normal air, the carding room filled with clouds of fine choking dust and the wet spinning room with the hot damp deadly atmosphere of a tropical forest. In the first department you would see average healthy factory workers alert and cheerful; in the last two, the women and children, some of them palpably under age, with dull eyes and feverish cheeks, stand or sit listlessly by their machines, stolidly going through the mechanical routine which brings them daily nearer to the inevitable end. The factory inspector had made his visit a few days before mine; but being neither a medical man familiar with the symptoms of tuberculosis, nor a sanitary engineer, versed in the laws of ventilation, he found no fault except to suggest that the few insufficient ventilating fans which had been installed should be put in operation. When I went through the factory some of them were running and some were not; and as the superintendent told me of the admirable quality of twine he was turning out I could not but feel that the cost as paid in human lives was far too high.

These are isolated cases only. Granted. Yet I believe that in the discussion this afternoon the members of this Association may add many more from their own experience. We have already enough in my judgment to warrant us at least in looking further. We need exact knowledge of conditions here in Massachusetts. We want the State census of 1905 so planned as to furnish statistics of occupation mortality which shall be full and accurate. We want the Legislature to appropriate money for a special investigation of the risks and dangers of factory life by the State Board of Health, which, having solved the fundamental problems of water supply and sewage disposal, should be our pioneer in these new fields. With the facts once in hand, the members of this Association will not be slow to apply the needful remedies. It is the pride of sanitary science that it is founded on the unchanging rock of Nature's laws. Yet we study the world as it is only to make it better; and I believe that the informing motive of our profession, whether we are conscious of it or not, is a deep-rooted enthusiasm for the progress of that humanity which in such diverse individuals is so mysteriously one. These twin impulses, the love of truth and the love of man, are together irresistible, both should impel us to remove the cruel conditions which make it necessary for even one individual to barter the health of tomorrow for the livelihood of today.

THE CHAIRMAN: Mr. Winslow's very interesting paper is before you for discussion. I hope it may give rise to questions and to additional information.

DR. BECKWITH: I would like to ask if the reader of the paper or any one else knows whether people working in celluloid factories have their health impaired. I have seen two or three cases in which there has been a great loss of strength and weight, and also some impairment of the kidney function. In fact, I have found two or three cases where there was a good deal of albumen in the urine, and it has seemed to me as though there was something in the process of making celluloid that perhaps caused this.

THE CHAIRMAN: Have you come across that, Mr. Winslow?

MR. WINSLOW: I have not.

THE CHAIRMAN: Dr. Abbott, I think you might say something to the point.

DR. ABBOTT: The reader of the paper has covered the ground so fully that I have but little to add to what he has said, except to amplify one or two points. I will answer the last speaker, in regard to celluloid, that I visited a celluloid factory in the village of Zylonite, part of the town of Adams, some years ago—I think it is not in existence now—and went through the whole factory, noting the different processes. It seemed to me that the principal danger there, aside from the tremendous danger of fire, was that of breathing the spirits of camphor. I understood the superintendent of the factory to say that occasional cases of headache and some irritation of the throat were about all that really were to be feared. The fact is, as the reader said, we do very little about this subject in this country in consequence of the want of information upon the subject. Any sanitary body has to have, of course, information first, and then it can go ahead with prevention afterwards. The information is almost all foreign. The laws in Massachusetts put this whole work in charge of the district police, but the district police—perhaps through want of funds—have not, as they have in other countries, any efficient and intelligent medical authority under their control to supervise the work; so that the laws which have been framed at their instance have been mostly laws in regard to ventilation, plumbing, etc., which, of course, are important, but there is not much of anything upon other points. The general term "sanitary" appears in those laws, but that term needs to be more specifically defined, in order to amount to anything. The occupations which the reader has spoken of as most dangerous to health are those which have to do with the metallic poisons, lead, arsenic and corrosive sublimate, also the poison of phosphorus which is involved in the trade of match making, and the dust producing occupations. Then another occupation which is a source of danger is that of persons who are exposed to alcoholic excess—that is, bartenders and saloon-keepers. Every life insurance man knows very well that a bartender or saloon-keeper will not be taken as a risk except under restricted limitations.

Some years ago I visited a paper mill in Maine, where I was surprised to see that the people were far better protected than in any mill I have ever seen in this State. That was Mr. Warren's mill, the Cumberland Mill.

THE CHAIRMAN: He was a Massachusetts man.

DR. ABBOTT: Yes, sir. The fact is, in the paper mills there are two classes of people, one class which is exposed to danger and one class which is not. The first class comprises persons who take the rags and dust them. The dusting men, perhaps, first of all, and then the women who sort the rags in the mill, are constantly exposed to danger from dust. Also, as Dr. Withington found in an inquiry made for our board some fifteen years ago, there is the exposure to small-pox, which is not so great as it used to be since greater precautions are taken in paper mills with reference to the vaccination of employees.

In the sorting room of Mr. Warren's mill where the women sort the rags, every person has in front of her a machine, or a part of a ventilating apparatus, which is connected with a general shaft running through the room by which all the dust is taken away from the mouths and faces of the operators and deposited in a shaft outside the building. The other class in the paper mills that handle the finished paper after it has been through the various processes are not exposed to any danger whatever. The clean paper has been thoroughly disinfected by the processes to which the rags have been subjected.

With regard to arsenic, I can say this. I visited some ten years ago a mill in this State where 200 pounds of paris green were then made annually. The complaint then had nothing to do with the operatives, but it came from the people outside who were afraid of the arsenic being distributed around the surrounding region for a quarter of a mile. One farmer allowed his whole crop of hay to rot on the ground for fear his cows would be poisoned by eating it. But the condition of the operatives in that mill surprised me. Almost every man in that establishment had sores upon the face, eyes, nose, ears, mouth, hands and other parts of the body, due to the neglect of the greatest of all laws, the law of cleanliness—absolute cleanliness—which has more to do with this subject than anything else. People handle these metallic poisons and then take their lunch without washing—that is where the trouble very largely comes from, handling poisons and then contributing those poisons to the food every day, right along, day after day. I have seen the same thing in other factories of similar nature.

The figures, it has been said, are unreliable in this country. There are no figures in this country upon this subject that really amount to anything except, perhaps, those of some of the great industrial insurance companies. One reason for this unreliability is this. In this State the statistics on this subject were begun in 1842, and were continued for nearly forty years. They were published in the registration reports for all that time, but they gave the average age at death, which does not amount to anything. It has no significance whatever upon the subject. Let me illustrate. A major general dies at seventy years of age, we will say, as a general rule, and a lieutenant dies at perhaps thirty or forty years of age. Is that of any value to show that the position of a major general is any more healthful than that of a lieutenant? Not one bit. It is a question of age. In an old ladies' home the average age at death is seventy; in an infants' asylum it is two. Is one for this reason to be considered any more healthful than the other? Not a bit. These figures were on a wrong basis. When we can get down to the proper basis of comparing the deaths in each industry at certain ages with the living at similar ages we shall have something to rely upon.

PROF. SEDGWICK: In view of the paper which has been read and the fact that members of this Association are stationed as sanitary pickets, as it were, all over the State, I hope that any one within whose knowledge there may come information regarding cases of damage to health due to special occupations will be kind enough to communicate with Mr. Winslow and inform him of the fact. And in view of the statements which have been made by the secretary of the State Board of Health that we lack authentic information even in this State, which is noted for its leadership in sanitary science, I would like to suggest the passage of a resolution requesting the Legislature to set in motion some machinery looking toward the gathering of accurate information. It so happens that this is a very good time to do this, inasmuch as there is a committee of the Legislature now considering just such questions, namely, the Committee on Relations of Employers to Employees. With this idea in mind I am going to submit for your consideration, and if possible for your adoption, the following resolutions which, if they should come with the authority of this Association, might, I believe, do a real good at the present juncture in bringing about legislation looking towards the end desired. I should like to move, Mr. President, that this Association adopt, and through its secretary forward to the proper persons, the following resolutions:

"Whereas, investigations in other countries have shown that certain trades and industries, when conducted without due sanitary supervision and regulation, are injurious to the health of the operatives employed; and

"Whereas, exact information is lacking with regard to the extent of such evils, if any, in Massachusetts, be it

"Resolved, That the Massachusetts Association of Boards of Health, in Boston assembled, April 28, 1904, respectfully urge the General Court to direct the State Board of Health, with such aid as it may require from the chief of the District Police and the Bureau of Statistics of Labor, to investigate and report upon the sanitary conditions of factories, workshops and other places of employment in the Commonwealth of Massachusetts, with respect to all conditions which may endanger the life and limbs or be prejudicial to the health of persons employed therein."

THE CHAIRMAN: You have heard the resolution introduced by Prof. Sedgwick. What is the pleasure of the Association with regard to them?

DR. SMITH: It seems to me better that this Association should not undertake to get information concerning the dangers to life and limb of employees. It seems to me we have got enough to do to give our attention to unsanitary conditions and to those conditions which lead to certain diseases, and I would move an amendment, that that particular phrase be stricken out.

PROF. SEDGWICK: I am willing to accept that amendment, Mr. President.

THE CHAIRMAN: Do I understand that it is the pleasure of the mover of the resolution to so amend it that it shall read, "all conditions which may endanger the life or be prejudicial to the health of persons employed therein?"

PROF. SEDGWICK: I think Dr. Smith wished to omit "life and limb" both.

THE CHAIRMAN: "With respect to all conditions which may be prejudicial to the health of persons employed therein." I understand that is the form you are now willing to leave it?

PROF. SEDGWICK: Yes.

THE CHAIRMAN: The essential part of the resolutions then will now read, "to investigate and report upon the sanitary conditions of factories, workshops and other places of employment in the Commonwealth of Massachusetts with respect to all conditions which may be prejudicial to the health of persons employed therein." It is moved and seconded that these resolutions be adopted.

DR. MILLER: I was going to suggest that we leave in that word "life." I think it is important to have it in there—"life and health."

DR. SMITH: I simply made the suggestion to narrow down the inquiry to matters of sanitation. If the Association intends to go into the question of accidents it seems to me that is somewhat beyond our scope. It belongs to an entirely different body —to a body of engineers—to determine the conditions that endanger the limbs of persons, and not an association of this kind. The two functions, it seems to me, are quite distinct. While I think that we should certainly support these resolutions, as being of very great importance, it seems to me that what I suggest is much simpler than the broader statement that is contained in the original draft. All conditions that militate against the health of individuals may in the long run affect life of individuals. It seems to me the two terms, health and life, are more or less synonymous.

THE CHAIRMAN: What is your pleasure with regard to these resolutions? It is moved that they be adopted. If that be your pleasure you will signify it by saying aye.

(The motion was carried.)

THE CHAIRMAN: It seems to be the unanimous sense of this Association. The next paper upon our programme is by Dr. S. J. Russell, city physician of Springfield, on "Trichinosis."

(EDITOR'S NOTE.—Dr. Russell's paper, describing certain cases of Trichinosis, was read, but was not submitted for publication in time for use in this issue.)

THE CHAIRMAN: Dr. Russell's paper is before you for discussion.

DR. CHAPIN: I should like to ask one or two questions. Was this animal fed on offal?

DR. RUSSELL: It was fed on offal from the city of Springfield.

DR. CHAPIN: Then I want to know whether all the pork was from one animal, and also how the pork was cooked that caused the trichinosis.

DR. RUSSELL: On the first examination I questioned the patients about the pork. They said they had eaten very little, and it was well cooked. I forgot to state that the blood examinations, made in every case, showed an increase of eosinophiles, ranging from sixteen to sixty per cent.

DR. CHAPIN: Did you find on further investigation that the pork they had eaten was cooked a long time in the ordinary manner, like roast pork or friend ham or boiled ham—just how was it cooked?

DR. RUSSELL: I found that some of the pork was in the form of sausages which were eaten raw, but they claimed that most of the pork was very well cooked. Some ate raw pork and others ate the sausages raw.

DR. CHAPIN: Was it your opinion that some of them ate only the well cooked pork, or do you think all of those that were affected ate pork which was practically raw?

DR. RUSSELL: I think most of the pork was under-done.

DR. CHAPIN: Was there more than one animal infected?

DR. RUSSELL: Just one.

DR. CHAPIN: Did any other people eat of that who were not taken sick?

DR. RUSSELL: There were a few who ate a very little of it and were not taken sick.

DR. SMITH: This disease, while it seems to be comparatively rare in our own country, is yet more prevalent than is generally supposed. It is probable that mild cases occur, which are diagnosed as something other than trichinosis, and the true facts in the case are not discovered unless the body of the person should reach the dissecting room, and there the trichinosis may be found. Dr. Williams of Buffalo has made a rather careful study of the prevalence of trichinosis in our country, and he found that not less than five per cent. of the bodies that were examined contained trichinæ. This would indicate that the infection is commoner than we suppose, but that the dose is also less than that which people consume who eat meat raw. In Europe, as probably most of you remember, the outbreaks were at one time very extensive. The manner of the meat distribution there is so different from that which subsists in this country that outbreaks are traced more easily to their source. In the smaller towns and villages the animals that are slaughtered are consumed on the spot, so that a single pig may reach a large number of consumers, and epidemics in which hundreds of people have been involved, and in which the mortality has been relatively very high have been traced to single pigs. With reference to the cooking of meat, it is probable that now and then large masses of meat, although apparently well cooked on the surface, still retain living trichinæ near the bones. A few years ago my attention was called to some cases of trichinosis in one of our charitable institutions in the State. So far as was known at that time, the meat was thoroughly cooked. All precautions were being taken, and yet unquestioned cases of trichinosis occurred in this institution. The hogs were examined by removing small bits of tissue with a harpoon, and I think in over half of the cases trichinæ were found. Hence it may occur that infection with trichinæ will take place in families where pork is usually very well prepared, but where certain portions of it have not been subjected to the heat necessary to kill the trichinæ, where in other words the pork is underdone. This may account for the five per cent. of cases which have been found in the dissecting room and at autopsies by Dr. Williams. Of course the remedy is in all cases to thoroughly cook the pork. In fact, that is probably the the only remedy, unless the industry of raising hogs should be completely changed, and that of course would greatly augment the price of this kind of meat. Trichinosis in this country was practically unknown until the habit of certain foreigners of eating meat underdone or raw was brought with them. In France the disease is practically unknown, because the people cook all their meat, though, so far as we know, the statistics of the examination of pork show that the pigs in France are no less infected than in other countries. Practically the only remedy we have is to instruct the people to cook the meat as thoroughly as possible.

THE CHAIRMAN: If there is nothing else to be said upon this subject, we will proceed to the next paper on the programme, "The Transmission of Infection by means of Footwear," by Dr. Francis P. Denny and Mr. J. Albert C. Nyhen of Brookline.

THE TRANSMISSION OF INFECTION BY MEANS OF FOOTWEAR.

BY DR. FRANCIS P. DENNY AND MR. J. ALBERT C. NYHEN
Brookline Board of Health Laboratory.

The experiments which are here reported were carried out by the writers in the Brookline Board of Health Laboratory, with the object of determining in a general way how readily infectious material will adhere to shoes, and how long and how far it will be carried in that way.

These experiments, which have been of a very simple nature, have consisted chiefly in putting some growth of the Bacillus prodigiosus (a red-pigment-producing non-pathogenic organism) on various parts of our shoes before going out from the laboratory to attend to our regular duties. On returning to the laboratory after varying intervals of time, each part of the shoe which had been infected was thoroughly rubbed with a moist cotton swab, and then the swab was rinsed in a tube of melted gelatine, which was then plated. The bacilli, if recovered from the shoes, appeared in the plates as characteristic red liquefying colonies.

The parts of the shoes which were inoculated were the under surface of the sole and heel, the lower edge of the side of the sole, the instep, and a few tests were made by inoculating some of the small holes in the O'Sullivan rubber heels. When entering the laboratory on our return, care was taken to avoid having the parts of the shoe which we had inoculated come in contact with the floor, which might have become infected with B. prodigiosus from some of the earlier experiments. In a number of control plates made from the parts of the shoes which had not been inoculated, B. prodigiosus was never found.

The tests were made during all the different seasons and under very varying conditions of weather and temperature. The amount of walking that was done while the bacilli were on the shoes varied considerably, but was usually more than that of the average physician for the same length of time.

The total number of tests made was 126. The results are given in the following table:

Duration of Tests.	Sole		Heel		Instep		Side Sole		Rubber Heels		Rubber O'rshoes	
	+	—	+	—	+	—	+	—	+	—	+	—
½ hour	1	1	1	.	.	.	.	.	.	.	.	.
1 "	5	13	5	7	.	1	2	.	.	.	2	2
1½ "	4	5	4	1	1	1	.	.	.	.	.	.
2 "	3	3	2	1	.	1	1	.	.	.	.	.
3 "	1	3	1	1	3	1	.	.	.	.	.	6
4 "	.	.	.	.	3	.	4	.	.	2	.	.
5 "	.	.	.	.	1	.	.	.	.	.	.	.
6–8 hours	.	2	.	.	.	2	.	.	.	.	.	.
8 to 12 "	.	2	.	1	2	.	2	.	4	1	.	.
24 "	.	1	.	.	2	1	2	1	.	.	.	.
48 "	.	.	.	.	1	1	.	1	.	.	.	.
72 "	.	.	.	.	1	1	.	2	.	.	.	.
5 days	.	.	.	.	.	1	.	.	.	.	.	.
8 "	.	.	.	.	1	.	.	.	.	.	.	.
9 "	.	.	.	.	.	1	.	.	.	.	.	.
	14	30	13	11	15	11	11	4	4	3	2	8

Some of these data may be summarized as follows:

In thirty-seven tests where the *soles* were inoculated and where plates were made after intervals varying from one to three hours, the bacilli were found in thirteen (35 per cent.)

In twenty-two tests with the bacilli on the *heels* for a similar length of time, the plates were positive in twelve (55 per cent.) This would seem to show that bacteria will remain longer on the heel than on the sole, although the number of tests made is rather small to justify that conclusion.

In twenty-six tests where the *instep* was inoculated and plates were made after intervals varying from one hour to nine days, the results were positive in fifteen (58 per cent.)

In fifteen tests with the bacilli on the lower edge of the *side of the sole,* eleven were positive after intervals varying from one to seventy-two hours (73 per cent.)

As was to be expected, we found that the bacilli remained on the side of the sole and the instep for a much longer time than on the sole or heel. In ordinary walking on the sidewalks there is very little friction on the instep and the side of the sole. In some of the tests we could actually see for several days the growth which we had put on the instep. On the contrary, cross-country walking will very quickly remove any material from the instep or the side of the sole.

In seven tests where the *holes in the rubber heels* were inoculated, four were positive after intervals of four to nine hours.

Ten tests were made with the bacilli on the soles and the heels of *rubber overshoes* which were worn when there was snow on the ground. Of four tests with a one hour interval, two were positive and two negative. Of six with a three hour interval, all were negative.

With the exceptions about to be mentioned, the bacilli used in these tests were from fresh blood serum cultures. Eight of the tests were made using bacilli, which had been dried and pulverized. The powdered bacilli were put on a sheet of paper on the floor, and the foot was pressed over them. Six of the eight tests were positive after intervals of one to one and one-half hours.

Six tests were made using mucus, in which some growth of B. prodigiosus had been mixed; three were positive and three negative.

It seems probable that the bacilli actually persisted on the shoes in a much larger proportion of cases than would appear from our results, for many conditions were present to prevent all the bacilli appearing in the plates. Thus, all the bacilli were not necessarily removed from the shoe by the cotton swab, and probably all the bacilli removed on the swab were not washed out by the melted gelatine. Furthermore, some of the bacilli were doubtless overgrown by other bacteria, especially by some very abundant forms which rapidly liquefied gelatine.

These experiments having shown that footwear experimentally infected with bacilli will carry the infection to a distance, it remains to consider: (1.) under what conditions are shoes likely to become infected; (2.) what is the danger of the transmission of disease by the feet; (3.) what precautions should be taken to prevent the transmission of disease in this way.

INFECTION OF THE FEET IN THE VICINITY OF CASES OF CONTAGIOUS DISEASE.

It is certain that the floor of a room occupied by a contagious case becomes infected. Flugge* and others have shown that fine bits of secretion are given off as a spray in the act of coughing, sneezing and loud talking. These droplets disperse themselves to varying distances from the patient, and then sink onto the floor and other surfaces. Fine particles of epidermis from persons desquamating also find their way to the floor. In unmodified smallpox some of the many thousand scabs given off from each patient during desquamation are sure to drop on the floor despite the watchfulness of the attendants. If one looks carefully, one can actually see these scabs on the floor about the bed of a small-pox patient who is at the height of desquamation. What is true of such gross particles will be equally true of the smaller particles of epidermis in scarlet fever and others of the exanthemata.

---

*Deutsch. med. Wochen. Oct. 14, 1897, p. 665.

From the results of our experiments, it is certain that a person walking over an infected floor may carry off some of the infectious material on his shoes. One of the writers found a scab clinging to the foot of a patient in a small-pox hospital, and also on the sole of a rubber overshoe, which he himself was wearing in visiting the hospital. Wright and Emerson* found diphtheria bacilli on the soles of the shoes of three nurses in the diphtheria ward of the Boston City Hospital.

It is often possible for a physician to visit a contagious case without coming in contact with any infected objects, except with his hands in examining the patient, and with the soles of the shoes on the floor. The hands are always disinfected on leaving the patient, but the feet are usually neglected.

Is it necessary or desirable that precautions should be taken by physicians and others visiting a contagious case, to guard against carrying away infection on the feet? In many instances we believe it is unnecessary, for the reason that while it is possible for pathogenic organisms to be carried from the room on the feet, there is comparatively small chance for the infection to pass from the floors to which it has been carried to the mucous membranes of susceptible persons.

Under the following conditions it seems to us important that precautions should be taken:

(1.) *In the more serious contagious diseases,* and those which from the point of view of the public health are especially important; for example, small-pox, plague and foot-and-mouth disease.

(2.) *Under any circumstances, where it is considered necessary to have a strict quarantine;* for example, if it is considered necessary to keep a sheet wet with a disinfectant at the door of the patient's room, then certainly care should be taken to prevent infection being carried out on the feet of those leaving the room.

(3.) In scarlet fever and diphtheria, where a physician or other person is going very directly from a contagious case to rooms or nurseries where there are small children who play on the floor.

---

*Centralblatt fuer Bakteriologie. 1894. XVI. p. 112.

(4.) *In contagious hospitals.* In a hospital where a large number of contagious cases are collected together, the floors must be very thoroughly infected, and if persons are passing back and forth from one part of the hospital to another, for example, from the scarlet fever to the diphtheria side, without taking any precautions with their feet, there is great opportunity for the transmission of the contagion. It is not necessary that persons should actually pass from one side of the hospital to another, in order to have the infection transmitted by the feet. This may take place if the attendants from different sides use any rooms or corridors in common. In some contagious hospitals, which are considered models of their kind, the nurses from different departments use dining rooms and other rooms in common. It seems to us very important that in the construction of a contagious hospital provision should be made for the complete separation of the nurses caring for the different diseases.

PRECAUTIONS TO GUARD AGAINST CARRYING INFECTION ON THE
FEET FROM ROOMS OCCUPIED BY CONTAGIOUS CASES.

On leaving the room the soles of the shoes may be immersed in a disinfectant, or the sole may be thoroughly wiped with a towel or cloth wet with a disinfectant. Rubber overshoes afford a very convenient and satisfactory method of protecting the shoes from infection as they may be put on before entering the sick room or hospital and taken off on leaving. They are easily disinfected themselves by immersion in a disinfectant solution. The nurse who is taking care of a patient isolated at home may put on rubber overshoes in passing through the house on going out for her daily exercise.

INFECTION OF FOOTWEAR FROM SPUTUM.

The habit of spitting on the sidewalk and floors of public places is still very common. On almost every sidewalk which is much used one can see sputum at intervals of only a few yards. Mucus adheres readily to the sole of the shoe, and if a person steps on fresh sputum it may cling to the edge of the sole or low instep, and so be carried for a long time. It is not necessary here to speak of the dangers from sputum. It is well to remember that besides tubercle bacilli, other pathogenic bacteria may be present, for example, the influenza bacilli, pneumococci, and the diphtheria bacilli.

It is certain that any bacteria which are on the sidewalks may be carried to the floors of our own houses. In this way persons ot refinement are exposed to disease through the filthy habits of others. To protect the public, therefore, spitting on the sidewalk should be an offence punishable by law, and this law should be enforced. It is our belief that footwear plays an important part in the dissemination of the tubercle bacillus.

INFECTION OF THE FEET FROM FECAL MATTER AND URINE.

Shoes may become contaminated in fields and gardens with fecal matter used as fertilizer and also in alleys and other more or less secluded places. Fecal matter is very likely to become adherent to the instep where it will be carried for a long time. The chief danger of fecal contamination is from typhoid bacilli.

The work of Richardson* and others has shown that typhoid bacilli in large numbers are often present in the urine in typhoid fever, and that they persist for a long time—months and sometimes years after recovery. Persons urinate out of doors much more frequently than they defecate and often in places where persons walk. The soles of the shoes may become contaminated with urine, and especially with soil saturated with urine.

If typhoid bacilli are brought into houses in material on the shoes, they may then be carried to articles of food by means of flies.

In military camps the feet probably play an important part in the spread of typhoid fever. If from lack of discipline or the indifference of the commanding officers, the men do not always use the sinks, the excreta (urine and feces) may become thoroughly disseminated in the camp by the soldiers' feet.

---

*Journal of Experimental Medicine. Vol. iii. No. 3. 1898.

The report of the committee* appointed to investigate the prevalence of typhoid fever in the camps during the Spanish War calls attention to this means of spreading the disease. The conditions of camp life, and especially the exposure of food to flies, are very favorable for the transmission of typhoid in this way.

FOOTWEAR IN THE TRANSMISSION OF ANIMAL DISEASES.

Feet probably play an important part in the transmission of animal diseases. The floors of barns and stables are sure to become contaminated with excreta, which is carried about on the shoes of the men and on the feet of the animals. If pathogenic organisms are in the excreta or on the floor, the animals' fodder is likely to become contaminated, as hay and ensilage are often walked over and tossed about on the floors.

Veterinarians and other visiting barns infected with foot-and-mouth disease should take special precautions to avoid carrying the infection on their shoes to other herds.

The point which we wish to emphasize most is the importance of footwear in disseminating tubercle bacilli. There is a great deal of sputum on our sidewalks, much of it is tubercular. We are carrying it about on our shoes and into our homes. The prevention of spitting on surfaces where people walk should receive the attention of all who are engaged in public health work.

THE CHAIRMAN: Before proceeding to the discussion of this paper I should like to call the attention of the Association to the fact that at the time of our annual summer outing with the authorities of the city of Boston in Boston Harbor—I may say one of the most agreeable occasions of the year—the laboratory of the State Board of Health for the preparation of vaccine matter and anti-toxin will be in operation. The building is externally complete, and will be occupied probably in June, so that in July we shall be able to show the members of the Association the establishment in actual operation. The building is at Forest Hills,

---

*Vaughan ; Boston Medical and Surgical Journal. May 18, 1899. p. 480.

within 10 minutes of the South Station by the quick trains of the New York, New Haven & Hartford Railroad, and the building at Forest Hills is a distance of only two or three minutes walk from the railroad station. It would be very possible for the members of the Association, as they come to Boston, to spend an hour or two in the inspection of that establishment before taking the steamer for the island in Boston Harbor, and I hope the members of the Association will take advantage of the opportunity offered. The paper of Dr. Denny is now before you for discussion or question.

DR. HARRINGTON: Dr. Denny's very interesting results suggest to me the desirability of the extension of such an investigation so as to determine how much danger of carrying infection may reside in women's skirts, through the senseless custom of dragging them over dusty sidewalks and staircases, gathering up all manner of filth which must necessarily be carried into the household. I know that it is a common practice on getting home to shake the skirt, in order to detach as much as possible of the dirt that has adhered during the walk. I hope that Dr. Denny will look into this matter, for it seems to me that there may be even greater danger of transmission of infection by skirts than by footwear. Another suggestion occurs to me. In place of putting on rubbers in passing to and from a contagious case, why would it not be well to use some sort of sandal made of stout paper, which, after use, could be burned? When one wears rubbers they must afterwards be disinfected, whereas with a very cheap sort of paper sandal the necessity of disinfection would be done away with.

DR. CHASE: I would like to say a word about the practical carrying out of these suggestions of Dr. Denny as to shoes. At the Brookline Board of Health Hospital we have two or three pairs of rubbers in the robing room at the entrance of the diphtheria ward, and also of the scarlet fever ward, and I find it a very easy matter to slip on one of these pairs of rubbers; and if another physician is along he does the same; but if his feet do not fit the rubbers he wipes off the soles and heels of his shoes with a solution of corrosive sublimate on a towel after finishing the visit to the scarlet fever ward. In visiting private patients we do not always do this; but now that our patients with dangerous contagious diseases are more and more generally cared for in hospitals, it is worth while, and is more necessary than ever to take this precaution to prevent cross infection. We all know the comparative frequency with which physicians bring home scarlet fever to their younger children, the children going around on all-fours. Within a year I have had in my care the one-year old child of a physician, who is very sure he himself brought home scarlet fever to his baby. He was taking care of a number of scarlet fever patients at the time, and it is very possible he brought home the infection on his feet. It is so easy and simple a matter to adopt Dr. Denny's timely suggestion that I hope others will try it as we have in Brookline.

MR. WINSLOW: In connection with this scheme it is worth while to recall the typhoid fever epidemic in Springfield in 1892. I think the experts believed that the infection was carried from a tobacco field, in which typhoid bacilli occurred in human excreta, to a well in which milk cans were sunk. In that case infection was carried on the feet of workingmen.

DR. SWARTS: The reader of the paper might have mentioned one other opportunity of investigation, made possible by the introduction of water filtration by means of what is called the sand-bed filtration, where the surface of the bed must necessarily be scraped at intervals, and the employees who do the scraping must necessarily tread upon the cleansed surface of the bed as they remove the scum of the bed, and after passing over a field well fertilized with night-soil it would seem to be possible that the footwear might carry a considerable quantity of innoculating material by which the whole of the filtering bed might become infected in this way. That is one of the objections to the use of sand-bed filtration, as compared with mechanical filtration, where it is not necessary to tread upon the bed in order to cleanse it. I would like to ask of the representatives of the

State Board of Health having control of all water supplies in the State whether they extend their labors to the control of the changing of shoes by those operatives who are scraping the beds; if not, whether it would not be a good idea to control such a condition.

THE CHAIRMAN: I seem to be left as the representative of the Board to speak upon that matter. It does not seem to me a matter of any consequence, because we assume that the typhoid bacilli do get upon the surface of that bed in any case. It is exactly what the sand bed is there for—but they don't get through it.

DR. DURGIN: I would like to ask Dr. Chase if he recollects what stage of scarlet fever this child was in when the foot-wear of the doctor was supposed to take the infection away.

DR. CHASE: He had quite a number of scarlet fever patients at the time, and they were in various stages of the disease. He could not tell from which patient he brought the contagion home, but he was positive he himself brought it to his child.

DR. CHAPIN: Dr. Denny's paper is a very interesting one, and investigations of this kind cannot help being extremely suggestive and useful. But at the same time I cannot but feel that we should be very careful in making deductions from them. Of course, it must be admitted from what he has told us today that the infection of a number of diseases can be transmitted from one place to another on the feet; but, as Dr. Denny himself well said, what we want to know is what are the chances of that infection getting from the feet to other living beings. What we want to know in all these investigations—and in all our study of the infectious diseases—is the exact mode by which the virus passes from the sick person to the well. We want to know the path followed in the majority of cases. I wish we were sure of this, but it does not seem to me that at present we really know very much about it. It appears that most of our notions are guess work. Now, it is possible to guess that the shoes are an important factor in carrying the disease from one person to another. It is possible to guess that the clothing is an important factor—that money, library books and school books are important factors—that the disease germs may be blown in the air from one person to another, and the disease spread in that way. So far as actual knowledge is concerned we appear at present to be very much at sea. Now, instead of guessing that the disease may be spread in the way mentioned, we are at liberty to guess that it is very rarely spread in any such way. We are at liberty to guess that, as a rule, the transmission of infection is pretty direct; that the disease poisons, the bacilli in diphtheria, for instance, are almost invariably transmitted in a pretty direct manner from the sick person to the well. Thus a person who is infected with diphtheria bacilli drinks out of a tumbler and some one else drinks out of the same tumbler shortly after before it is dry. A person who is infected with diphtheria puts a pencil in his mouth, and some one else puts that same pencil in his mouth within a few minutes and becomes infected. Those are direct means by which the bacilli are carried from one person to another. Now, one may guess that this is almost the sole manner in which disease is spread from the sick to the well. That guess has a good deal back of it. There is much to make us think that this guess is correct. Thus we find that it is not very easy for a person who has scarlet fever or diphtheria to infect others. All of you have noted plenty of instances where persons with scarlet fever or diphtheria have mingled freely with susceptible persons for days and weeks, and perhaps only one or two have become infected from them. Furthermore, we know that in diphtheria there are a large number of unrecognized cases of the disease, a very large number of persons who are not sick at all, but who are yet infected, and who are mingling freely with people in every walk of life and on all occasions, and it seems to me that opportunities for direct infection are very great indeed. So when we see that very often when there is close communication between sick and well, infection does not take place, that the infection appears to be somewhat difficult, and is not readily carried from one to another, we should be very chary of attributing very much importance to the carrying of the poison of diphtheria and probably of scarlet fever and the other diseases, on clothing or books or shoes or anything of the kind. Of course, we must admit that such a thing is possible. There is no doubt but that it occasionally occurs. But if we place so much stress upon the carrying of disease in fomites, as is usually done, are we not straining at a gnat? It seems to me that we are, and that we are drawing away public attention from the real source of the trouble, the real source of the extension of the contagious disease, namely, the existence of a very large number of unrecognized cases which are not sick at all, but are yet infected with the bacilli or other organism causing the disease. We know that this is the case in diphtheria. We have every reason to believe that it is so in other diseases, and I think we should hesitate very much before we unduly alarm people about any danger which may come from carrying the disease germs on the feet or on dresses or clothing or books or money or things of that kind, where there are a number of changes between the sick and the well and where considerable time elapses.

Of course, it is very much easier to blame inanimate objects, like books and shoes and clothing, for carrying disease than to blame a person who is perfectly well. No one who is perfectly well, who has had no sign of sore throat or eruption, likes to think that he can be the bearer of disease; but we know that can happen in diphtheria, and we believe that it can in other diseases. It is these persons themselves, it seems to me, that do the harm, and not the clothing or other material things carried by them.

Where a doctor brings home diphtheria to his children—which by the way, it seems to me, is a very rare thing, for I have almost never known of a physician carrying contagion in my experience of twenty years, and I have been on the lookout—is it not infinitely more likely that the physician has the diphtheria bacilli growing in his throat, that he has been infected himself from some one of his patients and has carried it home to his children in that way than that he has carried it home on his overcoat or his whiskers or his shoes? As regards scarlet fever we do not know that it is a bacterial disease, and we do not know with certainty the seat of infection, but we have reason to believe that the mucous secretions are infectious as they are in diphtheria, and also that well persons may have an infected throat or nose. In the case mentioned by Dr. Chase is it not more likely that the physician carried the disease home on his mucous membranes than on his clothing? It seems to me that in most instances it is the living person rather than inanimate objects that carry contagion, and that this is what we ought to teach.

THE CHAIRMAN: Is there anything else to be said on the subject of this very interesting paper?

DR. DENNY: I would like to say that I agree wholly with what Dr. Chapin has said—that infection is usually transmitted very directly from person to person, and usually from mild and unrecognized cases, and I don't think that the public should be stirred up about things of this sort. I should not think of bringing such a subject to the attention of the public. But it seems to me worth while to call to the attention of men who are engaged in preventing the spread of contagious disease the possibility of such a transmission, and especially the possibility of the transmission of tuberculosis. We don't know certainly how much danger there is from the sputum, which is around on the sidewalks or on the floors of our houses. Possibly we get infected more directly from other cases, but still, at the present time, when so much is being said and done to prevent the spread of tuberculosis from sputum, it seems to me as though we ought to consider the possibility of tuberculosis sputum being carried about in this way.

THE CHAIRMAN: If there is nothing more to be said upon this subject? Is there any other business to be brought before the Association at this time?

THE SECRETARY: I move we adjourn.

THE CHAIRMAN: If that be your pleasure, I will declare the Association adjourned.

ABSTRACTS, REVIEWS, NOTES AND NEWS.

Boards of Health are asked to send the Managing Editor notes of not more than one hundred and fifty words relating to new regulations passed, legal cases prosecuted, outbreaks of infection, unusual problems encountered, or other matters the publication of which may further the attainment of the objects of the Association.

References are indicated by numbers. See list at end of column.

ANTI-VIVISECTION BILL AGAIN DEFEATED.—House Bill No. 174 of this year, which forbade any animal experimentation whatever to Municipal Board of Health or Hospital laboratories throughout the State, and permitted to the State Board of Health only inoculation tests, was reported "leave to withdraw" by the Committee on Probate and Chancery, May 4th, 1904. Substitution of the bill for this report was rejected in the House by a vote of 90 to 35, or 72 per cent. against the bill.

This bill required the appointment of a Commission of three to supervise animal experimentation, "one of whom and only one" should be a physician. Ex-Governor Brackett, who supported the bill at the hearings, sat beside the Speaker during the debate. Dr. Wheatley of Abington, a member of the Massachusetts Association of Boards of Health, Mr. Grady of Boston, the leader of the Democrats in the House, Mr. Cox of Boston and Mr. James Clark of Medford all spoke against the bill. Dr. H. L. Plummer and Mr. A. L. Gavin, both of Boston, also opposed the bill. Mr. McManus of Natick supported the bill, and so did Mr. Woodhead of North Adams, notwithstanding that the Board of Health of North Adams signed the protest against it.

Thereafter, in the Senate, substitution of the bill for the adverse report was urged, May 11th, by Senator Callender. The bill was again defeated, 16 to 7, or about 70 per cent. against it.

At the hearings, Dr. Harold C. Ernst appeared against the bill as the representative of the various Massachusetts Colleges and Universities, Hospitals and Boards of Health, presenting for the latter the official protests of Boards of Health from 31 of the 33 cities of the Commonwealth, and from 50 of its towns. The Boards of the remaining two cities also signified their opposition to the bill, but failed to sign the protest.

AGAINST THE TOY PISTOL.—At a meeting of the Berkshire District Medical Society, Feb. 26, 1904, it was voted that;

"Whereas, 406 deaths from tetanus were reported as occurring in the United States in July, 1903, as a result of fourth of July celebrations, 363 of these deaths having been caused by toy pistols loaded with blank cartridges, and 17 by cannon crackers,

"Resolved, That the Berkshire District Medical Society is in favor of any legislation and municipal ordinances which will effectively stop the sale and use of toy pistols, blank cartridges and cannon crackers.   *L. C. SWIFT, Secretary."*

IMPORTANT HEARING RELATIVE TO THE PROTECTION OF WATER SUPPLIES.—By a recent statute the State Board of Health of Massachusetts was authorized to "make rules and regulations to prevent the pollution and to secure the sanitary protection of all such waters as are used as sources of water supply." Acting under the provisions of this Statute (Revised Laws, Chapter 75, Section 113), the State Board of Health has made rules and regulations for several of the public water supplies of cities and towns, including Salem, Cambridge, Marlboro, Haverhill, Taunton, Pittsfield, Fitchburg, the Metropolitan Water District and several other places.

The density of the population in Massachusetts has increased to such a degree that it has become necessary to provide every possible safeguard for the many sources of water supply in order to protect them from the inevitable pollution which the collection of human beings in the neighborhood of such sources is bound to produce.

The city of Taunton acquired the right to take the waters of some of the great ponds in Lakeville, the largest fresh water areas in the State. But the natural beauty of these lakes had already induced a considerable number of summer cottagers to acquire land and erect buildings upon the immediate borders of these lakes, and for this reason an application was made to the State Board of Health to make such regulations as would protect these waters from pollution. Hence an attempt is being made by these property owners, among whom are several Indians, who claim direct descent from Massasoit, through seven or eight generations, to repeal the statute already mentioned. As the general tendency of legislation since 1878 has been to give greater, rather than less protection, to public water supplies, it can hardly be expected that this attempt will prove successful. The experience of Pennsylvania towns, in which the most serious epidemics have occurred in consequence of water pollution, was due largely to the absence of such statutes as Massachusetts fortunately possesses.

A hearing was held at the State House on Monday, May 2, at which the petitioners were heard, asking for the enactment of a new statute, the effect of which would seriously impair the value of such regulations. At the time of going to press the result of the hearing was not known. *S. W. ABBOTT, M. D.*

UNDERTAKING AND EMBALMING.—By a resolve of the Legislature, March 28, 1904, the Massachusetts State Board of Health was directed to investigate the necessity for a desirability of legislation to regulate undertaking and embalming. The Board reported May 4, 1904. We give below the paragraphs from the report bearing most explicit on the matter.

"As a result of this investigation (of the existing laws and conditions relating to undertaking and embalming) it is apparent that there is already vested in local Boards of Health a power in such matters exceeding that conferred upon the State Board of Health, and entirely adequate to ensure that the undertaking business will continue to be carried on, as at present, in a manner generally satisfactory to the community." * * *

"In regard to the question of embalming, the Board is distinctly of the opinion that, whatever value this practice may have in other respects, it cannot be regarded as necessary for, or contributing to, the protection of the public health. In the absence, then, of any necessity for new legislation to ensure the safe conduct into or through other States, of dead bodies shipped from this State in accordance with the requirements of existing statutes, and in the freedom from menace to the public health under existing conditions, the Board respectfully suggests that if for any reason new regulations to control the business of undertaking and embalming appear to be desirable, it must depend upon issues foreign to those upon which the Board feels itself competent to report."

AERIAL INFECTION FROM SMALLPOX HOSPITALS.—In the course of a suit, the Attorney-General and Others vs. the Mayor, Aldermen and City of Nottingham, England, recently heard before Mr. Justice Farwell, (Feb., 1904), much evidence concerning the extent and manner of distribution of infection from smallpox hospitals was considered. The Medical Officers of Health of the Essex County Council, of Basford, of Glasgow, of Bradford, and of Lambeth, testified that in their opinions aerial convection of the infective agent of smallpox is a serious source of danger in the neighborhood of such hospitals. The M. O. H.'s of Nottingham, Liverpool, Brighton, Staffordshire and others, did not agree with this, but believed that the spread of smallpox from a smallpox hospital is almost always to be ascribed to mal-administration in permitting intercourse with the people of the neighborhood to continue to a greater or less extent.

In summing up, Mr. Justice Farwell gave a long and closely reasoned opinion, and dismissed the case with costs, on the ground that the aerial convection of smallpox was not established by the evidence.

This case is interesting on account of the conflicting testimony given, but also because of the evidence that some smallpox hospitals at least so not spread infection.

FEDERAL REGULATIONS CONCERNING VACCINES AND ANTITOXINS.—Rosenau, in a letter to *American Medicine,* calls attention to the act, signed July 1, 1902, "to regulate the sale of viruses, serums, toxins and analogous products in the District of Columbia, to regulate interstate traffic in said articles, and for other purposes."

This law requires that all establishments, native and foreign, engaged in such work, shall hold an unsuspended and unrevoked Government license, and prohibits interstate commerce in any product made in an illicit or unauthorized manner. It requires that every package of any such product shall bear the name, address and license number of the manufacturer, together with the name of the product, and the date beyond which it may become inert. False labelling is punishable by $500 fine, or imprisonment up to one year, or by both.

The U. S. Pub. Health and Marine Hosp. Service must detail an officer to inspect establishments having interstate commerce, and the Surgeon-General of this service, together with the Surgeon-Generals of the Army and Navy, constitute a board which may make rules, etc., controlling the licenses. The Director of the laboratory of this Service must examine the products, and licenses may be revoked for faulty methods of manufacture, faulty construction, faulty administration, impurities or weakness of products; already during a little over a year of operation of this law, four licenses have been revoked, and others have been refused, pending the making of indicated reformatory changes.

A STANDARD ANTITOXIN UNIT FROM AMERICAN SOURCES.—In the letter of Rosenau, just quoted, it is stated that his laboratory is engaged in the preparation of a standard toxin, after the character of Ehrlich's standard toxin, and that this standard toxin will be distributed to all interested in testing antitoxins. At the present time American laboratories depend principally on Ehrlich's laboratory for their supplies of such standard toxin. The ready determination of antitoxic strength in terms of a standard unit having general acceptance will be of considerable advantage to the whole country.

DIPHTHERIA MORTALITY WITH ANTITOXIN.— The Chicago Board of Health has recently published statistics concerning 7435 cases of diphtheria, which received antitoxin. Amongst these the death rate was 6.5 per cent., while in the remaining, non-antitoxin cases, the death rate was 35 per cent., or more than five times as great. In other words, eight deaths out of ten in the latter group occurred simply from neglect of a simple and readily obtainable form of treatment, available to the poor as well as to the rich.

THE TWENTY-NINTH ANNUAL MEETING OF THE NEW JERSEY SANITARY ASSOCIATION was held Dec. 4, 1903. The proceedings have been published and are all excellent. We cannot forbear quoting a few paragraphs from the brief address of the President, Dr. John S. Leal, Health Officer of Paterson, N. J., although all interested in scientific hygiene should read the article itself. "We must teach that the great sanitary bugbear of the past—filth, filthy water and filthy air— are in themselves of little sanitary importance, and that measures directed against them alone, however commendable they may be, are not demanded by sanitary science.

"True sanitary science wars against infection whether it chances to be in filth or in purity, in filthy air or water or in that which is pure. It is just as dangerous, if not more so, in what is pure as in what is filthy. The measures used against it may incidentally aid in accomplishing other good things, but their prime and true object is the destruction of the infection.

"The converse is also true that measures which properly belong to public decency, public comfort and public policy may also incidentally aid in the fight against infection."

THE STATE LABORATORY OF HYGIENE OF NEW JERSEY, now under the directorship of R. B. Fitz-Randolph, late Associate-Director of the Hoagland Laboratory, Brooklyn, has reached a high standard of efficiency, but while enjoying the confidence of the State Board of Health and of public hygienists throughout this country, it has received scant financial support from the Legislature of the current year. The same Legislature was prevented only by the Governor's veto from wrecking the excellent Sanitary Inspector law, emanating from the New Jersey Sanitary Association and approved by the well-known sanitarian, Dr. Henry Mitchell, secretary of the State Board of Health, passed one year ago, and received with general acclaim by the leading hygienists of New Jersey.

We would assure such legislators that they need not fear prosecution for adulteration should they mix brains with their legislation, notwithstanding the fact that, strictly speaking, such a compound might often properly come within the scope of the clause forbidding the addition of "substances foreign to the well-known article under whose name they are offered for consumption."

A CHANGE IN THE BOSTON BOARD OF HEALTH.— The Hon. Edwin L. Pilsbury, whose term of office expired May 1, 1904, failed of reappointment. Mr. Pilsbury, whose capacity and courtesy all members of this Association will remember with admiration and pleasure, has been a member of the Board for about twelve years, and has proved an excellent and efficient public servant. Political pressure at the last moment was alone responsible for his non-appointment. We cannot but regret the reason as well as the fact.

His successor, Dr. T. B. Shea, chief medical inspector, was selected by the Mayor independently of the political movement referred to, and his appointment illustrates two excellent principles—promotion of an officer who has proved his efficiency in a subordinate position and the choosing for a responsible technical and professional position one with training and experience for its important duties.

THE MAYOR OF SAN FRANCISCO has made it his business to deny the existence of plague in that city, and to obstruct all efforts against its spread. He has recently removed the whole City Board of Health, in whom the people had confidence, and has replaced them by men in sympathy with his policy. Six cases of plague were reported by the U. S. P. H. and M. H. S. as present in the city during February, 1904. (8.)

We cannot but regret that the distinguished visitor from the East should so far forget the courtesy due to the chief executive of the only American city which has yet shown him extended hospitality as to overstay his welcome, especially when that chief executive takes pains to state that the distinguished visitor has never been present at all. We suggest that the plague—or the Mayor—should align himself with the real facts as soon as possible.

DR. PETER H. BRYCE, for many years the Secretary of the Provincial Board of Health of Ontario, has recently been appointed Medical Inspector of Immigration, under the Dominion Government. He has established a detention hospital in Quebec, and is building also a hospital for the treatment of emigrants. He is in charge of the Medical Service to the Indians throughout the Dominion. His successor in the Secretaryship is Dr. Charles H. Hodgetts, of whom we hope a conduct of affairs reaching the high standard set by Dr. Bryce. The reports of the Board contain much of interest, particularly the recent one describing the work of Dr. John A. Amyot, Bacteriologist to the Board, on sewage purification at Berlin. If Dr. Hodgetts will inaugurate his term of office by an appeal to the Government to print his reports on paper, and with type, not quite so wholly disreputable as Dr. Bryce has been compelled to use, he will confer a great favor on those at a distance, whose chief acquaintance with the Provincial Board of Health work must necessarily be had from their pages.

DR. U. O. B. WINGATE, whose name has long been a household word in hygienic circles, a well-known member of the

American Public Health Association, and a thoroughly sound and efficient public health officer, was recently removed from his position as Secretary of the Wisconsin State Board of Health because, as one of the members of the Board put it, "the plum should be passed around." To Dr. Wingate this "reason" involves a tribute, since no one can imagine that it would have been offered had a better one been available. To Wisconsin and to its State Board the "reason" is a disgrace not easily to be forgotten or forgiven by the hygienic world.

DR. E. A. DE SCHWEINITZ died in Washington, Feb. 15th, 1904, of uræmia. He was chief of the Bio-chemic Division, Bureau of Animal Industries, U. S. Department of Agriculture, and was known everywhere for the high character of his work, particularly in the bacteriology and chemistry of tuberculosis.

MR. GEORGE C. WHIPPLE, at one time Biologist to the Boston Water Board, and for the last six years Biologist and Director of Mount Prospect Laboratory, Brooklyn Water Department, has recently resigned to go into private practice as a Sanitary Expert in New York City.

CHEMICAL DETECTION OF RAW MILK.—Raw milk, treated with a solution of orthomethylaminophenol sulphate, followed by hydrogen peroxide, develops a brilliant deep red color. If heated at a temperature of 75 C. for half an hour, the milk will no longer react. Higher temperatures destroy the reaction more rapidly, but a temperature of 70 C. for an hour does not prevent the reaction. Raw milk, masquerading as scalded or Pasteurized, can be recognized by this method. So delicate is it that one per cent. of raw milk added to scalded milk can be detected. (5.)

AN INDIAN SNAKE-STONE.—The well known stories concerning stones capable, when applied to snake bites, sometimes to mad-dog bites, of adhering to the wound and absorbing the

poisons, have been put to the test by H. Watkins-Pitchford, Gov_
ernment Bacteriologist in Pietermaritzburg, Natal. The stone
tested came from India, accompanied by a statement from the
(white) owner that he had obtained it from a native whose life
the stone had saved in his (the owner's) presence.

Careful tests on rabbits, using the venoms of various poisonous snakes, and following in the application of the stone the cer-
emonies described, exactly in the native fashion, showed, as
might have been expected, that the stone had absolutely no effect
whatever upon the symptoms or fatality caused by the snake
poison. (7.)

A NEW METHOD OF GROWING ANAEROBES.—B.
R. Rickards, 1st Asst. Bacteriologist, Boston Board of Health
Laboratory, devised the simple plan of inverting ordinary tubes
of solid media, inoculated in the ordinary way, in the ordinary
solution of pyrogallol and alkali, contained in a tumbler or other
convenient receptacle. For liquid media, a U-tube, with one end
sealed, and this half filled with the inoculated medium, is similarly inverted with the unsealed end in the pyrogallol. For plates,
the liquefied nutrient jelly is poured into a sterile erlenmeyer, and
after solidification of the jelly, the flask is likewise inverted. In
all cases, the pyrogallol solution rises in the medium container
as the oxygen is absorbed. A fuller account is to be found in the
Centrablatt fuer Bakteriologie.

SEWAGE PURIFICATION TESTS IN COLUMBUS,
O.—About $50,000 have been appropriated for the testing of the
various known methods of purification, the tests to run for a
year from about July 1, 1904. The object is to determine the best
conditions for Columbus, but the broad views shown in the planning of this work, and the character of the men who will conduct it, ensure that much will be added to the general stock of
knowledge on this subject.

Mr. George A. Johnson, who was a member of the laboratory
force which conducted the well-known water-filtration experi-

ments in Louisville in 1895-96, under Mr. George W. Fuller, and who has since been engaged in similar work in Cincinnati, Washington, St. Louis and other cities, will be in charge. Mr. A. E. Kimberly of the Lawrence Experiment Station of this State will be First Asst. Chemist. The First Asst. Bacteriologist has been selected, we believe, but his name has not yet been made public.

DISEASE, OTHER THAN TYPHOID FEVER, FROM MILK.—During an outbreak of acute sore throat in England, traced by Vincent to one of two dairies, from which the infection had been distributed, a death occurred also from acute septic colitis, and Vincent convinced himself that this also was due to the use by the patient of the infected milk. (6.)

PNEUMONIA HAS BEEN PLACED ON THE REPORTABLE LIST in New York City, for the first time, it is said, in any city of this country. This is a marked recognition of the infectious nature of the disease, and of its increased ravages in late years.

The impression seems to be growing that even the ordinary colds are infectious, but these, as well as pneumonia, require a lowered condition of vitality in some form in the recipient before simple transmission of the infective agents becomes significant. We suggest that those Boards of Health which feel inclined to place pneumonia on the reportable list should be prepared to support their views by statistics, showing the average number of cases which can be traced to a single original case, amongst members of the same household and others closely associated with the patient, as has been done in tuberculosis.

TUBERCLE BACILLI IN OLD LIBRARY BOOKS.— Those who are in the habit of separating stuck-together leaves in public library books with finger-tips moistened with their own saliva, may, if well, become infected with tubercle bacilli, or if consumptives themselves, place their bacilli where others, following the same practices, may remove them to their own mouths.

Mitelescu, examining the books of a public library, chiefly from the fiction department, found that one-third of those over two years in use yielded tubercle bacilli from the leaves, when these were washed, and the washings centrifugalized and injected into guinea-pigs.

On clean paper the bacilli die out readily, from drying, but when dirty leaves stick together, evaporation is impeded, and the bacilli live longer. They were not found in books less than two years old (although we do not understand why), nor on the covers of any of the books. (10.)

It must not be forgotten that consumptives may infect books in the mere act of coughing, or even laughing and talking, when the book is open before them, and that such infection is more likely to remain active, shielded as it is from the action of sunlight and air when the book is closed, than similar infection of ordinary exposed surfaces. While it is unlikely that any large number of people become infected from this source, the handling of library books with moistened hands, a bad habit at best, receives additional condemnation from these results.

REGISTRATION OF TUBERCULOSIS.—Lecturing for the Phipps Institute, Dr. Herman M. Biggs of the New York Health Dept. points out that the objections to this can be met easily by providing that no action will be taken in the cases reported, unless the circumstances are such that administrative interference is necessary or desirable.

This is the principle on which the Boston Board of Health has proceeded since registration was made compulsory and comparatively little difficulty has been found in securing registration under this understanding.

FREE HOSPITALS FOR CONSUMPTIVES IN TORONTO.—This hospital, situated about ten miles outside of Toronto, is to be opened as soon as the necessary funds for furnishings, etc., are secured. A site near the new buildings of the University of Toronto Medical Faculty has been decided upon for a free dispensary for consumptives. So far about $400,000 has been expended in anti-tuberculosis work in Ontario by the National Sanitarium Association.

A PUBLIC TUBERCULOSIS CLINIC has been opened by the New York Health Department, near its headquarters, 55th Street and 6th Avenue. Diagnosis, circulars of information, treatment, sputum cups, etc., are offered free to indigents. A special corps of trained nurses is provided to care for poor patients at their homes. The co-operation of charitable organizations for the supply of fuel, ice, etc., has been secured. Suitable cases are sent to hospitals or sanitaria. Special attention is paid to preventing the spread of the disease, particularly amongst the children of the infected families. (9.)

ARE ALL SPECIES OF ANOPHELES HARMFUL?— Hirschberg throws doubt on *Anopheles punctipennis* as a transmitter of malaria, while confirming the capacity of *Anopheles maculipennis* in this direction. His method was to permit the mosquitoes to bite patients suffering from malaria in favorable stages, and then after waiting the proper interval, to section the mosquitoes and search for the parasites within them. In 58 tests with *A. punctipennis* he did not succeed in finding parasites at all, while in 48 tests with *A. maculipennis,* 8 positive results were obtained. (2.)

DENGUE, OR BREAK BONE FEVER, a hitherto mysterious affection of the Far East, is now ascribed by Dr. Graham of Beirut to a parasite transmitted by mosquitoes after the manner of malaria.

MEDICAL INSPECTORS APPOINTED.—Forty medical inspectors have been recently appointed by the Health Department of Philadelphia, pursuant to a recent act passed by the City Council. These medical inspectors are to give their entire time to the city, and each is placed in charge of a certain district. It is his duty to report all cases of infectious diseases, to trace the source of epidemics, to report any unhygienic conditions, to inspect public schools, etc. Each inspector is to receive a salary of $1200 per annum. (3.)

INSPECTION OF SCHOOL CHILDREN IN CHICAGO. —It is proposed in Chicago to thoroughly inspect the school children in each of the city schools. Teachers and principals must report for medical examination any pupils they believe physically defective, deformed, or afflicted with a functional disorder, The rules provide that the examinations shall be made by a school medical inspector in the office of the principal and under the latter's supervision. (3.)

VACCINATION OF PUBLIC SCHOOL CHILDREN in New York State, according to the decision of Attorney-General Cunneen, need not take in order to satisfy the legal requirements. It is evidently sufficient, in New York, to have "the form of godliness without the power thereof."

A PERMANENT EXHIBIT OF A HYGIENIC HOME, containing everything tending to promote the welfare of its inhabitants, particularly designed to meet the requirements of the working man, is maintained in Berlin. This idea might well be adopted in the larger cities in this country.

DR. JOHN N. HURTY, the well known Secretary of the State Board of Health of Indiana, has recently been unanimously re-elected for a period for four years. Dr. Hurty is in charge of the Hygienic Exhibit at the St. Louis Exposition.

EPIDEMIC CEREBRO-SPINAL MENINGITIS, known familiarly as "spotted fever," is reported from Hartford, Conn., to the extent of fifty-eight cases and thirty-two deaths in April. Strict measures of isolation have been carried out by the Board of Health.

COMPULSORY REGISTRATION OF TUBERCULOSIS as a contagious disease was voted down by a tie vote in a recent meeting of the Philadelphia County Medical Society.

LECTURES FOR MEDICAL INSPECTORS are being conducted under the auspices of Director Martin of the Philadelphia Board of Health.

TYPHOID BACILLI ISOLATED FROM DRINKING WATER.—In a previous issue we recorded various findings of this organism in water. To make the list more complete, we have below starred a few additional names quoted in the article of Konradi (see below), and have added the references for all.

Fischer and Flatau	Cent. f. Bakt., Ref. Abt.		1,	29
Genersich	"	"	"	27
Hankin	"	"		26
*Hanriot		Ref.		29
*Konradi	"	" Orig.		35
Kubler and Neufeld	Zeit. f. Hyg.,		Bd. 31	
Loesener	Arb. a. d. kais. Gesundheit.		Bd. 11	
*Tavel	Cent. f. Bakt., Orig.			33
Wesbrook	Rep. Minn. St. Bd. Health for '95-'98			
*Bonhoff (doubtful)	Cent. f. Bakt., Orig. Abt.		1,	33

B. R. RICHARDS.

TYPHOID FEVER DIAGNOSTICUM.—Under this name Ficker has placed in the hands of a manufacturing chemist for sale a slightly turbid fluid for use after the fashion of the Widal test, for the diagnosis of typhoid fever. To a little of this fluid the physician adds a drop of the patient's blood. In a short time the liquid shows a flocculation, and in time becomes clear by sedimentation, if the reaction be present. The test does not require a microscope, and can be applied at the bedside, while the fluid remains good for nine months. (11.)

Ruediger of Chicago has recently recommended for use in the same manner cultures of typhoid bacilli, killed by the addition of formalin. He claims for this method saving in time, as well as in trouble, over the usual method with living cultures. (12.)

TYPHOID BACILLI IN WELL PERSONS.—Juergens, examining the members of households where typhoid fever was present, found the bacilli, not only in the sick members, but also in those but slightly affected, and even in well persons associated with the clinically developed cases. (13.)

TYPHOID FEVER FROM CREAM IN WILLIAMS-TOWN, MASS.—The investigation of thirteen cases of typhoid fever which occurred at Williamstown during November, 1903, among the students of Williams College, shows that the probable source of infection was from a can of heavy cream, this being the only article of diet common to all the patients.

The cream supply was primarily obtained from Hoosick, N. Y., being shipped daily to the North Adams Milk Co., and subsequently delivered by eight different routes, seven of which were in North Adams and the other in Williamstown. No cases of the disease occurred among people using the regular supply at North Adams, and the investigation did not show the exact source of infection in the cream which went to Williamstown. A portion of this cream, returned daily to the milk depot, was used as a special supply for afternoon orders, and seven cases of typhoid fever occurred at North Adams among those who might have received the cream in this way. As additional evidence of the cream being the source of infection it was found that one member of the Tufts College football team, which played at Williamstown during the period when the infection of these patients probably occurred, and who had access to the cream, was subsequently taken ill with the disease.

On account of the length of time which elapsed from the date of the patient's going to bed to the reporting of the cases to the State Board of Health, the investigation could not be called complete, and it was not possible to obtain information which would point to the exact source of infection, on account of this lapse of time and the consequent loss of important connecting facts.—

F. L. MORSE, M. D.

TYPHOID FEVER FROM MILK IN PLYMOUTH, MASS.—On Feb. 1 the attention of the State Board of Health was called by the Board of Health of the town of Plymouth to the presence of an unusual number of cases of typhoid fever in the town, and it was asked that an investigation be made as to the cause of the disease.

From Jan. 2nd to Feb. 3rd 28 patients were found to have gone to bed ill with typhoid fever, 18 of them previous to the 15th of the month, and the remainder up to and including the 26th. All these patients had resided in the town for some time, and none had been away on any vacation, while with but one exception all had taken milk of one producer by the name of Finney. This exception was a young woman to whom the milkman was paying attention.

In the milkman's family five members were sick with the disease on Feb. 1st, the father, mother and three children. The milk barn is located about a mile from the home, and there are accommodations for twenty head of cattle, the milking being done by two of the boys. The milk was brought directly to the house, placed in a 100-qt. mixing can, cooled, and subsequently turned into 8-qt. cans for delivery. A small amount was placed in quart cans for the use of special customers, but ordinarily the milk was dispensed by measure at the house of each customer.

One of the boys doing the milking was taken ill on Jan. 9th, but continued to work until Jan. 15th, when he gave up work entirely, and three days later, on account of the appearance of the disease among the customers the milk supply was voluntarily suspended.

There have been four deaths in the course of the epidemic. One of the early cases to become ill was a patient living in a house located on the shores of Town Brook Pond. The attending physician did not give instructions relating to the disinfection of the discharges, and they had been thrown sometimes into a privy located on the water's edge, and at other times upon the ice which had formed upon the pond.

During the month of January about 1000 tons of ice had been

cut on this pond, 700 tons to be used for refrigerating purposes only, and 300 tons to be used in the fish business. The harvesting of the latter supply was completed on Jan. 28th, and ice was taken from the pond within 20 feet of the privy already mentioned. A sample of ice was obtained at a point near this locality and sent to Lawrence for examination. It showed numerous bacteria present, and upon the advice of the State Board of Health all of the ice was prevented from being used.—

F. L. MORSE, M. D.

TYPHOID EPIDEMIC IN WATERTOWN.—Information from Watertown, N. Y., March 10, says: George A. Soper of New York, the sanitary expert who is in charge of the typhoid fever situation here, says that there is a marked improvement in conditions. The number of cases reported daily shows a decided decrease, and the total number of cases is considerably less. The number of cases now in the city is less than 500. Arrangements have been practically completed for supplying the city with pure spring water. A number of tank wagons will be put into commission, and kept until the filtration plant is in operation next fall.

LEPROSY ON CAPE COD.—A case of leprosy has been discovered at North Harwich, the patient being a Portuguese 38 years of age, who has resided in this country for twelve years. His father, mother and sister are said to have died with the disease before his arrival in this country. His symptoms developed about five years ago with the formation upon the forearms of tubercles, which afterwards ulcerated. He has been treated at New Bedford by two different physicians, but the disease was not recognized by them. At the present time the face is covered with small tubercles the size of the tip of the little finger, with numerous ulcerations on the upper and lower extremities. Numerous cicatrices are present upon the forearms, indicating old ulcers which have subsequently healed. The roof of the mouth and nasal passages are also ulcerated, and there is considerable swelling of the face and hands.

The slight infectious character of this disease must be apparent when it is known that this man has been free to go and come in the past five years, during which time he has been in an infectious state, without giving rise to any other case. He is at present quarantined by the Board of Health of the town.

F. L. MORSE, M. D.

SMALLPOX IN LEOMINSTER.—A case of smallpox was reported from the town of Leominster on May 2nd, this being the first case of the disease existing in the eastern part of the State for a period of about two months. The patient is a French Canadian 34 years of age, who has never been vaccinated.

F. L. MORSE, M. D.

MERCURIC BICHLORIDE, AS A DISINFECTANT, NOT HARMFUL THROUGH VAPOR.—Bertarelli has investigated during two years the effect of disinfection by mercuric bichloride, on the disinfectors, and on the persons living in rooms after such disinfection, in Turin, where solutions of one to one hundred strength are used regularly.

The urine and feces were examined, and animals, enclosed in experimental chambers treated with the solutions, were observed.

He concludes that no risk of mercurial poisoning need be feared from the emanations of premises thus disinfected.

The solutions of "bichloride" used in this country rarely approach in strength the figures quoted for Turin, so that it appears proper to dismiss any haunting qualms which may have existed in their use. Of course, precautions against accidental swallowing of the solutions require the same attention as heretofore. (4.)

COAL SMOKE CONSISTS of solid matter and gases. The solid matter is made up of about equal parts of carbon and coal-ash, rather less than two pounds of each being thrown off in the burning of each ton of coal.

The gaseous matter consists of carbon dioxid, from 2 to 11 per cent by volume; carbon monoxid, .3 to 0 per cent.; oxygen, 7 to 18 per cent.; nitrogen about 80 per cent., and traces of hydrogen and of a large variety of hydrocarbons.

Smoke-consuming devices remove the solid matters largely, but not the gases. The economy of these devices lies, not, as is often supposed, in the saving of the carbon otherwise wasted, which is too small an item to be of much value, but in the added efficiency gained from the use of the methods of firing necessary to secure smokelessness, and in the smaller amount of hired help required. Under ordinary conditions, one pound of coal evaporates from 5 to 6 pounds of water, but under smokeless conditions, from 6 to 7 pounds. The total saving is put at 15 to 30 per cent.—(*From notes furnished by Prof. A. H. Gill.*)

ANTHRAX IN LYNN.—*The Boston Medical and Surgical Journal* of April 21st, 1904, states that fifteen cases of anthrax have occurred in Lynn, Mass., during the last three or four years, and urges investigation, with a view to prevention.

OYSTERS AND CLAMS.—"Seventy-seven samples of oysters have been examined by the New Hampshire State Board of Health Laboratory for boric acid and in thirty-four cases it was present. When the inspection was first commenced every sample of tub oysters contained boric acid, and the results obtained from samples from Dover, Portsmouth, Manchester and Concord showed conclusively that it was the practice of Boston wholesalers to add boric acid, or a preparation known as 'Preservaline' and containing boric acid, to every tub of oysters they sent out. A vigorous correspondence with dealers in Norfolk and Providence River tub oysters produced such beneficial results that on the last inspection of oysters from the above-named cities but little boric acid was found. The practice of preserving oysters by the liberal use of boric acid permitted the small grocer or marketman to keep oysters on his counter, without ice, in warm weather, as long as any remained unsold. We must conclude that a preservative active enough to arrest decay in such perishable articles as oysters, under such conditions, would not fail to arrest, in a like manner, the action of the digestive ferments.

"Clams are equally liable to adulteration by preservatives, and because of their less common use may contain even larger quantities of boric acid.

"The action of the wholesale houses in quickly abandoning the use of boric acid when notified by their customers that they were not allowed to sell goods so treated, proves the practice to be unnecessary." (1.)

NEW MILK REGULATION.—The Boston Board of Health has amended its milk regulations of 1898 by the addition (April 29, 1904,) of a paragraph relating to bacteriological examinations and control as follows:

Art. IV., sect. 1.—No person, by himself or by his servant or agent, or as the servant or agent of any other person, firm, or corporation, shall bring into the city of Boston for purposes of sale, exchange or delivery, or sell, exchange, or deliver any milk, or cream which contains more than 500,000 bacteria per cubic centimeter, or which has a temperature higher than fifty degrees Fahrenheit.

Routine bacteriological examinations of the Boston milk supply are now being arranged for at the Boston Board of Health Laboratory.

References.

New Hampshire San. Bull.
    1. January, 1904.
Johns Hopkins Hospital Bull.
    2. February, 1904.
American Medicine.
    3. Feb. 27, 1904.
   14. March 18, 1904.
   16. March 5, 1904.

Zeit. f. Hyg.
    4.   1903, xlii.
    10. 1903, p. 397 (Abs., Pratt, *Boston Medical and Surgical
         Journal*, April 23, 1904).
British Medical Journal.
    5.   March 21, 1903.
    6.   Feb. 6, 1904.
    7.   Feb. 20, 1904.
Journal American Medical Association.
    8.   March 12, 1904.
    13. April 23, 1904.
Boston Medical and Surgical Journal.
    9.   March 3, 1904.
Berl. klin. Wochen.
    11. 1903, No. 45.
Journal Infectious Diseases.
    12. Vol. 1, No. 2, 1904.

BOOKS.

ELEMENTS OF WATER BACTERIOLOGY.—Prescott
(S. C.), and Winslow (C. E. A.)   John Wiley & Sons.   1904.
Price, $1.00.

For a long time there has been an urgent need of a treatise on
Water Bacteriology, which would not only give the methods in
use in Europe, but also the especially facile procedures which
have been worked out in American laboratories.   The authors
have met this need with a well-arranged and practical volume of
125 pages.

Some criticisms may be made of the mediocre press work, of
the ambiguous wording in one or two places and of the rather
poor proof reading.   For example, in the diagram on Page 7,
one of the two "Nitrates" should be "Nitrates."   On Page
9, it is stated that "A good river water under favorable conditions should thus contain only a few hundred bacteria."   Would
not the reader get the impression that all waters with less than

a few hundred bacteria are good, and all with a few thousand bacteria (unpolluted muddy streams) are bad?

In the first paragraph on Page 38 there are two indistinct letters and a split infinitive. On Page 45 it would be better to say "more common"; and "the latter" refers to a word four lines back. It would perhaps be better to give the date of Johnson's paper, Page 75.

The subject matter itself in the book is excellent. One can only be impressed with the careful presentation of the subject. Especially praiseworthy is the bibliographical work and the convenience of the references. Especially well balanced are the chapters on the Significance of the Presence of *B. coli* and Other Intestinal Bacteria in Water. The authors take the sound position that a sample of water free from *B. coli* is undoubtedly safe, and that its continued presence in 1-c. c. samples is an index of serious pollution.

Chapter IX, which treats of intestinal bacteria other than *B. coli,* is an excellent summary of the present knowledge of the sanitary significance of this class of bacteria. Much of this chapter is new. The authors say that the presence of *Streptococci* is valuable confirmatory evidence of dangerous pollution.

The methods given for the examination of water are excellent. Many of them are the same as those recommended by the American Public Health Association. The other methods are largely supplementary or are new methods not discussed by the Association. The outline of the methods is very well given and is in general very clear. One might ask if double dilution (Page 28) were not the best method for handling samples rich in bacteria. On Page 44 it is stated that bacteria develop very little at the body temperature after 24 hours of incubation. Can this be strictly true?

While reading Page 54 one will ask if natural immunity does not protect the human race to some extent.

In the last chapter the value of bacterial methods is, set forth very well. However, the authors are inclined to overestimate the accuracy of the various methods. The reading is easier than the doing. Again, there is perhaps a tendency to forget that while the bacterial examination in many cases is a sanitary *sine qua non,* it is seldom the *ne plus ultra.*

Everyone interested in the analysis of water should own a copy of this little book. It is the best of its kind in any language, and with the minor errors eliminated in the future editions, should have a wide circulation.—*R. S. W.*

GENERAL PATHOLOGY.—By Sidney Martin, M. D., F. R. S., F. R. C. P., Professor of Pathology at University College; Physician to University College Hospital, London. With numerous woodcuts from micro-photographs, and other illustrations, including many in colors. Philadelphia, 1904. P. Blakiston's Son & Co. Pages, 495, with index, preface and introduction.

Based on lectures delivered at University College, and intended primarily for students, this book seems to us better fitted for those already somewhat familiar with the subject than it is for the beginner, to whom detailed explanations are necessary if he is to secure any consecutive and logical view of the whole. Nevertheless the author has succeeded in covering the chief fields of modern pathology in clear language. We are particularly pleased with his advocacy of physiological pathology, believing that the term pathology is too often restricted to the mere anatomy of disease. Disease is a process in a machine, the autopsy revealing merely a vertical section through the process, with the machine stopped. The divorcement of clinical research and teaching from pathological research and teaching not infrequently results in the student receiving the impression, not formularized, but latent, that every disease possesses a dual personality; he carries two distinct pictures of pneumonia, say, with him; one, the pneumonia of his clinical teacher, existing only in the hospital ward; the other, the pneumonia of his pathological teacher, existing only in the autopsy room. To substitute a proper composite picture these two are the real basis of successful medical teaching.

SANITARY ENGINEERING NOTES.

ROBERT SPURR WESTON, M. A.,
Assoc. M. Boston Soc. C. E.

REPORT OF THE SPECIAL COMMISSION ON THE WATER SUPPLY OF SPRINGFIELD, MASS., 1904.—The present Ludlow and Jabish Brook supplies are subject to very numerous growths of organisms, principally anabæna, which give rise to disagreeable tastes and odors in the water. Consequently the improvement of the present supply, or the taking of a new supply from another source, is becoming a pressing question.

The recent report by Samuel M. Gray, M. Am. Soc. C. E., and George W. Fuller, Assoc. M. Am. Soc. C. E., with the appended report of E. E. Lochridge, Resident Engineer, discusses the whole problem in a thorough manner.

Experiments by Mr. Lochridge demonstrated that the present supply could be purified by double filtration, together with repeated aeration. This purified supply would be good for 15,000,-000 gals. per diem, and could be supplemented by filtered Connecticut River water from above Holyoke. This combination would be the cheapest method of supplying the city with 25,000,-000 gals. per diem.

The engineers considered supplementing the Ludlow water with that of the Scantic River (filtered), and investigated the practicability of supplying the city solely with filtered Connecticut River water. They also studied the Westfield River at Huntington.

The estimated cost of the various supplies per million gallons, on a basis of 25,000,000 gals. per day, is as follows:

Ludlow Reservoir and Connecticut River . . .	$25.44
Westfield at Huntington	27.76
Ludlow and Scantic	26.89
Connecticut River	27.08

In view of the extreme difficulty of purifying the Ludlow water, the necessity of pumping the Connecticut River supply, the small amount of pollution of the Westfield—a gravity supply

—and the slight differences in cost, the engineers have recom-mended the most desirable supply, namely, the Westfield River at Huntington. The estimated cost of this construction is $4,-303,990, which, although about $1,000,000 above the cost of the Ludlow and Connecticut River scheme, is well within the means of the Water Department, particularly if the excessive consumption of water be lessened.

It is gratifying to note that the engineers have recommended that all water, even the upland water, be filtered. However, the names of the engineers were a guarantee that this modern position would be taken. The so-called "unpolluted" watersheds which are available for water supply are not numerous.

THE EFFECT OF POLLUTED RIVERS UPON THE NEIGHBORING GROUND WATER.—Wolf, K. (Arb. aus den Kgl. hygien. Instituten zu Dresden. Vol I, 1903, p. 291.)— The Dresden water supply is taken from the gravel layers, which extend underneath the Elbe River. At times of flood the numbers of bacteria in the ground water rises to several thousand per cubic centimeter. Several of these bacteria were isolated from the ground water. Two of them were determined to be *B. coli* and *B. vulgaris,* respectively. The author suggests that the water of filter galleries and wells adjacent to rivers should be analyzed at all stages of the river before deciding upon the ground water as a source of supply.

NEW METHOD FOR THE DETERMINATION OF THE VELOCITY OF GROUND WATER FLOW.—Slichter. (Jour. f. Gas. und Wasserversorgung, 1903, No. 12, p. 230.) —In place of studying the rate of passage of salt or dye stuff through the ground, the author introduces ammonium chloride at the higher of the two points in the ground water table, and brings them into an electric circuit, thus measuring the electro-conductivity of the soil, which, on the appearance of the ammonium chloride at the second and lower observation point, shows a sudden change.

A NEW COAGULANT FOR USE WITH RAPID FIL-
TERS.—In several rapid filter plants, for example, Lorain, O.,
and Danville, Ill., the use of sulphate of alumina has been stopped
and lime and ferrous sulphate have been used in its place, thereby effecting a considerable cost saving, with continuance of good
bacterial results. A. C. Brown (Engineering Record, Vol. 48,
p. 701, 1903) describes his experience with this coagulant as used
at Lorain.

BACTERIA IN SOIL IN RELATION TO INFILTRA-
TION GALLERIES FOR WATER SUPPLY. G. C. Whipple.
(Engineering Record, Vol. 48, p. 501-2.)—Experiments were
made to determine the efficiency of the soil for removing bacteria
from water collected by filter galleries, which galleries
were constructed of vitrified pipe, laid with open joints, in
trenches from 10 to 20 ft. deep, and surrounded with gravel or
broken stone. One typical experiment is selected for an example.

Depth Below Surface (Ft.)	Bacteria per Gram of Soil.
0.	136,000
0.5	115,800
1	6,800
2	2,850
3	885
4	380
5	60
6	00
7	00
8	00

Mr. Whipple concludes that "The sand below 5 ft. in depth
never contains more than a very small number of bacteria. Tests
for *B. coli* were negative."

These experiments confirm the belief that wells are most frequently contaminated from the surface, and seldom through
sandy soils. Fissured soils, however, may allow the direct passage of water from a source of pollution to a well.

SEWAGE DISPOSAL IN IOWA. A. Marston. (Jour. Western Soc. E.)—Reviewed in American Chemical Research, Vol. X, No. 4, by L. P. Kinnicutt.) This paper gives a detailed account of the eleven sewage disposal plants in the State of Iowa. They are all modern plants, using the septic tank. The reader is referred to Prof. Kinnicutt's review or the original paper for a fuller account.

FILTERS, VERSUS CONTACT BEDS AND SEWAGE PURIFICATION. *Municipal Engineer.* Vol. XXVI, p. 111-117; also Journ. Am. Chem. Research, Vol. X, No. 4.)—In this paper the author concludes that the septic tank is a necessary preliminary to sewage purification. It is to be noted that the English practice is to provide from one to one and one-half days' storage in the septic tank, while the American practice is to store the sewage from one-half to one day only. Regarding the treatment of the septic tank effluent, whether by means of sand beds, contact beds, or trickling beds, the author states that the tendency of the English practice is away from the contact beds and toward the trickling bed. These latter are built of coarse material, and the sewage is applied continuously in the form of a spray. In cold climates there would be danger of freezing were trickling beds used.

THE TARRING OF MACADAMIZED ROADS TO PREVENT DUST. Schottelius and Guglielminetti (Muench, med. Wochenschrift, 1903, No. 25, p. 1068.)—The authors note that pneumonia, influenza, diphtheria, etc., are increased by breathing dust. They show this by adequate statistics. They describe the process for preventing the same by covering the road with a layer of tar in the following manner.

On a dry and warm day the cleaned and rolled macadam is given one or two coats of coal tar previously heated to 60 degrees C. After two to three hours the tar is strewn with dry sand. The tar absorbs rapidly, and it is claimed that dust is diminished. It is said that one pound of tar will cover 5 sq. ft., and that it would cost about $150 to tar a mile of road 18 ft. wide. Petroleum is not a satisfactory substitute for tar.

CIDER VINEGAR AND SUGGESTED STANDARDS OF PURITY. (Albert E. Leach and Herman C. Lythgoe. *Journal American Chemical Society,* Vol. XXVI. p. 375.)—The authors give analyses of many true and also many sophisticated vinegars, and describe the methods used for analyzing the same. As a result of their experience they suggest the following standard:

"The acetic acid shall be more than 4.50 per cent.; the cider vinegar solids more than 2 per cent.; the ash should constitute at least 6 per cent. of the solids; the alkalinity of 1 gram of ash should be equivalent to at least 65 c. c. of tenth-normal acid; at least 50 per cent. of the phosphates in the ash should be soluble in water. The reducing sugars should be the same in amount after as before inversion, and should not exceed 25 per cent. of the solids. The polarization, expressed in terms of 200 mm. of undiluted vinegar, should lie between -0.1 degree and -4.0 degree Ventzke. Malic acid should be indicated by both calcium chloride and the lead acetate test."

"Aside from the test for acid and total solids, by far the most important tests are the polarization and the tests for malic acid."

POPULAR ESSAYS ON HYGIENE AND SANITATION.

(A Series of Leaflets designed to teach in simple language some of the more important Lessons of the Time concerning Health and Disease.)*

SERIES A.   ON DIRT AND DISEASE.

No. 1.   WHY DIRT IS DANGEROUS.

Dirt and disease are apt to go together, but until lately no one knew why.   Today we know that dirt and disease are often closely connected, because dirt is generally not merely dead earth but rather a kind of *living earth,* crowded with unseen and almost countless *germs* or *microbes,* many of which may be dangerous and even deadly.

WHAT IS DIRT?   We use the term dirt for various things: for "earth," for "soil," and for "stains" and "spots" of many kinds, but dirty dishes, dirty faces, dirty clothing, dirty shoes and dirty streets often mean something foul or filthy.   The word dirt itself comes from an older word drit (meaning dung or excrement), and, strictly speaking, the word "dirt" should not be used for good clean earth, or virgin soil, or sands and gravels, such as are found in sea beaches or sandbanks or deserts. It really ought to be kept for dung or excrement or filth, or for earth, soil or sands polluted or stained with dung, excrement or filth.

---

*Prepared and published by the Sanitary Research Laboratory of the Massachusetts Institute of Technology in Boston, at the request and by the Gift of a Friend of Science and Education.
The present is the first (No. 1) in SERIES A.   ON DIRT AND DISEASE.
Some of those to follow are:—
No. 2. WHY DIRTY MILK IS DANGEROUS.
No. 3. WHY DIRTY WATER IS DANGEROUS.
No. 4. WHY DIRTY STREETS ARE DANGEROUS.
No. 5. WHY DIRTY PERSONS ARE DANGEROUS.
Other Leaflets may eventually be prepared upon " Microbes,— Good and Bad ; " " Some Common Diseases : How they Come and how to Avoid them ; " " Farm Sanitation ; " " Why Flies are Filthy and Dangerous ; " and other practical sanitary and hygienic topics.
It is hoped that Boards of Health, School Boards, Hospital Authorities, Charity Workers, Health-Education Leagues, Anti-Tuberculosis Societies and other Educators or Philanthropic Persons and Organizations may make use of this Leaflet and those which are to follow in that campaign of Sanitary education in which all civilized peoples must sooner or later participate.
Reprints of the Essay here published (SERIES A, No. 1—WHY DIRT IS DANGEROUS) may be had (postpaid) by addressing the Biological Department, Mass. Institute of Technology, Boston, Mass., and enclosing postage stamps according to the following schedule :—
One to fifty copies . . . . .2 cents each.
Fifty or more copies . . . . .1 cent   "

WHY DIRT IS DANGEROUS. Dirt is dangerous chiefly because it is very often dung, excrement or filth, and as such may be the carrier of disease germs or microbes from diseased human beings or other animals to persons who, though well, are able to catch a disease.

In typhoid fever, for example, germs peculiar to that disease are thrown off (excreted) in the bowel discharges, urine and spit of the patient. These excreta, as they are called, may thus become carriers of typhoid fever, because they carry its germs, and linen, bed-pans, spittoons, handkerchiefs and the like, soiled or dirtied by any of these excreta, may be bearers of the living poisonous germs of this terrible disease from a patient to a laundress, a maidservant, a nurse, or to anyone whose hands become dirty by handling such articles or excreta. From hands so soiled contagion may be carried to plates, cups, saucers, spoons, and above all, food.

HOW DIRT IS DANGEROUS. Dirt being often really dung, excrement or filth, is dangerous because it passes so readily and in so many ways from the patient to the public. We have just spoken of laundresses and others whose hands may become dirty by handling dirty linen, dirty bedpans and the like. Such persons are themselves in great danger from this dirt and often actually "catch" the disease. But if the urine or bowel discharges of typhoid fever patients are thrown into a brook leading to a reservoir of drinking water, the lives of all the people of the town or city using that water are endangered. Again, if such dirt finds its way into milk there is grave danger for anyone who drinks that milk, or if into a sewer emptying upon an oyster bed for anyone eating oysters thus sewage-polluted; or if such sewage is used to water a celery or lettuce or strawberry patch then anyone eating such dirtied celery, lettuce or strawberries may run the risk of losing his life.

WHY DIRTY STREETS ARE DANGEROUS. Dirty streets are dangerous because the dirt in this case may cling to shoes

or other articles of footwear and be carried from the streets
into houses where, either as fresh dirt or more often as dry
dirt (dust), it may find its way to foods or other articles
which either enter or touch the mouths of members of the
household.   Street dirt is also dangerous when dried up and
pulverized or turned into dust, which may be readily lifted
and blown about by winds, thus finding its way perhaps directly into the mouths of human beings, or through cracks
and crevices or open doors and windows into human habitations and finally into human bodies upon articles of food or
drink.

Insects, such as flies and mosquitoes, may also carry dirty
particles from dirty streets into houses and deposit them upon
food materials in the pantry or upon the table.

We need only stop to think for a moment how really dirty
the dirt of a street may be, to understand how dangerous it
may become.   If we remember that the streets are constantly
used by dirty horses, dogs, cats, birds (such as sparrows and
pigeons) and occasionally by other animals, when we remember how many people of all sorts thoughtlessly spit in the
streets or on the sidewalks,—using the gutter as a kind of
spittoon,— when we consider how many loads of manure and
other dirty materials are hauled through the streets and how
many careless people throw into the streets rubbish of all
sorts, such as papers, orange-peel, banana-skins, cigar-stubs
and the like, when we realize that a certain number of the
animals or human beings whose droppings, spit or rubbish are
cast into the streets are suffering from diseases (and sometimes
loathsome diseases) and especially from consumption, diphtheria,
colds or other complaints, then we can easily see how and why it
is that street dirt is dangerous.

WHY DIRTY WATER IS DANGEROUS. It is still easier to
understand that water which contains dirt or excreta may be
very dangerous, because in no way are the germs of disease
more readily taken into the human body than with food and
drink.   We shall shortly publish in this series a special circu-

lar upon drinking water and disease and all who are interested may procure and read that leaflet.

WHY DIRTY MILK IS DANGEROUS. Dirty milk is dangerous because the dirt most often found in milk is cow dung or else dirt derived from dirty milkmen who have handled the milk with dirty hands. Then, too, milk is good food for some germs or microbes, very much as it is for human beings, and germs will therefore grow and multiply in milk more readily than in water. There will be later a special leaflet in this series upon this subject and all who are interested may procure a copy of it.

DIRTY HANDS AND FACES AND WHY THESE ARE DANGEROUS. Human hands go only too readily almost everywhere and thus very easily become dirty. Children, for example, having soiled their hands may perhaps the next minute put their fingers upon their faces or into their mouths and thus carry dirt, and with that the germs of disease, directly into the body itself. Frequent washing of the hands is a great sanitary safeguard, and for this reason no one should sit down to a meal at which food will be "handled" without having first carefully washed his hands. Workingmen away from home, taking their dinners from a dinner-pail, should be particularly careful to wash their hands, especially if they have been handling paints or other poisonous substances, or dirt in any of its thousand forms.

CLEANLINESS IS NEXT TO GODLINESS. This is an old saying which has come down to us as a result of long and painful experience. Why, of all things, should cleanliness be placed next to godliness? Why should not honesty, or industry, or any one of a thousand things rather than cleanliness, be placed there? The reason probably is that very much as godliness is believed to give to the godly eternal life in the world to come, so cleanliness, as shown by experience, tends to give to the cleanly long life in this world. Dirt and disease, danger and death have been found by hard experience to go together, while cleanliness tends toward safety, health, comfort and long life.

HOW DIRTY PEOPLE KEEP HEALTHY. Everybody who stops to think knows that some dirty people do appear to keep healthy and live long, and some may wonder that this is so. The reason appears to be this: Some people are so strong, robust, hearty and healthy that they can resist almost all ordinary causes of disease. They can get "soaked through" in a rain without catching cold; they can go with wet shoes and stockings, or thinly clad, and yet seem to be none the worse: they may even sometimes be exposed to contagious or infectious diseases without catching them. All this is at first sight hard to explain, but if we remember that the human body is after all a good deal like a machine, such, for example, as a watch or a wagon, we can perhaps realize that, like most machines, some specimens are stronger than others and when exposed to rough usage stand the strain wonderfully well, while some, though looking just as strong, break down easily. It is true that some few human beings are so strong and robust that they can thrive for a time, even in dirt, but these are the exception and not the rule, and even for them dirt is always a danger; for if these same strong people get overworked, or run down, or become dissipated in any way, they, too, generally suffer, just like their weaker neighbors, from dirt and filth.

(A copy of this Essay may be secured free of cost by addressing the Biological Department Massachusetts Institute of Technology, Boston, and enclosing a stamped, addressed envelope.)

JOURNAL OF THE

MASSACHUSETTS ASSOCIATION OF BOARDS OF HEALTH

AND

AMERICAN JOURNAL OF PUBLIC HYGIENE.

ORGANIZED 1890.

[The Association as a body is not responsible for statements or opinions of any of its members.]

| VOL. XIV. | August, 1904. | NO. 3 |

THE MASSACHUSETTS ASSOCIATION OF BOARDS OF HEALTH was organized in Boston, March, 1890, with the following objects: the advancement of sanitary science; the promotion of better organization and co-operation among local boards of health, and the uniform enforcement of sanitary laws and regulations.

All communications concerning the ASSOCIATION should be addressed to the Secretary of the Association, JAMES C. COFFEY, CITY HALL, WORCESTER, MASS.

All bills not relating to the Journal, and MEMBERSHIP DUES $2.00 per year), should be sent to the Treasurer of the Association, DR. JAMES B. FIELD, 329 WESTFORD ST., LOWELL, MASS.

THE JOURNAL OF THIS ASSOCIATION has for fourteen years faithfully reflected the views of the public hygienists of Massachusetts. With the October issue of the year 1903, a policy of expansion was adopted, and the encouragement received from a great many hygienic quarters led to still further expansion, as may be seen in this issue.

The dates of publication are FEBRUARY, MAY, AUGUST *and* NOVEMBER *of each year.*

THE JOURNAL will contain the papers read at the meetings of · the Association, papers contributed by hygienists, reports of the discussions, editorials, abstracts, reviews and hygienic notes of professional interest. Subscription rates, $1.00 per year. Reprints furnished at cost price.

All communications concerning the JOURNAL, copy, proof, subscriptions, advertisements, etc., should be addressed to the Managing Editor, DR. H. W. HILL, 739 BOYLSTON ST., BOSTON, MASS.

EDITORIALS.

SCARLET FEVER ISOLATION.

The length of time that a patient ill with scarlet fever should be isolated is a very important matter, and has been the subject of careful study by those who have the charge of infectious diseases. The practice in different localities varies very considerably; as for instance, in Glasgow the time is much longer than in England and in this country. The so-called return cases are a source of annoyance to the physician and an injury to the public. Some physicians go so far as to say that the desquamation is not infectious, but that the contagium of scarlet fever is in the discharges from the mucous membranes and from the ears. This is a little too radical an opinion and is not in accordance with clinical experience. There is no doubt that during the active stage of primary desquamation scarlet fever is infectious. There is very grave doubt if the secondary desquamation is infectious. In scarlet fever, bacteriology is of no assistance because, as yet, the organism that causes the disease has not been definitely discovered. Mallory's work in this direction is of very great value from a scientific point of view, and while he has proved that a protozoön is the cause of the disease, the length of time required to find the organism deprives Mallory's discovery of much practical benefit. The other organisms found in scarlet fever have never been definitely shown to be the cause of the disease. It must be taken as an accepted fact that scarlet fever is infectious from the commencement of the attack, even before there is an eruption. It has also been proved that the disease is not so infectious at this stage as later in the course of the attack. There is also abundant clinical experience proving that scarlet fever without an eruption, with marked throat symptoms, is infectious. In many of the so-called return cases, investigation has shown that some member of the family had a sore throat, presumably scarlatinal in its nature, which was the cause of the outbreak of the disease and not the patient who was discharged from the hospital.

In 1898 the Metropolitan Asylums Board of London commenced a series of investigations on this point. The investigation was made by Dr. W. J. R. Simpson and was very carefully conducted for a period of six months. His report was referred to a committee of the Royal College of Physicians, England. The conclusions reached briefly were as follows:

1. "The committee have carefully considered Dr. Simpson's report and the documents referring thereto, for the purpose of expressing an opinion as to whether, and if so, under what conditions, the present period of detention of patients in the hospitals of the Metropolitan Asylums Board could consistently with public safety be shortened."

2. "The committee are impressed with the small percentage of those cases which, on investigation, were found to have given rise to fresh infection, viz., 1.1 per cent on the total cases discharged from hospital of diphtheria and scarlet fever taken together. They also note that of these, no fewer than 80 per cent were suffering from some mucous discharge, either during their stay in hospital or shortly subsequent to their return home."

3. "The total number of return cases of diphtheria was 21, equal to a percentage of .5 on the cases of diphtheria discharged. With reference to the length of detention after diphtheria, the committee are of opinion that this can only be left to the discretion of the several medical superintendents. The importance of the question of return cases mainly turns on the length of detention of scarlet-fever cases, which are more numerous than those of diphtheria. The proportion of the return cases in diphtheria is small, viz., .5 per cent of the patients discharged after suffering from that disease; and apart from the difficulty which is occasionally experienced in respect to the recognition of the specific bacillus, a difference of opinion exists as to the practicability of regulating a patient's detention by bacteriological examination alone."

4. "The total number of return cases of scarlet fever was 90, giving a percentage of 1.3 of the total number discharged. In endeavoring to arrive at a definite conclusion as to the necessary length of detention in scarlet fever, there are two points on which elucidation is required.

The degree of infectivity attaching to—

(*a*) The desquamation of the skin.

(*b*) Any mucous discharge occurring during convalescence."

"In respect of the infectivity of the later desquamation of the skin in scarlet fever, it is to be observed in Dr. Simpson's investigation that in only 2.7 per cent was there any reason to suspect desquamation of the skin as the cause of secondary infection. The relatively high degree of infectivity of the mucous discharges, as compared with the later desquamation of the skin in scarlet fever, as shown in the report, is one which is obtaining an increasing support among those of the profession who have had much to do with infectious diseases. It would suggest that possibly too much importance has been hitherto attached to the infectivity of the skin during the later weeks of scarlatinal convalescence. The committee have communicated with the authorities of many hospitals in other large cities in this country, in America, and in Germany, and have ascertained that the period of detention insisted on is of somewhat shorter duration than is practiced in those of the Metropolitan Asylums Board. Unfortunately no corresponding record of the incidents of return cases is available for comparison with that recently obtained for the Metropolitan Asylums Board."

In the *London Lancet* of March 12, 1904, is an extremely interesting paper by R. E. Lauder, F.R.C.S. Edinburgh, D.P.H. Medical Officer of Health of the County Borough and Port of Southampton; Medical Superintendent of the Borough and Port Fever Hospital.

Dr. Lauder takes a very decided stand regarding the infectivity of discharges from the mucous membranes and does not place so much stress upon the contagiousness of the desquamation. Dr. Lauder says that in 1902 no cases of scarlet fever were discharged from the hospital until all peeling had ceased, but that during 1903 he has acted on the belief that the infection is in the respiratory tract, that the constitutional condition, and particularly the rash, are only the result of toxic products, and that therefore the desquamation of the skin is not *per se* a source of danger.

He gives the following tables:

TABLE I.

Year	Cases Notified.	Removed to Hospital.	Discharged from Hosp'l.	Av. Period in Hospital.	No. Causing "Return" Cases	Cases Treated at Home.
1902	261	208	164	48 days	7	53
1903	427	353	325	34 "	7	74

TABLE II.

	Discharged.	Av. Duration in Hospital.	No. Causing "Return" Cases
1. Without peeling or complications .	33	33	0
2. Peeling without complications . .	204	28	2
3. Cases with compl.cations	88	50	5
Total	325	34	7

A glance at Table 1 shows that in 1902 the average period of detention in the hospital was 48 days, while in 1903 it was 34 days. In 1902 there were 208 patients admitted to the hospital and there were 7 instances of return cases, while in 1903 there were 353 cases admitted and 7 instances of return cases. In Table II he gives the number discharged without peeling or complications; the number peeling without complications, and the cases with complications. It is interesting to note that there were no return cases where there was no peeling nor complications; that where there was peeling without complications there were two instances of return cases; that where there were cases with complications there were five instances of return cases. This paper of Dr. Lauder's is an extremely valuable one, but from the comparatively small number of cases it seems as if it would be hardly safe to accept his deductions.

In other words, in view of the immense amount of clinical experience proving the infectivity of desquamation, it would harldy be a wise procedure to discharge patients from isolation as long as there was any peeling. This question, however, is one that should receive more attention from boards of health.

At the South Department of the Boston City Hospital the average length of time that a patient remains in the hospital is 50 days. No patient is discharged who has any discharge from the nose or any abnormal condition of the throat.

In 1903, 650 patients were discharged from the scarlet fever ward. There were 15 instances of alleged return cases. Investigation, however, failed to show anything abnormal in the condition of the individuals discharged. There was a certain number of alleged return cases where it was demonstrated that the source of infection was not the patient who had been discharged from the hospital, but from patients who were suffering from mild and unrecognized attacks of the disease. In order to prevent the possibility of return cases, the following circular is given to each patient on his discharge from the hospital:

THE BOSTON CITY HOSPITAL,

South Department,

745 Massachusetts Avenue,

Boston, December 16, 1902.

Advice to the Parents of Patients who are Discharged from the Wards Set Apart for Infectious Diseases:

1. To avoid any possible danger of the communication of scarlet fever, measles or diphtheria to other members of the family, it is much safer for any person who has just been discharged from the wards used for these diseases to sleep alone for *at least one week*, and preferably for *two weeks*.

2. These diseases are especially likely to be spread by means of discharges from the ears or nose, or from any running sore on the body, long after the patient is otherwise entirely well. Therefore, if at any time during two weeks after discharge from the hospital the patient shows any such trouble, he should immediately be brought back to the hospital for examination, and in the meantime should keep as much as possible away from others, and should not use the same towel, brush, comb or other toilet article that others use. When there is any such discharge, handkerchiefs, etc., that are used should be burned when it is possible; when this is not possible, they should be thoroughly boiled. It is better that separate toilet articles be used even if there is no apparent trouble.

3. When a person comes home from an infectious ward, clothing, toys, books, etc., used by him at the time he was taken sick should not be brought out again unless it is certain that they were *thoroughly* disinfected.

This advice is especially important in cases of scarlet fever.

In very many instances the alleged return cases of scarlet fever have no connection with the discharged patient, as the following quotation from the Report of the Metropolitan Asylums Board proves:

1. "Lily T. returned home from hospital where she had been treated for scarlet fever for 45 days. Later, Ida and Dudley T. were reported as suffering from scarlet fever. On investigation it was ascertained that Elsie, a cousin living in the same house, had been attacked with scarlet fever *one day before* Lily returned, and that the probable cause of Elsie's attack was infection from a mild case that had been kept at home and not sent to hospital."

2. "Harry G. returned convalescent from hospital after 51 days' detention in hospital for scarlet fever. A few days afterwards Winifred W. and Clara G., living in the same house, were reported suffering from scarlet fever. On inquiry it was found that Winifred W. had been removed to hospital for scarlet fever *about half an hour before Harry arrived home.*"

3. "Alfred G. was treated in hospital for diphtheria, and was detained there 63 days; 17 days after his return home, Lily G. was attacked with scarlet fever. The possible source of Lily's infection was from cases which occurred amongst children on the opposite side of the street."

4. "Theodore W. was attacked with scarlet fever 16 days after the return of his sister from hospital, where she had been detained 76 days. On her return she remained in excellent health. For the first week she slept with two of her sisters, aged 17 and 7 respectively. The sister aged 7 was the delicate one of the family. Neither of these were attacked. Later Grace slept with Theodore. On the twelfth day after her return, a dressed doll which Grace played with while in bed, and which was put away when she was taken to hospital, was brought out and played with by Grace and Theodore. Grace washed the flannel clothes of the doll, and Theodore washed his face and mouth with the flannel clothes. Two days after this Theodore began to complain, and on the fourth day the rash of scarlet fever appeared on him."

5. "Thomas P. and William L., members of different families, were attacked with scarlet fever 14 days after the return of Amy C., who belonged to a third family living in the same house. Amy C.'s

three brothers and sisters, with whom she came much in contact, remained quite well. Eleven days' after Amy's return, Thomas P. and William L. were permitted to go downstairs and play with her, and, to amuse them, Amy's books and satchel, which she used when ill in bed, before she was taken to the hospital, were brought out from a cupboard in which they had been lying since her removal to hospital. Three days after both children were attacked with scarlet fever."

Many instances of a similar nature occurring in Boston during the past few years might be cited.

After a careful consideration of Dr. Lauder's paper, after a study of the report of infectious hospitals, both in this country and abroad, it seems evident:

First: That in scarlet fever discharges from mucous membranes are infectious.

Second: That desquamation is also infectious.

As a corollary to the foregoing conclusions, it may be said that no patient should be removed from isolation as long as there is any discharge from the mucous surfaces, or as long as there is any primary desquamation.

There can be no definite time limit, but the average time in the majority of cases of scarlet fever, from the commencement of the initial fever until the process of desquamation is completed, is about 50 days. In certain rare instances, particularly in very young children, the time may be somewhat less.

COPPER SULPHATE vs. ALGAE.

For the past few weeks the professional and lay press has contained many references to the Department of Agriculture bulletin on this subject,* and many unauthorized claims of excellence have been made for the results reported by the authors.

The bad odors and tastes produced in water by growths of algæ have long been recognized. Sometimes they are so persistent and extensive for short periods, that the most elaborate systems of aëration combined with double filtration, fail to remove the odor completely.

As the result of a series of brilliant studies, the authors have devised a method which consists in adding minute yet alga-toxic quantities of copper sulphate to the water under consideration, with the result that the odor-producing algæ are quickly killed. In practice only .25 parts of copper sulphate per million are required to kill such organisms as anabaena and uroglena. Drs. Moore and Kellerman give evidence of the harmlessness to man of these minute quantities of copper, such as would be applied to water contained in reservoirs. The method has been under observation for over a year, and undoubtedly will prove a valuable tool in the hands of sanitary experts and engineers.

The first reservoir treated was one under the observation of the present writer, at Winchester, Ky. At one time during July, 1903, this reservoir contained nearly 9,000 organisms, and the water was offensively putrescent because of the presence of anabaena. On July 9 of the same year the reservoir was treated with .25 parts of copper sulphate per million, the salt being applied from a sack which hung over the stern of a rowboat, which latter was made to traverse practically the whole surface of the reservoir. The results were as follows:

Date.	Volumes per c.c.
July 6	3,400
" 9	(Day of treatment.)
" 10	54
11	8
13	0
15	0
20	0 .

It was thought by some sanitary experts that the cold, wet season of 1903, rather than the treatment, was responsible, in part, for the disappearance of the organisms, but in July, 1904, the reservoir was still free from anabaena, and a second treatment of .12 parts of copper sulphate per million resulted in the disappearance of nearly all the grass-green algæ as well. There was left in the water only harmless crustace and a few pediastra. Jamaica Pond, Boston, which at this time of the year usually contains about 1,500 organisms per c.c., was also treated with copper in 1903. This summer the organisms number less than 100 per c.c.

At Elmira, Caird† reports a successful trial of this method, but as he used about five times the ratio of copper sulphate used at Winchester, a few fish were killed. At present Dr. Moore advises a greater dilution (1.3 parts per million) than that used at Elmira. The cost of treatment at Elmira was less than 75 cents per million gallons.

Many other reservoirs have been treated this year, among them the reservoirs at Cambridge, N.Y., Butte, Mont., and Belchertown, Mass., with success in each case, it is believed.

The authors also studied the effect of copper sulphate upon mosquito larvæ and pathogenic intestinal bacteria. They state that 10 parts of copper sulphate per million suffice to kill *B. typhosus* and *Microspira comma* (the cholera bacillus), at room temperature, in less than 5 hours. Furthermore, mosquito larvæ are readily killed by this reagent.

The authors state that the method is not one for a novice to apply, as the nature of the organism must be known before treatment can be prescribed. Each reservoir must be treated specially, and the authors believe that the advantage to the public health promised, warrants this special treatment. The cost for treating a reservoir semi-annually would not be a serious factor.

The treatment is not designed to replace efficient means of filtration, since it hardly affects the turbidity of the water, but is to be an aid where such treatment alone does not suffice. It probably would be of special value during typhoid epidemics.

It is specially stated in the bulletin that "it would be a matter of regret if the method proposed here should ever be regarded as a universal panacea to be used by every one, regardless of the organism to be eradicated and the condition of the water."

It has been suggested to the authors that the therapeutic value of copper sulphate for the treatment of typhoid fever should be carefully investigated.

* G. T. Moore and K. F. Kellerman. Bulletin No. 64, Bureau of Plant Industry, U. S. Dept. of Agriculture.

†Eng. News, 1904, LII, 34.

A PARADOX IN THE DEATH-RATE IN VARIOUS DISTRICTS IN NEW YORK.

Under the foregoing title, *American Medicine*, June 4, 1904, publishes an item showing marked disparity in the death-rates of certain wards in the city of New York (the seventh, tenth, eighteenth and twentieth). In these selected wards it appears that the death-rate was lower in those which are most densely settled (the seventh and tenth) than it was in the less densely settled eighteenth and twentieth wards.

The explanation of this apparent paradox is undoubtedly to be found in the fact that sanitary conditions, such as overcrowding, uncleanliness, etc., are by no means the only conditions which influence the death-rate. The *age distribution* must always be borne in mind in considering this question. The effect of immigration also is apparent, since it introduces a large number of healthy persons at ages when the death-rate is low. For example, a colony of male Italians, living in a certain ward and laboring upon public works, should have a low death-rate (not over 6 or 8 per 1,000), and this fact influences the death-rate of the whole ward. Many of these laborers are unmarried and have no children. Consequently the death-rate is also low.

The presence of large hospitals and other public institutions also raises the death-rate. Ward 18, in New York has three of the largest hospitals.

A method of comparing the death-rate of different communities in which the age distribution differs, may be found in the report of the State Board of Health of Massachusetts for 1902 (34th Annual Report), in which the death-rates of 20 cities are corrected upon this plan.

The only definite figures quoted in this item, upon which one may found an opinion, are those of the seventh and twentieth wards, each having a population of about 90,000, but one having 1,300 deaths in a year, and a consequent death-rate of 14.4 per 1,000, and the other having 2,000 deaths, and a death-rate of 22.2. These two wards both show a wonderful improvement since the publication of Dr. Billings' excellent maps and tables of New York

City in the U. S. Census Report of 1890. In this report the death-rates of the seventh ward was very heavy, 33.7 per 1,000, and that of the twentieth was 33.5. The lowest rate in any district of these two wards was 27.9 per 1,000 in one district of the seventh.

As an instance of the marked effect of age distribution, there are two adjoining towns in Massachusetts, of nearly equal size, one of which had a death-rate in 1902 of 13.3 per 1,000, and the other, 122.2 per 1,000, or nearly ten times as great, the latter being due to the presence of a large public institution in which there are collected large numbers of old people, and also many infants born in the institution. The death-rate of each of these classes being very much above the general death-rate.

JULY QUARTERLY MEETING
OF THE
Massachusetts Association of Boards of Health.

The quarterly meeting of the Association was held on Thursday, July 28, 1904. In the morning, àt the invitation of the State Board of Health, members inspected the new laboratories for the manufacture of diphtheria antitoxin and vaccine lymph at the Bussey Institute. Shortly after noon the steamers "Vigilant" and "John H. Howard" took them to Gallup's Island, Boston Harbor, where, by the courtesy of the City of Boston, dinner was served.

After dinner a business meeting was held under the chairmanship of Dr. H. P. Walcott. The reading of the records of the previous meeting was dispensed with, and the following members were elected:

F. J. Hanley, M.D., Whitman; J. E. Richardson, Somerville; William Craig, Brookline; William P. Gesner, Boston; A. E. Mossman, M.D., Westminster; Luke H. Howard, Taunton; James O. Jordan, Boston; Edwin P. Gleason, M.D., Brockton; N. C. B. Haviland, M.D., Holliston; William R. Morrow, M.D., Framingham; C. P. Holden, M.D., Melrose; E. L. Grundy, Melrose; G. Houston Smith, Melrose; F. E. Stone, M.D., Lynn.

THE PRESIDENT. The first paper, the only one upon the program, is a paper upon the "Etiology of Leprosy." I am requested to say that after a discussion of this subject by certain gentlemen who are familiar with cases of this disease, Dr. Carson will exhibit a specimen, an individual afflicted with leprosy, to the Association. I now have the pleasure of introducing to you Dr. Smith.

PROFESSOR SMITH. Mr. President and Gentlemen of the Association: Certain reasons have made it desirable that I should look over the recent literature of leprosy in order to see whether our knowledge concerning its transmissibility had in any way changed in recent years. There is no special reason why I should stand here to-day and read a paper on leprosy, because I know very little about it. I only saw one case in my life. That was ten years ago, in Berlin. There are those among you who have seen more. But the paper which I shall read may be considered a kind of summary of our existing knowledge, which will be a very good introduction to a general discussion on your part, and I trust that you will take the paper in that light.

[EDITOR'S NOTE.— Owing to the very regrettable loss of the manuscript of this paper, and the absence of a duplicate, the publication has been delayed. Dr. Smith has kindly promised to rewrite the article, if possible, for our next issue.]

THE PRESIDENT. It is always a pleasure upon these occasions to call attention to the great obligations that the state of Massachusetts is under to the city of Boston for the protection which the city of Boston gives to the public health of this commonwealth. In the matter of leprosy, of course the most of our leprous patients have been in the control of the city of Boston, and concerning the policy of the city of Boston in such cases, I think we should all be glad to hear from Dr. Durgin, who fortunately has had control of them for a great many years.

DR. DURGIN. Mr. President and Gentlemen: There are but few words I may say with regard to leprosy as having been cared for in the City of Boston. Within the last thirty odd years I have known but four cases personally, and only that number has come under the notice and care of the Boston Board of Health. One of these was found in East Boston, living as any other member of a family. He had lived in Honolulu, where he evidently took the disease, and had been suffering from it for some years, was in quite an advanced stage, even to the necrosis of his toes and fingers. There were suppurative ulcerations going on, so that he had to be bandaged to protect the family and to prevent the oozing of the. matter upon furniture and other things about the house. It was an astonishing thing to me in those days to find one of these cases so ill-cared for, to appearances, as this, in the midst of a family, that is, in his own family. He was taken at once to the island here and kept, and while his appearance indicated that he might live only for a few months, he lived about three years and a half. How much was due to good nourishment and good care I cannot say, but I have learned since, that such patients live on far beyond any ordinary prognosis that you would be likely to give. The protective measures against the spread of the disease are easier applied here than they could be in a less isolated place.

Another case which came was found, so far as the Board of Health is concerned, in a large charitable institution in Boston. I don't think it will hurt the institution any for me to say here what is was. It was the Massachusetts Charitable Eye and Ear Infirmary, where he went to have his eyes treated, they being some-what affected in this case. We took him here, and under the extraordinary treatment by Dr. Carson, he cleaned up so well that he ran away, thinking himself well. And he certainly was strong. He pulled himself away in a stone boat. We found him and took him back. When he was still further recovered, so that he looked smooth and free from anything of this sort of disease, he ran away again, and we were not very sorry, because he was in good shape and perhaps free from the disease.

Another case, which we found ashore, is present to-day, and will be shown you. His environment and much that may be said can better be said to you by Dr. Shea, who had the oversight of the case. In fact, Dr. Shea has seen and looked after the others to a considerable extent.

One case, in which Dr. Shea is still more interested, was the one which I want to mention as the only one which we have ever taken from a vessel in the harbor. She came from Sweden, and was in very bad shape, passed two English physicians at Liverpool, but was very quickly detected by Dr. Shea as quarantine physician here at that time. Photographs were taken, and she was held here at the island for some months and then returned to Sweden.

The policy of the Board has been to take these patients as early as convenient and isolate them. Their treatment until within the last year or two has been simply the supporting treatment, and good, nourishing and clean care. In ulcerative cases we have found it right to cover them with mosquito netting to keep the flies away, keep them out of doors on the piazza as much as possible in suitable weather, and cover them in their chairs with netting. The treatment as given by Dr. Carson may be interesting to you, and also the environment and the method of picking them up by Dr. Shea.

DR. SHEA. Mr. President and Gentlemen: As Dr. Durgin has told you, in the last fifteen or twenty years I have had charge, for the Department, of five cases of leprosy. The very important thing for this Association, and especially for Boston, to determine is what we ought to do with these lepers. Look at the financial end of the question. It is very serious, financially, to have to take a patient and maintain him for three, four or five years. It means a great expense to the city. And as far as I can learn from my observation in the last fifteen or twenty years, especially the study of these cases, I have yet to find that any of them did any particular harm.

The first case that Dr. Durgin mentioned to you was that of the Swedish woman. Her family was living in one of the towns adjacent to Boston for a great many years, and I personally had an observation kept over the children for ten years after she was sent back to Sweden. She had a very large family, eight or ten children, and at the time they were discharged they were free from all signs of the disease. Again, in these other cases that we have picked up in Boston, it could never be said that the people were infected in this country. The infection, it has been fair to say, has been contracted elsewhere. Three cases were among seafaring men, who had at some time in their life been in Honolulu, where the disease is endemic.

We all know the policy adopted by the Board of Health of New York about five or six years ago. They began by taking a leper to North Brothers Island. Within a few years they had quite a colony there, I think about ten lepers, and the question of expense immediately had to be considered. These men seemed to thrive, and the outlook was that they would live there for years. The Board of Health of New York discharged these lepers, and within a few days they turned up at different charitable institutions. I don't know what the final result was, but I think that the Health Department of New York had to receive them again.

Probably the gentlemen might be interested, especially the medical men of the Association, with the differential diagnosis of this disease. Years ago there was always an element of chance in these cases, but thanks to bacteriology, leprosy is one of the most simple diseases now that a health official has to deal with. This last case that we have, that we are about to show you here, was under treatment by a physician in Boston connected with a hospital. He had given the patient a very thorough specific treatment, and was rather disappointed at not obtaining any results. He asked me to see the man, who was a Chinaman, and from his history I was rather suspicious of leprosy. At that time, I took one of the nodules and sent it down to Dr. Hill, and he gave me a diagnosis within twenty minutes. He found the lepra bacillus. Of course, for a differential diagnosis, we would have to consider syphilis and lupus. The bacteriologist can tell you whether you are dealing with lupus, or leprosy. The question of syphilis could be decided by thorough specific treatment for a time.

If a patient with leprosy could be placed under proper surroundings, for example, the surroundings of a modern hospital, I do not see how he could be any danger or menace to the immediate family or anybody in the community, if proper precautions are taken with the discharges, and in early cases I cannot see how there could be any danger. Where the case is well advanced, and the lesions are many, and the ulcerations have broken down, I think that probably as a matter of safety, if the patient cannot get the care that a modern hospital could afford him, it is time for the health authorities to act and remove him. That has been the policy of this Health Department. Unfortunately, all our cases have been cases which have required hospital treatment and could not be isolated at home, and we have been obliged to take them, at a great expense, as I said before, to the city.

Whether or not the disease is communicable, a very interesting case happened while I was at the quarantine station, that throws some light upon the question. I boarded a vessel one morning, and the captain told me, as I was about to leave that I probably would, in a week or two, board another vessel that was coming from the same port, Dutch Guiana, and that there would probably be there as passengers two boys. Before he had left he had been asked to take these boys as passengers and had made arrangements, but had been told before he sailed that the father was a leper. Fearing that he might be held up in Boston and undergo a long quarantine, he refused the boys. Within a week or two, as he had foretold, the boys arrived. They were being sent to the states to school. One of them was about twelve, and I think the other was fourteen years of age. I examined them. As far as I could see, they were perfectly normal, healthy boys, with the exception of one, that I thought was inclined to be tuberculous. We held the boys that day—it was a Sunday, I remember very well—till I could communicate with the authorities and with the people with whom they were to board in the city. The Board determined that we could not hold them, as they were free from disease; but we did determine to keep them under observation, which we did, and within a year one of them came down with leprosy and was sent back home. The history, as I remember, that the boys gave me at that time was that their father had been sick for six years. They had lived on a very large estate there, and had not seen him; he had lived in a hut, or, rather, a more pretentious building, built for his exclusive use, and he had his own servants, and no connection at all with the immediate family. In all these cases we have to take what our experience brings to us to aid us in forming an opinion. Of couse, this case would be very strong evidence on the question of heredity, but still, on the other hand, there were these other cases, where it is only fair to suppose that the infection was direct from visiting these countries, such as Honolulu, where there is more or less leprosy.

I think the question for the boards of health of this state to decide, and especially for Boston, is, Is it necessary to isolate these patients, especially such a case as that we are going to show you to-day,—a very early case? Probably three or four years from now, if this man doesn't improve under treatment, he would be a fit case for the Board of Health to take and maintain in a hospital; but in his present condition I am very strongly of the opinion that if he is so situated at home that he could have the facilities of a modern hospital and the care and treatment that a hospital would give, it would not only be a hardship, but I think it would be cruel to send him, as he has been sent, to this island to pass the remainder of his days.

DR. H. W. HILL. The only thing that strikes me, not covered by previous speakers, is Dr. Shea's reference to my making a diagnosis in twenty minutes. It is true that bacilli can be quite readily found in many cases, and yield very fair evidence of the conditions, especially when taken with the clinical evidence. It is unlikely that tubercle bacilli would be found in tubercular lesions in such number and so arranged as to be confused with lepra bacilli; but to clinch the diagnosis and make it final, we have made a practice, in the few cases we have seen, of inoculating a guinea pig, so as to exclude possible tuberculosis entirely. There is no harm in being as safe as one can be, when one has all the facilities. Of course, the guinea pig is a very sensitive test for tuberculosis, but with leprosy it shows nothing whatever. In the course of four or five weeks—five better than four—the guinea pig is chloroformed and autopsied. If no lesions whatever are found, one can rule out tuberculosis, leaving the diagnosis leprosy. Various differences in staining between tubercle and lepra bacilli are described by the authorities, but the differences are hardly marked enough for us, with the necessarily limited experience which we have had, to base so important a diagnosis on them alone. One should keep in mind, also, the various forms of acid-fast bacilli, smegma bacilli, etc., as possible sources of error, but these are not likely to make trouble.

DR. CHAPIN (Providence). Mr. President, I am happy to say that we have only had one case in Rhode Island.

Two years ago Dr. Swarts called my attention to a patient whom he had in the Rhode Island Hospital, and on whom he had already made the diagnosis of leprosy, so that I was not troubled on that score. I think it was of the anæsthetic type. He had contracted the disease some eight years before, if I remember rightly, in Pernambuco, South America. He had been living in Providence nearly all the time since then. The bacilli were found in great profusion in the secretions from the nose. The problem of what to do with him fell to me, and for the next few hours I was a good deal disturbed in my mind. Perhaps my trouble was a little increased by the fact that he was a well-known business man and an acquaintance and neighbor of mine. The problem, however, was soon solved by his escape from the hospital. He went to some isolated place in Pennsylvania, near the boundary between New Jersey and New York, thinking that there he could be safe from officious health officers by going from one jurisdiction to another.

After the very clear and concise way in which Dr. Smith has presented the present status of the leprosy question, it seems to me that we must all be agreed that the only thing to do is to secure the isolation of these patients. The real problem, though, is how to bring it about, and certainly this is a very difficult problem for us. It seems to me that the best solution would be to have a national leper home for the isolation of these occasional cases that occur in this part of the country.

Take a case like the one that we had in Providence. I had made up my mind that if his family were willing to take the trouble, it would be perfectly simple and easy for them to isolate him in their home, but the event, as it turned out, showed how risky that would have been. This man is not isolated at all now. Where he is, I do not know, but I imagine in New York City. That appears to be a haven for lepers at present. They can go there and go freely about their business, and are not interfered with. They can easily conceal themselves in that city, and apparently the Board of Health of New York City does not care much about isolating them. Of course, with poor patients, it will be necessary, as Dr. Shea said, for the town or city to take them in hand and maintain them in isolation, which is a very expensive and difficult matter. As we know, even in Boston, they sometimes escape, even when they are kept on an island. I have no sympathy with that view which would permit the lepers to go about. It seems to me we are running a very great risk indeed to do so.

I have heard it said that, because it is apparently difficult for leprosy to be transmitted from one person to another, it is unreasonable to be strict in the isolation, that we might just as well isolate every person with tuberculosis as to isolate every person with leprosy. I think that the comparison is an unfair one. We have no leprosy in the country at the present time, to speak of, and we should take every precaution that it should not become as common with us as tuberculosis is. If the United States were as free from tuberculosis to-day as it is from leprosy, certainly every case of tuberculosis that appeared on our shores should be, and I think would be, put into the strictest isolation, and we should in one way or another secure the isolation of all cases of leprosy.

DR. MORSE. Mr. President and Members of the Association: I cannot offer anything further except corroborative evidence of what has already been said.

Early in the spring, I think in the month of April, a leper was found in the town of Harwich, down on Cape Cod, and one of the local physicians made a correct diagnosis of the case. The man was one who had come from the Cape de Verde Islands about nine years ago, and from his family history it was ascertained that his mother and two sisters had died of leprosy before his sailing for this country. He landed at New Bedford, apparently free from the disease, and since that time he has lived successively in New Bedford, Fall River and Harwich. He has been free to go wherever he pleased, although during the last five or six years he has shown active symptoms and lesions of the disease at all times. He has been variously treated by different physicians for syphilis and for constitutional diseases, but with no apparent result. He has a large family. Although he has been in this country only about ten years, he is the father of nine children, the youngest one about three months of age now, so that every facility has been given for the transmission of the disease to his own family. At the present time, neither his wife nor any of his nine children show any evidence of the disease, which again impresses us with the very slight infectious character of it.

The case is certainly not an advantageous advertisement for the town of Harwich, where many summer people go, and it was the intention of the town authorities to get rid of the patient at the earliest opportunity. They brought the question before the Attorney-General, but got very little relief. Finally, an act was passed by the Legislature in its closing days, giving the State Board of Charity authority to remove this patient, if they so desired, but up to the present time he has been allowed to remain in the careful hands of the selectmen of the town of Harwich. He has been separated from his family, and at present is in a house all by himself. The town sees that he has plenty to eat, and not being of the class of people who have very high ideals in life, he has no desire to escape. His one accomplishment seems to be music, and the town has very properly provided him with an accordion on which to play, and he takes great pleasure in doing that. He has worked in the cranberry bogs during the fall, and in the woods during the winter. Although he has resided in this country and in this state a number of years, he has never become a citizen of the state and has never paid any taxes, and is consequently a state case. But the expense of caring for him is very slight, and I believe that although he has an opportunity to escape every hour of the day, he is content to remain where he is.

Dr. Carson then brought in the patient referred to, and demonstrated him to the Association, the members examining freely and asking questions, which were answered by Drs. Carson and Shea.

Adjourned.

ABSTRACTS, REVIEWS, NOTES AND NEWS

Boards of Health are asked to send the Managing Editor notes of not more than one hundred and fifty words relating to new regulations passed, legal cases prosecuted, outbreaks of infection, unusual problems encountered, or other matters the publication of which may further the attainment of the objects of the Association.

AN EXPERIMENT WITH COPPER SULPHATE, THE NEW ALGACIDE.

In connection with the use of copper sulphate in reservoirs, as an algacide, the writer has noted that while concentrations of only .25 parts of copper sulphate per million of water* have sufficed to destroy the anabaena and kindred organisms, some other objectionable algæ† survive in a solution one thousand times as concentrated, and that if enough copper is added to kill these more resistant organisms, the fish in the reservoir will be killed.‡

Most species of fish do not survive a concentration of copper sulphate of ten parts in one million of water. What causes their death? Experiments with warm-blooded animals show them to be less susceptible. It is not possible that the proteid cell contents of the gills of fish are precipitated by copper sulphate in certain concentrations? The writer isolated cell albumin from both animal (egg white—diluted and filtered) and vegetable (yeast) sources, and observed that this substance is precipitated by as little as ten parts of copper sulphate in one million parts of water, and is not precipitated, apparently, by such concentrations as suffice to kill anabaena; namely, one part or less in one million.

It would seem, therefore, that in reservoirs which are over-treated with copper‖ the fish have been killed by the precipitation of albumin in the superficial cell layers of the gills, thereby strangling the fish.

From the classic work of Drs. Moore and Kellerman one would

---

* At Winchester, Kentucky, July, 1903, and July, 1904.
† Moore and Kellerman, Bureau of Plant Ind., Bul. No. 64.
‡ Caird, Eng., *News.*
‖ Elmira, N. Y., 1903. *Eng. News*, loc. cit.

deduce that the death of algæ is produced by this same precipitation, and that the difference in resistance among algæ is probably due to differences in the structures of different vegetable cells.

The concentration which will kill most fish may be detected by the tongue of the casual observer, and the writer and three others were able to detect as little as two parts of copper sulphate in a million of distilled water, one-fifth of the above.

The writer believes that even if the applied copper should remain long in solution, which it does not, its presence in excessive amount would be detected by taste. Therefore, it may be used by competent hands with entire safety.

ROBERT SPURR WESTON.

THE NATIONAL ASSOCIATION FOR THE STUDY AND PREVENTION OF TUBERCULOSIS organized June 6 at Atlantic City, N. J., during the meeting of the American Medical Association. The officers elected were: President, Trudeau; vice-presidents, Osler, Biggs; executive committee, Hurty, Otis, Klebs, Ravenel, Devine; directors: Massachusetts, Bowditch, Otis; Connecticut, Foster; New York, Biggs, Trudeau, Devine, Knopf; Pennsylvania, Flick, Ravenel, Anders, Pearson; New Jersey, Hoffman; Maryland, Welch, Osler, Jacobs, Fulton; District of Columbia, Sternberg; North Carolina, Minor; Colorado, Soley; Illinois, Klebs, Babcock; Minnesota, Bracken; Mississippi, Porter; Indiana, Hurty; Michigan, Vaughan; Ohio, Probst; California, Briggs; Texas, Smith; U. S. P. H. & M. H. S., Wyman; U. S. Army, Bushnell.

The objects of the society are: The study of tuberculosis in every detail; the dissemination of knowledge concerning every phase of the disease,—cause, treatment and prevention; and the encouragement of scientific treatment and prevention.

We are rather struck by the relatively small number of public hygienists amongst the directors, although those selected are preëminently well fitted to deal with the subject. Since tuberculosis is peculiarly a preventable disease, and much of the work of its suppression must be in the hands of those officially charged with the conservation of the public health, it seems to us that at least every official state hygienic society or association in this country should have in its own hands the election of a director of the National Society from its own membership. Only in some such way can the full benefit of coöperation and advice be secured.

INOCULATION OF SMALLPOX VIRUS NEGATIVED BY VACCINATION.—Fink, civil surgeon in Burma, gives notes* regarding vaccination preventing inoculation smallpox, which quite equal in interest the classic experiments made in Massachusetts early in the nineteenth century. It seems that the Burmese outside of the large cities and towns practice and have great faith in, the inoculation of the powdered scabs from mild cases of smallpox as a preventive, and were slow to accept vaccination as a milder and equally efficient substitute, until convinced by the following experiments: During 1900 and 1901, 144 children were vaccinated. Of these, 123 were inoculated by the native saya, or medicine man, in 1903. None of them contracted the disease, nor did any one of the remaining 21 children, who, although not inoculated, were exposed to infection without the smallest precaution.

THE "CONSCIENTIOUS OBJECTOR" IN LONDON.— Collingridge† comments on the law passed in 1898, known as the "Conscientious Objectors' Act," as follows: "The decline in the proportion of conscientious objections during a year when smallpox was epidemic is some indication of the little faith the average anti-vaccinationist attaches to his own teachings, when face to face with the disease."

Smallpox was prevalent in London from 1900 to 1902. The ratio of infants exempted from vaccination in the city of London under the Conscientious Objectors' Act of 1898 is given by Collingridge, thus:

In 1898, 7.0 % of the births   In 1901, 2.6 % of the births
In 1899, 2.3 % of the births   In 1902, 0.6 % of the births
In 1900, 1.9 % of the births   In 1903, No cases of objection(!).

S. W. Abbott, M. D.

---

* *British Medical Journal*, July 16, 1904.
† Rep. Med. Off. of Health of City of London, 1903.

It may be suggested that perhaps the lack of objection in 1903 was due less to the conversion of the objectors than to their demise during the epidemic. It will be remembered that "antis" of all descriptions are particularly hard to convert, showing little mental reaction to facts. At least four more or less prominent anti-vaccinationists in this country, one of them "Citizen George Francis Train," suffered in their own persons from smallpox during the late outbreak. The only one of these whose opposition to vaccination came to an end as the result of his personal experience was the Chicago man. He died during the attack.

MAJOR REED'S RESULTS IN YELLOW FEVER.— The incorporation of a society, of which Dr. Daniel C. Gilman is president, to provide for the erection of a monument to Dr. Walter Reed, recalls the principal points established by the classical work on yellow fever of himself and his associates, Carroll, Lazear and Agramonte. These were as follows:

1. The specific agent of yellow fever (as yet unknown) resides in the blood of the patient for the first three days of the attack only. During this period only can the patient serve as a source of infection, and only in two ways: by direct (always experimental) transfer of his blood into the circulation of a susceptible person; and by indirect transfer, through a mosquito, *Stegomyia fasciata*.

2. This mosquito, to become infected, must bite the patient during the first three days of the attack. The mosquito's bite thereafter is harmless, until about twelve days later, after which, and so long as the mosquito lives, it may infect by biting.

3. There is no other natural method for the transmission of yellow fever than through the bite of an infected mosquito; fomites are not a factor in the transmission of this disease, and disinfection, except as directed against the mosquitoes, is quite useless as a preventive.

THE ASSOCIATION OF EXECUTIVE HEALTH OFFICERS OF ONTARIO held its nineteenth annual meeting at Sarnia, Ontario, July 13 and 14. Dr. Hodgetts, the new secretary of the Provincial Board of Health, read a paper on consumption, which resulted in the passing of a resolution requesting the government to make notification of tuberculosis compulsory throughout Ontario.

AN UNRECOGNIZED SOURCE OF TYPHOID INFECTION.

—Barringer* states that over 85,000 persons travel each mile of railway roadbed in the United States annually. The excreta must of necessity foul the roadbed, since the deposits are made just outside the track, favoring rapid desiccation and dissemination by the wind. Students arriving at the University of Virginia in the fall usually furnish from one to three cases of typhoid fever in each year, all appearing within a fortnight after the railway journey, and apparently due to infection contracted *en route*.

"The remedy lies in the retention closet. A good, dry earth closet would suffice, and could be used on every train. It would prevent soiling the roadbed, and be inoffensive."

S. W. ABBOTT, M.D.

RELATIVE EFFICIENCY OF CARBOLIC ACID, FORMAL-DEHYDE AND CYLLIN AGAINST B. PESTIS.

Experiments undertaken by Dr. E. Klein (*Public Health*, June, 1904, p. 563) to determine the action of carbolic acid, formaldehyde and cyllin (a trade-marked creolin) against a virulent strain of *B. pestis*, originally derived from the bubo of a fatal case in a man in Cardiff in 1901, led to the following conclusions: 1. Phenol 1 in 80 is a stronger disinfectant for *B. pestis* than formalin 1 in 30. 2. Phenol 1 in 80 stands in about the same position as cyllin 1 in 2400, inasmuch as both failed to completely devitalize the *B. pestis* in 5 minutes, though they both succeeded in doing so in 10 minutes. Expressed in a different form, cyllin possesses for watery emulsions of *B. pestis* a disinfecting power which is more than 27.5 (in fact, about 30) times as great as that of absolute phemol.

CHARLES HARRINGTON, M. D.

NOTES ON FORMALDEHYDE.

Formalin is commonly described as a 40 per cent solution of formaldehyde in water, but it is well known that that is the maxi-

* *Medical Record*, Dec. 19, 1903.

mum possible strength and that the commercial article is rarely as strong. The analysis of 21 samples is reported by E. F. Ladd (*North Dakota Agricultural Experiment Station, Bulletin, No.* 60), who found from 21.6 per cent to 38.47 per cent, and in a majority of the samples about 33 per cent.

With regard to the influence of temperature in formaldehyed disinfection, Bonhoff (*Berliner klinische Wochenschrift,* 1904, No. 19) makes the interesting statement that, in winter, anthrax spores are not destroyed even when larger amounts of formaldehyde than usual are employed. He believes that the influence of temperature is underestimated and that it is important in cold weather to raise the temperature of the room, rather than to increase the dose.

A case of suicidal poisoning by formalin is reported by Dr. L. A. Levison (*Journal of the American Medical Association,* June 14, 1904). The amount taken was estimated at 2 or 3 ounces, and the victim died in about 20 minutes, after intense suffering. The stomach, esophagus, duodenum, and all organs and tissues in contact with the stomach were found to be hardened like leather.

CHARLES HARRINGTON, M. D.

TYPHOID FEVER OUTBREAK AT KINGSTON, ONT.— Kingston receives its water supply from the main current of the St. Lawrence River, conducted through a pipe, the intake of which is about 1,500 feet out from the shore. The sewer outlets open into the river at the shore line. Amyot, provincial bacteriologist, analyzed water sent by the Kingston authorities chemically and bacteriologically. The chemical results were indefinite, but the water was found to contain colon bacilli and streptococci. He was commissioned to investigate the conditions. He found that the sewage discharged at the shore line was swept downstream so rapidly that it did not extend outward to the water intake, despite the short distance between the outlets and the intake. Colon bacilli and streptococci were absent at the intake and for about 700 feet inward along the course of the pipe, when they began to appear. Investigation of the pipe was suggested, and finally a bad leak was located about 500 feet from the shore, and hence in the sewage-infected area. The leak was traced to the efforts of two tugs to release a ship's anchor which had fouled at this point. The tugs gave up after the chain broke, and both chain and anchor were found, the latter lying under the bent pipe. The pipe was repaired with cement and iron hoops, the colon and streptococci disappearing almost at once from the city water, and the typhoid fever diminishing two weeks later.

The experience of Kingston calls attention once more to the folly, already well established at Toronto and at Chicago, of carrying a water supply, however pure, through a sewage-polluted area, without perfectly sound methods of protecting the water in transit, as well as at its source. It is to be hoped that Kingston will not rest content with the repaired pipe, but remodel its system of water conductors to the point where the lives of the inhabitants are not at the mercy of every passing ship.

DEATH OF A NOTED SANITARIAN.—Sir John Simon died at his house in Kensington Square, London, on Saturday, July 23, in the eighty-eighth year of his age. His medical career, which began in 1833, continued until 1848, when he was elected to the newly constituted post of medical officer of health to the city of London, an appointment which may be credited with having turned his studies in the direction of preventive medicine. In 1855 he was appointed to another newly created office, that of medical officer to the Privy Council. Subsequently, he was for a short time a member of the local government board. He resigned the office in 1876 and was made a crown member of the General Medical Council, from which he retired in 1895. He has been the recipient of many degrees and honors. Sir John Simon was preëminent among English health officers, and his death removed another of the pioneers of sanitary science.

R. S. WESTON.

INDUSTRIAL DISEASES.—Whitelegge* reports upon the cases of lead poisoning, phosphorous poisoning, arsenic and mercurial poisoning, and from anthrax in different industries in

* Ann. Rep. Chief Inspector of Factories and Workshops, 1904, London, June, 1904, p. 264.

England in 1903.   Under the operation of the recent act requiring notification of these forms of illness, it appears that the cases of lead poisoning have been reduced from 1,258 in 1899 to 614 in 1903, or to less than half.   Of these cases, 37 occurred among smelters of metals, 13 among printers, 24 in file cutters, 18 in tin and enamel workers, 109 in white-lead workers, 97 in china and earthen-ware makers, 28 in makers of electrical accumulators, 39 among paint and color workers, 74 in coach makers, 24 in ship-building, and 151 in other industries.

There were 5 cases of industrial arsenical poisoning, 8 of mercurial poisoning, and 47 of anthrax.

A summary of the cases of anthrax is given for the 5 years, 1899–1903.   The whole number of reported cases was 211, most of which were among workmen in wool, horsehair, hides and skins. The situation of the pustule in the persons attacked was upon the neck in 84, the cheek in 31, the forehead in 14, the forearm in 16, the upper eyelid in 12, the angle of the jaw in 8.

S. W. Abbott, M.D.

SANITARY ENGINEERING.

BY ROBERT SPURR WESTON, M. A.,

Assoc. M. Am. Soc. C. E.

SEWAGE DISPOSAL AT YORK, ENGLAND. CHANGES IN METHOD DURING THE PAST TEN YEARS. (Alfred Creer, A. M. Inst. C. E., "The Surveyor," 1904, pp. 623 to 631.)

In 1894 York, England (population 79,114 in 1902), completed a chemical precipitation works at a cost of about $135,000. These works were in operation as precipitation tanks, using lime and alumino-ferric, until April, 1899, when some of the tanks were transformed into open septic tanks, and experiments were started with a hope of improving the character of the effluent, which was then causing complaint. Using the precipitation system, the cost of treating 1,000,000 gallons by the original process, exclusive of interest and sinking fund, but inclusive of sludge pressing, was about $9.74 a million U. S. gallons. The experiments, all on a large scale, may be outlined as follows:—

Experiment No. 1.—Covered Septic Tank and Single Contact. Tank, 48,000 gals. capacity; four filters, each 40 ft. x 20 ft. x 3 ft. Cycle, 8 hours; medium clinker, ¾ in. to 1½ in.; rate, 250,000 to 700,000 gals. per acre per 24 hours.

Experiment No. 2.—Crude Sewage and Double Contact Beds.— No. 1 bed, 90 ft. x 30 ft. x 2.75 ft.; medium clinker, 1¼ x 3 in. No. 2 bed, same size as bed No. 1, filled with medium clinker, ⅜ x 2¾ in. Cycle, 8 hours principally.

*Experiment No. 3.—Ladder Filter, Crude Sewage and Multiple Contact Bed.—*Filter made up of 10 compartments, each 4 ft. x 3 ft. 5 in. x 2 ft. Medium clinker, ⅜ in. to ¾ in. The 10 compartments were arranged in steps, each 6 inches below the one immediately above it. The sewage passed from the first compartment to the second, and so on through the series.

Experiment No. 4.—Open Septic Tank and Continuous Filter.— This filter, which is still in operation, is circular, 67.5 ft. in diameter, and was specially constructed, with perforated walls and drains so that free access of air to all parts of the bed might be maintained.

A distributor delivers the sewage in the form of small jets equally over the area of the filter. The sewage trickles down through the filter, emerging at the floor level as a clear and bright liquid, totally devoid of smell and purified to a greater degree than was the effluent in any of the other experiments.

Experiment No. 5.—Open Septic Tank and Double Contact.— The sewage used during these experiments analyzed about 30 parts of "Oxygen Consumed" and 4.6 parts of "Albuminoid Ammonia" per million.

Results.—Experiments Nos. 1, 2, 3 and 5 were discontinued in August, 1901, as Experiment No. 4 was so successful. Experiment No. 4 was interrupted between March 12 and May 7, 1902, to allow the construction of a grit chamber in the connected septic tank. This grit chamber increased the efficiency of the filter. The filter, previous to the end of March, 1904, had been in operation for three years and nine months, and is still producing an excellent effluent at the rate of about 2,200,000 gallons per acre per 24 hours.

The city has recently constructed a second continuous filter, having over twice the area of the first one. Experiments with filtering material point to the probable superiority of coke and clinker over broken bricks and the so-called honeycomb slag.

The operation of the septic tank gave some valuable data. Mr. Creer thinks that the sludge should be removed once in every two or three weeks. He found that one cubic yard of sludge, containing 55 per cent of non-combustible mineral matter, was produced for each 348,000 gallons of sewage.

The period of storage in septic tank was between 19 and 20 hours, but repeated analyses showed very little, if any, reduction in the oxygen consumed and albuminoid ammonia after 13 hours of storage.

The action of this septic tank upon suspended solids is interesting because of the total quantity entering the tank, 75 per cent was organic and 25 per cent mineral water, but on leaving the tank the suspended solids had been reduced to 58 per cent composed of 73 per cent of organic and 27 per cent of mineral matter.

SHEFFIELD, ENGLAND. In this connection it is interesting to

note that the city of Sheffield, England, has decided to adopt the septic tank and contact bed system. This decision also was based upon the result of a series of experiments. Sheffield has acid sewage, while that of York is distinctly alkaline. These facts are evidence that no one system has been devolved which will treat successfully the sewage of all localities, and that each locality should follow the scientific method, as have these two English cities.

TREATMENT OF PLUMBO-SOLVENT, MOORLAND WATERS IN WAKEFIELD, ENGLAND. (Smith and Chaplin, Brit. Assoc. W. W. Eng., Hull meeting, July, 1904.)

Houston (Supplements to Reports Loc. Gov. Bd., 1900 to 1902) showed that by contact with peat water acquires that acidity which enables it to dissolve lead pipe, and that this acidity is probably produced by bacterial growth.

At Wakefield, the water is treated temporarily with sodium carbonate, 415 pounds being sufficient for 1,000,000 gallons of water. This reduces the plumbo-solvency of the water in a satisfactory manner.

Experiments were conducted to determine upon some other, and, if possible, a more economical method. Sand beds were found to neutralize the water for a short time only, or until the alkalinity of the filtering material was neutralized. It was arranged to give the water a treatment with chalk, following the treatment with filtration and a second treatment with clear lime water. Fifteen parts of chalk and from 15 to 30 parts of lime per million of water gave satisfactory results.

POLLUTION OF STREAMS BY WOOD PULP. (Jour. Franklin Inst., June, 1904.)

The U. S. Geological Survey, coöperating with Prof. F. E. Robinson of Bowdoin, is continuing its investigation into the pollution of the Androscoggin and Penobscot rivers. Twenty-five analyses have been made, but as yet no record of conditions which existed during dry summer seasons has been obtained. The work which the Survey now proposes to undertake will be directed toward a determination of the effect of wood pulp wastes upon natural waters. Pollution of streams in the vicinity of Lake Champlain has brought the subject to the fore.

The plans made contemplate a precise determination of the characters of sulphite and soda pulp wastes and their respective stabilities. Having determined the characters of the wastes, it is important to note whether each waste is of itself highly putrescible, or whether it has characteristics similar to those of strawboard waste, stable itself, but affording abundant opportunity for the decomposition of matters brought in contact with it. The effect of wood pulp waste upon streams will also be studied. Already it has been found that these wastes have a bad effect when discharged into streams which are used afterwards in connection with the cloth-dyeing industry.

SOLUBILITY OF ATMOSPHERIC OXYGEN IN SEA WATER AND IN WATER OF DIFFERENT DEGREES OF SALINITY. (F. Clowes, Jour. Soc. Chem. Ind., 1904, XXIII, p. 358.)

It is usual to measure the injurious effects produced by the discharge of sewage into bodies of water by ascertaining the extent to which the dissolved oxygen has become reduced in amount by the addition of foreign liquids. It has been known that sea water dissolves about 80 per cent as much oxygen as does distilled water. Experiments show that the solubility of atmospheric oxygen diminishes regularly with the addition of sea water to distilled water.

NUMBER OF BACTERIA IN THE WATER OF THE NORTH SEA, AND THE EFFECT OF SEA AND RIVER WATER AND OF BIOLOGICAL TREATMENT ON THE NUMBER OF BACTERIA PRESENT IN SEWAGE. (F. Clowes. Jour. Soc. Chem. Ind. Loc. cit.)

The author has made a careful investigation of the bacterial flora of the North Sea in the part known as the Thames Estuary. The results show that the average number of 7,443,000 bacteria per c.c., which were present in the sewage effluents discharged from the Barking and Crossness outfalls, had become reduced by the action of the river water to 4,840 at a distance of 21 miles from Crossness, and that off Southend, 31 miles from Crossness, a further reduction to 379 has taken place. When the Nore Lightship is reached the bacteria number only 186 per c.c. It also appeared that the intestinal bacteria in the sewage effluent were not found in the water at 27 miles below the point at which they had been introduced into the stream.

As is well known, the sludge from the London precipitation tanks is discharged into the estuary of the Thames from the holds of sludge steamers. The number of bacteria in a cubic centimeter of the discharged sludge is about 130,000,000, while the number found in the water after the discharge of the sludge was only 1,940. The number of bacteria in the river during an incoming tide, which represents the estuary water mingled with the sludge discharged into the estuaries, was only 458 per c.c. The water from the open sea contains an average of 287 bacteria per c.c. and what are ordinarily considered intestinal organisms were not found.

Experiments with the biological sewage purification plant showed that the settling tank effected a reduction of 15.8 per cent, and the effluent from the coke contact beds showed a reduction of 32.2 per cent, over the numbers of bacteria contained in the crude sewage. Samples of the effluent from the Barking coke bed show that this device had effected an 89 per cent reduction in the numbers of bacteria contained in settled London sewage.

The author concludes, therefore, that "no one has a right to consider the sewage bed as a means of increasing the number of bacteria. The bacteria rather appear to carry out their active functions in the bed and to pass away in large numbers in the effluent in a lifeless condition."

———

SEPTIC TANKS IN OHIO. (R. Winthrop Pratt, Mun. Eng., 1904, July, p. 34.)

There are 26 sewage purification works in Ohio, while 18 more will be in use in the near future. Of these, 26 plants, 8 use the septic tank; of the 18 proposed plants, 14 will use it. Mansfield, with a population of about 20,000, has the largest septic tank and contact bed system. It is designed to treat 1,000,000 gallons per 24 hours. Descriptions of the construction and operation of several of the Ohio plants are given.

PANAMA CANAL: NATURAL CONDITIONS AFFECTING ITS CONSTRUCTION. (Gen. H. L. Abbott, Eng. Magazine, August, 1904.)

General Abbott, of national reputation, has compiled the meteorological data of the isthmus in an interesting article, in which he also discusses the sanitary conditions which will affect the construction of the Panama Canal. He says that "much wild exaggeration has been circulated, in great part founded on the experience of ill-acclimated laborers engaged in surface soil excavation." He quotes the excellent hospital records which were kept by the new canal company, which records show that during recent years the percentage of disease and mortality has not exceeded that on any large work in any country.

SPRING-WATER INSPECTION AT SPRINGFIELD, MASS.

All vendors of drinking water are required to have a license from the City Board of Health, which, before granting such license, analyzes the water, inspects the source of supply, and also the methods of collection and distribution.

UTILIZATION AND DISPOSAL OF MUNICIPAL WASTE. (William F. Morse. Jour. Franklin Inst. June, 1904.)

Municipal waste, comprising garbage, street sweepings, ashes and rubbish, is divided into the following approximate proportions:

	Percentage. By Volume.	Ash By weight.
Ashes	65	57
Street Sweepings	17	12
Garbage	10	10
Rubbish	8	30

The amount of municipal waste varies greatly in different localities, as shown by the following table: ∴

City.	Lbs. per Capita.
New York	4.
Philadelphia	3.5
London	1.6
Hamburg	1.1
Berlin	0.9

Analyses of these various components of municipal waste are given. The average American city garbage is made up of

Moisture	65%
Solids	25%
Foreign Substances	6%
Grease	4%

The author gives the history of various methods for the disposal of garbage; namely, feeding to hogs, dumping, ploughing into ground, reduction and cremation. He evidently believes that the "utilization of such parts of the refuse as may be sold for conversion of manufacture into other forms of usefulness and the disposal of the worthless residuum" is the best method for large cities. In England some steam power is derived from the burning of garbage. Mr. Morse believes that the destruction of American waste in furnaces of the best English type may be achieved successfully without the use of fuel.

Hitherto, however, there is no record of a furnace which will consume garbage during the green-corn season without the aid of some other and better combustible.

EXAMINATIONS FOR SANITARY INSPECTORS IN NEW JERSEY.

All candidates for the positions of Sanitary Inspector or Health Officer in New Jersey cities must pass an examination and receive a certificate from the State Board of Health. The first examination under the new law was held in June. The subjects for examination were sanitary law, preventable diseases, isolation and quarantine, disinfection, nuisances, collection and disposal of refuse, vital statistics, milk supply, etc. The first examinations were not very severe, as might have been expected, but the step is one in the right direction.

TYPHOID FEVER AT THE STATE HOSPITAL FOR THE INSANE AT MENDOTA, WIS. (Eng. News, 1904, LII, p. 94.)

The hospital had two sources of supply; namely, an artesian well and the lake water. The latter was sewage polluted. In spite of warning, the employees drank the lake water because it was more agreeable to their taste. An outbreak of typhoid fever followed.

SEWAGE POLLUTION OF QUAHAUGS, OR ROUND CLAMS, AT NEW BEDFORD.

Owing to pollution of the beds by sewage, the Massachusetts State Board of Health has requested the Fish and Game Commission to prevent the further taking of shellfish from New Bedford Harbor and from Clark's Cove. This ruling will seriously affect the "Little Neck" clam industry in these localities. It is a well-known fact that this family of shellfish congregates most thickly about the outlets of sewers.

PREVENTIVE THERAPEUTICS.

BY HERBERT D. PEASE, M. D.,

Director, N. Y. Antitoxin Lab., Albany, N. Y.

DIPHTHERIA ANTITOXIN.—A committee of bacteriologists engaged in antitoxin production, and some others, was selected in the fall of 1902 by Prof. J. P. Remington, chairman of the committee on revision of the U. S. Pharmacopœia, to advise with him concerning the introduction of diphtheria antitoxin into the next issue of the U. S. Pharmacopœia. This committee has recently reported, advising that diphtheria antitoxin be introduced, suggesting its proper dosage, and the conditions under which it should be issued and distributed. If the committee on revision adopt these suggestions, diphtheria antitoxin will be one of the first remedies, if not the first, requiring a physiological test for the determination of its therapeutic activity which has been included in the Pharmacopœia. The committee consisted of Dr. Theobald Smith as chairman, and Drs. W. H. Park, J. J. Kinyoun, E. M. Houghton, M. J. Rosenau, H. A. Hare, H. D. Pease, and Surgeon Craig of the Army Medical Srvice.

The committee on antitoxic and immunizing sera of the laboratory section of the American Public Health Association, composed of the same gentlemen, except Drs. Houghton, Craig and Hare, and with the addition of Dr. Joseph McFarland, are undertaking the standardization of the technic of testing the specific antitoxic strength of diphtheria antitoxins.

TETANUS ANTITOXIN.—Marie and Morax* have shown experimentally that tetanus toxin is absorbed and passed on towards the central nervous system by both motor and sensory nerves, through their axis cylinders, and is also absorbed by the sympathetic nerves in the same manner. The toxin enters the axis cylinders only through the distal nerve terminations. Certain nerves absorb toxin more rapidly and allow

---

* Ann. de l'Inst. Pasteur Tome XVII., No. 5.

it to flow through them faster than others. In general, the length of nerve determines the rate of passage. The motor branch of the trifacial nerve in the horse absorbs toxin with great rapidity, and this fact probably explains the precocious appearance of trismus in horses infected with tetanus.

Meyer and Ransom* confirm the work of Marie and Morax, and further show that antitoxin present in or introduced into the circulating fluids of the body does not come into contact with any tetanus toxin present in the axis cylinders. In effect, the nerves are insulated throughout their course to all transfusion, either of toxin or antitoxin. The latter also does not seem to be adapted for absorption by the nerve terminations, as is the toxin. The authors, therefore, recommend the injection of tetanus antitoxin directly into the large nerve trunks in cases of this disease, as being the only method, in their opinon, of bringing the antitoxin directly into contact with the toxin already in the nerves.

Elting‡ has obtained temporary amelioration of the general convulsions in tetanus through injection, by the lumbar puncture method, of large doses (up to 50 c.c.) of tetanus antitoxin. These large doses produced no lesions demonstrable at autopsy.

Scherz† reports the use of immunizing doses of tetanus antitoxin in 436 injured persons, none of whom developed tetanus, while in the hospitals of the same region during the same period of time 7 cases of tetanus were found in persons who had not received prophylactic injections of serum.

Pease‖ classifies 53 cases of tetanus, occurring in New York state in 1903, according to their severity, into 3 groups: acute, subacute and chronic. Thirty-three were acute cases, 14 of which were, and 19 were not, treated with tetanus antitoxin. All the acute cases ended fatally. He places 12 cases in the subacute class, and of these, 7 died. Of these 7, 4 had been treated with antitoxin, and 3 not. Of the 8 chronic cases, 5 died, 3 having been treated with antitoxin, and 2 not so treated. No case not treated with antitoxin recovered, but the manner of collecting the records of the cases may have influenced this statistical result.

---

* Archiv fur Exp. Path. und Pharm., Band XLIX., Heft 6.
† *Albany Med Ann.*, January, 1904.
‡ Centralb. fur Bakt. Erst Aht Ref. XXXIV., Nos. 18 and 19.
‖ *Med. Rev. of Rev.*, June, 1904.

"Local" tetanus, or early and distinguishable spasms of the part or member injured, occurred in 10 out of 46 cases in which observations on this point had been made. It is generally considered to be a rare symptom in man.

As indicating the time of year in which tetanus is most likely to occur, a study of the cases gave the following results: January and February, 1 case each; March, 4 cases; April, 6; May, 2; June, 10; July, 24; August, 6; September and October, 5 cases each; November, 4, and December, 2 cases. Eighteen of July's 24 cases were due to Fourth-of-July injuries.

RESEARCH IN JAPAN.—An interesting illustrated pamphlet has been issued in connection with the combined exhibits of the institutes for infectious diseases and serum and vaccine production of the Imperial Government of Japan at St. Louis. These institutes are presided over by Professor Kitasato, and indeed their existence is largely due to his work and efforts.

The first of these institutes consists of an infectious-disease hospital,—a dormitory, laboratory, stable and disinfecting plant devoted to original investigation and teaching. The results obtained are given as follows:

Diphtheria antitoxin used on 4,556 persons, with a death-rate of 10.5 per cent.

Tetanus antitoxin used on 74 persons, with a death-rate of 55.4 per cent.

Pasteur's hydrophobia treatment on 428 persons, with a death-rate of .24 per cent.

Prophylactic injections of so-called vaccines and of "antitoxins," and the therapeutic use of the latter in hospital cases and epidemics of cholera, typhoid fever and dysentery, are reported. Investigations into the treatment of tuberculosis, leprosy and erysipelas, and the etiology of malaria, beriberi, cancer and syphilis, have also been carried on.

For this institute an appropriation of about $30,000 was made in 1903.

The serum institute for producing antitoxins and vaccines (except for smallpox) consists of a main laboratory, plague laboratory and the stables and outbuildings. The illustrations and descriptions of these buildings show them to be of a high order and very attractively situated.

The tabulated results obtained from the use of diphtheria anti-toxin in Japan, from 1889 to 1902, show the usual 50 per cent reduction of the death rate in this disease, although the number of cases of the disease has greatly increased since 1896.

Plague serum production is described, and the results of its use in Formosa in 1901 are given as follows: Cases treated, and those not treated, 56 each. Death-rate of the treated cases, 33 per cent; not treated, 62 per cent. Plague vaccine is also produced, and in 200,000 inoculations, but few cases have been known to occur subsequently.

The appropriation for this institute was over $50,000 for 1903. The work of the lymph or vaccine institute is described, and the method of producing the non-humanized lymph of Umeno is given in detail. This institute receives about $28,000 a year. Dr. M. Miyashima, of the latter institute, came to this country in charge of this exhibit at St. Louis, and has been making a tour of the various vaccine and antitoxin laboratories here.

SERUM USED PER CASE OF DIPHTHERIA IN NEW YORK STATE.—In a forthcoming report of the New York State Department of Health for the year 1903, a table appears showing the relative frequency with which the physicians of that state use the different sized packages of diphtheria antitoxin. The serum is issued in two sizes, of 1,500 units and 2,500 units respectively, and the table shows that 45 per cent of the individual doses were of the latter size, 10 per cent were of 3,000 units, and another 10 per cent were of 4,000 units or over. The death-rate in 1,033 cases was 8.6 per cent.

VETERINARY SANITATION.

BY VERANUS A. MOORE, D. V. M.,

Cornell University, Ithaca, N. Y.

MUZZLING DOGS TO PREVENT RABIES.—The Board of Agriculture of Great Britain began six years ago to enforce the muzzling of dogs.   In 1895, 672 cases of rabies in dogs were reported; in 1896, 438 cases; in 1897, 151 cases, and in 1901, only 1 case.

VACCINATION AGAINST TUBERCULOSIS IN COWS.—The Pennsylvania State Live Stock Sanitary Commission recently reported progress for the year at the Harrisburg meeting.   Cattle vaccinated against tuberculous and exposed thereafter for a year to daily contact with tuberculous animals remained sound, as also did vaccinated calves allowed to run with tuberculous mothers, and using their milk.   Control animals succumbed.

ANTHRAX IN ONTARIO.—In the summer of 1902 on a farm adjoining the village of Ancaster, three cows died after a very short sickness, and were pronounced anthrax by the local veterinarian.   A fourth cow, dying at the same time, was autopsied under the impression that it did not have anthrax.   During the autopsy, which was done on the barn floor, a considerable amount of bloody fluid ran down into the root-cellar below.   The first three cows were burned, but the autopsied cow was buried in an oat field.

In the fall mangolds were stored in the root-cellar, and fed to the cattle during the winter.   About the time that the mangolds in contact with the floor were reached, three cattle died.   Anthrax was suspected, and the bodies were burned.   A fourth cow was buried in quicklime, but one foot was left exposed.   Amyot, provincial bacteriologist, was sent to investigate.   He found anthrax bacilli in the projecting foot of this cow, in the body of the cow burned in the oat field, and on the walls of the root-cellar, down which the autopsy fluids had run.   In tracing the origin of the anthrax, he found that for thirty years or more batches of three or four cattle had died mysteriously at intervals of one, two or three years.   Poisoning had been suspected.   The farms where deaths occurred were almost without exception in a district of low land subject to flooding from a small stream.   The exceptions could be traced to the pasturing of cattle from other farms on this low land in droughty seasons, or to "nice black soil" carted thence to high-lying farms.   Evidently this low-lying land had been infected in some way. Inquiry showed that up to twenty-five years before, a large woolen mill, employing 150 hands, and dealing to some extent with foreign wools, had been in operation on the banks of the stream mentioned, and above the infected area.

Amyot points out the longevity of the infection, renewed, doubtless, from time to time by the small outbreaks, and calls attention to the necessity for investigating the conditions in factories, tanneries, etc., which handle "foreign" wools and hides. He states that six large Canadian tannery districts are now infected with anthrax, and urges action to restrict the extension of the disease.

PERSISTENCE OF ANTHRAX SPORES.—Von Szekeley* found anthrax spores, alive and virulent to white mice, in gelatin cultures inoculated eighteen and one-half years before and kept at ordinary room temperatures, in diffuse daylight, and under conditions favoring moderately rapid drying. The spores of the bacillus of malignant œdema also remained alive and virulent under simular conditions for the same period.

MUNICIPAL SANITATION.

BY CHARLES V. CHAPIN, M. D.,

Superintendent of Health, Providence, R. I.

IMMUNIZATION AGAINST DIPHTHERIA.—Early in the year the Dept. of Health of the City of New York issued to physicians a circular, setting forth the value of this procedure. It was stated that of 13,000 persons in New York City immunized with diphtheria antitoxin, and presumably exposed directly to the disease, only 40, or .3 per cent contracted diphtheria, and only 1 of these cases died. It was strongly urged that when diphtheria occurs in a family, every well child be at once immunized. The dose recommended for this purpose is 300 units for children under two, and 500 units for all persons older than this. No details are given in the circular in regard to the above data, but from other sources it may be inferred that cases occurring within

---

Zeit. Hyg. u Inf. 1903, XLIV., No. 3.

twenty-four hours, or later than thirty days after immunization are not reckoned as failures. J. S. Billings, Jr., gives* many interesting facts in regard to the use of antitoxin in the city of New York. He states that of 5,479 persons immunized by department inspectors, from March 1, 1902, to Jan. 1, 1903, 17 were taken sick between two and thirty days after immunization, and 7 before two or after thirty days. This makes, all told, only a little over .4 per cent in which immunization was followed by diphtheria. A study of the chance of secondary cases occurring in an infected family shows that if no immunization had been practiced, probably from 700 to 800 cases of diphtheria would have developed, instead of the 24 reported. The results obtained by private physicians are not quite as favorable. Of 2,864 cases of immunization, the disease occurred in 1.4 per cent. The experence of New York, as well as other cities, seems to indicate that to obtain the most prompt and general use of antitoxin, it is necessary that it be not only furnished but also administered by health-department officials whenever requested. In New York the department goes so far as to urge personally, or by telephone, upon every physician reporting diphtheria, the prompt use of antitoxin on both sick and well. In Baltimore,† of 1,151 cases of immunization, 6 cases, or a little over .5 per cent, were attacked. The usual dose was 500 units, but in the 251 cases where 1,000 units were used, there was no recurrence. The latter dose is recommended in that city.

NUTRITIVE VALUE OF FOODS.—Boards of health are generally active in the prevention of the sale of decayed, diseased and adulterated food materials. Of late they have undertaken a campaign of education in regard to proper methods of producing and handling milk, and in some instances, at least, have entered upon the business of distributing to infants sterilized or clean milk. One important phase of the food problem seems thus far to have been neglected by health officials. It is important for all, but especially for the wage-earning class, that money spent for

---

* *N. Y. Med. Jour.*, Dec. 12, 1903.
† *Rep. Health Dept.*, 1902, p. 141.

food should bring the greatest possible return. A vast amount of data has of late been collected in regard to the nutritive value of foods as related to cost. It would appear to be time for this knowledge to be popularized, and the York (England) Health and Housing Reform Association have issued, for general circulation, a small sheet, on which is represented graphically the nutritive value of the more common food materials. There is also some explanatory matter in easily understood language. This form of sanitary education is one which might well be taken up by health officers in this country.

MILK AND FOODS.

BY CHARLES HARRINGTON, M. D.,

Asst. Prof. of Hygiene, Harvard Med. School.

IS ANY PART OF A MILKING BACTERIA-FREE?—One sometimes hears it stated that the milk that is drawn after the "fore-milk" is, to all intents and purposes, free from bacteria; and again, on the contrary, that even the "strippings" may be fairly rich in bacteria,—even 500 per cc. Recent studies by A. Lux* support the latter contention, and demonstrate further that the first milk drawn often contains fewer bacteria than the middle milk and strippings. The element of time appears to have considerable influence, for milk drawn from the same teat, after intervals of varying length (two to twenty-four hours), yielded them the more generously the longer the interval. Thus, in one instance, the range was from 65 to nearly 3,000 per cc., and in another, from 22 to more than 1,200.

BACTERIA OF MILK DUCTS.—It is generally understood that the small residuum of milk in the ducts after milking acts as a pabulum for the teat bacteria, enabling them to go on multiplying during the periods of rest; but if Uhlmann is correct in his assertions,† milk is never present in the capillary ducts, except in minute amounts, and is commonly absent. Upward of a one thousand

---

* *Centralb. fur Bakt. u Parasit.*, 2 Abth., XVII., pp. 195 and 267.
† *Thesis.* Jena, 1903.

sections of thirty-five teats were stained and studied. Although milk was commonly basent, every section showed bacteria, chiefly micrococci, in small, and occasionally in large, numbers.

ACTION OF FORMALDEHYDE ON THE DIGESTI-BILITY OF MILK.—Certain eminent German and English authorities have recently advocated the chemical treatment of milk as a means of diminishing the bacterial content thereof, and thus bringing about a diminished infantile death-rate. Formaldehyde has commended itself to their consideration as an agent which, contrary to general belief, is incapable of exerting any harmful influence on the digestibility of the casein. That this agent does exert such an influence has been proved once more by Trillat,‡ who found that casein from fresh, untreated milk was from 5 to 6 per cent more digestible than that from milk to which formaldehyde had been added to the extent of 1 part in 20,000 (about a half of a teaspoonful of commercial formalin to 5 gallons), and about 30 per cent more so than casein that had been treated with dilute formaldehyde (1:20,000 water) after it had been separated by means of rennet. The local action of the antiseptic in the stomach is additional ground for prohibition of its use.

THE FATE OF TYPHOID BACILLI IN BEER.

Professor Surmont of Lille, France, has been testing the beer made there, in respect to its effect on typhoid germs. He found that the cultures of typhoid bacilli added to the beer were all killed in one-half to 67 hours, the bactericidal effects being most pronounced in proportion to the amount of lactic acid in the beer; the acetic acid had also a lesser influence of the same kind. The beer, as it is manufactured, is evidently a hygienic drink, but when water is mixed with it, as frequently occurs, the germs in the water may prove a source of infection. Beer weak enough to allow survival of bacteria becomes more bactericidal as it ripens, as the bacilli in it generate more lactic acid, which in turn has a destructive action on them.—*Public Health*, June, 1904, p. 529.

Compt. rend., 1904, CXXXVIII., p. 720.

MEAT POISONING AND PARATYPHOID.

In 1901 there was, in Düsseldorf, an outbreak of more than 50 cases of meat-poisoning due to eating horsemeat in an almost or quite raw state. One of the victims, a boy of nine, died, and from his spleen was isolated a very motile, short, thick bacillus, with rounded ends. This proved to be highly pathogenic for mice and guinea pigs. Dr. H. Trautmann (*Zeitschrift für Hygiene,* Vol. XLV., p. 139), who isolated it, has made a comparative study of this and other forms of bacteria obtained by others from other outbreaks, and of various strains of paratyphoid bacilli of types A and B, and has come to the conclusion that though differing widely in shape, size, growth, staining, spore formation and behavior on culture media, they show no fundamental difference and are merely varieties of the same organism; so he puts them all under the general head of *Bacillus paratyphosus* and divides them into five groups according to their agglutinating properties, the members of one group exerting a greater influence upon one another than against members of the other group. All of the most widely known meat-poisoning bacteria, as Van Ermengem's *B. botulinus,* Gaertner's *B. enteritidis,* and Basenau's *B. bovis morbificans,* are included.

ANOTHER CAUSE OF BERIBERI.

According to G. Maurer (*Geneeskundig Tydschrift voor Nederlandsch-Indie,* XLIII., p. 336, through *Biochemisches Centralblatt,* May, 1904, p. 542), both beriberi and psilosis are consequences of intoxication by oxalic acid produced in the intestine. Von Uchermann (*Centralblatt für innere Medizin,* June 18, 1904), after an investigation of cases occurring aboard ships, is convinced that the disease is an intoxication and not an infection; that it is closely related to scurvy, and that it is caused by the exclusive use of preserved foods. In this connection, it is interesting to note that M. Coplans (*The Lancet,* June 18, 1904) attempts to show that scurvy in adults is probably a specific bacterial disease rather than the result of the lack of particular kinds of food. He instances an outbreak of the disorder in a military camp in South Africa, where the food was identical in quality and kind with that of other camps in which no scurvy occurred. In the camp in question, the sanitary condition was very bad, and those who were seized were neglectful of personal hygiene.

DESTRUCTION OF TUBERCLE BACILLI IN MILK.

After it had been asserted by Hesse and others, that milk containing tubercle bacilli could be rendered harmless by heating to 60° C. for 20 minutes, it was shown by Professor Theobald Smith that the pellicle which forms on the surface may offer such protection to the bacilli that they do not succumb to an exposure of a half hour to 65° C.; and now Dr. W. Rullmann (*Münchener medicinische Wochenschrift*, 1903, No. 31, p. 1342) reports that even with constant agitation as a preventive of the pellicle and with the observance of every precaution, including that of maintaining a constant temperature, he was unable to destroy added bacilli in a half hour with a temperature of 65° C.

NEW SOURCES OF LEAD POISONING.

Attention is called by Dr. Y. C. Gibson (*Australasian Medical Gazette*, April 20, 1904) to the possibility of painted rails and walls as frequent sources of lead poisoning in children, especially those who bite their nails and suck their fingers. He says that cases are most numerous during hot weather, when the paint is softened and less adherent. Another source of poisoning, according to Dr. Lefour (*Presse Médicale*, May 14, 1904), is wallpaper. He reports the case of a woman whose urine showed 1 milligram of lead per liter, the cause of which was thought to be the wallpaper, which contained considerable lead. He obtained a lot of different papers from a dealer and found that most of them contained lead.

PREVENTING THE BACTERIAL CONTAMINATION OF MILK.

MILK.—Investigations conducted by Fraser* to determine the relative effect of the different dairy operations upon the bacterial content of the milk, point to the cow herself, and particularly to the udder, as the chief source of bacteria and of dirt. Agar plates were exposed, usually for one minute, near the milkpail during

* *Ill. State Bull.* No. 99, p. 219.

numerous tests showed reduction of the bacteria, from washing the udder before milking, from 578 bacteria to 192. The dirt was also directly estimated. Taking the amount of dirt found in the milk after thorough washing of the udder as a standard, unwashed udders, apparently clean, yielded three and one-half times, slightly soiled udders, eighteen times, and grossly dirty udders, ninety times, as much dirt. B. R. RICKARDS.

LABORATORY WORK.

Laboratory men are invited to send brief notes of laboratory news, authors' abstracts, new apparatus, new technic, summaries of results, etc., to the Managing Editor for this column. Line drawings, capable of reduction to 3″ x 4,″ will be inserted when necessary.

THE BACTERIOLOGICAL LABORATORY OF THE BOSTON BOARD OF HEALTH has been transferred from its old outgrown quarters in the Sudbury Building, occupied since 1898, to the Boylston Chambers, 739 Boylston Street, Room 501, telephone 1500 Back Bay, where greater space and conveniences have been secured.

In addition to the diagnostic work, which has increased very much since the laboratory was established, the bacteriological examination of the Boston milk supply has been recently undertaken, involving the examination of about six hundred samples each month.

THE BACTERICIDAL ACTION OF TYPHOID SERUM.— Stein and Kirk* add to fresh, untreated rabbit serum a dilution of a twenty-four-hour broth culture of typhoid bacilli, and varying amounts of treated typhoid serum, at 36.5° C. After three hours, plate. Normal human serum could not be diluted more than 1 to 200 to secure bacteriolysis by this method, while typhoid sera produced bacteriolysis in much higher dilutions,—even in 1 to 50,000 in some cases. No connection between agglutination and bacteriolysis was detected, the later developing the earlier in the course of an attack, and promising a valuable means of early diagnosis of typhoid, especially when the Widal reaction cannot be obtained.

Berl. klin. Wochen, 1904, No. 9, p. 213.

AUTOMATIC DISINFECTION OF CLINICAL THERMOME-
TERS.—Denny* reports experiments to show that 2 or 3 drops of
ordinary commercial formalin, 40 per cent, dropped upon cotton
packed into the bottom of the thermometer case, will sterilize the
thermometer completely in five to twenty minutes, so long as a
strong odor of formalin can be detected at the mouth of the case.
Denny points out that this method should not be used when the
thermometer is passed rapidly from mouth to mouth, since sufficient
time for disinfection by this method will not then be had. The
thermometer should be rinsed to remove the formalin taste
before placing it in the patient's mouth. Denny attributes the
excellent germicidal effect obtained in the short time mentioned
upon *Staph. pyogenes aureus, B. typhosus, B. subtilis* (spores) and
B. diphtheriæ to the high humidity reached and to the relatively
high temperature obtained when the case is carried, as is usual, in
the vest pocket.

TO AVOID "SPREADERS" ON AGAR PLATES.—At 37° C,.
agar plates, especially if the atmosphere of the incubator be
saturated, as it should be, with moisture, are prone to "spread,"
involving great annoyance in plating for isolation, and a considerable loss of "counts" in routine counting work on milk, sewage,
water, etc.

To avoid spreaders, several plans are followed. One consists
in the inversion of the Petri dish after the agar has hardened, but
this is far from uniformly successful. Other methods involve the
use of 20–22° C., instead of 37° C., for agar, or even reject agar
entirely, substituting for it gelatine at 22° C.

In plating for isolation, it is often necessary, or at least preferable, to use the higher temperature, while the liquefaction common
in gelatine plates from mixed cultures introduces for them a dis-
advantage almost as undesirable as the spreading of agar. In
plating for counts, the higher temperature offers the further great
advantage of uniformity, since constancy of temperature is readily
secured at this point, while constancy at 20–22° C. is almost not to
be had in most laboratories; and time-saving, since 24 hour
counts at 37°C. are practically final counts.

---

* *Boston Med. and Surg. Jour.*, June 2, 1904.

In order to secure the advantages of agar plates at 37° C. for milk counts, while avoiding the objection due to spreading, Hill (Boston Board of Health Bacteriological Laboratory) suggested the use of a porous cover for the Petri dish, instead of the glass cover now almost universally employed. For this purpose, he found the earthenware "fern saucer" of the pottery trade very satisfactory, one of the regular sizes on the market happening to fit the standard Petri-dish capsule almost as if made for it. Dr. F. H. Slack, of the same laboratory, made careful comparative tests with the usual Petri dish and this modified form, in the routine milk counting of the laboratory, with the following results:

Atmosphere of incubator dry.

No. of plates with glass covers.	Spread.	No. of plates with porous cover.	Spread.
45	15%	46	2+%

Atmosphere of incubator moist to saturation.

86	36%	46	11%

The spreading under the glass covers was generally extensive and harmful, while in one-half of the porous-covered plates recorded as spread, the spreading was slight and negligible. Since the success or failure of the porous cover as a preventive of spreading depends on its absorptive powers, thorough drying of the earthenware after washing is essential, and is easily achieved by merely prolonging somewhat the dry sterilization employed for Petri dishes of the original type.

With this form of Petri dish it is not necessary to invert the dish after cooling the agar.

The "fern-saucer" is good, but it is probable that an earthenware or porcelain cover, made for the purpose, would prove even more satisfactory. Buttons placed at regular intervals on bottom of the dish inside, after Whipple's design for glass covers, would secre ventilation of the dish, as recommended by him.

WHY DIRTY MILK IS DANGEROUS.*

WHY IS DIRTY MILK DANGEROUS? Everyone knows how milk looks and how it tastes, and that it comes from cows, sheep, goats and other domesticated animals, and yet very few really know what milk is, or how it is made by animals, or how dangerous it can be when it gets dirty.

WHAT IS COWS' MILK? Cows' milk is a whitish, opaque liquid specially prepared in a milk organ (the "bag," or "udder") by living cells fed and nourished by the hot blood of the animal. As it comes from the cow, milk is warm, rich and sweet. It is *warm*, because it comes from the body of a warm-blooded animal. It is *rich*, because it contains a kind of invisible liquid meat, besides fats which, when milk stands, rise as *cream*. It is *sweet*, because it contains considerable sugar (milk sugar). It is also salty.

FRESH, PURE MILK. Milk like that just described is fresh and pure. It is *fresh*, because it has just come from the cow. It is *pure*, because it is milk, the whole milk, and nothing but the milk. Milk which has been robbed of its fat, or *skimmed*, is not whole, but skimmed, milk. Milk which has been "watered" or "doctored" is *adulterated* milk.

* The present is the second (No. 2) of **POPULAR ESSAYS ON HYGIENE AND SANITATION,**—a series of leaflets prepared by Workers in the Sanitary Research Laboratory and Sewage Experiment Station of the Mass. Institute of Technology by the request and at the expense of a friend of sanitary education, and designed to teach in simple language some of the more important lessons of the time concerning Health and Disease, and especially the Prevention of Disease.

Some of the other leaflets of the present series, **SERIES A. ON DIRT AND DISEASE**, are :
No. 1. WHY DIRT IS DANGEROUS, (Ready.)
No. 3. WHY DIRTY WATER IS DANGEROUS. (Ready in November.)
No. 4. WHY DIRTY STREET SARE DANGEROUS. (In Preparation.)
No. 5. WHY DIRTY PERSONS ARE DANGEROUS. (In Preparation.)

Other leaflets may eventually be prepared upon "Microbes,—Good and Bad;" "Some Common Diseases : How they Come and how to Avoid them;" "Farm Sanitation;" "Why Flies are Filthy and Dangerous;" or other practical sanitary and hygienic topics.

It is hoped that Boards of Health, School Boards, Hospital Authorities, Charity Workers, Health-Education Leagues, Anti-Tuberculosis Societies and other Organizations, Philanthropic Persons and Educators may make use of these leaflets in that campaign of education in sanitation and hygiene in which all civilized peoples are now engaging.

Copies of the Leaflets may be had (postpaid) by addressing the Biological Department, Massachusetts Institute of Technology, Boston, Mass., and enclosing money or postage stamps according to the following schedule :—
One to fifty copies .2 cents each.
Fifty or more copies . . . . .1 "   "
Larger quantities by special arrangement.

IMPURE MILK. Milk may be made impure not only by skimming, watering or doctoring, but also by *dirt*, which gets into milk from dirty stables, dirty milkmen and dirty pails, cans, bottles, strainers, or other utensils and receptacles.

BABY MILK. The sucking calf gets from its mother pure, fresh and whole milk. The human baby thrives best also on its mother's milk; but when this fails, it may do very well on cows' milk, sometimes slightly altered to suit its needs. Above all, the bottle-fed baby needs *fresh, pure* and *clean* milk; and this, unfortunately, is often hard to get.

STALE MILK. Milk that is pure and fresh contains a few microbes, but only a few, and these chiefly harmless or even useful *souring microbes*, which slowly *curdle* the milk and are helpful in cheese making. As milk becomes *stale*, these microbes multiply enormously, and seriously alter the milk, so that the milk sugar disappears and an acid (*milk acid* or *lactic acid*) comes in its place. Every one knows that babies need sweet milk rather than sour milk, and it is easy to see why stale milk, which is much less sweet and pure than fresh milk, is not, therefore, good for babies.

· **DIRTY MILK.** Like most white things, milk very easily gets soiled or dirty, but, unlike most white things, it does not easily *show* soil or dirt. If, instead of a pailful of milk (which is a thick and foamy white liquid), a pailful of downy or fluffy pure white cotton or wool were drawn from an animal in an ordinary cow stable, it would be easy to see how particles of dust and dirt getting into the pail from the air of the stable, or the hide of the cow, or the hands or clothes of the milker, would soon make the cotton or wool dirty, and also how hard it would be to get the dirt out, once it had got in. Now it is a fact, that milk which is fresh, looks pure, and would be pure if it were only clean, is often grossly impure simply because it is *dirty*.

WHAT IS DIRT? The word "dirt" comes from an older word, "drit," meaning *dung* or *excrement* and, strictly speaking, clean soil or clean earth should never be spoken of as dirt, for dirt means excrement, filth or dung, such as cow dung. Dirt (dung) is always rich in microbes, most of which cause milk to spoil quickly, and some of which may be dangerous and even deadly. (For more facts about dirt, see Leaflet No. 1 of the present Series.)

HOW COW'S MILK GETS DIRTY. Milk as it comes from the cow is not only warm, rich, and sweet, but also perfectly *clean.* But with cow *stables* it is different. These are generally dirty, and too often the cows have no good care but must stand and lie in their own filth, which sticks to their hair, and later dries and drops off into the milk pail while the milker is milking. Too often also the dust from the hay, and dirt from the unwashed hands of the milker, fall into the pail ; and too often the pails, strainers and milk cans are themselves dirty.

WHY DIRTY MILK IS DANGEROUS. Dirty milk is always dangerous, either for babies or for adults. It is dangerous for babies for two reasons : first, because dirty milk quickly gets stale and spoils, thus becoming unlike mothers' milk, which is always fresh, pure and clean. Cholera infantum, which kills many bottle-fed babies in very hot weather when milk spoils rapidly, is probably largely caused by stale baby milk. In the second place, dirt sometimes contains germs of dangerous and deadly fevers, such as typhoid fever, scarlet fever and diphtheria. Epidemics of these diseases even among children have been known to come from dirty milk.

Dirty milk is dangerous for adults as well as for children, chiefly for the second reason just given, namely, that it is liable to contain the germs of typhoid fever, diphtheria and other infectious or contagious diseases.

HOW MILK CAN BE MADE SAFE. Any milk not actually sour and spoilt can be made safe for drinking by heating it to the boiling point, cooling it, and using immediately. For babies, however, pasteurized milk is generally better than boiled milk. To pasteurize milk for babies, the milk should first be got *as pure, fresh and sweet as possible;* it should then be put into bottles or tins which have been thoroughly scalded and scoured. These bottles or tins should then be loosely stoppered or covered, and set into a vessel of water, which should be heated nearly, but not quite, to the boiling point, and kept there for half an hour. If a thermometer can be had, the milk (not the water outside of it) should be kept at 160° for at least twenty minutes. The milk should then be cooled and kept, on ice if possible, until it is used, but it should never be used in hot weather for babies after it has stood more than a few hours. The feeding bottle, nipple and tube are very apt to get dirty or sour, and should be scalded frequently.

HOW CAN WE GET BETTER MILK? Cleaner, fresher, and therefore, sweeter and safer, milk is greatly needed in all our cities and towns, and this can only be secured by greater cleanliness on the part of farmers and milkmen.

Buyers should refuse to take milk that is stale, dirty, sourish, or "cowy" in odor; but, on the other hand, consumers, especially those having babies to bring up, should be willing to pay somewhat more for clean, sweet and pure milk, because it costs the farmer more to produce and deliver such milk, and he is not likely to take the pains to do this unless his customers ask for it and are willing to pay more for clean milk. It is unreasonable and absurd to spend money on luxuries and yet refuse to pay a little more for milk that is pure, fresh, and free from cow dung.

All milkers should wash their hands before sitting down to milk. The cows should be given plenty of fresh air and exercise and groomed or otherwise cared for, as horses are. It is absurd to treat horses, which we use chiefly for work or for pleasure, better than we do cows that give us food to drink. All pails, cans, bottles, strainers and other utensils should be *thoroughly* cleaned by *scalding* water before they are used for holding milk.

Ashby
E. A. Hubbard, M. D.

Avon
R. A. Elliott, M. D. 2
E. P. Linfield, M. D. 1

Arlington
E. E. Stickney, M. D. 2

Athol
W. H. Brock

Attleboro
George K. Roberts, M. D. 2

Andover
Charles E. Abbott, M. D. 2

Belmont
W. Lyman Underwood. 1
H. A. Yenetchi, M. D.

Boston
S. W. Abbott, M. D. 13*
Silas H. Ayer, M. D.
J. W. Bartol, M. D.
David D. Brough, M. D. 4
Alex. Burr, M. D. V. 8
D. A. Cheever, M. D.
J. W. Cosden.
Robert Cox.
B. F. Davenport, M. D.
S. H. Durgin. M. D. 1
H. C. Ernst, M. D.
Langdon Frothingham, M. D. V.
W. P. Gesner.
E. F. Gleason, M. D.
Charles Harrington, M. D. 11
Edward M. Hartwell.
Dennis J. Hern. 2
W. L. Hicks.
H. W. Hill, M. D. 5
Everett D. Hooper, M. D.
L. H. Howard, D. V. S.
James O. Jordan. 17
Thomas Jordan. 7
S. C. Keith, S. B.
W. H. Mitchell.
Frank L. Morse, M. D. 4*
Austin Peters, D. V. S. 14*
E. B. Phelps, S. B.
E. L. Pilsbury.
W. H. Prescott, M. D.
Mrs. Ellen H. Richards.
B. R. Rickards, S. B. 5
Geo. B. Robbins.
Howard P. Rogers, M. D. V.
Prof. W. T. Sedgwick.
T. B. Shea, M. D. 2
Agnes C. Vietor, M. D.
Robert S. Weston, S. B.
George M. Whitaker, 16
George Whiting.
C. E. A. Winslow, S. B.
John F. Worcester, M. D.

Bondsville
D. B. Sullivan, M. D.

Brighton
E. S. Hatch, M. D.
Horace E. Marion, M. D.
Otis H. Marion, M D.
F. W. Rice, M. D.

Brookline
H. L. Chase, M. D. 6
James M. Codman, Jr. 1
Nathaniel Conant. 2
William Craig. 2
Francis P. Denny, M. D. 5
Robert W. Hastings, M. D.
Edward A. McEttrick. 13
J. Albert C. Nyhen. 5
F. H. Osgood, M. R. C. V. S. 8,11
H. Carlton Smith, 17
Willard E. Ward. 15
John K. Whiting.

Brockton
George E. Bolling. 5
F. H. Burnett, M. D.
Charles H. Cary. 3
Edward P. Gleason, M. D. 10
J. H. Lawrence, M. D. 1
A. W. Packard.
F. J. Ripley, M. D.
F. Herbert Snow, C. E.
S. Alfred Spear. 12

Cambridge
Lewis L. Bryant, M. D.
E. R. Cogswell, M. D.
John Crawford.
Edwin Farnham, M. D. 4
Charles Harris.
John G. Hildreth, M. D.
Goodwin A. Isenberg. 1
Ross McPherson, M. D.
J. Arnold Rockwell, M. D.
E. H. Stevens, M. D.
H. P. Walcott, M. D. 1*
Roswell Wetherbee, M. D. 2
Charles F. Whiting.

Charlestown
C. H. Hood.
Nelson M. Wood, M. D.

Chelsea
Frank E. Winslow. 3

Clinton
W. P. Bowers, M. D.
C. C. Crowley.
C. L. French, M. D. 1
J. J. Goodwin, M. D.
E. H. Mackay, M. D. 10
James H. McGrath. 2
G. L. Tobey, M. D. 2

Cohasset
Oliver H. Howe, M. D.
Herbert A. Tilden.

Concord
John M. Keyes. 1
Thomas Todd. 2

Dedham
E. W. Finn, M. D. 2

Duxbury
Alfred E. Green. 1
N. K. Noyes, M. D.

East Bridgewater
A. L. Shirley, M. D.

Everett
R. E. Brown, M. D.
George W. S. Dockum. 2, 13
A. A. Jackson, M. D.
E. J. Newton, M. D. 2
N. B. Smith. 1
George E. Whitehill, M. D.
E. W. Young, M. D.

Fall River
Charles A. Hicks, M. D. 2

Falmouth
Russell S. Nye. 2
Asa R. Pattee, M. D. 2
T. L. Swift, M. D. 1

Fitchburg
J. F. Bresnahan. 7
E. L. Fiske, M. D. 1
Henry M. Francis. 2
Fred R. Houghton. 3, 6
A. P. Mason M. D. 5
Charles H. Rice, M. D.
D. S. Woodworth, M. D.

Framingham
N. I. Bowditch.
Charles M. Hargraves. 2, 13
William R. Morrow, M. D. 2

Gloucester
H. L. Belden.

Haverhill
J. F. Crostan, M D. 2

Holyoke
J. J. Linehan. 2, 6
A. B. Wetherell, M. D. 1
Frank A. Woods, M. D. 2, 13

Hingham
Charles H. Marble. 1
J. Winthrop Spooner, M. D. 2

1, Chairman, Bd. Health ; 2, Member; 3, Clerk ; 4, Medical Officer ; 5, Bacteriologist; 6, Agent ; 7, Sanitary Inspector ; 8, Inspector of Animals ; 9, Quarantine Officer ; 10, City Physician ; 11, Milk Inspector ; 12, Supt. of Health; 13, Secretary ; 14, State Cattle Dept. ; 15, Disinfector ; 16, U. S. Dairy Inspector ; 17, Chemist ; 18, Examiner of Plumbers.
* State Officials.

AMERICAN JOURNAL OF PUBLIC HYGIENE

AND

JOURNAL OF THE .

MASSACHUSETTS ASSOCIATION OF BOARDS OF HEALTH

ORGANIZED 1890.

[The Association as a body is not responsible for statements or opinions of any of its members.]

| VOL. XIV. (New Series. Vol. I., No. 1.) | November, 1904. | NO. 4 |

THE MASSACHUSETTS ASSOCIATION OF BOARDS OF HEALTH was organized in Boston, March, 1890, with the following objects: The advancement of sanitary science; the promotion of better organization and co-operation among local boards of health, and the uniform enforcement of sanitary laws and regulations

THE JOURNAL OF THIS ASSOCIATION has for fourteen years faithfully reflected the views of the public hygienists of Massachusetts. With the November issue of the year 1904, the encouragement received from many hygienic quarters induced the Association to undertake the expansion of the Journal to a national standard' with the co-operation of many noted sanitarians as editors. A new title was selected, while the older and well-established title was retained also.

The dates of publication are FEBRUARY, MAY, AUGUST *and* NOVEMBER *of each year.*

THE JOURNAL will contain the papers read at the meetings of the Association, papers contributed by hygienists, reports of the discussions, editorials, abstracts, reviews and hygienic notes of professional interest. Subscription rates, $1.00 per year. Reprints furnished at cost price.

All communications concerning the JOURNAL, copy, proof, subscriptions, advertisements, etc., should be addressed to the Managing Editor, DR. H. W. HILL, 739 BOYLSTON ST., BOSTON, MASS.

All communications concerning the ASSOCIATION should be addressed to the Secretary of the Association, JAMES C. COFFEY, CITY HALL, WORCESTER, MASS.

All bills not relating to the Journal, and MEMBERSHIP DUES $2.00 per year), should be sent to the Treasurer of the Association, DR. JAMES B. FIELD, 329 WESTFORD ST., LOWELL, MASS.

LEPROSY.*

The occasional appearance of imported leprosy in our midst, the difficulty of knowing how to deal satisfactorily with it, and the frequent errors in diagnosis made before the true nature of such cases is recognized, may serve as an excuse for bringing up this somewhat foreign subject.

Leprosy may be regarded as one of the most ancient of maladies which has maintained itself up to the present. Though rare in highly civilized countries, it is quite well established in South America, Africa and Asia. Even in Europe there are persistent foci in Russia, the Balkan States and in Norway. Occasionally a slight tendency toward greater diffusion is noticed, as in Eastern Prussia in 1896 from the Russian provinces. The great diffusion and prevalence of leprosy throughout Europe in the Middle Ages and its equally remarkable shrinkage and gradual disappearance after the fourteenth century are unique facts in epidemiology. It seems scarcely credible that there were 19,000 leproseries in Christendom and that in France alone there were 2000. The disappearance of the disease is ascribed to the stringent measures applied toward lepers, which consisted either in casting them out of communities and making them vagrants or else in confining them in special hospitals. In the middle of the past century the theory that the disease is inherited rather than caught was promulgated and defended by two Norwegians, Danielsen and Boeck. The clinical history certainly tended to favor this view, but the discovery of the lepra bacillus in 1879 and 1880 by Hansen and by Neisser gradually put an end to this theory, although as late as 1894 Dr. J. C. White of Boston still considered it necessary, in view of the persistent prevalence of the theory of heredity to vigorously defend the theory of infection. In England some authorities believe that the consumption of fish stands in some relation to the disease.

*Kindly written by Dr. Theobald Smith, to take the place of his article on the same subject, read at the July meeting of the Association.

The causal relation of the Hansen bacillus has been firmly established by examinations made in many parts of the world on different types of the disease. The disease is not readily transmitted, however, and prolonged exposure, as in family life, seems necessary to successful infection. Yet even in the family infection does not always follow. Koch mentions a mother who nursed and lost a husband and four sons during a period of twenty years, but remained free herself. Hansen states that none of the children of the one hundred and seventy Norwegian lepers who migrated to this country became diseased. This apparent hesitancy of the lepra bacillus to invade a new subject must not shut our eyes to the fact that we have an infectious disease to deal with and one peculiarly offensive because of its prolonged duration and tendency to extreme mutilation of the body. The rapid diffusion of the disease in the Middle Ages, and in the Hawaiian Islands in the last century, indicates that perhaps some variety of this species of bacillus differing slightly from the one encountered today was responsible, and that some slight variation in the character of the bacillus may in part repeat the history of former centuries if our negligence permits it. Personal hygiene is not so highly developed in the densely crowded portions of our cities as to stand in the way of a spread if other conditions are favorable.

It is well known that leprosy appears under two clinically quite distinct types, the tuberculous and the anaesthetic. To this a third, the so-called mixed or intermediate type, has been added. The anaesthetic type, which is marked chiefly by lesions of the nervous system, is the type prevalent in those countries where leprosy has been endemic for long periods of time. The tuberculous is the more common type in foci of recent origin.

In the anaesthetic type bacilli are scarce in the lesions. In the tuberculous type they are as a rule abundant. Within recent years attention has been drawn to the lesions of the nasal mucous membrane and to the presence of large numbers of bacilli in the discharge from the nose as a possible source of infection. Thus Sticker gives the following statistics obtained by an examination of patients in Calcutta, India. Of fifty-seven cases of tubercular leprosy fifty-five showed bacilli in the secretions from the nose. In sixty-eight cases of nerve leprosy forty-five had demonstrable bacilli in the nose. In twenty-eight cases of the mixed type twenty-seven were discharging bacilli from the nose. Kolle examined a large group of cases in the leper hospital of Cape Colony with the following results: Lepra bacilli were found in the nose in all of forty-five cases of tubercular leprosy, in twenty-two out of thirty cases of the mixed type and in only twenty-one out of sixty-two of the anaesthetic type. (1.) These figures suffice to show that the large number of lepers are discharging bacilli even in those stages of the disease in which ulcers of the skin are absent.

A disease which propagates itself so very slowly, and which makes itself known only in rare, isolated instances, does not create apprehension, and hence preventive measures are usually neglected. We have been told that lepers in the past have moved freely about in our country, using public conveyances and even Pullman cars without hindrance. It seems to us that every leper should be under the constant vigilant care of public health authorities, and that some action should be taken by the General Government which will bring the lepers of the country together in some lazaretto or home where they will be humanely treated, where they may enjoy the society of their kind and perhaps do useful work. No State is at present in position to deal satisfactorily with these cases, as each has perhaps but one, or at most a few cases within its borders. In all the States there may be not over one hundred. In 1894 Hyde stated that up to that time five hundred and sixty cases had been reported in our country.

The success of segregation in leper homes supported by the Government is shown in the experience of Norway. There the admission to leper hospitals was at first voluntary, although every inducement was made to have the lepers leave their home. When they remained with their families they were compelled by law to occupy separate beds, and if possible separate rooms.

(1.) In a case of tubercular leprosy quarantined in this State, we found last summer large numbers of acid-fast bacilli, some in the form of the characteristic balls or so-called globi in the swabs from the nose.

Clothing and eating utensils were to be kept separate from those of the rest of the family. All dressings for wounds were to be burned. If these measures are neglected the patient is transferred to a leper home. This relatively mild treatment has been signally successful in gradually reducing the number of cases. In 1856 there were 2870 lepers; in 1900 only 577.

Though it may seem harsh and unnecessary to segregate and isolate those afflicted with a disease which incapacitates so litttle at first, and which seems so feebly contagious, the history of leprosy, imperfect as it is, bids us to protect the family and the public at large, and this can be done most humanely by providing for the lepers a well equipped hospital under the auspices of the National Government, where the patients may be treated and the disease studied from the most advanced standpoint. This would relieve the various States of the burden of establishing and duplicating what would necessarily be unsatisfactory institutions on account of the few to be cared for, and create a centre of information concerning this exotic malady.

THE PRESENT STATUS OF MORTALITY REGISTRATION IN THE UNITED STATES.

In the history of vital statistics in the United States during the past three years there is much to encourage those who have been trying to extend the registration area. The United States Census of 1880 secured reliable mortality data from the registration officers of but two States, Massachusetts and New Jersey. To the Census of 1890 the registration officers of eight States contributed aceptable data, though two at least of the six additional States had certainly not in 1890 as good mortality registration as Massachusetts and New Jersey had ten years earlier.

In 1900 the Census Bureau was more stringent about accepting the returns of local registration offices, and the States included in the so-called registration area were nine. The six New England States, with New York, New Jersey and Michigan, made up the number. For the first time a western State, Michigan, was admitted to the group of registration States.

At this time, in 1904, the list of registration States would probably include also Maryland, Indiana, Illinois, perhaps Ohio, and possibly Colorado. Six other States are making earnest efforts to secure complete and systematic registration of mortality. Of these the great State of Pennsylvania is one, so that in 1910 all that part of the country north of the Potomac and Ohio Rivers and east of the Mississippi may be expected to account for its mortality by means of effective local registration. The State of Delaware, perhaps, will be the one small spot of barrenness in this great area.

American mortality statistics are therefore likely to become useful in a larger way than heretofore, and with the prospect of a respectable mass of mortality statistics it is now time to consider the quality of our records and the methods of utilizing them. The Director of the Twelfth Census said of the records obtained from registration sources that they were in certain particulars less satisfactory and more difficult of analysis than were the returns of enumerators. The enumerators' returns were less complete in a quantitative sense, but they were more uniform in their contents; while the registration records, conforming to the varying acquirements of local registration, differed materially as to the items of information furnished, and were entirely silent as to certain data necessary to fit them to the statistics of population.

This observation brings in to view one of the reforms long needed in American registration, and now in a fair way to be accomplished, namely, practical agreement as to the essential items of information to be recorded on a death certificate. Substantial progress toward this sort of uniformity has been made in the last three years. A majority of the registration States now use a blank agreeing in contents with the standard form of certificates suggested by the Census Bureau. This form does not make such extensive inquiry, especially into the family history of descendants, as the Census Bureau sought to make in the organization of the Twelfth Census.

Several registration offices participated in the formulation of this certificate; it takes into consideration all the real difficulties of local registration, and asks no more information than all registration offices can easily obtain.

Another advantage recently accrued to American registration is the adoption of the International classification of causes of death. This classification has some very notable defects, but it is superior to any of the older classifications; it is used in a good majority of registration offices, and it is to be revised by an international congress every ten years.

With the Census Bureau established upon a permanent footing and with the best sources of vital data well conformed to practical standards, we may expect more satisfactory Census reports, both of population and vital statistics, than we have had hitherto. But it is not only for the sake of better Federal documents that recent advances in registration are welcome. Many of us have to consult occasionally the registration reports of other States and cities in the study of our own problems, and it is difficult to grow accustomed to the disappointments so often met. City registration reports are seldom worth consulting. They cover in several instances a good many years of time, but furnish extremely little information as to the causes of mortality. Among State registration offices only four record any long experience, and these four supply at present the best obtainable information concerning causes of death in the United States.

We are just now beginning to be able to accumulate quantities of useful data, and we should have some regard for the temper of the student who shall consult our tables at the end of another quarter of a century. If we plan our registration with some consideration of such long intervals our work will be all the better for current use. One of the first things upon which we should be agreed is as to recording the distribution of both population and deaths by ages.

The mortality of the first five years of life is usually divided in some fashion, and we should reach some agreement as to the manner of dividing this period. If but one division is to be made the age of two years is perhaps the best dividing line. It is preferable to divide this period twice, giving separate statements of the mortality under one, between one and two, and between two and five.

For ages above five it is the usual practice to state the mortality for quinquennial periods up to 25 or 30, and for decennial periods for ages above up to about 80, making one statement for the latest period of life. This arrangement makes it difficult or impossible to determine certain relations of important causes of death. It is quite as easy and far more satisfactory to employ quinquennial periods up to the age of 90 years.

When the mortality is given separately for the first 15 years of life, then by decennial periods up to 65, and for a final period of 65 years and over, one is apt to resent the locking up of important information by such an arbitrary arrangement. The age distribution of populations is usually given by quinquennial periods, and it is essential that the age distribution of mortality should be stated in the same way.

One wishes that registration offices were agreed upon at least a certain number and variety of separate tabulations, and that these might follow each other in a definite order, so that many volumes might be consulted without waste of time. It is doubtful if any man or group of men could propose an acceptable series of tables, but we should be agreed to publish at least one table covering the whole nomenclature, with distinctions of age, sex and race.

The rates and ratios published in registration reports are a source of continual annoyance and confusion to the student, because their factors are seldom stated. Just here it is permissible to remark upon the popular interest in death rates and ratios. Information (or misinformation) concerning current mortality has a stable news value. That part of public hygiene which hygienists most neglect is of most constant interest to the general public. Newspaper readers accept these statistical summaries as of equal reliability with the market reports and baseball scores. Explanations will be demanded when people discover, as in time they will, that the arithmetic of an official record of a minor league of baseball players is vastly superior to that of the average report upon vital statistics, and that American cities, whose records of current mortality are as prompt and complete as the score of a game, have no common rules and no settled practice in the statistical treatment of their records. The intelligent layman believes that the population and the mortality are the factors of a death rate. It will be a shock to him to know that registrars are not agreed upon a method of determining either the one or the other. The total mortality he supposes is accurately obtained by simply counting the deaths. He will agree that still-births should be excluded because these individuals never formed part of the population. For the same reason deaths of non-residents ought to be excluded, and here are two discounts against the total mortality. If he should ask for a definition of a still-birth or of a non-resident no authoritative or generally accepted definition can be furnished. If he asks whether the deaths abroad of individuals, who were in fact citizens and accounted for in the population, are also accounted for in the mortality, a truthful answer might surprise him. It might even transpire that the test of citizenship is not the same for a dead man as for a live one.

In the absence of any standard of practice there is no restraint upon the will or inclination of a city registrar to figure out a death rate precisely to suit his fancy, provided his fancy is not taken with a palpably fictitious death rate. Some of the large cities of this country publish rates which stagger the faith of experienced registrars, and it is a wonder that intelligent laymen do not oftener express doubt as to their truthfulness. Those who are accustomed to deal with vital statistics, life actuaries for instance, have very little confidence in the mortality figures of American cities. Occasionally municipal registrars have received from such expert sources very pointed observations upon statistical fallacies and misstatements, but no improvement is known to have followed such admonitions.

The Mayor of a certain great American city recently boasted that among the great cities of the world his own municipality expends the least money, and at the same time shows by the mortality records the largest profit upon the cost of its health department. This distinguished mayor might just as safely have prophesied his death rate for next year. The true death rate of last year being known, it is a simple matter to determine a slight modification of the local distinction between resident and non-resident decedents, or to choose a new radical for the estimation of population, and so with practical certainty work out a pre-assumed death rate.

Several large cities in this country have in fact very low death rates, which result entirely from the age constitution of their populations and not at all from any advantages of locality or government. But health departments have not been scrupulous to show the causes of low mortality though ever so explicit about the causes of occasional high death rates. The American public has been allowed to wander at will and without guide in the mazes of vital statistics where the expert must move warily. The crudest and loosest statements concerning death rates, mortality ratios, average age at death, and duration of life, are furnished year in, year out, and year by year, by health departments to the public prints, with the result that the statisticians themselves appear to be as ignorant of the meaning of these things as the unskilled layman. A health department having 40 years' experience in registration has the effrontery (or whatever qualification the act implies) to discuss at length its rising mean age at death, offering this to the too docile public as proof that the average duration of life has increased in the same way. If this be not an act of effrontery, then we must conclude that there are registration offices in this country where it is not known that nowhere from the beginning to the end of the age of man do the curves of age distribution of the living and of the dead make one step in parallel motion. It is shameful that the people are misled by or allowed to misinterpret the figures.

The variations of the average age at death are particularly interesting to the popular mind, but no one knows how the average age at death is determined. It is doubtful if any city statistician takes the sum of the ages of the decedents in any year, or if any two officials have ever expressly agreed upon a method of estimating the mean age of the decedents in each age period, or if any single office has consistently employed one method for twenty consecutive years.

In dealing with the particulars of mortality the registrars of this country (city registrars expecially) have not protected themselves or the public from serious misinterpretation of the raw data. They impute to death certificates more definiteness than these documents possess or else treat them as of fixed interpretation year after year. In tracing the progress of causes of death through periods of years changes in the practice of registration and in the science of medicine are as a rule ignored. It is not of necessity that these variations remain unconsidered, nor are they, as some declare, negligible; for their influence can often be traced and is often important. The history of that considerable mortality accounted for under the title "Unknown" or "Ill-defined" causes is full of interest and notably affects the course of certain better defined causes of death. It discloses in the practice of registration variations which are often not improvements, and reveals an amount of positive improvement in medical diagnosis quite sufficient to discredit the face value of the raw statistics of earlier years. If "unknown causes" are studied in connection with the other indefinite accounts found in the classification, one can often determine, and apply to the figures such corrections as will give a truer view of the cause of certain definite causes of death. The statistics of fevers show steady progress toward definiteness, both in certification and registration, so that the mortality accounts for successive years of typhoid fever, for instance, may be shown more truly if one takes into account the gradual disappearance or apparent decline of some twenty odd sorts of fever often reported by the physicians of earlier days. The typhoid fever account is indeed just now approaching definiteness. Its deficit in some parts of the country is even now about 40 per cent, but twenty-five years ago the recorded mortality from typhoid fever was in the whole country more than 40 per cent short.

"Pneumonia" is an example of a statistical title treated as if
it were quite definite, though it is in fact far less definite now
than formerly.   Thirty years ago the diagnosis of pneumonia
rested upon thoracic pain, fever, rapid respiration and rusty
sputum.   Few, very few, physicians recognized pneumonia in the
absence of any two of these "cardinal" signs.   In those days
pneumonia was rarely recognized in children, and its presence
in old persons frequently escaped detection.   Nowadays most
physicians recognize pneumonias occurring at any period of life
and not presenting the old signs.   Moreover we have become
acquainted with various pulmonary consolidations having
etiological relations just as various, and we call them pneumonias, distinguishing them in death certificates either very care-
lessly or not at all from the non-complicating pneumonia.   In
1889 a vigorous strain of influenza arrived in America, a most
energetic provider of secondary pneumonia.   We had at first a
furore of influenza mortality which passed into an obsession of
pneumonia mortality, and so disguised is still with us. Sensational
statements concerning the great and growing pneumonia mortality
appeared often in city dailies.   These publications probably had
a strong effect upon certifying physicians, giving the real pneumonias less chance to escape diagnosis, and in doubtful cases
perverting the judgment of the physician.   Meanwhile the business of industrial life insurance has greatly spread, and innu-
merable small concerns void their contracts if death results from
pulmonary tuberculosis.   The certifying physician, whose practice is among the industrial classes, finds that certificates of
death from tuberculosis are to be avoided if possible, while if
he divides his consumption mortality between bronchitis and
pneumonia definite satisfaction results to all concerned.

When the reported pneumonia mortality of the country is carefully studied, as Klebs has recently studied it, one finds that between the ages of 15 and 60 pneumonia has not increased but
diminished in late years.   The apparent increase is confined to
the periods of life under 15 and over 60, and if these periods
were in their turn carefully studied it might appear that the

pneumonia mortality has not increased at all or that the increase has a significance hitherto unsuspected. Those cities which have published alarming statements concerning the mortality from pneumonia have made no attempt to discover the more intimate relations of their figures.

It has often been remarked that notwithstanding the uncertainty attending the life of an individual, few things are less subject to fluctuation than the life history of men in large numbers. The time has come when vital statistics must be studied in detail, and by methods of amplification. The sanitary history of the twentieth century will no doubt make a mark or two before the decimal point, but in the present decade we shall record our net winnings on the hind side of that significant dot. Particular death rates will engage most of our attention from now on. We have expressed here our own opinion that the registration offices in this country are not now prepared to do such work in vital statistics as the time demands, and that the performances of city offices are especially poor. This may seem a harsh judgment, and we fear it is not becomingly pronounced, but we are convinced, by our own engagements with certain important inquiries, that the vital data of about 20 millions of people living in American cities, where accounts are kept exactly in step with current mortality, offer to the student material of less value than the little State of Rhode Island supplies for half a million people from mortality accounts always a month late.

JOHN S. FULTON.

THE VALUE OF RESTRICTIVE MEASURES IN THE CONTAGIOUS DISEASES.

In these days when the efficacy of so many of the accepted methods of fighting these disease is being questioned, it is important and gratifying to be able to point to facts which plainly show that what has been done thus far has really been productive of most excellent results. Nearly every municipal health officer whose records go back for 25 years is able to show a decided decrease in scarlet fever and diphtheria, and this he rightly feels is evidence of the value of restrictive measures. There is a chance of error in such figures, in that the character of the disease may have altered during the period in question or new therapeutic or diagnostic methods may have been introduced. Therefore if contemporaneous data from communities where restrictive measures are, and are not enforced, can be compared, additional and stronger evidence of the efficacy of such measures, if they really are effective, is likely to be forthcoming. Data of this character, and data which ought to have a wider circulation are to be found in the annual reports of the State Board of Health of Michigan. The writer not long since had the opportunity, through the courtesy of Dr. Baker, of examining the original reports of the health officers from which these tables are compiled, and was impressed with the reliability of the deductions drawn from them. In the report for 1901 the reports of outbreaks of contagious disease in Michigan for the 14 years 1887-1900 are classified according to the completeness with which restrictive measures were carried out. In this tabulation the reports from the larger cities as Detroit, Grand Rapids and Lansing, are omitted because in these cities the diseases in question are permanently epidemic. Only those places are considered which have remained free from the disease for at least 60 days, and this unfortunately is never true of a city of any considerable size. The outbreaks reported are arranged in groups, one in which isolation and disinfection were both enforced, one in which they were both neglected and one in which the reports did not state with sufficient exactness what restrictive measures were carried out. The following is a summary of some of the tables in the report:

	Number of Cases for Outbreak.			Number of Cases for Outbreak.	
	Restriction Measures not Enforced.	Restriction Measures Enforced.		Restriction Measures not Enforced.	Restriction Measures Enforced.
Typhoid Fever, 10 years .	5.82	3.13	1900	6.72	2.22
Diphtheria, 14 years. . .	11.12	2.11	1900	4.85	1.71
Scarlet Fever, 14 years .	11.95	2.32	1900	10.43	2.53
Measles, 11 years	48.30	3.03	1900	27.60	4.67
Smallpox			1900	32.00	3.80

Several things are to be noted in connection with these figures. In the first place isolation and disinfection accomplish very much in preventing the extension of all of these diseases. The number of facts is so great, the outbreaks of each disease running into the hundreds, and the difference between good and bad sanitation is so manifest in each one of the years for each one of the diseases, that the success achieved must be a very real one. It appears certain that isolation and disinfection as practiced in the smaller communities of Michigan reduce the cases of contagious disease, in round numbers, from 45 to 95 per cent. There are, however, some things in these figures which are rather surprising. Thus one would hardly expect that isolation and disinfection would accomplish so much in typhoid fever, though to be sure less is accomplished than in the other diseases. In a large city with a complete sewer system it probably would make very little difference how strictly a typhoid case was isolated, but in a village community, with excreta disposal on the soil, it would make a difference whether the patient remained at home or was an ambulatory case going freely about the village. Moreover Dr. Baker's tables show that while isolation has some effect, disinfection, which means disinfection of the discharges chiefly, is of more consequence, for in 1900 in the 21 outbreaks where there was disinfection but no isolation, there were 1.24 cases per outbreak, but in the 99 outbreaks where there was isolation but no disinfection, the number of cases was 3.14 per outbreak. In scarlet fever, diphtheria, measles and smallpox isolation appears from the reports, as one would expect, to have very much more restrictive effect than disinfection. One of the things which appeared most remarkable to the writer in these reports is the apparently great restriction of measles. It has certainly been the experience in all our larger cities that restrictive measures, no matter how energetic, have had very little effect in reducing the mortality from this disease. But in the smaller communities in Michigan it appears that where isolation and disinfection are well carried out there is nearly 94 per cent. less cases per outbreak than where precautions are neglected.

But if one examines the original returns of the health officers it appears plain why such good results are obtained. If the first case of the disease coming to a community is early recognized and isolated the chances are good that the outbreak will be at once checked. The chances that such a case will be so recognized in a village are very much greater than in a city. If, however, the outbreak is not checked at its very outset the chances are, even in the country, that its extension will be very considerable. As a matter of fact a great many of the first cases coming to small communities are promptly recognized and isolated, and as a result an outbreak prevented. It is because outbreaks are in rural communities so often nipped in the bud that the application of restrictive measures in such communities makes such a good showing. What is true of measles is true also of the other diseases, particularly of scarlet fever and diphtheria. It is success in applying restrictive measures to the first case that is the principal cause of the apparent efficiency of these methods. If every appearance of contagious disease in these rural communities had gained some headway before restrictive measures were applied, the showing in their favor would not be nearly so favorable. In fact in the large cities in Michigan where these diseases are always epidemic, restrictive measures even of a very severe type have not enabled the health officers to "stamp them out." Thus in Detroit it has been the custom for many years to absolutely "quarantine" every house where there is scarlet fever or diphtheria. No one is allowed to go out, and the inspectors visit the house twice a day and furnish provisions for the poor at an expense of thousands of dollars annually. Yet these diseases have been no more "stamped out" in Detroit than they have been in Chicago or other cities where milder methods have prevailed. The chief reason for this seems to be that when a disease of this kind has existed for a time in a community, there are sure to be a large number of mild unrecognized cases, and it is these which keep the disease going, and will continue to do so no matter how strictly the known cases are isolated.

The conclusion seems to be that in large communities the strictest methods of isolation and disinfection will never eliminate those diseases, because such measures can only be directed against the recognized cases, and the unrecognized cases are very numerous, perhaps more numerous than the former. A certain amount of restriction is of great use in such cities, and it has resulted in reducing the death rate from these diseases very decidedly, but it seems to the writer that we have gone far enough, and too far in some directions. There is certainly at the present time a decided reaction against such measures as hospital treatment for all cases, or the keeping of wage earners from their work. Unnecessary severity causes the concealment of cases and ineffectual severity alienates the sympathy of the medical profession and of the laity.

On the other hand when contagious disease first appears in a village, small town or public institutions, strict isolation of the patients, "contacts" and "suspects" should be tried, and it will often be found that the attempt is successful and that the outbreak will be checked. Identical methods of managing these diseases are not applicable to all times and places.

CHARLES V. CHAPIN.

DR. SAMUEL WARREN ABBOTT was found dead Oct. 22, 1904. Few public hygienists in America have been more widely known or more generally held in high regard, personally or professionally. As vice-president of the Massachusetts Association of Boards of Health and a warm supporter of, and editorial writer for, its journal, his death is a great and direct loss to the public health circles in this State. Outside of Massachusetts as well as within it, material from his pen took the highest rank in statistical and hygienic literature, while the annual reports of the Massachusetts State Board of Health, to which he was necessarily a large contributor, have become standards of excellence throughout the world. He was born in Woburn, Mass., in 1837, graduated from Harvard Medical School in 1862, entered the navy during the war, then transferred to the army in order to see more active service, practiced for a time in Woburn, became coroner and later medical examiner in Middlesex county, and finally began in 1882 that connection with the public health service of the State. which terminated only with his death.

The appended note is only one of the many forms in which the public estimation of his career is recorded:

OFFICE OF THE BOARD OF HEALTH,

CITY HALL,

Fitchburg, Mass., Oct. 24, 1904.

S. H. DURGIN, M. D., Boston, Mass.

Dear Doctor: On behalf of the Board of Health of the city of Fitchburg I wish to extend to the Massachusetts Association of Boards of Health and to the family of the late Dr. Abbott our sympathetic regards as an expression of the high esteem in which he was held by members of this board during his long service as a public official. Very sincerely yours,

(Signed)   *E. L. FISKE, M. D., Chairman.*

OCTOBER QUARTERLY MEETING

OF THE

Massachusetts Association of Boards of Health.

The October quarterly meeting of the Massachusetts Association of Boards of Health was held at Mount Tom, Northampton, on Tuesday, Oct. 13, 1904.

In the absence of the president and vice-presidents, Dr. H. Lincoln Chase of Brookline was elected chairman. A cordial address of welcome was made by Mayor Chapin of Holyoke, after which the Hon. Christopher Clarke of Northampton spoke on the securing of Mt. Tom as a public reservation and the advantages to the people of such places in promoting health and recreation. The programme of papers was then proceeded with after the election of the following gentlemen: John I. French, M. D., Winchester; Albert R. Brown, Southbridge; Francis Hervey Slack, M. D., Boston; William L. Young, Springfield; Converse Ward, Athol; F. W. Farrell, Springfield; Charles King, Chicopee; E. W. Brown, Northampton; J. W. Hastings, Agawam.

THE NEW LABORATORY OF THE MASSACHUSETTS STATE BOARD OF HEALTH FOR THE PREPARATION OF DIPHTHERIA ANTITOXIN AND VACCINE.

BY THEOBALD SMITH, M. D.

Pathologist and Bacteriologist to the Massachusetts State Board of Health.

Mr. Chairman and Members of the Massachusetts Association of Boards of Health:

In 1895 a laboratory was opened in the Bussey Institution of Harvard University for the preparation of diphtheria antitoxin, although the work itself had been started in November of the year preceding at the State House by Dr. J. L. Goodale. Associated with it under the same roof was the laboratory of comparative pathology of the Harvard Medical School opened in 1896. The demand for antitoxin slowly increased and reached its acme in 1900 during a prolonged, severe epidemic prevalence of the disease. During the seven years beginning with 1897 and ending with 1903 about 400 gallons of serum were distributed. The existence of a free depot for antitoxin naturally enough increased the dosage over that in use elsewhere. For several years tetanus antitoxin was also prepared, but owing to the contracted quarters of the laboratory it was thought best to discontinue its preparation.

The necessity for a suitable laboratory soon made itself felt as the output increased. But there was no urgent reason for any additional outlay until in June of 1903 the State legislature, after a somewhat protracted discussion extending over two years, finally authorized the State Board of Health to prepare not only antitoxin but vaccine as well.

The need of a special building was thus created by this act of the General Court. But where could such a building be found? The environment should be rural. Such a laboratory should be surrounded by vegetation, rather than by human habitations. Fortunately for the State the President and Fellows of Harvard University, always ready to promote the public health by means within their power, agreed to erect a building on the grounds of the Bussey Institution, in a region ideally adapted for the purpose. The building was planned, erected and equipped and operations begun during the school year of 1903-1904. The severe winter greatly impeded the building operations, and postponed the opening of the laboratory three or four months beyond the expected time. The preparation of antitoxin was not interrupted by the transfer of the work from one building to another, and the preparation of vaccine was begun in July, at a time not well adapted on account of the disturbing effects of the summer temperature.

A satisfactory description of the building can hardly be given without the aid of plans and other illustrations, and hence this is omitted. All that it is necessary to state here is that the walls, ceilings and floors of the various rooms have been so constructed as to permit ready cleansing and disinfection. This is especially true of those rooms in which animals are kept and operated on.

The protection of the community against smallpox through vaccination involves two important processes, the preparation of an adequate supply of efficient lymph and the vaccination of the individual. Both are of equal importance. The greatest care on the part of the physician in vaccinating cannot make a poor lymph good, and the greatest circumspection and conscientiousness exercised in the vaccine laboratory cannot retrieve the failures of careless and indifferent vaccination or subsequent neglect of the vaccinal eruption. Granted the proper execution of both these processes—the preparation of an animal product and its final use upon the human subject—there may still be mysterious influences of season, food, age, etc., which act upon the animals yielding such products so as to modify these products in an unexpected manner. There is need, therefore, of constant vigilance on the part of the laboratory worker and the practicing physician. The State and municipal laboratories should stand in close touch with the physicians supplied by them, so that the mutual helpful criticisms, comments and suggestions may tend steadily to improve the quality of the services rendered and stimulate to improvements—not necessarily in containers, syringes, "points," etc.—but in the quality of the product itself and in its more effective and economical application.

The conditions under which vaccine is prepared at present and its inherent perishable qualities make it highly desirable that vaccinations be carried out at certain regular intervals, and that the population be thoroughly protected by vaccination. To wait for an impending epidemic before the people are vaccinated is not only dangerous, but it is prone to upset the operations of the laboratory by making demands which cannot be filled at once, since vaccine must first be satisfactorily produced and then stored for at least four to six weeks in order that the miscellaneous bacteria may become destroyed. The desultory, irregular and unexpected demands for vaccine are likely to lead to a large waste of a product, the preparation of which must go on whether it be used or not in order to provide for such demands. The energy saved in preventing waste can be applied to the improvement of the product itself. The conditions under which diphtheria antitoxin is prepared and distributed are wholly different, since the latter product may be stored under suitable conditions for months without undergoing any perceptible deterioration.

For the benefit of those unfamiliar with the method of preparing animal vaccine a few words on this phase of the subject may not be out of place. In the days of Jenner and for years after, the lymph was obtained from the arms of children. There was what is called arm-to-arm vaccination. In 1840 or thereabouts Negri in Italy began to use calves as a source of vaccine and with the introduction of glycerine as a preservative some years later the process reached that stage where it practically is today. Animal vaccine has almost wholly supplanted humanized vaccine, and the danger of transmitting diseases from child to child is thus eliminated.

The procedure as carried out today is, in brief, as follows: The cow, steer, or calf—in most institutes the latter—is thoroughly cleansed, tied upon a specially constructed table and the abdomen shaved. Linear incisions, very superficial, are made over the shaved area and the lymph rubbed in.

The incisions after several days begin to show signs of proliferation with the formation of vesicles. After four to six days the animal is again fastened to the table, the eruption, after thorough cleansing, is removed with a curette and ground with diluted glycerine in special machines into the final product. The animal, obviously enough, can be used but once. It is killed after the vaccine has been removed and carefully examined. If any disease should be found, the lymph is rejected. In the lymph after removal there are many bacteria. These gradually disappear under the influence of the glycerine. The bacteria themselves, however, are harmless, as was shown by a German Commission appointed to investigate this subject some years ago. After a time the vaccine may become sterile and still be active.

We have adopted the method, quite generally employed in this country and in Europe, of storing the vaccine in glass capillary tubes sealed in the flame. These are placed in containers suitable for storage and mailing.* The sealed tube is opened at both ends with a pair of forceps, wire pliers or cutters and a small rubber bulb supplied with the vaccine is used to force the lymph out of the tube upon the scarified area. I have brought with me a variety of lancets devised for scarifying. They all take into consideration the necessity of sterilizing the lancet before use upon every patient. Hence the lancets are supplied in each out-fit in from three to twenty-five or more. Here is one provided in a sealed glass tube. When the lancet is needed the ends are broken off and the sterile lancet slips out. Here is another which resembles a steel pen. A metal box full of these is provided. The whole can be sterilized in an oven. Each pen lancet is placed in a metal holder and used but once.

The simplest instrument for scarifying is a steel sewing needle. With this the area scarified can be made very small. The patent "points" supplied by dealers are as a rule too coarse to permit a delicate scarification, although they are very convenient for the busy practitioner. It is customary in Europe to make three small scarifications on the arm. Three relatively small vesicles are the result. If the scarification is made crudely it is apt to be too large and as the eruption grows in all directions it may become too large and heal with difficulty, besides giving extraneous infection better access. If two scarifications are made, both large, the vesicles may coalesce and make matters worse.

Besides the method of exposing the lower layers of the epidermis over a small area, linear incisions and punctures are also in use, especially in Europe. These tend to produce only a vesicle of limited width and lead to a less formidable lesion than with the flat scarification.

The vaccine issued from the new laboratory of the State Board of Health is numbered and a date is attached beyond which the vaccine is likely to become uncertain in its action. If the vaccine

---

*Local Boards of Health will confer a favor by returning from time to time unused and empty containers, which can be reissued after appropriate sterilization in the hot air oven.

fails to take in primary vaccination, we shall consider it a favor to be so informed. In that case no further issue of that number will be made. In a similar manner all antitoxin issued is pro-vided with a number which enables us to trace its source, and in case of unsatisfactory reports to remedy any defects.

DR. PALMER: I would like to ask Dr. Smith if he has had any experience in using vaccine hypodermically. I have seen it rec-ommended, but have never tried it.

PROFESSOR SMITH: I think the method of inoculating with a hypodermic syringe has been used in the vaccination of calves, but I do not know that it has upon human beings.

DR. F. G. WHEATLEY: I would like to inquire, Mr. Chair-man, in regard to the present condition of the State Board as to the distribution of vaccine virus. Is the State Board ready to distribute it?

PROFESSOR SMITH: We have a certain amount on hand now which is ready for distribution, and we probably shall continue to have, but whether the amount will be sufficient to satisfy all demands I cannot say, because it will be my object not to issue any until I am quite satisfied that it is efficient. But I think it is safe to say that we shall have enough to send to the boards of health. We hope sooner or later to devise some method by which single doses may be sent out without too much expense. We are also prepared to distribute the virus to those who vac-cinate on a large scale, in vials containing from twenty-five to fifty and even a hundred doses. This method is used very large-ly in the vaccination of large numbers, where the persons to be vaccinated come to a definite place for vaccination. This ob-viates the necessity of opening a small capillary tube for each person to be vaccinated.

BACTERIAL COUNTS OF BOSTON'S MILK SUPPLY.

BY HIBBERT WINSLOW HILL, M. D. Director, and FRANCIS HERVEY SLACK, M. D., 2d Assistant Bacteriologist, Boston Board of Health Bacteriological Laboratory.

On April 29th, 1904, the following regulation in regard to the milk supply was adopted by the Boston Board of Health:—"No.

person by himself or by his servant or agent, or as the servant or agent of any other person, firm or corporation, shall bring into the City of Boston for purposes of sale, exchange or delivery, or sell, exchange, or deliver any milk, skimmed milk, or cream which contains more than 500,000 bacteria per cubic centimeter or which has a temperature higher than 50 deg. F."

To secure the enforcing of this regulation, the Boston Board of Health, in April, 1904, authorized the preparations for making the necessary bacteriological counts, etc., the results of these counts being placed in the hands of Dr. Charles Harrington, Chief of the Bureau of Milk Inspection, for use in the notification, prosecution, etc., of cases of infringement.

The month of May was used in procuring and standardizing the necessary apparatus and in general preparation for the summer's work. The method decided upon after consideration of those employed in about 15 laboratories throughout this country was as follows: For media, one and one-half per cent. nutrient agar (B. C.), 10 cc to a tube, reaction plus 0.7. The collection outfit was devised anew and consists of a case for carrying the samples made of copper with double walls interlaid with one-half inch felting. This case is divided into three compartments; the central one for samples, the other two for ice. When iced and closed, a constant temperature of 34 deg. F. is maintained. The samples are carried in sterilized test tubes, the compartment holding eight racks of four tubes each. A smaller case was also made holding but three racks. These racks are made from copper tubing as suggested by one of us. (H. W. H.) Holes in the partitions of the case allow the ice water to circulate around the bottoms of the tubes. The use of the test tubes for carrying samples was suggested by S. C. Keith. For collecting, glass pipettes are used. These are carried in a detachable copper case, adapted for sterilizing, divided into two compartments, the upper for fresh sterile pipettes, the lower for the pipettes after use.

For plating the samples, the agar, after being melted, is kept in a water bath between 40 deg. and 45 deg. C. until needed. In order to bring down the actual number of colonies in a plate to a countable figure, a standard dilution of 1 to 10,000 is used. For dilution water, square eight-ounce bottles, marked at 100 cc., are used. This water is sterilized in the autoclave under 15 pounds steam pressure for 20 minutes at a temperature of about 250 deg. F. Two bottles are used for each sample, giving a dilution of 1 to 10,000, with 1 cc of milk. Each dilution is shaken 25 times for thorough mixing, as is also the sample. A sterile pipette marked to contain 1 cc and calibrated in the laboratory is used at each stage, three being required for each sample. After expelling the milk into the first bottle, the pipette is rinsed to the 1 cc mark in the dilution water; 1 cc from the first dilution bottle is transferred to the second dilution bottle; then 1 cc from the second dilution bottle is transferred to the petri dish. The agar is then carefully added, mixed with the diluted milk in the plate and allowed to harden.

The plates are incubated in a saturated atmosphere at 37 deg. C. for 24 hours. The colonies in a saturated atmosphere are not only more numerous, as shown by Whipple, than in a dry atmosphere, but also larger and therefore more easily ·counted; 37 deg. C. is used in preference to room temperature because the latter requires more time for satisfactory development of the colonies, and is also so variable as to give no standard for the comparison of results. The 24-hour incubation is used in preference to the 48-hour because, though the latter shows a slightly higher average count, the counts are not sufficiently higher to materially change the report. One thousand consecutive plates incubated at 37 deg. C and counted at 24 and 48 hours gave the following results:

679 or 68 per cent. showed an increase in the number of colonies at the 48-hour count.

In 195, or 19.5 per cent., the count remained the same; 126 or 12.6 per cent. showed a decrease.

799 or 80 per cent. of these plates had counts below 100.

The average 24-hour count on these plates was 15 1-2; the average 48-hour count 18 1-4.

193, or 19 per cent., had between 100 and 1000 colonies averaging at the 24-hour count 275, and at the 48-hour count 283.

Eight plates, about 1 per cent., had over 1000 colonies each, averaging 1287 at the 24-hour and 1334 at the 48-hour count.

Only 13 plates changed their relation to the legal limit, nine going from below to above 500,000 and four decreasing.

In many plates, the count is lower with the 48-hour incubation on account of small colonies becoming obscured in the growth of larger ones. There are also more spreaders.

This annoying difficulty with spreaders, frequently met with even in the 24-hour plates, we now overcome by the use of earthenware petri covers suggested by one of us. (H. W. H.)*

Spreading seems to be caused principally by water condensing on the petri covers and agar. The dry porous earthenware covers absorb this condensation water, still leaving the atmosphere saturated, as proven by the large size of the colonies. Organisms having an inherent tendency to spread from unusual motility are not prevented from spreading by this method.

IN COUNTING.—A box, a child's slate, a reading glass and a "lumber counter" are used.

The box is 6x6x5 inches, with open bottom, glass front, and a four-inch circular opening in the top, painted black within and without, except the glass front.

The slate has a circle cut in the surface, 4 1-2 inches in diameter, divided into 10 equal segments, the lines filled with red lead.

The reading glass is a common four-inch lens magnifying about two diameters.

The petri dish is placed over the circle on the slate and uncovered. The box fits over the circle, the reading glass over the box, thus protecting the plate, keeping a constant focus and setting both hands of the operator free.

A slight pressure of the thumb for each colony seen on the lumber counter accurately adds and records the count. As the dilution is 1 to 10,000, the actual count must be multiplied by 10,000 to obtain the number of bacteria in 1 cc of the milk.

*Journal Medical Research. Nov.. 1904.

Having thus briefly outlined our laboratory methods for the collection and examination of milk samples, it is of interest to consider the milk itself, those who deal with it, and the various processes it goes through before reaching the consumer:

Boston's milk supply comes from dairy farms situated all over New England. It is impossible for each of these farms to be directly under our supervision, yet to secure a clean milk supply, these producers must be induced to produce clean milk.

Clean dairymen, clean cattle, clean barns, clean utensils, clean handling and proper cooling are necessary.

Reform in these directions can be most readily accomplished through the dealer, who, being fined for dirty milk, will be forced either to educate his dairymen, regularly inspect the milk and handle it in a proper manner himself, or leave the business.

Dealers may be divided into five classes:

First—The large contractor who deals in milk by the train load, controlling the buying in districts situated along his line of road, and selling to stores, restaurants and milk pedlers as well as direct to consumers.

Second—The small contractor who collects one or two car loads from some particular town or section, selling to stores, restaurants, milk pedlers and direct to consumers.

Third—The independent dairyman, owning a dairy farm in or near the city, and selling direct to the consumers.

Fourth—The milk pedler who purchases a certain number of cans each day from the contractor, selling to stores, restaurants and direct to consumers.

Fifth—The store or restaurant buying from the contractor or milk pedler and selling direct to consumers.

Beginning the first of June, samples have been taken continually. Most of these samples have been secured from the milk as it arrives in the city. Such samples as have been taken from stores show that the average storekeeper has yet to learn how to properly care for milk. This part of the work will soon receive more attention.

This table shows temperature of samples taken in June, July, August and September.

MONTH	Number of Samples Taken	Between 30° and 40°	Between 40° and 50°	Between 50° and 60°	Between 60° and 70°
June	539	2.25%	68%	27.75%	2%
July	620	1.50%	49%	38.50%	11%
August . . .	626	4%	39%	47.25%	9.75%
September . .	609	8%	43%	43.50%	5.50%
Totals . .	2394	4%	49.25%	39.50%	7.25%

Below 50° F. the law-limit, 53.25%.   Above 50° F. 46.75%.

This table shows number of samples taken, with results, for June, July, August and September.

MONTH	No. of Samples Taken	Below 100,000	Between 100,000 and 500,000	Between 500,000 & 1,000,000	Between 1,000,000 and 5,000,000	Above 5,000,000	Uncountable Spreaders	Below Law-Limit	Above Law-Limit
June . . .	539	49%	23%	7.5%	13%	5.5%	2%	72%	26%
July . . .	620	29%	33%	12%	15%	10.5%	.5%	62%	37.5%
August . .	626	46%	31%	9%	11%	2.5%	.5%	77%	22.5%
September .	609	45.5%	30.5%	10.5%	12%	1.5%	. .	76%	24%
Totals .	2394	42%	29.75%	9.75%	12.75%	5%	.75%	71.75%	27.50%

The greater part of the milk is brought to the city in 8 1-2 quart cans, but in some cases cans holding over 20 quarts are used for special purposes. When the milk reaches the contractor, it is supposed to be from 6 to 18 hours old. A few contractors deliver this milk at once to the consumer the majority, however, after mixing, store it in ice until the following morning. Milk should be cooled at once after milking. Rushed warm from the dairies and allowed to stand for hours at some country depot, then thoroughly cooled on the cars, it often reaches the city with a temperature of 40 deg. F. and a bacterial count of several millions. Occasionally a contractor with an extra supply of milk on hand will keep some over to the third day before being delivered, and on the evening of the fourth day it is sold in the tenement districts.

The contractor takes more care of the milk which is to be bottled for family trade than of the rest of the milk, and it is safe to say that if the same solicitude was shown for all the milk as for that used for the family trade, there would be very little milk coming to the city that would not be within the present standard. There are a number of places in the City of Boston where carloads of milk arrive in which it would be difficult to find a sample containing over 500,000 bacteria per cc. Since this care can be and is taken for a certain portion of the milk, why should it not also be extended to the rest?

MIXING THE MILK is a custom generally followed as it furnishes a fairly standard supply from day to day; the law has, in fact, forced this by requiring a certain standard of fats and solids. Some dairies mix the milk before putting it into cans in order that every can may show an average product. Some milk is mixed or even pasteurized in the towns where it is collected before being sent to the city. The milk pedler who purchases of the contractor, taking his supply directly from the cars, usually has a mixing room and ice chest connected with his stable. The contractor himself mixes the milk in large quantities, keeping a separate mixer for the family trade. The milk is usually strained as it is poured into the mixer; variations are seen in this from no strainer at all to several thicknesses of cheesecloth or cotton. In summer, millions of flies hover around some of these mixing rooms. Indeed, when the cans are opened dead flies from the farms are sometimes found in them.

TASTING is a necessary pirt of the program for the detection of the poor milk, poor that is from the standpoint of taste, which must be set aside. The methods are many—one man asserts that by lifting the can and taking a sip, the sense of smell is also educated to detect poor milk. Some sip the milk from a ladle. A spoon is frequently used, the only cleansing it receives being on the visit to the mouth between cans. Licking the under part of the stopper is a practice generally followed, the stopper being then thrown into a box, the mixed milk drawn off into the emptied cans, and the dirty stoppers again inserted. It is said that one milkman arranges his cans in a row, removes the stoppers, inserts a finger with great dexterity into each can and thence to his mouth in rotation. In one place, the largest cans are tasted by dipping in the hand instead of a ladle. It is easy to see how a taster with diphtheria in his throat, or typhoid on his hands, might infect a whole community. So long as these methods are allowed, only healthy men should be permitted to taste milk, but the methods should be changed. In want of a better device, a supply of common wooden tongue depressors would do, carried in a double box; the clean on one side, the used on the other. These could be bought at a trifling cost and easily cleansed. One man has suggested the use of paraffine straws. Most of the tasters spit also. To see tasters spitting the milk from the mouth in the midst of the open cans, even though care is taken not to spit into the same, is not an agreeable spectacle for the prospective consumer.

PASTEURIZATION is carried on by but few Boston contractors, and even by them not for their whole supply. The milk is in the pasteurizing machine about four minutes, and passes through three processes. First, it is heated to about 165 deg. F., then cooled by ice water, and finally cooled by brine. Milk keeps much longer after this process because most of the bacteria are thus destroyed. However, a milk kept sweet by cleanliness and cold is much to be preferred to a pasteurized supply filled with lifeless organisms and their by-products. One contractor wishing to show what interest he took in furnishing a bacteria free supply of milk to his patrons showed a report from a bacteriologist stating that the milk before going through the pasteurizing process at his plant in a distant town contained 7,000,000 bacteria per cc; after the process but 4000. Consider for a moment the condition this milk was allowed to reach before pasteurization was used to prevent further development.

THE MILK CAN may be held responsible for many high counts. Some milk cans, each time the milk is emptied from them, are thoroughly cleansed and sterilized before being sent back to the producer, but as a rule this is not true. Such a can usually has the following history—purchased new it is kept for a while on the car for family trade and is carefully attended to, but as age advances it gives way to brighter and better looking cans, and takes its place among the store cans. The farmer cleans it with hot water as best he can. He does not mind the dents in the side, for the dented can holds less milk. When the can is filled with warm milk, the bacteria, lodged in inequalities, broken seams, etc., multiply rapidly, the spring water in which the can is usually set not cooling the milk sufficiently to prevent bacterial growth. After the early morning ride to the stations and a wait on the station platform, the milk is cooled in the car on its journey to the contractor, where it arrives say about 10 A. M. If still sweet, to the taster's tongue, the milk is poured into the mixer, and the empty uncleaned can filled with the mixed milk and stored in ice until early the following morning, when it is delivered to the storekeeper. He disposes of the milk during the day, returns the empty dirty can the following morning to the contractor, who, without cleaning, ships it to the farmer and the round begins again. To furnish clean milk, some contractors have two lines of cans—one for the farmer sent back the morning it is received and reaching him with what milk is left in it perfectly clean and sweet; the other set receiving the mixed milk and being sent to the customers. These cans are carefully cleansed and sterilized each time they return. The contractor finds but little sour milk when the cans are thus cared for, and the inspector finds but few bacteria.

THE MILK CAN STOPPER deserves a few words in passing; being generally of wood, it absorbs the milk sooner or later into its pores, becomes filled with bacteria, and if not properly cleansed with boiling water each time it is used, readily infects the fresh milk. Split one of these old stoppers and you will see how the milk has penetrated the pores of the wood. The wooden stopper fits the can tightly, and if properly cleansed has no superior while sound, but the places where it is properly cleansed are few. Metal stoppers of the same material as the cans are now used to some extent. This is a step in the right direction.

Some of the contractors seem anxious to do what they can to furnish a pure milk supply. Dairymen are learning the two C's—Cleanliness and cold. The outlook is favorable. We expect the time will soon come when it will be difficult to find amongst Boston milk dealers milk containing more than 500,000 bacteria per cc.

THE CHAIRMAN: Gentlemen, the paper is before us for discussion. The Chair will be glad to hear from some representative of the milk firms on this subject. We would like to know something from their point of view.

MR. CHARLES WHITING: I am very glad to say that the milk contractors are very glad to have the interest of the Board of Health and to have its assistance in bringing about cleanliness for the Boston milk supply. In the past years something has been done to bring about an improved supply, and with the aid of the Board of Health this work can go on much faster than it has done. I know of several cases where the notice of the Board of Health to the farmer has already been productive of good. The farmer respects the authority of the city of Boston and is hastening improvement. The contractors of Boston, I can say, will work gladly in co-operation with the Board of Health.

I should like to inquire if any tubercle bacilli have been found in any of the samples or any other pathogenic germs.

DR. SLACK: We have been so busily engaged in doing the routine work that we have had no time to differentiate as yet the different species of bacteria which we have found.

MR. RICKARDS: I would like to say that the results obtained by Dr. Slack have been turned over to Dr. Charles Harrington, the chief of the Bureau of Milk Inspection, who manages the notification of those whose milk is worse than the standard, and as Dr. Harrington is unable to be here today he has asked me to present for him his contribution to this discussion, as follows:

DR. HARRINGTON: I have been asked very frequently what is to be the policy of the Bureau of Milk Inspection in the matter of enforcement of the regulation establishing a bacterial standard, and I have heard some criticism and even insinuation that no actual legal enforcement is intended, because thus far no persons have been prosecuted. It was not deemed good public policy to proceed criminally against morally innocent persons without any warning whatsoever and without attempting to bring about improvement by gentler methods. Since the work began in June last, about 400 warning notices have been sent to contractors and retail dealers, but for the most part to the former. The notices to the contractors set forth the dairy mark of the can examined, and the person receiving them can send, therefore, directly to the producers with such comments, directions or warnings as he may choose to make. The good results of these notices have been demonstrated repeatedly, for in many instances later examinations of specimens from warned dairies have shown a very great diminution in the bacterial count. The sending of warnings to shopkeepers has not been accorded the same measure of approval by one of the contractors, whose own premises are anything but cleanly, that he gave to the plan of warning the producer. The reason is plain: The producer has nobody back of him to complain to, but the shopkeeper can and does have something to say to the one who sells him dirty milk, which may be the basis of a criminal action. This particular contractor deems it unfair to take any action, even so much as a warning, in the case of a retailer, until, as he puts it, "all the milk comes down from the country in proper shape." In other words, let us throw all the blame on the farmer, who cannot strike back, and not interfere with the contractor's customers until the millenium. Some contractors are economical of ice; at least one, to my knowledge, has no conception of the word cleanliness. If only the producer is to be held to answer for his lack of care, the others who are careless will probably not exert themselves.

In the case of several shopkeepers second warnings have been sent with the addition of these words: "Second and final warning. Further violation means prosecution."

After due warning, not of every man, but of a reasonable proportion of those engaged in the business (for a double warning to each dealer would be the same as licensing each to break the law twice with impunity), the issuing of notices as a routine process will be discontinued, and every dealer will be held responsible for the condition of the milk he sells, be he contractor, pedler or shopkeeper. It is the business of every dealer to see that the milk supplied to him is free from adulteration; he is responsible in the eye of the law; it is equally his duty to see that the person back of him in the chain supplies him with a product that is decently clean.

To conclude, the policy of the Bureau of Milk Inspection will be to enforce sanitary regulations equally with statute standards.

PROFESSOR SMITH: Mr. Chairman, the papers presented to-day have been very interesting and of great importance. It seems to me that there is no one subject that needs such constant attention and discussion as the milk supply. If we bear in mind that the milk is very rich in protein substances, which are favorable media for many of the pathogenic as well as the ordinary bacteria that may be present, we can realize the danger that confronts children and infants in taking this milk into their system. While in our country the importance has been realized by sanitarians for a long time, it must be remembered that in a democratic country like ours proper safeguards cannot be established until we have educated the public who elect representatives to frame, pass and enforce the necessary laws. In Europe a proper appreciation of the importance of a pure milk supply has also been gaining ground, but there, of course, matters can be dealt with, perhaps, in a more summary manner than with us. I was talking yesterday with a prominent scientist and sanitarian who was sent here by the German Government to investigate the milk supply of this country, to see what we were doing from a sanitary point of view, and to report to his government, so that they also might take a more active part in the regeneraion of the milk supply of large cities. He told me that some years ago he presented statistics which showed that in one year more infants were lost in Germany than men during the wars of 1866 and 1870. This fact greatly startled the people who listened to this address of his, and their attention now is focussed more or less upon the milk supply. There the large cities are beginning to feel the difficulties that we have felt for some time past, namely the long distances over which milk has to be carried to reach the large centres of population.

THE CHAIRMAN: I am sorry that the short time left makes it necessary to close this discussion. I will call on Dr. Brough for his paper.

TWO RECENT OUTBREAKS OF TYPHOID FEVER IN BOSTON.

DAVID D. BROUGH, M. D.
Asst. Medical Inspector Boston Board of Health.

Typhoid fever is an infectious and largely a preventable disease. If we could find the origin in every case the disease would soon be eliminated. In recognition of this fact the Board of Health of Boston endeavors to find the cause if possible in each case. A series of questions is asked each individual, and the answers are noted on the card which contains the sanitary condition of the house, and these are filed for reference.

These questions relate to the occupation and place of business, the milk supply, what water other than city has been drunk, the exact duration of the illness and the time of taking to bed, the boarding place, whether the patient has been out of the city before being ill. If there is any store for the sale of food or drink in the building where the illness occurs, this is also noted.

From this method of examination we find that a certain large percentage of cases are infected outside the city. The shore, the mountains, the country, other cities and states and even foreign countries are found to be the real sources of infection. A certain number are secondary to some previous case. Others occur in which the most searching inquiry fails to show any known cause. The nationality and location of the residence of the patients have to be given careful consideration.

The information obtained in this way often gives the clue that leads to the discovery of the cause of occasional groups of cases. I desire to show the main features of two recent local outbreaks of typhoid. The investigation of the first was conducted by Dr. T. B. Shea and Dr. A. Burr, who supplied these, facts.

Early in August our sanitary inspector reported that two cases of typhoid had been drinking water from a spring in Mattapan. On this information the district was immediately visited. The supposed spring was found to be water drawn from a trench where a sewer was under construction. This sewer was being built by two contractors. Their places of work were situated at the end of the trench some eighth of a mile apart. Both contractors were using pumps for drawing the inflowing water from the trench—one had a steam and the other a hand pump. The water as it flowed was cool, clear and apparently pure. A large number of people had drunk from both places. A printed notice was at once prominently displayed forbidding the use of the water for drinking purposes. The contractors were also seen and told to see that the order was carried into effect. A sample of the water was taken and analyzed. The chemical examination showed the water to be badly polluted.

Special inquiry was now made to find what cases of typhoid fever had ever drunk this water. The old cases of typhoid were seen at their homes and all the hospital cases were examined. From these and the subsequent cases that developed, twenty-nine persons in all were found to have been infected. Cases were found in East Boston, Roxbury, Roslindale, Milton and the North End.

The course of the investigation developed the interesting fact that only those who had taken water from one particular part of the trench became ill. This was where the water was drawn up by the hand pump. No cases were found among those who drank only the water from the steam pump, nor did any cases of illness occur among those working at this end of the trench. It seemed evident that the infection had occurred at the other section where the hand pump was used.

It was found that about twenty men were employed at this part. They were in the habit of urinating in the trench, and thus directly contaminated the water. A privy used by these workmen was situated on the top of the trench where the work had recently been completed and had been filled with loose stones and gravel. This was not more than twenty feet from where the water was pumped up. The soil was loose and the deposits from this closet ran directly into the trench. This closet was used by the workmen only.

The first case reported and found to be from the infected water was Aug. 2, and the last Sept. 6. The symptoms began in the earliest case on July 22 in the last on August 20. The infection must have occurred before July 22. Three workmen were found ill, two of whom became ill on July 29 and 30. These two had apparently been infected from drinking the water. The third, it was found, had been ill for eight days prior to July 22, when he stopped work. During this time he had urinated in the trench, and as he was suffering from diarrhoea, had used the closet. After leaving work he was ill for a month. The history of the case showed that this man undoubtedly had typhoid, and it is fair to presume that he was the original cause of this outbreak, and had infected the water in the early stages of the disease.

In all, including the original case, there were twenty-nine cases, some of these of a severe type. It is interesting to note that all were males, the location of the pump being such that a woman would not drink there.

At nearly the same time another outbreak occurred, which I was enabled to investigate.

About the middle of August a number of cases of illness appeared among the Hebrew residents of the city. These persons were scattered over various districts. There was no common acquaintanceship amongst them. There was, however, one common story with all. They had attended a golden wedding reception given a venerable Hebrew gentleman on August 7th. Besides the cases that were reported to our Board, we found several cases of illness which were under physicians' care that had never been reported. It was with extreme difficulty that we found some of the cases, as no list of the guests had been kept. It is supposed that from one hundred to one hundred and fifty were present.

The history of the illness was similar in all cases. They were taken ill rather suddenly; there was fever, headache, prostation and pain in the bowels. Some had diarrhoea. In a number of cases the onset was so sudden that the patients went to bed immediately and remained there. In others there were prodromal symptoms lasting a few days before going to bed. Besides the cases in Boston, twelve occurred in other cities, these patients having visited Boston only on the night of the wedding and remaining in the city only during that evening. In all thirty-four. cases of illness were directly traced to the reception. It is plain that these people coming from many different places, having nothing in common but this reception, and being attacked by the same form of disease, must have received the infection at the reception.

Seventeen of the cases I examined at their homes, and the seven more were examined at the Boston City and Massachusetts General Hospitals, where I obtained their histories. In the rest of the cases only a history was obtained. In eight of the cases seen at home there was an abundant crop of rose spots, tympanites, high fever and characteristic stools. In those seen at the hospital there was tympanites, enlarged spleen and rose spots. Positive Widal reactions were obtained. Two of the cases developed acute middle ear trouble. Otherwise there were no especial complications. The duration of the disease varied. In some cases it lasted only from two to three weeks. In the

majority of cases it ran from three to five weeks before couva-
lescence. So far as could be found no deaths occurred. These
thirty-four cases were clearly all typhoid fever of a mild type.
The infection having been at the dinner, it must have been
through some food or drink. So far as we could find the colla-
tion of the evening consisted of chicken and chicken soup, bread,
cake, chopped liver, fruit, potatoes, tonics and water. There
was no tea, coffee, milk or ice cream. Milk and meat are not
used together by orthodox Hebrews. All the persons who had
the handling of the food were examined and no one was found
to have been ill. The water was from the ordinary city supply
and was above suspicion. The chickens were bought alive and
freshly killed for the party; the soup was made from the chickens.
The liver was from a steer killed the day before at the abattoir.
The cake was made by the family of the old gentleman, all of
whom were well. The bakery where the bread came from was
inspected and no one was found ill. No suspicion could be found
attaching to the fruit or vegetables.

The tonics, consisting of soda water with various fruit flavors,
were prepared especially for the evening. We visited the establishment where the tonic was manufactured, and while the
sanitary conditions were found to be bad, affording abundant
opportunity for infection, if there had been a case among the
workmen, yet no case was found. While the Board of Health
ordered various improvements to be made in the sanitary condition of the place, yet there was no direct evidence to show that
the tonic was the source of infection.

All the cases occurred in children or young adults, and with
one exception all were under twenty-five years. The youngest
was four years old, most of them being between ten and twenty
years. The older people, of whom there were a number, were
not attacked. As a rule the disease was milder in the children
than in the adults.

The important point of this outbreak was that we were able
to get the exact period of incubation. By incubation is meant the
time from the entrance of the infection into the system to the

appearance of the first symptoms. We found two were taken ill within four days; seven were taken ill on the fifth day; five were taken ill on the sixth day; nine were taken ill on the seventh; three were taken ill on the eighth day; one was taken ill on the ninth day; two were taken ill on the eleventh day; five were taken ill on the twelfth to the twentieth day. Twenty-six cases or more than two-thirds of the whole number were taken ill between the third and eighth day after the reception. Practically all were taken ill within eleven days. It would seem that under certain conditions typhoid fever can develop more rapidly than is commonly supposed. In some of the recorded instances I found that where the time of infection was definitely known the period of incubation was very brief.

These two outbreaks represent some features of typhoid investigation. In the first we were able to discover the place and the exact cause of the infection. The second illustrates the extreme difficulty of positively stating what has been the cause, even when the time and place of infection have been definitely proved.

MILK AND FOODS.

DR. CHARLES HARRINGTON, M. D.
Secretary, Mass. State Board of Health.

MILK AND DIARRHOEAL DISEASES.—In a report on the work of the Liverpool Health Committee's depots for the preparation of "humanized" (sterile) milk, Hope* refers to the high death-rate among infants under one year of age. In 1903, the general death-rate of Liverpool was the lowest ever known, and the infantile death-rate was 159 per thousand, against an average of 178 for the last preceding three years. The plan of supplying sterile milk began early in 1901, and by the end of 1903, 6295 infants of an average age of three and a-half months had been supplied. Among the 4453 supplied during 1903, the mortality was but 78 per thousand, while the best districts of the city had

*Journal of State Medicine, May, 1904. Page 313.

an infantile death-rate of from 88 to 118; the worst districts, 212 to 215, and the whole city 159 per thousand. The committee maintains four depots in the city. The milk is supplied in bottles containing single feedings, the size varying, of course, according to the age of the child. The applicant must agree to continue its use regularly, to send for it at a stated hour, and to refrain from using any stale residues in place of opening fresh bottles as needed. Any disagreement of the milk with the child must be reported. The cost to the applicant is about 35 cents per week in advance.

Newman,* Medical Officer of Health for Finsbury, says that he has made inquiry into the feeding of 190 infants dying of diarrhoea within his district, and finds that 20.5 per cent were breast-fed, 34.7 per cent were fed wholly or partly on condensed or other artificial milks, and 44.7 per cent were fed wholly or partly on cow's milk. That is to say, 79.4 per cent of the infants dying of diarrhoeal disease in Finsbury were fed on milk which is liable to great contamination.

Dr. Arthur Newsholme has recently restated his views on this topic in his annual report as Medical Officer of Health for Brighton for 1903, wherein he gives figures which bear out his previously expressed opinions.

Newsholme says: "The deaths of suckled children were about one-ninth of what ought to have occurred on the supposition of average distribution of diarrhoea; the deaths of those suckled and having also farinaceous foods were about one-third; the deaths of those having only cow's milk were about three times, and the deaths of those having condensed milk were about seventeen times the number that ought to have occurred on the supposition of average distribution of diarrhoea among infants fed in different ways. If we assume that feeding plays no part in the causation of diarrhoea, these differences are difficult to explain; if, as is practically certain, it plays an important part, then suckling is a very potent means of minimizing its incidence, the

---

*British Medical Journal, Aug. 27, 1904.

use of cow's milk, under present conditions, greatly increases its incidence, and the use of condensed milk still further increases its incidence."

MILK AND SEPTIC SORE THROAT.—Chalmers, M. O. H. for Glasgow, reports* an interesting outbreak of septic sore throat due to infected milk. The circumstances were as follows: On April 23, 1904, a new cow was added to a herd of 72, which was divided into a number of groups, each in charge of one milker. The new cow was placed first in one group and later was transferred to another. Before the end of the month, the first group began to suffer with an eruption of the teats, and soon it was found that the second group was similarly affected. By May 6, about 30 per cent of the cows were attacked; and during the course of the outbreak, the hands of four of the eight milkers were likewise involved. During the week ending May 7, eight persons connected with Belvidere Hospital were attacked with septic sore throat; in the course of the next week (May 7-14) nineteen more; and during the next (May 14-21) nine more were attacked. The milk consumed in the hospital came from the dairy above-mentioned, which supplied also a portion of a neighboring village, where similar cases were found. The milk supplied to one section of the hospital was sterilized on and after May 17, and no more of the inmates of that portion were attacked; that which was used in the other part was, through misunderstanding, not scalded until May 23, and but one case occurred thereafter. Dr. Chalmers concluded that the sore throats were a direct result of the teat eruption, the infective nature of which was shown by its spread among the cows and transmission to the milkers' hands.

It will be recalled that, in May, 1902, an outbreak of what was then thought to be milk-borne scarlet fever, occurred in Lincoln, England, the 200 and more patients suffering with sore throat, vomiting and slight fever, and some showing a rash. Most of the victims drank milk from the same dairy, where, however, no

*Public Health, Sept., 1904. Page 771.

case of scarlet fever existed, and it was given out that the outbreak was a second "Hendon epidemic," due to a teat disease, which was supposedly capable of causing scarlet fever in the human subject. Lately a report has been issued by the Local Government Board, from which it appears that Dr. Mair, who investigated the matter, concluded not only that the disease was not scarlet fever, but that it was a special disease, due possibly to a form of yeast found in many of the fields, where the cows were pastured, the spores adherent to the udders being transferred to the milk in the process of milking.

MILK-BORNE SCARLET FEVER.—A series of cases of scarlet fever from a common source is reported by Mussen,* by whom the outbreak, which occurred at Liverpool, was investigated. During the first week of February, 16 cases of the disease were reported from a suburban district which had been comparatively free from the disease, and it was found that there was but one condition common to all, and that was the milk supply. About the middle of January, a child of the dairyman was taken ill, but was not given medical attention, and was allowed to come downstairs about a week before the first case was reported. On February 6, when the investigation began, there was slight oedema of the feet and ankles, with copious desquamation from the hands and feet. The child was removed, all milk and cream in the dairy was destroyed, and the house and contents were thoroughly disinfected. Cases of the disease continued to be reported until February 23, but no attacks occurred after February 10 in houses not previously infected, outside of four cases, in each of which there was proof of close association with patients in other houses. In all there were 59 cases, 55 of which could be traced to the dairy, the others arising through contact.

Another milk-borne outbreak of the same disease, due in great part to official carelessness, has been recently reported.† The milk was supplied from dairies which could not pass inspection two years previously by Buffalo physicians, and investigation

---

*Public Health, Aug., 1904. Page 687.
†The Journal of the American Medical Association for Sept. 24, 1904.

showed that a number of cases of the disease existed at one of the dairies. The supply was not stopped immediately on the discovery of this state of affairs, and at least one death was recorded, in which case the infection occurred during the period while the milk was still being used in spite of this knowledge. Another outbreak of 10 cases was traced to a similar cause and condition, and the sale of milk from the infected dairy was promptly stopped.

Another outbreak attributed to milk is described by Tingvall.* In four days, 27 cases were reported from 18 houses in the same quarter of a town, where no cases had previously existed. The families affected obtained their milk from a shop supplied by a farm on which were several cases of the disease.

PUS AND BACTERIA IN MILK.—In 1900, it was pointed out by Professor D. H. Bergey that a high cellular and bacterial content of milk appears to be associated with some inflammatory process within the udder. Since then he† has studied the milk of several cows during an entire period of lactation, in order to obtain information concerning the relation of the period of lactation to the cellular and bacterial content. The milk of one of the cows selected for observation showed, previous to the close of the preceding period of lactation, a slight amount of pus in association with staphylococci. That of cow No. 2, examined for the first time after calving, showed no pus, but merely the normal leucocytic content, which is equivalent to the presence of not more than 10 cells per field of a one-twelfth immersion lens. Cow No. 3 was suffering with contagious mammitis, and her milk after calving showed large amounts of yellow pus and very large numbers of streptococci. The milk of all three of these cows was examined at intervals of one or two months, until the close of the period of lactation—a period of nine months. The results of the investigation appeared to warrant the following conclusions:

1—The occurrence of pus in cow's milk is probably always

Hygienische Rundschau, Feb., 1904. Page 109.
†*University of Pennsylvania Bulletin*, July-August, 1904.

associated with the presence in the udder of some inflammatory reaction brought about by the presence of some of the ordinary pyogenic bacteria, especially of streptococci.

2—When a cow's udder has once become infected with the pyogenic bacteria, the disease tends to persist for a long time, probably extending over several periods of lactation.

3—Lactation has no causative influence *per se* upon the cellular and bacterial content of cow's milk, though it probably tends toward the aggravation of the disease when the udder is once infected.

4—The so-called "gelbe galt," or contagious mammitis of European writers, appears to be merely a severe form of mammitis due to a variety of streptococcus, which, on account of its chromogenic properties, gives to the milk its peculiar golden-yellow color.

PREVENTIVE THERAPEUTICS.

BY HERBERT D. PEASE, M. D.,

Director Antitoxin Laboratory, N. Y. State Dept. of Health, Albany, N. Y.

VACCINE AND VACCINATION—Power, N. H.,* reports an increased observance of the vaccination law of England and Wales concerning the vaccination of new born infants during the year 1901. Not only did the percentage of successful vaccinations to birth in every one of the 43 counties increase, but the percentage of cases of conscientious objections did not increase, and in one-half the counties decreased. The Welsh counties show nearly as favorable a result.

Blaxall and Frembin (Page 652) report the results of their work on the "Properties of Lymph as Collected from the Calf on Successive Days After Vaccination." Up to the end of forty-eight hours the collectable lymph gave variable results. From the third to the seventh day it was capable of producing typical vesiculation. From the latter time to the fourteenth or fifteenth

----

*Thirty-Second Annual Report Local Government Board, Medical Officers' Report 1902-03.

days the vaccinating power declined and the lymph finally became innocuous. The vesicles began to show evidence of drying on the seventh day, and the number of extraneous bacteria in them greatly increased from then on.

Green (Page 659) reports on the "Use of Chloroform in the Preparation of Vaccine." The method described consists in triturating one part by weight of vaccine pulp with from two to three parts of sterile distilled water. This emulsion is next subjected to chloroform in the following manner: A constant current of sterile air is passed through pure liquid chloroform, whereby the former becomes charged with chloroform vapor. This mixture is then passed through the vaccine emulsion, and the water of the latter takes up the chloroform to saturation. This process is best carried on at a temperature of 20 degrees C. This method was devised to overcome the injury done to the specific organism in vaccine if it comes into contact with pure chloroform. When the latter is first dissolved in water there is no appreciable injury inflicted on the vaccine organism. Of 45 vaccines treated by this process and used to vaccinate 48,027 cases, the percentage success was for primary vaccinations 97.8 per cent and revaccinations 97.1 per cent.

Concerning the effect of the chloroform on the extraneous bacteria, the author shows that by passing the chloroform air mixture through the vaccine for two hours, and allowing it to stand sealed in the refrigerator up to 42 hours, or by passing the air-chloroform mixture for six hours, agar plates inoculated with the vaccine remained sterile. Before the vaccine is issued the chloroform may be removed from the emulsion by passing sterile air through the latter. The emulsion may then be mixed with the proper amount of glycerine if glycerinated vaccine is desired.

THE PASSAGE OF ANTITOXIN THROUGH THE INTESTINAL WALLS OF INFANTS—Stimulated by the work of Behring and his pupils on the possibility of the immunization of infants by feeding them with the raw milk from cows artificially immunized to tuberculosis, Salge* endeavored to ascertain

---

*Jahrbuch fur Kinderheilkunde, Band 10, Heft 1, July, 1904.

whether antitoxins are absorbed from the alimentary canal un-
changed and the conditions surrounding such absorption.

Romer working on horses and rabbits found that the antitoxin
in the milk of females of these species actively immunized to
diphtheria, was absorbed into the circulation of the offspring receiving it. With the colt, however, such absorption was for a
limited period. The antitoxin in mare's milk fed to a rabbit
was not absorbed into the circulation of the latter. Antitoxic horse serum fed to the colt when older did not result in
the absorption of antitoxin into its circulation. As he found
some antitoxin in the feces and intestinal contents he believes
there is some anatomical barrier in the intestinal walls to the
absorption of antitoxin by adults.

Salge considering that Romer disregarded the possible differences between the antitoxin in milk and those in serum, and
that he also failed to use in all cases homologous proteids, undertook a line of investigation on young infants.

By careful, well controlled methods he shows that nine infants, ranging from five days to six months, failed to absorb
diphtheria antitoxic horse serum fed with various kinds of proper
food. He then demonstrated that the normal diphtheria antitoxic
properties present in a certain woman's milk were transferable
to the blood of a nursing infant. The amount of antitoxin in
the circulation of the latter was increased by the subcutaneous
injection of antitoxic serum into the nursing woman.

The lack of absorption of antitoxin when fed as serum and
its apparent ease of absorption when fed in the form of homologous milk, speaks strongly against Romer's theory of
an anatomical barrier to absorption in the intestinal mucous
membrane.

The difficulty lies either in a difference between the antitoxin in
milk and that in serum or to the use of antitoxin proteids from
hetrologous sources. To establish the possible influence of the latter factor Salge is about to feed infants with the milk of actively
immunized animals.

THE BEST METHOD FOR THE ADMINISTRATION OF DIPHTHERIA ANTITOXIN—Cruveilhier* investigated to determine which of the following methods of injection of diphtheria antitoxin would produce the most certain and the most rapidly favorable results; subcutaneous, in single or repeated doses; or intravenous. His method was to inoculate guinea pigs with fatal amounts of either cultures or the bacteria — free diphtheria toxin, and then determine the last hour when it was possible to save them by a given dose of antitoxin administered by the various methods.

He concludes that in general the injections of toxin, as compared with the bacteria, require the earlier use of the serum.

With toxin injections the single injection of a small dose of serum intracerebrally was usually slightly superior in results to a larger dose given subcutaneously. Excessively large single doses subcutaneously were no better than the ordinary large doses. Large doses subcutaneously, and repeated, were superior to repeated small doses intracerebrally.

Large doses intravenously were much superior to any of the other methods tested.

This work is of considerable interest. But little actual knowledge exists as to the relative rates of absorption of antitoxin from different kinds of tissues—muscle, subcutaneous, etc. Any one who has seen at autopsy large amounts of physiological salt solution injected fifteen hours before death unabsorbed, and distributed throughout an area of subcutaneous fat, will realize with the writer, that antitoxin injected into similar tissues is all but wasted.

Antitoxin should be injected into tissues with a rich blood supply in order that its absorption may be as rapid as possible. Whether the average physician is properly equipped to give antitoxin intravenously is questionable.

In hospitals and in the hands of surgeons this method might be used to excellent advantage.

---

*Annales de l'Institut Pasteur, Tome XVIII, No. 1, 25 Janvier, 1904.

ANTIDYSENTERIC SERUM—Rosenthal* after reviewing the work of Shiga and Kruse on the production and use of anti-dysenteric serum, reports the results of his work on the immunization of the smaller experimental animals, the rabbit, guinea-pig and dog, and follows with the results of tests made upon artificially infected laboratory animals with the antidysenteric serum of horses, and the report ends with the results obtained by the use of this serum in the treatment of 157 cases constituting a portion of those occurring in an epidemic of dysentery in Moscow in 1903.

The author by his tests of the horse serum on guinea-pigs and rabbits claims to show that the serum possessed not only strong specific bactericidal properties for dysentery bacilli, but also antitoxic properties for the toxin produced by this species. This serum was used at the Alt-Catharinin-Spital during the epidemic on over 157 cases, but many were excluded on account of surely fatal chronic diseases existing with the dysentery. The death rate in these cases, where the attack of dysentery was in the nature of a terminal infection, was from 50 to 75 per cent.

The ages of these 157 cases were as follows: 10-20 years, 30 per cent; from 20 to 40 years, 50 per cent, and from 40 to 80 years about 20 per cent.

While it was impossible to examine all the cases for the presence of the dysentery bacillus in the stools, forty cases were so examined and the bacillus always found present.

As to the stage of the disease when first treated; 15 per cent were treated within three days, 50 per cent in the latter half of the first week, 25 per cent in the second week and 10 per cent later. The dose of serum varied from 20 to 40 cubic centimetres. When given early the favorable results were strikingly rapid. When given later the decrease in the symptoms was later, but ultimately satisfactory. There was a marked contrast between the cases receiving the serum and those not so treated. Under the influence of the injection the pain and tenesmus lessened within twenty-four hours, the stools less frequent, the blood disappeared from

*Deutsche medicinische Wochenschrift, 5 Mai, 1904, S. 691.

them, the course of the disease was shortened and the continuation of the disease into a chronic stage much less frequent.

Of the 157 serum treated cases eight died, and one was complicated with tuberculosis, giving a fatality of 4 1-2 per cent. All the fatal cases were over 19 years of age. Three were first treated by the end of the first week; four by the end of the second.

For ten years previously the death rate in Moscow hospitals from dysentery was from 12 to 17 per cent. In the same hospital in forty cases, belonging to this epidemic, treated before the serum treatment began, the death rate was 10 per cent. As with Shiga the death rate was ,therefore, reduced more than one-half.

Todd* calls attention to the well known fact that in dysentery the causative bacilli are not found in the body outside of the intestines and mesenteric glands. This coupled with the clinical picture strongly suggests a severe poisoning. He first set about the production of a true toxin freed from the bacteria, and was, like Lentz, Conradi, Neisser and Shiga and others, very successful. The effects of his toxin when injected into animals were practically the same as those caused by the injection of cultures.

The most important result of this work is the demonstration that anti-dysenteric serum is antitoxic in its action.

ACTIVE IMMUNIZATION OF MAN AGAINST THE TYPHOID BACILLUS.—The bacteria-free filtrate of a suspension of typhoid bacilli in sterile physiological salt solution after heating of one hour at 60 degrees C., and two days in the incubator at 37 degrees C., was used by Shiga† for the subcutaneous injection of himself and Dr. Lipstein in two doses of .05 and .25 cubic centimetres respectively.

The serum of both was found to have acquired a high agglutinating power and also bactericidal properties for typhoid bacilli.

DUNBAR'S ANTITOXIN FOR HAY FEVER.—Glegg‡ gives an excellent review of the recent investigations on the

*Journal of Hygiene, Volume 4, No. 4, October, 1904.
†Berliner klinische Wochenschrift, 25 January, 1904.
‡Journal of Hygiene, Volume 4, No. 3, July, 1904.

cause, prevention and treatment of hay fever. Dunbar's hay fever antitoxic horse serum used locally in the eye and nose in the form of a fine powder, is apparently able to ward off attacks of the disease in a large majority of cases, occurring both in America and Europe. Used locally in this way it requires the frequent application of the remedy in advance of or at the first suggestion of the onset of the attack.

It is inadvisable to use the serum subcutaneously on account of the skin disturbances, which, in a varying percentage of persons, follow the subcutaneous injection of any horse serum.

Glegg gives the results of the use of the remedy in 222 cases from all parts of Europe. Of these 127 cases, or 57 per cent., obtained entirely successful results by its use. In 71 persons, or 32 per cent, a partially favorable result was obtained. In 24 persons, or 11 per cent, no effect was produced. The latter group was only 1.4 per cent after deducting the cases not using the serum properly.

In America the results were as follows in the 63 cases reported. Positive result in 44, or 70 per cent; partial in 12, or 19 per cent; negative in 7, or 11 per cent.

Mohr* considers the value of Dunbar's antitoxin to consist in the modification of individual attacks. This requires the use of the antitoxin during the period when the patient is usually afflicted. His conclusions are in harmony with those of Glegg.

VETERINARY SANITATION.

VERANUS A. MOORE, M. D.
Professor of Comparative Pathology, Cornell University, Ithaca, N. Y.

TUBERCLE BACILLI IN THE MILK OF COWS THAT REACT TO TUBERCULIN.—In view of the many examinations of milk of tuberculous cattle for tubercle bacilli, and the almost uniform positive results obtained, the results of Stenstrom† are significant by contrast. Stenstrom's experiments

*Deutsche medicinische Wochenschrift, 21 January, 1904.
†Zeit. f. Heisel und Muld Hygiene, May, 1904. Page 277.

were made in the laboratory of the Separator Company in Hamra on cows for slaughter. The milk was passed through a separator, and the sediment (slime) and the cream were mixed and inoculated into the abdominal cavity of guinea pigs and rabbits. The milk from fifty cows that had reacted to tuberculin, and later were proved by post mortem to be tuberculous, was examined. Sixty-eight rabbits and fifteen guinea pigs were used. One rabbit died of peritonitis. All the others were examined within five months and not one was found to be tuberculous.

PREVENTION OF FOWL CHOLERA.—One of the interesting experiences in the prevention of animal diseases that has been recently reported in this country is given by Ward[*] in his account of checking the spread of fowl cholera. The method followed was thorough and frequent disinfection of the poultry houses, and putting corrosive sublimate, 1 part to 2000, in the drinking water to prevent the spread of the virus by that channel. The results were highly satisfactory. The most interesting and perhaps surprising feature is that the fowls were able to drink water so highly charged with mercuric chloride.

RAPID METHOD OF DIAGNOSING RABIES.—Moore and Way[†] have recently published the results of their work in diagnosing rabies by the method suggested by Van Gehuchten and Nelis. They have been able to diagnose the disease in a number of cases, all they have tried, within forty-eight hours. In all cases control inoculations were made to confirm the results of the histological examinations. The method had already been confirmed by Ravenel and Valle.

The importance of a rapid diagnosis in this disease, from the sanitary point of view, was emphasized. The authors stated that in New York, where the quarantine of dogs was not enforced until after the diagnosis was made, it is of the greatest importance that the nature of the disease be determined before the exposed dogs develop the disease. They cited outbreaks of rabies in the Empire State that had resulted from the spread of the in-

[*] *Bulletin* 156, California, April, Exp. Station.
[†] *Am. Vet. Review.* Oct., 1904. Page 658.

fection while waiting for a positive diagnosis by the animal inoculation method.

The method consists of a microscopic examination of sections of the plexiform ganglion. In cases of rabies the ganglion cells atrophied and became infiltrated with small cells. These lesions are very readily detected in animals that have *died* of rabies, and they appear to be characteristic.

RECOVERY FROM RABIES.—Remlinger and Effendi* have reported recovery in two cases of experimental rabies. The first case was in a dog inoculated intravenously with 5cc of a milky suspension of fixed virus, previously passed through fine muslin. It developed rabies, was paralyzed but recovered. Some weeks later this recovered dog was bled and the serum mixed with fixed virus, and after acting for 24 hours two rabbits were inoculated. They survived for several days longer than usual. A dog was inoculated with a large dose of the treated virus and it remained well. The second case of recovery was a dog inoculated with 8cc of a suspension of fixed virus in the jugular. It developed characteristic lesions but recovered. This suggests the possibility of vaccinating dogs against rabies by way of the jugular vein, as formerly done by Krasmitski. The effect of the serum indicates that possibly a therapeutic serum for this disease may be procured.

TUBERCLE BACILLI IN MILK.—Koch is quoted as having recently said while on a visit to Paris, that he had abandoned the human-bovine tuberculosis question, and left its settlement to others. Those who maintain the danger of bovine tubercle bacilli to the human animal, particularly to children, seem to be decidedly in the ascendent. That tubercle bacilli are found infectious in the milk of tuberculous animals has been determined, as shown below, in many cases where the udders were not affected; in cases where the udders are affected, the milk should unquestionably be rejected, but it is not always possible to determine such udder infection clinically. It is estimated that somewhat less than 1 per cent

*Ann. de l'Institut Pasteur, 1904. Page 241.

of cows have infected udders. The danger of distribution from these, however, is greatly extended by the practice of mixing milk, which obtains largely in the milk trade of the present day. Moreover cattle having lung or intestinal tuberculous excrete the bacilli through the feces, and when the proportion of cow manure likely to reach the milk in an average dairy farm, as at present conducted, is considered, an appreciable source of danger from tuberculous animals, the udders of which are not affected, is evident.

The United States Department of Agriculture in Bulletin 44, Bureau of Animal Industry, 1903, published results of experiments conducted by the department on cows, 56 in number, reacting to tuberculin, but not showing lesions of the udder; injection of guinea pigs yielded positive results from 19.6 per cent of the cows at some time or other during the experiment, which lasted three months. The bulletin quotes the results of 57 other similar investigations made in this country and abroad with similar results, by microscopic, feeding and inoculation experiments. The bibliography, to the date of publication, is fairly complete.

MUNICIPAL SANITATION.

CHARLES V. CHAPIN, M. D.

Superintendent of Health, Providence, R. I.

INFANTS' MILK DEPOTS.—G. F. McCleary* in a recent article has given a very interesting and candid account of the use and value of stations for the gratuitous distribution of milk for infant feeding. The first of these institutions, known as the "Goutte de Lait," was established in Belleville, France, in 1892, and there are now in that country over 60 towns provided with one or more such stations. The Strauss milk charity in New York was organized in 1893, and has been copied in a number of American cities. In the United States, as in France, most of these stations are operated by private charity. In England on the contrary all but one of the stations are municipal affairs,

---

*Journal of Hygiene, July, 1904. Pages 329-368.

such important cities as Liverpool and Bradford having adopted this plan. The only city in this country having municipal stations is Rochester, where they were established in 1897. In the French and English stations the milk is sterilized, and in American cities it is pasteurized with the exception of Rochester. (2) In that city since 1899 the Health Department has each summer established a farm station where the milk is produced under modern conditions, and is delivered to the customers without either pasteurization or sterilization. It averaged not over 14,000 bacteria per cubic centimetre. Statistics from many cities are offered to show that these milk depots have effected a great saving in infant life. McCleary criticises to some extent the deductions usually drawn from these figures, but on the whole believes that the stations are productive of a great deal of good. McCleary also comes to the same conclusion as Park and Holt (3) in New York, that a great deal of the value of these stations is due to the opportunity afforded for the instruction of mothers in the proper care of their children. The article contains descriptions of methods and a number of illustrations.

TYPHOID FEVER FROM POLLUTED WELLS.—Woodward, health officer of the District of Columbia, relates (4) a case of this kind. The infected wells were not more than 8 or 10 feet deep, and were probably contaminated by a leaky privy box on the premises where the first case occurred. The water tasted of the carbolic acid used to disinfect the stools.

PERIOD OF ISOLATION IN DIPHTHERIA.—It is not often that a time limit for the termination of isolation in diphtheria is deliberately chosen, but in Fall River (5) the placard is now removed two weeks after the disappearance of the membrane. It may, however, be removed earlier if two successive negative cultures are obtained from both throat and nose.

.]   Ann. Rep. Dept. Pub. Health, Rochester, 1902.
.]   Med. News, Dec. 5, 1903.
[2.] Rep Health Officer, D. of C., 1903, p. 29.
[3.] Rep. Bd. Health, Fall River, 1903, p. 85.

VITAL STATISTICS.

JOHN S. FULTON, M. D.
Secretary Maryland State Board of Health.

CENSUS BULLETIN NO. 15 is by Dr. John Shaw Billings, and is entitled "A Discussion of the Vital Statistics of the Twelfth Census." If the Bureau can supply considerable amounts of statistical data as good as this Bulletin contains, students of vital statistics will acknowledge a service of very great value. Whoever has undertaken to collect statistical information on particular causes of death by consulting the reports of States and cities, and in the course of such work has wrestled (whether to success or defeat) against vagaries, elisions, ambiquities, discontinuities and sophistications, will have delight in the possession of statistical data concerning the mortality experience of many places, during eleven successive years, shown in all their major relations.

One great distinction of Dr. Billings' work on the Tenth and Eleventh Censuses was that he discarded the older methods of statement and gave us the figures in the most serviceable modes. In the matter of space he wrung large concessions from unwilling hands, and in utilizing that space he exercised most excellent discrimination. In the Bulletin now before us the same characteristics appear. As many subjects as can be satisfactorily treated are considered and no more. The tables include a statement of populations and gross death rates of 130 cities for the year 1900, with the death rate from eleven principal causes of death by color; a statement of deaths and death rates per 1000 population at all ages and under 5 years for each of the eleven years, 1890 to 1900, in 83 cities; the annual death rates from consumption per 100,000 population in 27 cities, from 1890 to 1900; similar statements concerning pneumonia in 25 cities, concerning typhoid in 30 cities and concerning diphtheria and croup in 30 cities.

The pamphlet concludes with a series of life tables for the cities of Baltimore, Boston, Brooklyn, Washington, New York and

Philadelphia, and the States of Massachusetts and New Jersey. These give expectation of life as derived from the census of 1880, the six years, 1884 to 1890, and the census of 1900, for whites of each sex and both sexes. Dr. Billings calls attention to the incomplete enumeration of children under 5 years, and especially of children under 1 year, as the most serious cause of error in the calculations.

THE HEALTH DEPARTMENT OF CHICAGO has published in one volume the vital statistics of the city for the years 1899 to 1903 inclusive. Chicago's parsimony toward her Health Department is notorious. Time was when valuable reports were published, but for several years past the Health Department has issued nothing but the weekly Bulletin, the most insignificant looking public document in existence, widely quoted, interesting always, and useful in Chicago, but disgraceful nevertheless as the only printed record of sanitary operations in a city of the first rank.

It is good to have from Chicago once more a detailed presentation of recent mortality experience, even though the story of five years has been compressed into one hundred and twenty-eight pages without one line of comment or discussion. More than 130,000 records of death enter into the construction of these tables, and those who habitually handle such records know what perplexing questions arise in their statistical treatment. The tabular statements, when completed, have an appearance of veracity which their makers know is exceedingly fallacious.

To be deprived of the critical obesrvations of those who have constructed such tables is to lose the better part of the value of their labors. Still, if the parsimony of a great city allows but 128 pages for a report upon the analysis of 130,000 death certificates one must admit that in the long run editorial comment can be spared better than the numerical statements. The mortality statistics of Chicago are worth 100 pages a year.

The tabular exhibits in this report are of great interest and of considerable variety. Like most American cities, Chicago states the age distribution of both the living and the dead by ten year periods above the age of 10 years. The figures for the age period 5 to 10 are separately given, and below the age of 5 each year receives separate statement. Statements of age distribution by 5 year periods to the end of life would simplify very much the study of special causes of death, and the comparison of living populations. One can see in the prevalent form of statement that urban populations present in their age distribution certain characteristics which distinguish them from rural populations, and that certain features distinguish large cities from small ones; but in the statement of age distribution by 5 year periods certain distinctions appear among large cities, and these distinctions have weight in comparing mortality experience.

The nomenclature of the Chicago tables is that which has been used in the earlier reports. It is understood that Chicago will in future employ the international classification. The statistics will gain much by the change, though it must be admitted that something will also be lost. One great advantage to be derived from the change of nomenclature can be shown by reference to one of the statistical summaries. Table XVIII shows, among other things, that the mortality from the so-called zymotic group of the old classification has been reduced in 19 years to less than one-fourth of its earlier importance. In the first half of this period the mortality rates in this group showed a tendency to increasing importance, ranging from 4.6 to 6.05 per 1000; but in 1895 the rate fell below 2 per 1000, and has maintained a lesser importance since that time. The ratios to total mortality tell the same story. Of the causes of death included in the zymotic group two only have appreciably yielded before the advances of modern hygiene, but the extinction of these two would be required to eliminate three-fourths of the mortality of the whole group.

It has happened in Chicago, as everywhere else, that medical certification and statistical treatment of causes of death have both altered in 20 years; the former progressively; the latter with noticeable jerks. The apparent decline of the zymotic diseases is, as insurance men say, " a good talking point," and indeed

Chicago has made good use of modern resources against certain causes of death included in the zymotic group; but the chief significance of these figures is that by the wear and tear of progress the fabric of the old nomenclature was cut clean through at a particular spot and in the year 1895 or thereabouts.

A singular feature of Chicago's mortality tables appears in the fact that of the 130,219 deaths accounted for not one escaped diagnosis. There is not in the book a word about death from unknown causes. Whether the unique skill indicated by this circumstance is possessed by the medical profession or by the registration officers, or is a joint property, one cannot learn from the report.

In some great cities the combined efforts of the medical man and the registrar send 10 per cent of all certificates into the unknown account. Elsewhere, such is the diagnostic acumen of the registrars, that but one-tenth of one per cent of death certificates fail of classification under definite heads. But in Chicago, apparently, the death certificate is absolutely blunder proof.

The report contains no statement of still births. Premature birth is credited with 1481 deaths, a little more than one per cent of the total mortality.

THE FRIENDS OF REGISTRATION IN MARYLAND have been somewhat uneasy of late about the operation of a law enacted by the last General Assembly. Under the provisions of this act the resident or attending physician of any hospital, sanitarium, school reformatory, asylum, or like institution may, on application to the County Commissioners, be qualified to issue burial permits, and may collect a fee of 50 cents for each permit issued.

The responsibilities of these institutional physicians for the return of records to the State Registrar of Vital Statistics is in all respects the same as that of other local sub-registrars. One can readily see that if a death in a hospital should occur under circumstances suggestive of negligence or crime, the attending or resident physician, having authority to write a certificate of death and to issue a permit to bury the body, would have power to screen the circumstances against investigation. Or, if suspicion concerning the cause of a death should arise outside the hospital, and it should appear that all the records in the case, including the permit to dispose of the body, had been made by the attending physician, such records would be the poorest possible defense and might indeed strengthen the pre-existing suspicion. Clearly such unmeasured responsibility is to be avoided by a careful physician. On the other hand, a physician engaged in the criminal practice offered by a great city would find in such an arrangement a most convenient and effective defense.

The evil results anticipated in Maryland have not, however, appeared. Physicians apparently recognized the compromising nature of these combined professional and magisterial responsibilities, and up to this time, six months after the law became operative, but two physicians have asked for authority to issue burial permits. Thus through the common sense and discretion of institutional physicians Maryland may avoid the anticipated evil results of a bad bit of legislation.

CANADIAN NOTES.

JOHN A. AMUYOT, M. D.
Provincial Board of Health of Ontario, Toronto, Ont.

TORONTO UNIVERSITY DIPLOMA OF PUBLIC HEALTH. During the last year the University of Toronto has established a post-graduate course in public health, at the termination of which, after qualification by examination, a diploma of public health will be given. The university unites with the Provincial Board of Health in giving the course, making use of the laboratories of the Provincial Board of Health and field inspection under the supervision of the Provincial Board of Health.

The first summer session will be devoted to laboratory work in: 1. Sanitary chemistry. 2. Bacteriology. 3. Parasitology. The winter session will be devoted to: a. Advanced general hygiene. b. Advanced general pathology, including theory of immunity and comparative pathology. c. Elements of geology, meteorology and climatology in their relation to public health. d. Sanitary engineering. e. Sanitary legislation and vital statistics. f. Clinics on contagious diseases. g. History of preventive medicine and epidemiology.

The second summer session shall be devoted to a course of Practical work in Public Health under the supervision of the Provincial Board of Health, including the methods of dealing with infectious diseases, inspection of schools and other public buildings, factories and dairies, inspection of water supplies and sewage disposal plants and other forms of municipal sanitation.

PUBLIC HEALTH REPORTS. In future it has been decided to publish the doings of the Provincial Board of Health, the vital statistics of the Province and the proceedings of the executive health officers association of the Province of Ontario in a quarterly magazine form under the leadership of the President and Secretary of the Provincial Board of Health, instead of separately and annually as has been done in the past.

COUNTY MEDICAL HEALTH OFFICERS. The agitation of the institution of the county medical health officers' system instead of the township and municipal health officer one as at present, is being pushed along, and with considerable hope of its success in the near future. It is becoming more and more apparent that the present system does not give the results. That the local man is hampered by localisms, the endangering of his practice and most of all by the time he is required to devote for a paltry or no monetary remuneration.

"THE PLAGUE OF PATENT POTIONS." The following resolution was submitted at a meeting of the Canadian Medical Association, held in Vancouver in August of this year:

It is a well known and established fact that many of the most popular and salable patent and proprietory medicines contain large quantities of alcohol and noxious drugs, which are very

injurious to the health of those making use of them, not only
petite for their continued use, which lead to the loss or disability
by their direct influence on health but by creating a depraved ap-
of many valuable lives, and that the sale of these medicines is
largely due to the manner in which they are advertised, their
venders making exaggerated and misleading statements through
the general press, literature posters and pamphlets as to their
healing virtues and life-saving qualities, thereby inducing sufferers from disease to purchase them to their very great injury,
morally, mentally and physically. The great and growing increase of the consumption of these drugs is daily impressed on
our profession by our observations of the injurious effects which
are produced by them on a large and daily growing number of
our population, and we feel that some urgent and effectual
means ought to be adopted by those who are responsible for the
health and welfare of the people that will control and restrict the
sale of these most injurious and pernicious preparations.

And this association, composed of the leading medical men
from one end of the Dominion to the other, feels that the time
has arrived when this great and growing evil to the public health
must be suppressed; and this association would strongly urge
the Federal Government, through the department having the
control and jurisdiction over matters of this nature, to take immediate steps to thoroughly investigate the nature and contents
of these preparations, and to suppress the pernicious and misleading form of literature and advertising by which this sale is
so largely brought about, and adopt such general and effectual
measures in connection with this matter as will insure the safety
of the public health, and that a copy of this resolution be forwarded to the department of the Government having control of
such matters.

The laboratory of the Provincial Board of Health of Ontario
has during the last year been working on these lines and endeavoring by the publication of the results to inform the public
at least of the condition of affairs.

BOOK REVIEW.

FOOD INSPECTION AND ANALYSIS.*

BY ALBERT E. LEACH, S. B.

This long needed book is written for public analysts, health officers, sanitary chemists and food economists by the present analyst of the Massachusetts State Board of Health, and gives in a clear, concise and well-illustrated manner the methods of food analysis selected and developed by the author, his predecessor and his assistants.

"Special prominence is given to the nature and extent of adulteration in the various foods, the methods of analysis for the detection of adulterants, and to some extent also to the machinery of inspection." Along these lines the author very sanely refuses to take sides on the value of various food substitutes, such as glucose preserves, lard substitutes, oleomargarine, etc., believing that if the public is protected by accurate labels, it has a right to buy a substitute in place of the genuine, provided the healthfulness of the article is not questionable.

The microscopy of foods, and especially spices and condiments, is developed to a high point in this work, as are also the various refraction methods.

An illustration of the newness of much of the material is the paragraph on the Zeiss immersion refractometer—a very recent and extremely useful instrument. The composition and analysis of foods is also very carefully treated, and nearly all of the important analytical and statistical tables are inserted in the text. Considerable space has also been given to tables showing the feeding values of various foods.

The author has performed a great service in compiling from widely separated sources—such as, for example, German treatises and U. S. Department of Agriculture reports—a series of well elaborated, practical analytical methods, most of which

---

*Large 8 vo.—XIV. 787 pages, 120 figures, 40 full page half tones. Cloth, $7.50. John Wiley & Sons, New York, 1904.

would stand cross-examination in court. In most cases one method alone is given, and readers may ask the reason for certain omissions. Many alternate methods could not be included in the text, however, without increasing the size of the book—rather large for the laboratory as it is.

The book is of excellent appearance and the illustrations of apparatus look like devices really seen in laboratories, not like those illustrated in apparatus catalogs. The micro-photographs are very well taken and reproduced, and the excellent illustrations from Moeller lend clearness to the descriptions.

A good bibliography accompanies each chapter, and a very good index follows the appendix, but, unhandily, precedes the plates, which are at the end of the book. As a whole, the work commands respect, and it is difficult to see how the subject could be better treated in any volume of this size. It should be in the hands of every food analyst and student.

WHY DIRTY WATER IS DANGEROUS.*

VARIOUS KINDS OF WATER.   There are in the world many kinds of water, such as rain water and dew, sea water, spring water, well water, river water, lake water, pond water, mineral water, drain water, sewer water, manure water—besides many other kinds.

MOST WATERS ARE MIXTURES.   Almost all of these are not water merely, but rather mixtures of water with various other things.   Sea water, for example, is a mixture of water with large amounts of common salt; mineral waters are mixtures of water with various mineral matters (such as Epsom salts) or gases (such as carbonic acid gas or sulphuretted gases); and sewer water (sewage) is a mixture of water with the excrements and wastes of life.

*Prepared and published by Workers in the Sanitary Research Laboratory and Sewage Experiment Station of the Massachusetts Institute of Technology in Boston, at the request and by the Gift of a Friend of Sanitary Science and Education.

The present is the third (No. 3) of **POPULAR ESSAYS ON HYGIENE AND SANITATION,**—a series of leaflets designed to teach in plain and simple language some of the more important lessons of the time concerning Health and Disease.

Series A, On Health and Disease, is as follows :

No. 1. WHY DIRT IS DANGEROUS. (Ready.)
No. 2. WHY DIRTY MILK IS DANGEROUS (Ready.)
No. 3. WHY DIRTY WATER IS DANGEROUS.
No. 4. WHY DIRTY STREETS ARE DANGEROUS. (In February.)
No. 5. WHY DIRTY PERSONS ARE DANGEROUS. (In Preparation.)

Other leaflets may eventually be prepared upon "Microbes,— Good and Bad ;" " Some Common Diseases, How they Come and how to Avoid them ;" " Farm Sanitation ;" "Why Flies are Filthy and Dangerous ;" and other practical sanitary and hygienic topics.

It is hoped that Boards of Health, School Boards, Hospital Authorities, Charity Workers, Health Education Leagues, Anti-Tuberculosis Societies and other Organizations and Philanthropic Persons or Educators may make use of this Leader, and those which are to follow, in that campaign of Sanitary education in which all civilized people must soon participate.

Reprints of the leaflet here published (SERIES A, ON DIRT AND DISEASE, No. 3.—WHY DIRTY WATER IS DANGEROUS (may be had (postpaid) by addressing the Biological Department, Mass. Institute of Technology, Boston, Mass., and enclosing money or postage stamps according to the following schedule :—

One to fifty copies . . . . .2 cents each.
Fifty or more copies . . . . .1 "   "
Larger quantities by special arrangement

WATER IS A GREAT ABSORBENT. Everyone knows that water absorbs or dissolves many things, such as salt and sugar, and that these things when absorbed, though still present and recoverable by evaporation, are lost to view, and if present in very small quantity cannot be detected in the water by taste or smell. Everyone knows also that water readily soaks into and mingles with most substances, sometimes softening them, and even detaching and floating them. It is for this reason that we use water for washing, for the object of washing is to soak up and float off or, as we say, "wash away" dirt from sidewalks, or floors, or soiled clothing, or our own hands, faces and bodies.

WATER IS A REMARKABLE VEHICLE. Water is not only a great absorbent but very few substances in Nature are as much in motion or as *active* as water is. The waters of the seas and great lakes, with tides, waves and currents, are never at rest; rivers rush swiftly to the sea; brooks and creeks run or pour themselves into rivers, and rains sprinkle the earth. Even in the ground, the water which supplies wells and springs has come from rain, and ground water moves slowly but ceaselessly through the earth, and at last finds its way to the sea. Now, because water is very abundant and a great absorbent, readily mingling with most things; and because it is almost never at rest, but nearly always moving; it is easy to see that water must be a very common and convenient vehicle for all sorts of substances. It is, in fact, the ready carrier, not only of ships, rafts, logs and chips, which float upon it, but also of mud, clay and dirt which mingle with and float in it, as well as of dish water, slops, and the wastes of factories and cities which are absorbed and transported by lakes, ponds and running streams.

PURE WATER. It is, therefore, no wonder that perfectly pure water (that is to say, mere water, or water free from all admixture of other substances) is very scarce in Nature, and probably never occurs except in freshly fallen rain or snow on high and lonely mountain peaks far above all human habitations, and above that atmospheric dust which rises even into the upper air. Rain or snow falling from the upper sky is really Nature's distilled water, and can only be duplicated in the chemical laboratory. Most natural waters are mixtures, and therefore not, in the language of chemistry, strictly pure. The sanitarian, however, uses the term "pure" in another sense, namely, as signifying clear and harmless water. Some mineral waters are clear but so heavily charged with salts as to be unwholesome, that is, unfit for drinking. Sea water belongs to this class. On the other hand some waters may be turbid with clay or clean mud and yet be entirely harmless.

CLEAN WATER. When rain strikes the earth it washes away with it material from the soil, but such water will be *clean* even if muddy, if the ground where it falls is clean, and if the rivers and ponds are clean through which it flows, for it will then have been in contact only with clean natural earth. Such clean waters are found in uninhabited regions, in forests and on uninhabited prairies.

DIRTY WATER. By "dirty" water is generally meant any water that is muddy, milky or turbid. But, as we have already shown in Leaflets No. 1 (*Why Dirt is Dangerous*) and No. 2 (*Why Dirty Milk is Dangerous*) of the series to which the present essay belongs, the word *dirt* comes from an older word *drit,* meaning excrement or filth. Strictly speaking then dirty water is water containing excrements, or substances thrown off from animal bodies, such as spit, urine or bowel discharges, and muddy or turbid water is not always, by any means, really dirty. Some muddy or turbid waters are entirely safe and harmless for domestic use, but no truly dirty water ever is—as we shall soon see. Water of this kind, contaminated or dirty with excrements, is often described as *polluted.*

SEWER-WATER OR "SEWAGE." In modern towns and cities the dirtiest, or most polluted, water is found in the sewers, because into these are emptied not only the waste waters from sinks and drains, the washings of laundries, stables, butcher shops, and the like but also the discharges of bath tubs, water closets and hospitals, the contents of spittoons, and sometimes the washings of streets and gutters. The mixture of all these and many other wastes with water, in sewers, is called *sewage,* and sewage is generally turbid and evil smelling and, if in any way it finds entrance into the body in polluted drinking water or milk, upon food or otherwise, it is dangerous to human life.

WHY DIRTY WATER AND ESPECIALLY SEWAGE IS DANGEROUS. If we understand by "dirty" water, water polluted with animal excrements, then it becomes very easy to see exactly why and how such water is dangerous; for such excrements often contain and may at any time contain parasites and micro-parasites—living organisms and micro-organisms— capable of producing certain well known diseases in man. One of these diseases is typhoid fever, and a large majority of the cases of this disease have in the past probably arisen from the use of dirty drinking water. Many epidemics of Asiatic cholera have also come from drinking water polluted with excrement. Diarrohoea and dysentery are believed to arise also frequently from the same source, and it is more than likely that dirty drinking water may and does cause some cases of diphtheria and tuberculosis. Patients with the sore throat of a beginning diphtheria, or with the cough and spitting of consumption, may spit in the street, the spittoon or the water closet, and these spittings mingled with water may pass into the sewers; and if this sewage or any of it finds its way into drinking water the diseases in question may be communicated to fresh victims.

Sometimes the water of a stream or pond becomes so dirty that the waste matters decaying in it produce foul odors, and small rivers into which much sewage has been discharged are sometimes a nuisance to those who live along their banks.

Generally, water is not allowed to become so dirty as this and is not dangerous as long as it remains in its natural channels. The peril arises when dirty water is used for drinking. Any

water which has been fouled by the wastes of human life is likely to contain germs of disease. The bacteria, minute microscopic
parasites, which cause the infectious and contagious diseases, are
thrown off in the bowel and other discharges of sick persons,
and may be present in water which is not dirty enough to show
any sign of impurity to the eye. When such water is drunk by
those in the right condition the germs enter their bodies and cause
the disease. Sometimes a heavy rain or a thaw washes a large
amount of dirt into a reservoir at once, and a sharp epidemic
of typhoid fever follows, as recently happened at Ithaca, N. Y.,
and Butler, Pa. Large and prosperous cities like Philadelphia
and Pittsburg have regularly used a dirty stream as a source of
water supply and suffered from thousands of cases of typhoid
every year in consequence.

In other places dirty water carries the germs of diarrhoea or
dysentery and causes those diseases, and it is probable that some
diphtheria and consumption may be spread in the same way.

HOW CLEAN WATER BECOMES DIRTY OR
POLLUTED. Clean river waters, brooks, creeks and the like
readily become polluted because they are the natural drains of
some region, and it is easy and convenient to empty into them all
kinds of wastes, such as the sewage of towns, villages and cities,
the discharges of factories, the drainage of manured fields, of
barnyards, stables and the like. Too often, also, privies are made
to overhang them, and in short all manner of excrement and filth
besides less objectionable wastes, such as rubbish and ashes, are
thrown or dumped into streams, which thus become polluted and
dirty. Wells dug near barnyards, privies, sewers or in dirty soil
may easily yield water which, though it *looks* clean and bright,
is really polluted and dirty, especially if as often happens excrement finds its way in at the top of the well. Springs, even, if
badly situated, may yield water which, though bright and spark-
ling, is really dangerously polluted with excrementitious matters.

It is a common habit to throw waste materials into the nearest
stream or pond, and in civilized communities the sewers which
carry off the water fouled by water closets, urinals, sinks, tubs

and so on, often reach the same destination. Single houses discharge sink drains into water courses. Privy vaults are built so as to overhang them. The very ground where many people live near together becomes dirty, so that the rain water as soon as it falls becomes polluted. In thickly settled regions practically all streams and many ponds are dirty. Even water in wells may be fouled by wastes which are washed in from the top or pass below through crevices in rocks or fissures in the soil.

WATER THAT LOOKS CLEAN IS OFTEN DIRTY. A drop of ink let fall into a pail of water, though present, is lost to sight. A drop of sewage let fall into a pail of good drinking water escapes detection, even by a chemist, and yet it is there and may cause typhoid fever or diarrhoea among persons drinking the water.

THE APPEARANCE OF WATER IS NO SAFE GUIDE TO ITS PURITY. It may even happen that a turbid, muddy or *dirty-looking* water is purer than one which *looks* clean. This is a fact never to be forgotten.

HOW CAN SUSPECTED WATER BE MADE SAFE FOR DRINKING. There are several ways in which sewage can be purified, but the purification of sewage will require an entire leaflet for its consideration. For the purification of suspected water there are also many devices.

If the supply of an entire city or town is under suspicion the community may filter the water before serving it at all to the public. This is now done in many places, for example in London, England, in Berlin Germany, in Albany, N. Y., Lawrence, Mass., and in many cities and towns in the Mississippi valley.

Water for family use may be made safe by boiling for a half hour and then cooling. This is the only absolutely safe method. But if possible all water admitted to cities, and especially to dwelling houses should be above suspicion from the start and derived from sources free from all traces of dirt (excrement) and sewage pollution, however small or remote.

President, HENRY P. WALCOTT, M. D.

Vice-Presidents, S. H. DURGIN, M. D., S. W. ABBOTT, M. D.

Treasurer, JAMES B. FIELD, M. D.   Secretary, JAMES C. COFFEY

Executive Committee — 1903-1904, G. L. TOBEY, M.D., W. H. GOVE, C. A. HICKS.
M. D., G. H. ELLIS, C. V. CHAPIN, M. D., 1903-1905, H. C. EMERSON, M. D.
D. S. WOODWORTH, M. D., F. W. KENNEDY, M. D., W. S. EVERETT, M. D.
W. C. KITE, M. D.   Also the officers of the Association, ex-officio.

*Any person interested in Hygiene may become a member by election
at a regular meeting of the Association.*

Agawam
J. W. Hastings.
Ashby
E. A. Hubbard, M. D.
Avon
R. A. Elliott, M. D. 2
E. P. Linfield, M. D. 1
Arlington
E. E. Stickney, M. D. 2
Athol
W. H. Brock
Converse Ward.
Attleboro
George K. Roberts, M. D. 2
Andover
Charles E. Abbott, M. D. 2
Belmont
W. Lyman Underwood. 1
H. A. Yenetchi, M. D.
Boston
S. W. Abbott, M. D. 13*
Silas H. Ayer, M. D.
J. W. Bartol, M. D.
David D. Brough, M. D. 4
Alex. Burr, M. D. V. 8
D. A. Cheever, M. D.
J. W. Cosden.
Robert Cox.
B. F. Davenport, M. D.
S. H. Durgin, M. D. 1
H. C. Ernst, M. D.
Langdon Frothingham, M. D. V.
W. P. Gesner.
E. F. Gleason, M. D.
Charles Harrington, M. D. 11
Edward M. Hartwell.
Dennis J. Hern. 2
W. L. Hicks.
H. W. Hill, M. D. 5
Everett D. Hooper, M. D.
L. H. Howard, D. V. S.
James O. Jordan. 17
Thomas Jordan. 7
S. C. Keith, S. B.
W. H. Mitchell.
Frank L. Morse, M. D. 4*
Austin Peters, D. V. S. 14*
E. B. Phelps, S. B.
E. L. Pilsbury.
W. H. Prescott, M. D.
Mrs. Ellen H. Richards.
B. R. Rickards, S. B. 5
Geo. B. Robbins.
Howard P. Rogers. M. D. V.
Prof. W. T. Sedgwick.
T. B. Shea, M. D. 2
F. H. Slack, M. D. 5.
Agnes C. Vietor, M. D.
Robert S. Weston, S. B.
George M. Whitaker, 16
George Whiting.

C. E. A. Winslow, S. B.
John F. Worcester, M. D.
Bondsville
D. B. Sullivan, M. D.
Brighton
E. S. Hatch, M. D.
Horace E. Marion, M. D.
Otis H. Marion, M D.
F. W. Rice, M. D.
Brookline
H. L. Chase, M. D. 6
James M. Codman, Jr. 1
Nathaniel Conant. 2
William Craig. 2
Francis P. Denny, M. D. 5
Robert W. Hastings, M. D.
Edward A. McEttrick. 13
J. Albert C. Nyhen. 5
F. H. Osgood, M. R. C. V. S. 8, 11
H. Carlton Smith, 17
Willard E. Ward. 15
John K. Whiting.
Brockton
George E. Bolling. 5
F. H. Burnett, M. D.
Charles H. Cary. 3
Edward P. Gleason, M. D. 10
J. H. Lawrence, M. D. 1
A. W. Packard.
F. J. Ripley, M. D.
F. Herbert Snow, C. E.
S. Alfred Spear. 12
Cambridge
Lewis L. Bryant, M. D.
E. R. Cogswell, M. D.
John Crawford.
Edwin Farnham, M. D. 4
Charles Harris.
John G. Hildreth, M. D.
Goodwin A. Isenberg. 1
Ross McPherson, M. D.
J. Arnold Rockwell, M. D.
E. H. Stevens, M. D.
H. P. Walcott, M. D. 1*
Roswell Wetherbee, M. D. 2
Charles F. Whiting.
Charlestown
C. H. Hood.
Nelson M. Wood, M. D.
Chicopee
Charles King.
Chelsea
Frank E. Winslow. 3
Clinton
W. P. Bowers, M. D.
C. C. Crowley.
C. L. French, M. D. 1
J. J. Goodwin, M. D.
E. H. Mackay, M. D. 10
James H. McGrath. 2
G. L. Tobey, M. D. 2

Cohasset
Oliver H. Howe, M. D.
Herbert A. Tilden.
Concord
John M. Keyes. 1
Thomas Todd. 2
Dedham
E. W. Finn, M. D. 2
Duxbury
Alfred E. Green. 1
N. K. Noyes, M. D.
East Bridgewater
A. L. Shirley, M. D.
Everett
R. E. Brown, M. D.
George W. S. Dockum. 2, 13
A. A. Jackson, M. D.
E. J. Newton, M. D. 2
N. B. Smith. 1
George E. Whitehill, M. D.
E. W. Young, M. D.
Fall River
Charles A. Hicks, M. D. 2
Falmouth
Russell S. Nye. 2
Asa R. Pattee, M. D. 2
T. L. Swift, M. D. 1
Fitchburg
J. F. Bresnahan. 7
E. L. Fiske, M. D. 1
Henry M. Francis. 2
Fred R. Houghton. 3, 6
A. P. Mason M. D. 5
Charles H. Rice, M. D.
D. S. Woodworth, M. D.
Framingham
N. I. Bowditch.
Charles M. Hargraves. 2, 13
William R. Morrow, M. D. 2
Gloucester
H. L. Belden.
Haverhill
J. F. Crostan, M D. 2
Holyoke
J. J. Linehan. 2, 6
A. B. Wetherell, M. D. 1
Frank A. Woods, M. D. 2, 13
Hingham
Charles H. Marble. 1
J. Winthrop Spooner, M. D. 2

1, Chairman, Bd. Health ; 2, Member; 3, Clerk ; 4, Medical Officer ; 5, Bacteriologist; 6, Agent ;
7, Sanitary Inspector ; 8, Inspector of Animals ; 9. Quarantine Officer; 10, City Physician ; 11, Milk
Inspector ; 12, Supt. of Health; 13, Secretary ; 14, State Cattle Dept. ; 15, Disinfector ; 16, U. S.
Dairy Inspector ; 17, Chemist ; 18, Examiner of Plumbers.

* State Officials.
**

Holliston

N. C. B. Haviland, M. D. 2

Hyde Park

Edwin C. Farwell.
John A. Morgan, M. D.
William W. Scott. 2
Charles F. Stack, M. D. 1

Hanover

A. L. McMillan, M. D.

Jamaica Plain

Theobald Smith, M. D. 5*

Lancaster

Chester C. Beckley, M. D. 2
Allen G. Butterick. 2
Albert E. Harriman, M. D. 1

Lincoln

Stephen H. Blodgett, M. D. 2
Joseph S. Hart, M. D.

Lexington

George O. Whitney.

Lawrence

William Berger.
Charles E. Birtwell, M. D.
A. D. V Bourget. 1
John T. Cahill, M. D.
T. J. Daly, M. D.
George S. Fuller, D. V. S.
Stephen de M. Gage. 5 *
F. W. Kennedy, M. D. 2
John A. Magee, M. D.
Victor A. Reed, M. D.
George W. Smith. 6
J. F. Winchester, V. S. 8

Leominster

C. E. Bigelow, M. D. 1
Fredson N. Grey. 2
H. N. Spring. 2, 6.

Lowell

William C. Doherty.
James B. Field, M. D.
J. Arthur Gage, M. D.
Thomas F. Harrington, M. D.
Leonard Huntress, M. D.
William B. Jackson, M. D. 2
H. H. Knapp. 6
W. P. Lawler, M. D.
J. N. Marston, M. D.
Thomas B. Smith, M. D. 5

Lynn

R. E. Hillard. 2
W. E. Holbrook, M. D. 2
F. E. Stone, M. D. 2
W. R. Woodfall, M. D. 1

Malden

C. W. McClearn, M. D. 1

Marshfield

C. W. Stodder, M. D. 2

Melrose

E. L. Grundy. 2
Clarence P. Holden, M. D.
Paul H. Provandie, M. D. 1
G. Houston Smith. 2

Milton

A. W. Draper, M. D. V. 2
Charles R. Gilchrist, M. D. 1
W. C. Kite, M. D.
Jacob S. Lincoln. 2
Samuel D. Parker.

Nahant

Joseph T. Wilson. 1

Needham

A. E. Miller, M. D.
A. M. Miller, M. D.

New Bedford

J. T. Bullard, M. D. 2
E. H. Gammons.
W. G. Kirschbaum. 1
L. H. Richardson. 7
Manuel V. Sylvia, M. D. 2, 9

Newport, R. I.

Joseph W. Sampson.

Norwood

E. C. Norton, M. D.

Newton

W. F. Harbach. 2
Arthur Hudson. 5, 11.
A. Stanton Hudson, M. D.
Harry A. Stone. 3, 6
E. R. Utley, M. D. 10

New York, N. Y.

Col. W. F. Morse.

Northampton

E. W. Brown.

No. Brookfield

T. J. Garrigan, M. D.

No. Abington

F. G. Wheatley, M. D.

Palmer

J. P. Schneider, M. D. 1

Plymouth

W. G. Brown, M. D.

Providence, R. I.

C. V. Chapin, M. D. 12
F. P. Gorham.
Gardner T. Swarts, M. D. 13*

Rockland

J. C. Batchelder, M. D.
Gilman Osgood, M. D.

Salem

G. Arthur Bodwell. 1
Wm. H. Colbert. 2
Martin T. Field.
W. H. Gove.
Raymond L. Newcomb. 3, 4
A. N. Sargent, M. D.
Benj. R. Symonds, M. D.

Somerville

A. C. Aldrich. 2
Robert Burns.
Allen F. Carpenter. 1
W. H. Hitchings, V. S.
Wesley R. Lee, M. D.
F. L. Lowell, M. D.
A. E. Merrill, M. D.
Caleb A. Page.
A. R. Perry, M. D.
J. E. Richardson. 11
Edmund F. Sparrow. 2

So. Framingham

L. M. Palmer, M. D.

Springfield

A. L. Brown, M. D. 2
T. J. Collins. 1
H. C. Emerson, M. D. 3
F. W. Farrell.

Edward B. Hodskins, M. D.
James Kimball. 6
B. D. Pierce, V. S.
W. L. Young.

Southbridge

Albert R. Brown.
Humphrey C. Moynihan. 1
Joseph G. E Page, M. D. 13

Three Rivers

Geo. J. Hebert. 2
S. O. Miller, M. D.

Taunton

Luke H. Howard. 18
Charles H. Macomber. 2
Edward J. Shannahan, M. D. 2
Henry H. Wilcox. 7

West Newton

Francis G. Curtis, M. D. 1
Geo. H. Ellis.

Waltham

H. D. Chadwick, M. D.
C. J. McCormick, M. D.
Marshall J. Mosher, M. D. 1
Charles A. Willis, M. D.

Watertown

Sumner Coolidge, M. D.
Julian A. Mead, M. D.

Waverley

L. B. Clark, M. D.

Westboro

D. P. Cilley, M. D.
Charles S. Knight, M. D. 2

Westminster

A. E. Mossman, M. D. 2

Weston

F. T. Hyde, M. D. 2
F. W. Jackson, M. D.
S. Sanford Orr, M. D.

Whitman

F. J. Henly, M. D.
C. E. Lovell, M. D. 2
A. A. MacKeen, M. D. 1

Winchendon

F. W. Russell, M. D. 1

Winchester

John J. French, M. D.

Winthrop

A. B. Dorman, M. D.
H. J. Soule, M. D.

Woburn

George Buchanan.
Dennis S. Doherty 2
William H. Kelliher, M. D. 1

Worcester

F. H. Baker, M. D. 5
Geo. W. Batchelder. 2
W. T. Clark, M. D. 1, 10
James C. Coffey. 2
May S. Holmes, M. D.
Prof. L. P. Kinnicutt.
W. W. McKibben, M. D.
L. F. Woodward, M. D.

Minneapolis, Minn.

F. F. Wesbrook, M. D. 5*
(Honorary Membe

Members are requested to send to the Managing Editor corrections or changes desired in the names, addresses or (where members are connected with a Board of Health) in the titles given in this list.

Members Massachusetts Association of Boards of Health.

OFFICERS FOR 1903.

President, HENRY P. WALCOTT, M. D.

Vice-Presidents, S. H. DURGIN, M. D., S. W. ABBOTT, M. D.

Treasurer, JAMES B. FIELD, M. D.   *Secretary,* JAMES C. COFFEY

Executive Committee — 1902-1904, G. L. TOBEY, M. D., W. H. GOVE, W. Y. FOX, M. D., C. A. HICKS, M. D., G. H. ELLIS. 1903-1905, H. C. EMERSON, M. D., D. S. WOODWORTH, M. D., F. W. KENNEDY, M. D., W. S. EVERETT, M. D., M. D., W. C. KITE, M. D. Also the officers of the Association, *ex-officio.*

Any person interested in Hygiene may become a member by election at a regular meeting of the Association.

Avon
R. A. Elliott, M. D. 2
F. P. Winfield, M. D. 1

Arlington
E. E. Stickney, M. D. 2

Attleboro
George K. Roberts, M. D. 2

Andover
Charles E. Abbott, M. D. 2

Belmont
W. Lyman Underwood. 1
H. A. Yenetchi, M. D.

Boston
S. W. Abbott, M. D. 13*
Silas H. Ayer, M. D.
J. W. Bartol, M. D.
David D. Brough, M. D. 4
Alex. Burr, D. V. S. 8
J. W. Cosden.
Robert Cox.
B. F. Davenport, M. D.
S. H. Durgin, M. D. 1
H. C. Ernst, M. D.
Langdon Frothingham, V. S.
E. F. Gleason, M. D.
Charles Harrington, M. D. 11
Edward M. Hartwell.
W. L. Hicks.
H. W. Hill, M, D. 5
Everett D. Hooper, M. D.
L. H. Howard, D. V. S.
Thomas Jordan. 7
S. C. Keith, S. B.
W. H. Mitchell.
Frank L. Morse, M. D. 4*
Austin Peters, D. V. S. 14*
E. B. Phelps, S. B.
E. L. Pilsbury. 2
W. H. Prescott, M. D.
Mrs. Ellen H. Richards.
B. R. Rickards, S. B. 5
Howard P. Rogers. M. D.
Prof. W. T. Sedgwick.
T. B. Shea, M. D. 4
Agnes C. Vietor, M D.
Robert S. Weston, B. S.
George M. Whitaker.
George Whiting.
C. E. A. Winslow, S. B.
John F. Worcester, M. D.

Brighton
E. S. Hatch, M. D.
Horace E. Marion, M. D.
Otis H. Marion, M. D.
F. W. Rice, M. D.

Brookline
H. L. Chase, M. D. 6
James M. Codman, Jr. 1
Nathaniel Conant. 2
Francis P. Denny, M. D 5
Robert W. Hastings, M. D.
Edward A. McEttrick. 2
J. Albert C. Nyhen. 5
F. H. Osgood, M. R. C. V. S.
Charles H. Pearson. 2
Willard E. Ward.
John K. Whiting.

Brockton
George E. Bolling. 5
Charles H. Cary. 3
J. H. Lawrence, M. D. 2
F. J. Ripley, M. D.
F. Herbert Snow, C. E.
S. Alfred Spear. 12

Cambridge
Lewis L. Bryant, M. D.
E. R. Cogswell, M. D.
John Crawford.
Edwin Farnham, M. D. 4
Charles Harris.
Goodwin A. Isenberg. 2
Ross McPherson, M. D.
William R. Peabody.
J. Arnold Rockwell, M. D.
E. H. Stevens, M. D.
H. P. Wolcott, M. D. 1*
Roswell Wetherbee, M. D. 2
Charles F. Whiting.

Charlestown
C. H. Hood.

Chelsea
Frank E. Winslow. 3

Clinton
W. P. Bowers, M. D.
C. C. Crowley.
C. L. French, M. D. 1
J. J. Goodwin, M. D.
James H. McGrath. 2
G. L. Tobey. 2

Cohasset
Oliver H. Howe, M. D.

Concord
John M. Keyes. 1
Thomas Todd. 2

Dedham
E. W. Finn, M. D. 2

Duxbury
Alfred E. Green. 1
N. K. Noyes, M. D.

East Bridgewater
A. L. Shirley, M. D.

Everett
R. E. Brown, M. D.
George W. S. Dockum. 2
A. A. Jackson, M. D.
E. J. Newton. 2
N. B. Smith. 1
George E. Whitehill, M. D.
E. W. Young, M. D.

Fall River
Charles A. Hicks, M. D. 2

Falmouth
Russell S. Nye. 2
Asa R. Pattee, M. D. 2
T. L. Swift, M. D. 1

Fitchburg
J. F. Bresnahan. 7
E. L. Fiske, M. D. 1
Henry M. Francis. 2
Fred R. Houghton, 3, 6
A. P. Mason M. D. 5
Charles H. Rice, M. D.
D. S. Woodworth, M. D

Framingham
N. I. Bowditch.
Charles M. Hargraves.

Gloucester
H. L. Belden.

Haverhill
J. F. Crostan, M. D. 2

Holyoke
J. J. Linehan. 1
A. B. Wetherell, M. D. 2
Frank A. Woods, M. D. 2

1, Chairman, Bd. Health ; 2, Member; 3, Clerk ; 4, Medical Officer ; 5, Bacteriologist; 6, Agent ; 7, Sanitary Inspector ; 8, Inspector of Animals ; 9, Quarantine Officer; 10, City Physician; 11, Milk Inspector; 12, Supt. of Health; 13, Secretary. State Officials are marked, *; 14, State Cattle Dept.

(Continued on page 98.)

Contributors of Regular Papers.

SAMUEL W. ABBOTT, M. D.,
Sec. Mass. State Bd. of Health.

DAVID D. BROUGH, M. D.
Asst. Med. Inspec. Boston Bd. Health.

ALEXANDER BURR, D. V. S.,
Veterinarian Boston Bd. of Health.

PAUL CARSON, M. D.,
Boston Port Physician.

CHARLES V. CHAPIN, M. D.,
Supt. Health, Providence, R. I.

W. H. CHAPIN, M. D.,
Springfield.

H. LINCOLN CHASE, M. D.,
Health Officer, Brookline, Mass.

H. W. CLARK,
Chemist, Mass. State Board of Health.

JAMES C. COFFEY,
Ex. Officer Springfield Bd. of Health.

FRANCIS G. CURTIS, M. D.,
Newton.

ELBRIDGE G. CUTLER, M. D.,
Boston.

FRANCIS P. DENNY, M. D.,
Brookline Board Health Bact. Lab.

SAMUEL H. DURGIN, M. D.,
Chairman, Boston Board of Health.

HARRISON P. EDDY,
Worcester Sewage Disposal Plant.

GEORGE H. ELLIS,
Wauwinet Farm.

PROF. HAROLD C. ERNST,
Harvard Medical College.

W. S. EVERETT, M. D.,
Hyde Park.

JAMES B. FIELD, M. D.,
Lowell.

G. W. FITZ, M. D.,
Cambridge.

X. H. GOODNOUGH, C. E.,
Engineer, Mass. State Board Health.

H W. HILL, M. D.,
Boston Board of Health Bact. Lab.

MAY S. HOLMES, M. D.,
Worcester Isolation Hospital.

S. .C KEITH, B. SC.,
Boston.

PROF. L. P. KINNICUTT,
Worcester Polytechnic Institute.

ATHERTON P. MASON, M. D.,
Fitchburg Board of Health Bact. Lab.

JOHN H. McCOLLOM, M. D.,
Boston City Hospital.

WILLIAM H. MITCHELL,
Boston.

FRANK L. MORSE, M. D.,
Medical Inspector, Mass. State Board
of Health.

COL. WILLIAM F. MORSE,
New York.

J. ALBERT C. NYHEN,
Brookline Board of Health Bact. Lab.

E. M. PARKS, M. D.,
New York Board of Health Lab.

AUSTIN PETERS, M. R. C. V. S.,
Mass. State Cattle Dept.

MRS. ELLEN H. RICHARDS,
Mass. Institute Technology.

MARK W. RICHARDSON, M. D.,
Boston.

B. R. RICKARDS, B. S.,
Boston Board of Health Bact. Lab.

PROF. WILLIAM T. SEDGWICK,
Mass. Institute Technology.

T. B. SHEA, M. D.,
Chief Med. Inspector Boston Bd. Health

PROF. THEOBALD SMITH.
Pathologist, Mass. State Board Health.

F. HERBERT SNOW, C. E.,
Brockton.

W. LYMAN UNDERWOOD,
Mass. Institute Technology.

JOHANNA VON WAGNER,
New York.

HENRY P. WALCOTT, M. D.,
Chairman, Mass. State Board Health.

EDWARD R. WARREN,
Boston.

ROBERT SPURR WESTON, S. B.,
Boston.

FRANKLIN W. WHITE, M. D.,
Boston.

Members Massachusetts Association of Boards of Health.

OFFICERS FOR 1903.

President, HENRY P. WALCOTT, M. D.

Vice-Presidents, S. H. DURGIN, M. D., S. W. ABBOTT, M. D.

Treasurer, JAMES B. FIELD, M. D. *Secretary,* JAMES C. COFFEY

Executive Committee — 1902-1904, G L. TOBEY, M. D., W. H. GOVE, W. Y. FOX, M. D., C. A. HICKS, M. D., G. H. ELLIS. 1903-1905, H. C. EMERSON, M. D., D. S. WOODWORTH, M. D., F. W. KENNEDY, M. D., W. S. EVERETT, M. D., W. C. KITE, M. D. Also the officers of the Association, *ex-officio.*

Any person interested in Hygiene may become a member by election at a regular meeting of the Association.

Avon
R. A. Elliott, M. D. 2
F. P. Winfield, M. D. 1

Arlington
E. E. Stickney, M. D. 2

Athol
W. H. Brock

Attleboro
George K. Roberts, M. D. 2

Andover
Charles E. Abbott, M. D. 2

Belmont
W. Lyman Underwood. 1
H. A. Yenetchi, M. D.

Boston
S. W. Abbott, M. D. 13*
Silas H. Ayer, M. D.
J. W. Bartol, M. D.
David D. Brough, M. D. 4
Alex. Burr, M. D. V. 8
J. W. Cosden.
Robert Cox.
B. F. Davenport, M. D.
S. H. Durgin. M. D. 1
H. C. Ernst, M. D.
Langdon Frothingham, M. D. V.
E. F. Gleason, M. D.
Charles Harrington, M. D. 11
Edward M. Hartwell.
Dennis J. Hern. 2
W. L. Hicks.
H. W. Hill, M. D. 5
Everett D. Hooper, M. D.
L. H. Howard, D. V. S.
Thomas Jordan. 7
S. C. Keith, S. B.
W. H. Mitchell.
Frank L. Morse, M. D. 4*
Austin Peters, D. V. S. 14*
E. B. Phelps, S. B.
E. L. Pilsbury. 2
W. H. Prescott, M. D.
Mrs. Ellen H. Richards.
R. R. Rickards, S. B. 5
Howard P. Rogers. M. D. V.
Prof. W. T. Sedgwick.
T. B. Shea, M. D. 4
Agnes C. Vietor, M. D.
Robert S. Weston, S. B.
George M. Whitaker.
George Whiting.
C. E. A. Winslow, S. B.
John F. Worcester, M. D.

Brighton
E. S. Hatch, M. D.
Horace E. Marion, M. D.
Otis H. Marion, M. D.
F. W. Rice, M. D.

Brookline
H. L. Chase, M. D. 6
James M. Codman, Jr. 1
Nathaniel Conant. 2
Francis P. Denny, M. D 5
Robert W. Hastings, M. D.
Edward A. McEttrick. 13
J. Albert C. Nyhen. 5
F. H. Osgood, M. R. C. V. S. 8, 11
Charles H. Pearson. 2
Willard E. Ward. 15
John K. Whiting.

Brockton
George E. Bolling. 5
F. H. Burnett, M. D.
Charles H. Cary. 3
J. H. Lawrence, M. D. 1
F. J. Ripley, M. D.
F. Herbert Snow, C. E.
S. Alfred Spear. 12

Cambridge
Lewis L. Bryant, M. D.
E. R. Cogswell, M. D.
John Crawford.
Edwin Farnham, M. D. 4
Charles Harris.
John G. Hildreth, M. D.
Goodwin A. Isenberg. 2
Ross McPherson, M. D.
William R. Peabody.
J. Arnold Rockwell, M. D.
E. H. Stevens, M. D.
H. P. Walcott, M. D. 1*
Roswell Wetherbee, M. D. 2
Charles F. Whiting.

Charlestown
C. H. Hood.

Chelsea
Frank E. Winslow. 3

Clinton
W. P. Bowers, M. D.
C. C. Crowley.
C. L. French, M. D. 1
J. J. Goodwin, M. D.
E. H. Mackay, M. D. 10
James H. McGrath. 2
G. L. Tobey, M. D. 2

Cohasset
Oliver H. Howe, M. D.

Concord
John M. Keyes. 1
Thomas Todd. 2

Dedham
E. W. Finn, M. D. 2

Duxbury
Alfred E. Green. 1
N. K. Noyes, M. D.

East Bridgewater
A. L. Shirley, M. D.

Everett
R. E. Brown, M. D.
George W. S. Dockum. 2, 13
A. A. Jackson, M. D.
E. J. Newton, M. D. 2
N. B. Smith. 1
George E. Whitehill, M. D.
EJ W. Young, M. D.

Fall River
Charles A. Hicks, M. D. 2

Falmouth
Russell S. Nye. 2
Asa R. Pattee, M. D. 2
T. L. Swift, M. D. 1

Fitchburg
J. F. Bresnahan. 7
E. L. Fiske, M. D. 1
Henry M. Francis. 2
Fred R. Houghton, 3, 6
A. P. Mason M. D. 5
Charles H. Rice, M. D.
D. S. Woodworth, M. D.

Framingham
N. I. Bowditch.
Charles M. Hargraves. 2, 13

Gloucester
H. L. Belden.

Haverhill
J. F. Crostan, M D. 2

Holyoke
J. J. Linehan. 2, 6
A. B. Wetherell, M. D. 1
Frank A. Woods, M. D. 2, 13

Hingham
Charles H. Marble. 1
J. Winthrop Spooner, M. D. 2

1, Chairman, Bd. Health; 2, Member; 3, Clerk; 4, Medical Officer; 5, Bacteriologist; 6, Agent; 7, Sanitary Inspector; 8, Inspector of Animals; 9. Quarantine Officer; 10, City Physician; 11. Milk Inspector; 12, Supt. of Health; 13, Secretary; 14, State Cattle Dept.; 15, Disinfector; State Officials are marked, *.

List of Members — Continued.

Hyde Park
Willard S. Everett, M. D. 2
Edwin C. Farwell.
William W. Scott. 2
Charles F. Stack, M. D. 1

Hanover
A. L. McMillan, M. D.

Jamaica Plain
Theobald Smith, M. D. 5*

Lancaster
Chester C. Beckley, M. D. 2
Allen G. Butterick. 2
Albert E. Harriman, M. D. 1

Lincoln
Stephen H. Blodgett, M. D. 2

Lexington
George O. Whitney.

Lawrence
William Berger.
Charles E. Birtwell, M. D.
A. D. V. Bourget. 1
T. J. Daly, M. D.
George S. Fuller, D. V. S.
F. W. Kennedy, M. D. 2
John A. Magee, M. D.
Victor A. Reed, M. D.
George W. Smith. 6
J. F. Winchester, M. D. 8

Leominster
C. E. Bigelow, M. D. 1
Fredson N. Grey. 2
H. N. Spring. 2, 6.
A. L. Whitney.

Lowell
James B. Field, M. D.
J. Arthur Gage, M. D.
Thomas F. Harrington, M. D.
Guy Holbrook, M. D. 1
William B. Jackson, M. D. 2
H. H. Knapp. 6
W. P. Lawler, M. D.
J. N. Marston, M. D.
Thomas B. Smith, M. D. 5

Lynn
R. E. Hillard. 2
W. E. Holbrook, M. D. 2
W. R. Woodfall, M. D. 1

Malden
C. W. McClearn, M. D. 1

Marshfield
C. W. Stodder, M. D. 2

Melrose
John Timlin, M. D. 2

Melrose Highlands
Clarence P. Holden, M. D.
Paul H. Provandie, M. D. 1

Milton
A. W. Draper, M. D. V. 2
Charles R. Gilchrist, M. D. 1
W. C. Kite, M. D.
Jacob S. Lincoln. 2
Samuel D. Parker.

Nahant
Joseph T. Wilson. 1

Needham
A. E. Miller, M. D.
A. M. Miller, M. D.

New Bedford
J. T. Bullard, M. D. 2
E. H. Gammons.
W. G. Kirschbaum. 1
L. H. Richardson. 7
Manuel V. Sylvia, M. D. 2, 9

Newport, R. I.
Joseph W. Sampson.

Norwood
E. C. Norton, M. D.
Lyman F. Bigelow, M. D. 1

Newton
John C. Brimblecom
W. F. Harbach. 2
Arthur Hudson. 5, 11.
A. Stanton Hudson, M. D.
Harry A. Stone. 3, 6
E. R. Utley, M. D. 10

New York, N. Y.
Col. W. F. Morse.

No. Brookfield
T. J. Garrigan, M. D.

No. Abington
F. G. Wheatley, M. D.

No. Andover
Charles P. Morrill, M. D.

Palmer
J. P. Schneider, M. D. 1

Plymouth
W. G. Brown, M. D.

Providence, R. I.
Ernest F. Badger.
C. V. Chapin, M. D. 12
F. P. Gorham.
Gardner T. Swarts, M. D. 13*

Rockland
J. C. Batchelder, M. D.
Gilman Osgood, M. D.

Salem
C. A. Ahearne, M. D.
G. Arthur Bodwell. 2
Wm. H. Colbert.
Joseph A. Fitzgerald. 1
W. H. Gove.
Raymond L. Newcomb. 3, 4
A. N. Sargent, M. D.
Benj. R. Symonds, M. D. 2

Somerville
A. C. Aldrich. 2
Robert Burns.
Allen F. Carpenter. 1
W. H. Hitchings, V. S.
F. L. Lowell, M. D.
A. E. Merrill, M. D.
A. R. Perry, M. D.
Edmund F. Sparrow. 2

So. Framingham
L. M. Palmer, M. D.

Springfield
A. L. Brown, M. D. 2
T. J. Collins. 1
H. C. Emerson, M. D. 3,
James Kimball. 6
B. D. Pierce, M. D.
J. C. Rausehousen.
S. J. Russell, M. D. 10

Southbridge
Humphrey C. Moynihan. 1
Joseph G. E Page, M. D. 13

Three Rivers
Geo. J. Hebert. 2
S. O. Miller, M. D.

Taunton
Charles H. Macomber. 2
Edward J. Shannahan, M. D. 2
Henry H. Wilcox. 7

West Newton
Francis G. Curtis, M. D. 1
Geo. H. Ellis.

Waltham
H. D. Chadwick, M. D.
C. J. McCormick, M. D.
Marshall J. Mosher, M. D. 1
Charles A. Willis, M. D.

Watertown
Sumner Coolidge, M. D.
Vivian Daniel, M. D. 2
Julian A. Mead, M. D.

Waverley
L. B. Clark, M. D.

Westboro
C. S. Henry. 2
Charles S. Knight, M. D. 2

Weston
F. T. Hyde, M. D. 2
F. W. Jackson, M. D.
S. Sanford Orr, M. D.

Whitman
C. E. Lovell, M. D. 2
A. A. MacKeen, M. D. 1

Winchendon
F. W. Russell, M. D. 1

Winthrop
A. B. Dorman, M. D.
H. J. Soule, M. D.

Woburn
George Buchanan. 2
Dennis S. Doherty 2
William H. Kelliher, M. D. 1

Worcester
F. H. Baker, M. D. 5
Geo. W. Batchelder. 2
W. T. Clark, M. D. 1, 10
James C. Coffey. 2
May S. Holmes, M. D.
Prof. L P. Kinnicutt.
W. W. McKibben M. D.
L. F. Woodward, M. D.

Minneapolis, Minn.
F. F. Wesbrook, M. D. 5*
(Honorary Member)

Chairmen are requested to send to the Managing Editor corrections or changes desired in the names, addresses or (where members are connected with a Board of Health) in the titles given in this list.

Contributors of Regular Papers.

SAMUEL W. ABBOTT, M. D.,
Sec. Mass. State Bd. of Health.

DAVID D. BROUGH, M.D.
Asst. Med. Inspec. Boston Bd. Health.

ALEXANDER BURR, D. V. S.,
Veterinarian, Boston Bd. of Health.

PAUL CARSON, M. D.,
Boston Port Physician.

CHARLES V. CHAPIN, M. D.,
Supt. Health, Providence, R. I.

W. H. CHAPIN, M. D.,
Springfield.

H. LINCOLN CHASE, M. D.,
Agent, Brookline Bd. of Health.

H. W. CLARK,
Chemist, Mass. State Bd. of Health.

JAMES C. COFFEY,
Ex. Officer Worcester Bd. of Health.

FRANCIS G. CURTIS, M. D.,
Newton.

ELBRIDGE G. CUTLER, M. D.,
Boston.

FRANCIS P. DENNY, M. D.,
Brookline Bd. Health Bact. Lab.

SAMUEL H. DURGIN, M. D.,
Chairman, Boston Board of Health.

HARRISON P. EDDY,
Worcester Sewage Disposal Plant.

GEORGE H. ELLIS,
Wauwinet Farm.

PROF. HAROLD C. ERNST,
Harvard Medical College.

W. S. EVERETT, M. D.,
Hyde Park.

JAMES B. FIELD, M. D.,
Lowell.

G. W. FITZ, M. D.,
Cambridge.

X. H. GOODNOUGH, C. E.,
Engineer, Mass. State Bd. of Health.

ROBERT W. HASTINGS, M. D.,
Brookline.

H W. HILL, M. D.,
Boston Bd. of Health Bact. .Lab.

MAY S. HOLMES, M. D.,
Worcester Isolation Hospital.

S. C. KEITH, S. B.,
Boston.

PROF. L. P. KINNICUTT,
Worcester Polytechnic Institute.

ATHERTON P. MASON, M. D.,
Fitchburg Bd. of Health Bact. Lab.

JOHN H. MCCOLLOM, M. D.,
Boston City Hospital.

WILLIAM H. MITCHELL,
Boston.

FRANK L. MORSE, M. D.,
Med. Inspec., Mass. State Bd. of Health.

COL. WILLIAM F. MORSE,
New York.

J. ALBERT C. NYHEN,
Brookline Bd. of Health Bact. Lab.

W. H. PARK, M. D.,
New York Board of Health Lab.

AUSTIN PETERS. R. M. C. V. S.,
Mass. State Cattle Dept.

MRS. ELLEN H. RICHARDS,
Mass. Institute Technology.

MARK W. RICHARDSON, M. D.,
Boston.

B. R. RICKARDS, S. B.,
Boston Bd. of Health Bact. Lab.

PROF. WILLIAM T. SEDGWICK,
Mass. Institute Technology.

T. B. SHEA, M. D.,
Chief Med. Inspec., Boston Bd. Health.

PROF. THEOBALD SMITH,
Pathologist, Mass. State Bd. Health.

F. HERBERT SNOW, C. E.,
Brockton.

W. LYMAN UNDERWOOD,
Mass. Institute Technology.

JOHANNA VON WAGNER,
Yonkers, N Y.

HENRY P. WALCOTT, M. D.,
Chairman, Mass. State Bd. Health.

EDWARD R. WARREN,
Boston.

ROBERT SPURR WESTON, S. B.,
Boston.

FRANKLIN W. WHITE, M. D.,
Boston.

President, HENRY P. WALCOTT, M. D.

Vice-Presidents, S. H. DURGIN, M. D., S. W. ABBOTT, M. D.

Treasurer, JAMES B. FIELD, M. D.　　*Secretary*, JAMES C. COFFEY

Executive Committee — 1903-1904, G. L. TOBEY, M. D., W. H. GOVE, C. A. HICKS, M. D., G. H. ELLIS, C. V. CHAPIN, M. D., 1903-1905, H. C. EMERSON, M. D., D. S. WOODWORTH, M. D., F. W. KENNEDY, M. D., W. S. EVERETT, M. D., W. C. KITE, M. D.　Also the officers of the Association, *ex-officio*.

Any person interested in Hygiene may become a member by election at a regular meeting of the Association.

Ashby
E. A. Hubbard, M. D.

Avon
R. A. Elliott, M. D. 2
E. P. Linfield, M. D. 1

Arlington
E. E. Stickney, M. D. 2

Athol
W. H. Brock

Attleboro
George K. Roberts, M. D. 2

Andover
Charles E. Abbott, M. D. 2

Belmont
W. Lyman Underwood. 1
H. A. Yenetchi, M. D.

Boston
S. W. Abbott, M. D. 13*
Silas H. Ayer, M. D.
J. W. Bartol, M. D.
David D. Brough, M. D. 4
Alex. Burr, M. D. V. 8
D. A. Cheever, M. D.
J. W. Cosden.
Robert Cox.
B. F. Davenport, M. D.
S. H. Durgin. M. D. 1
H. C. Ernst, M. D.
Langdon Frothingham, M. D. V.
E. F. Gleason, M. D.
Charles Harrington, M. D. 11
Edward M. Hartwell.
Dennis J. Hern. 2
W. L. Hicks.
H. W. Hill, M. D. 5
Everett D. Hooper, M. D.
L. H. Howard, D. V. S.
Thomas Jordan. 7
S. C. Keith, S. B.
W. H. Mitchell.
Frank L. Morse, M. D. 4*
Austin Peters, D. V. S. 14*
E. B. Phelps, S. B.
E. L. Pilsbury. 2
W. H. Prescott, M. D.
Mrs. Ellen H. Richards.
R. R. Rickards, S. B. 5
Howard P. Rogers. M. D. V.
Prof. W. T. Sedgwick.
T. B. Shea, M. D. 4
Agnes C. Vietor, M. D.
Robert S. Weston, S. B.
George M. Whitaker.
George Whiting.
C. E. A. Winslow, S. B.
John F. Worcester, M. D.

Bondsville
D. B. Sullivan, M. D.

Brighton
E. S. Hatch, M. D.
Horace E. Marion, M. D.
Otis H. Marion, M D.
F. W. Rice, M. D.

Brookline
H. L. Chase, M. D. 6
James M. Codman, Jr. 1
Nathaniel Conant. 2
Francis P. Denny, M. D. 5
Robert W. Hastings, M. D.
Edward A. McEttrick. 13
J. Albert C. Nyhen. 5
F. H. Osgood, M. R. C. V. S. 8, 11
Charles H. Pearson. 2
H. Carlton Smith, M. D.
Willard E. Ward. 15
John K. Whiting.

Brockton
George E. Bolling. 5
F. H. Burnett, M. D.
Charles H. Cary. 3
J. H. Lawrence, M. D. 1
A. W. Packard.
F. J. Ripley, M. D.
F. Herbert Snow, C. E.
S. Alfred Spear. 12

Cambridge
Lewis L. Bryant, M. D.
E. R. Cogswell, M. D.
John Crawford.
Edwin Farnham, M. D. 4
Charles Harris.
John G. Hildreth, M. D.
Goodwin A. Isenberg. 1
Ross McPherson, M. D.
J. Arnold Rockwell, M. D.
E. H. Stevens, M. D.
H. P. Walcott, M. D. 1*
Roswell Wetherbee, M. D. 2
Charles F. Whiting.

Charlestown
C. H. Hood.
Nelson M. Wood, M. D.

Chelsea
Frank E. Winslow. 3

Clinton
W. P. Bowers, M. D.
C. C. Crowley.
C. L. French, M. D. 1
J. J. Goodwin, M. D.
E. H. Mackay, M. D. 10
James H. McGrath. 2
G. L. Tobey, M. D. 2

Cohasset
Oliver H. Howe, M. D.
Herbert A. Tilden.

Concord
John M. Keyes. 1
Thomas Todd. 2

Dedham
E. W. Finn, M. D. 2

Duxbury
Alfred E. Green. 1
N. K. Noyes, M. D.

East Bridgewater
A. L. Shirley, M. D.

Everett
R. E. Brown, M. D.
George W. S. Dockum. 2, 13
A. A. Jackson, M. D.
E. J. Newton, M. D. 2
N. B. Smith. 1
George E. Whitehill, M. D.
E. W. Young, M. D.

Fall River
Charles A. Hicks, M. D. 2

Falmouth
Russell S. Nye. 2
Asa R. Pattee, M. D. 2
T. L. Swift, M. D. 1

Fitchburg
J. F. Bresnahan. 7
E. L. Fiske, M. D. 1
Henry M. Francis. 2
Fred R. Houghton. 3, 6
A. P. Mason. M. D. 5
Charles H. Rice, M. D.
D. S. Woodworth, M. D.

Framingham
N. I. Bowditch.
Charles M. Hargraves. 2, 13

Gloucester
H. L. Belden.

Haverhill
J. F. Crostan, M D. 2

Holyoke
J. J. Linehan. 2, 6
A. B. Wetherell, M. D. 1
Frank A. Woods, M. D. 2, 13

Hingham
Charles H. Marble. 1
J. Winthrop Spooner, M. D. 2

1, Chairman, Bd. Health ; 2, Member; 3, Clerk ; 4, Medical Officer ; 5, Bacteriologist; 6, Agent ; 7, Sanitary Inspector ; 8, Inspector of Animals ; 9, Quarantine Officer; 10, City Physician; 11, Milk Inspector ; 12, Supt. of Health; 13, Secretary ; 14, State Cattle Dept. ; 15, Disinfector.
* State Officials.

Hyde Park
Willard S. Everett, M. D. 2
Edwin C. Farwell.
William W. Scott. 2
Charles F. Stack, M. D. 1

Hanover
A. L. McMillan, M. D.

Jamaica Plain
Theobald Smith, M. D. 5*

Lancaster
Chester C. Beckley, M. D. 2
Allen G. Butterick. 2
Albert E. Harriman, M. D. 1

Lincoln
Stephen H. Blodgett, M. D. 2

Lexington
George O. Whitney.

Lawrence
William Berger.
Charles E. Birtwell, M. D.
A. D. V. Bourget. 1
John T. Cahill, M. D.
T. J. Daly, M. D.
George S. Fuller, D. V. S.
F. W. Kennedy, M. D. 2
John A. Magee, M. D.
Victor A. Reed, M. D.
George W. Smith. 6
J. F. Winchester, V. S. 8

Leominster
C. E. Bigelow, M. D. 1
Fredson N. Grey. 2
H. N. Spring. 2, 6.

Lowell
James B. Field, M. D.
J. Arthur Gage, M. D.
Thomas F. Harrington, M. D.
Guy Holbrook, M. D. 1
William B. Jackson, M. D. 2
H. H. Knapp. 6
W. P. Lawler, M. D.
J. N. Marston, M. D.
Thomas B. Smith, M. D. 5

Lynn
R. E. Hillard. 2
W. E. Holbrook, M. D. 2
W. R. Woodfall, M. D. 1

Malden
C. W. McClearn, M. D. 1

Marshfield
C. W. Stodder, M. D. 2

Melrose
John Timlin, M. D. 2

Melrose Highlands
Clarence P. Holden, M. D.
Paul H. Provandie, M. D. 1

Milton
A. W. Draper, M. D. V. 2
Charles R. Gilchrist, M. D. 1
W. C. Kite, M. D.
Jacob S. Lincoln. 2
Samuel D. Parker.

Nahant
Joseph T. Wilson. 1

Needham
A. E. Miller, M. D.
A. M. Miller, M. D.

New Bedford
J. T. Bullard, M. D. 2
E. H. Gammons.
W. G. Kirschbaum. 1
L. H. Richardson. 7
Manuel V. Sylvia, M. D. 2, 9

Newport, R. I.
Joseph W. Sampson.

Norwood
E. C. Norton, M. D.

Newton
W. F. Harbach. 2
Arthur Hudson. 5, 11.
A. Stanton Hudson, M. D.
Harry A. Stone. 3, 6
E. R. Utley, M. D. 10

New York, N. Y.
Col. W. F. Morse.

No. Brookfield
T. J. Garrigan, M. D.

No. Abington
F. G. Wheatley, M. D.

Palmer
J. P. Schneider, M. D. 1

Plymouth
W. G. Brown, M. D.

Providence, R. I.
C. V. Chapin, M. D. 12
F. P. Gorham.
Gardner T. Swarts, M. D. 13*

Rockland
J. C. Batchelder, M. D.
Gilman Osgood, M. D.

Salem
G. Arthur Bodwell. 2
Wm. H. Colbert.
Joseph A. Fitzgerald. 1
W. H. Gove.
Raymond L. Newcomb. 3, 4
A. N. Sargent, M. D.
Benj. R. Symonds, M. D. 2

Somerville
A. C. Aldrich. 2
Robert Burns.
Allen F. Carpenter. 1
W. H. Hitchings, V. S.
F. L. Lowell, M. D.
A. E. Merrill, M. D.
A. R. Perry, M. D.
Edmund F. Sparrow. 2

So. Framingham
L. M. Palmer, M. D.

Springfield
A. L. Brown, M. D. 2
T. J. Collins. 1
H. C. Emerson, M. D. 3,
James Kimball. 6
B. D. Pierce, M. D.
J. C. Rausehousen.

Southbridge
Humphrey C. Moynihan. 1
Joseph G. E. Page, M. D. 13

Three Rivers
Geo. J. Hebert. 2
S. O. Miller, M. D.

Taunton
Charles H. Macomber. 2
Edward J. Shannahan, M. D. 2
Henry H. Wilcox. 7

West Newton
Francis G. Curtis, M. D. 1
Geo. H. Ellis.

Waltham
H. D. Chadwick, M. D.
C. J. McCormick, M. D.
Marshall J. Mosher, M. D. 1
Charles A. Willis, M. D.

Watertown
Sumner Coolidge, M. D.
Vivian Daniel, M. D. 2
Julian A. Mead, M. D.

Waverley
L. B. Clark, M. D.

Westboro
C. S. Henry. 2
Charles S. Knight, M. D. 2

Weston
F. T. Hyde, M. D. 2
F. W. Jackson, M. D.
S. Sanford Orr, M. D.

Whitman
C. E. Lovell, M. D. 2
A. A. MacKeen, M. D. 1

Winchendon
F. W. Russell, M. D. 1

Winthrop
A. B. Dorman, M. D.
H. J. Soule, M. D.

Woburn
George Buchanan. 2
Dennis S. Doherty 2
William H. Kelliher, M. D. 1

Worcester
F. H. Baker, M. D. 5
Geo. W. Batchelder. 2
W. T. Clark, M. D. 1, 10
James C. Coffey. 2
May S. Holmes, M. D.
Prof. L. P. Kinnicutt.
W. W. McKibben, M. D.
L. F. Woodward, M. D.

Minneapolis, Minn.
F. F. Wesbrook, M. D. 5*
(Honorary Member)

Members are requested to send to the Managing Editor corrections or changes desired in the names, addresses or (where members are connected with a Board of Health) in the titles given in this list.

Contributors of Regular Papers.

SAMUEL W. ABBOTT, M. D.,
Sec. Mass. State Bd. of Health.

DAVID D. BROUGH, M.D.
Asst. Med. Inspec. Boston Bd. Health.

ALEXANDER BURR, D. V. S.,
Veterinarian, Boston Bd. of Health.

PAUL CARSON, M. D.,
Boston Port Physician.

CHARLES V. CHAPIN, M. D.,
Supt. Health, Providence, R. I.

W. H. CHAPIN, M. D.,
Springfield.

H. LINCOLN CHASE, M. D.,
Agent, Brookline Bd. of Health.

H. W. CLARK,
Chemist, Mass. State Bd. of Health.

JAMES C. COFFEY,
Ex. Officer Worcester Bd. of Health.

FRANCIS G. CURTIS, M. D.,
Newton.

ELBRIDGE G. CUTLER, M. D.,
Boston.

FRANCIS P. DENNY, M. D.,
Brookline Bd. Health Bact. Lab.

SAMUEL H. DURGIN, M. D.,
Chairman, Boston Board of Health.

HARRISON P. EDDY,
Worcester Sewage Disposal Plant.

GEORGE H. ELLIS,
Wauwinet Farm.

PROF. HAROLD C. ERNST,
Harvard Medical College.

W. S. EVERETT, M. D.,
Hyde Park.

JAMES B. FIELD, M. D.,
Lowell.

G. W. FITZ, M. D.,
Cambridge.

X. H. GOODNOUGH, C. E.,
Engineer, Mass. State Bd. of Health.

CHARLES HARRINGTON, M. D.
Milk Inspector, Boston Bd. of Health.

ROBERT W. HASTINGS, M. D.,
Brookline.

H. W. HILL, M. D.,
Boston Bd. of Health Bact. Lab.

MAY S. HOLMES, M. D.,
Worcester Isolation Hospital.

S. C. KEITH, S. B.,
Boston.

PROF. L. P. KINNICUTT,
Worcester Polytechnic Institute.

ATHERTON P. MASON, M. D.,
Fitchburg Bd. of Health Bact. Lab.

JOHN H. McCOLLOM, M. D.,
Boston City Hospital.

WILLIAM H. MITCHELL,
Boston.

FRANK L. MORSE, M. D.,
Med. Inspec., Mass. State Bd. of Health.

COL. WILLIAM F. MORSE,
New York.

J. ALBERT C. NYHEN,
Brookline Bd. of Health Bact. Lab.

W. H. PARK, M. D.,
New York Board of Health Lab.

AUSTIN PETERS. M. R. C. V. S.,
Mass. State Cattle Dept.

MRS. ELLEN H. RICHARDS,
Mass. Institute Technology.

MARK W. RICHARDSON, M. D.,
Boston.

B. R. RICKARDS, S. B.,
Boston Bd. of Health Bact. Lab.

PROF. WILLIAM T. SEDGWICK,
Mass. Institute Technology.

T. B. SHEA, M. D.,
Chief Med. Inspec., Boston Bd. Health.

PROF. THEOBALD SMITH,
Pathologist, Mass. State Bd. Health.

F. HERBERT SNOW, C. E.,
Brockton.

W. LYMAN UNDERWOOD,
Mass. Institute Technology.

JOHANNA VON WAGNER,
Yonkers, N Y.

HENRY P. WALCOTT, M. D.,
Chairman, Mass. State Bd. Health.

EDWARD R. WARREN,
Boston.

ROBERT SPURR WESTON, S. B.,
Boston.

FRANKLIN W. WHITE, M. D.
Boston.

Contributors of Regular Papers

AT THE ASSOCIATION MEETINGS.

SAMUEL W. ABBOTT, M. D.,
Sec. Mass. State Bd. of Health.

DAVID D. BROUGH, M.D.
Med. Inspec. Boston Bd. Health.

ALEXANDER BURR, D. V. S.,
Veterinarian, Boston Bd. of Health.

PAUL CARSON, M. D.,
Boston Port Physician.

CHARLES V. CHAPIN, M. D.,
Supt. Health, Providence, R. I.

W. H. CHAPIN, M. D.,
Springfield.

H. LINCOLN CHASE, M. D.,
Agent, Brookline Bd. of Health.

H. W. CLARK,
Chemist, Mass. State Bd. of Health.

JAMES C. COFFEY,
Ex. Officer Worcester Bd. of Health

FRANCIS G. CURTIS, M. D.,
Newton.

ELBRIDGE G. CUTLER, M. D.,
Boston.

FRANCIS P. DENNY, M. D.,
Brookline Bd. Health Bact. Lab.

SAMUEL H. DURGIN, M. D.,
Chairman, Boston Board of Health.

HARRISON P. EDDY,
Worcester Sewage Disposal Plant.

GEORGE H. ELLIS,
Wauwinet Farm.

PROF. HAROLD C. ERNST,
Harvard Medical School.

W. S. EVERETT, M. D.,
Hyde Park.

JAMES B. FIELD, M. D.,
Lowell.

G. W. FITZ, M. D.,
Cambridge.

X H. GOODNOUGH, C. E.,
Engineer, Mass. State Bd. of Health.

CHARLES HARRINGTON, M. D.
Milk Inspector, Boston Bd. of Health.

ROBERT W. HASTINGS, M. D.,
Brookline.

H W. HILL, M. D.,
Boston Bd. of Health Bact. Lab.

MAY S. HOLMES, M. D.,
Worcester Isolation Hospital.

S. C. KEITH, S. B.,
Boston.

PROF. L. P. KINNICUTT,
Worcester Polytechnic Institute.

ATHERTON P. MASON, M. D.,
Fitchburg Bd. of Health Bact. Lab.

JOHN H. MCCOLLOM, M. D.,
Boston City Hospital.

WILLIAM H. MITCHELL,
Boston.

FRANK L. MORSE, M. D.,
Med. Inspec., Mass. State Bd. of Health.

COL. WILLIAM F. MORSE,
New York.

J. ALBERT C. NYHEN,
Brookline Bd. of Health Bact. Lab.

W. H. PARK, M. D.,
New York Board of Health Lab.

AUSTIN PETERS. M. R. C. V. S.,
Mass. State Cattle Dept.

MRS. ELLEN H. RICHARDS,
Mass. Institute Technology.

MARK W. RICHARDSON, M. D.,
Boston.

B. R. RICKARDS, S. B.,
Boston Bd. of Health Bact. Lab.

PROF. WILLIAM T. SEDGWICK,
Mass. Institute Technology.

T. B. SHEA, M. D.,
Member, Boston Bd. Health.

PROF. THEOBALD SMITH,
Pathologist, Mass. State Bd. Health.

F. HERBERT SNOW, C. E.,
Brockton.

W. LYMAN UNDERWOOD,
Mass. Institute Technology.

JOHANNA VON WAGNER,
Yonkers, N Y.

HENRY P. WALCOTT, M. D.,
Chairman, Mass. State Bd. Health.

EDWARD R. WARREN,
Boston.

ROBERT SPURR WESTON, S. B.,
Boston.

FRANKLIN W. WHITE, M. D.
Boston.

C. E. A. WINSLOW, M. SC.,
Mass. Inst. Technology.

President, HENRY P. WALCOTT, M. D.

Vice-Presidents, S. H. DURGIN, M. D., S. W. ABBOTT, M. D.

Treasurer, JAMES B. FIELD, M. D.   *Secretary*, JAMES C. COFFEY

Executive Committee — 1903-1904, G. L. TOBEY, M.D., W. H. GOVE, C. A. HICKS, M. D., G. H. ELLIS, C. V. CHAPIN, M. D., 1903-1905, H. C. EMERSON, M. D., D. S. WOODWORTH, M. D., F. W. KENNEDY, M. D., W. S. EVERETT, M. D., W. C. KITE, M. D. Also the officers of the Association, *ex-officio*.

Any person interested in Hygiene may become a member by election at a regular meeting of the Association.

Ashby
E. A. Hubbard, M. D.

Avon
R. A. Elliott, M. D. 2
E. P. Linfield, M. D. 1

Arlington
E. E. Stickney, M. D. 2

Athol
W. H. Brock

Attleboro
George K. Roberts, M. D. 2

Andover
Charles E. Abbott, M. D. 2

Belmont
W. Lyman Underwood. 1
H. A. Yenetchi, M. D.

Boston
S. W. Abbott, M. D. 13*
Silas H. Ayer, M. D.
J. W. Bartol, M. D.
David D. Brough, M. D. 4
Alex. Burr, M. D. V. 8
D. A. Cheever, M. D.
J. W. Cosden.
Robert Cox.
B. F. Davenport, M. D.
S. H. Durgin. M. D. 1
H. C. Ernst, M. D.
Langdon Frothingham, M. D. V.
E. F. Gleason, M. D.
Charles Harrington, M. D. 11
Edward M. Hartwell.
Dennis J. Hern. 2
W. L. Hicks.
H. W. Hill, M. D. 5
Everett D. Hooper, M. D.
L. H. Howard, D. V. S.
Thomas Jordan. 7
S. C. Keith, S. B.
W. H. Mitchell.
Frank L. Morse, M. D. 4*
Austin Peters, D. V. S. 14*
E. B. Phelps, S. B.
E. L. Pilsbury.
W. H. Prescott, M. D.
Mrs. Ellen H. Richards.
R. R. Rickards, S. B. 5
Geo. B. Robbins.
Howard P. Rogers. M. D. V.
Prof. W. T. Sedgwick.
T. B. Shea, M. D. 2
Agnes C. Vietor, M. D.
Robert S. Weston, S. B.
George M. Whitaker, 16
George Whiting.
C. E. A. Winslow, S. B.
John F. Worcester, M. D.

Bondsville
D. B. Sullivan, M. D.

Brighton
E. S. Hatch, M. D.
Horace E. Marion, M. D.
Otis H. Marion, M. D.
F. W. Rice, M. D.

Brookline
H. L. Chase, M. D. 6
James M. Codman, Jr. 1
Nathaniel Conant. 2
Francis P. Denny, M. D. 5
Robert W. Hastings, M. D.
Edward A. McEttrick. 13
J. Albert C. Nyhen. 5
F. H. Osgood, M. R. C. V. S. 8, 11
H. Carlton Smith, 17
Willard E. Ward. 15
John K. Whiting.

Brockton
George E. Bolling. 5
F. H. Burnett, M. D.
Charles H. Cary. 3
J. H. Lawrence, M. D. 1
A. W. Packard.
F. J. Ripley, M. D.
F. Herbert Snow, C. E.
S. Alfred Spear. 12

Cambridge
Lewis L. Bryant, M. D.
E. R. Cogswell, M. D.
John Crawford.
Edwin Farnham, M. D. 4
Charles Harris.
John G. Hildreth, M. D.
Goodwin A. Isenberg. 1
Ross McPherson, M. D.
J. Arnold Rockwell, M. D.
E. H. Stevens, M. D.
H. P. Walcott, M. D. 1*
Roswell Wetherbee, M. D. 2
Charles F. Whiting.

Charlestown
C. H. Hood.
Nelson M. Wood, M. D.

Chelsea
Frank E. Winslow. 3

Clinton
W. P. Bowers, M. D.
C. C. Crowley.
C. L. French, M. D. 1
J. J. Goodwin, M. D.
E. H. Mackay, M. D. 10
James H. McGrath. 2
G. L. Tobey, M. D. 2

Cohasset
Oliver H. Howe, M. D.
Herbert A. Tilden.

Concord
John M. Keyes. 1
Thomas Todd. 2

Dedham
E. W. Finn, M. D. 2

Duxbury
Alfred E. Green. 1
N. K. Noyes, M. D.

East Bridgewater
A. L. Shirley, M. D.

Everett
R. E. Brown, M.D.
George W. S. Dockum. 2, 13
A. A. Jackson, M. D.
E. J. Newton, M. D. 2
N. B. Smith. 1
George E. Whitehill, M. D.
E. W. Young, M. D.

Fall River
Charles A. Hicks, M. D. 2

Falmouth
Russell S. Nye. 2
Asa R. Pattee, M. D. 2
T. L. Swift, M. D. 1

Fitchburg
J. F. Bresnahan. 7
E. L. Fiske, M. D. 1
Henry M. Francis. 2
Fred R. Houghton. 3, 6
A. P. Mason M. D. 5
Charles H. Rice, M. D.
D. S. Woodworth, M. D.

Framingham
N. I. Bowditch.
Charles M. Hargraves. 2, 13

Gloucester
H. L. Belden.

Haverhill
J. F. Crostan, M. D. 2

Holyoke
J. J. Linehan. 2, 6
A. B. Wetherell, M. D. 1
Frank A. Woods, M. D. 2, 13

Hingham
Charles H. Marble. 1
J. Winthrop Spooner, M. D. 2

1, Chairman, Bd. Health ; 2, Member ; 3, Clerk ; 4, Medical Officer ; 5 Bacteriologist ; 6, Agent ; 7, Sanitary Inspector ; 8, Inspector of Animals ; 9, Quarantine Officer ; 10, City Physician ; 11, Milk Inspector ; 12, Supt. of Health ; 13, Secretary ; 14, State Cattle Dept. ; 15, Disinfector ; 16, U. S. Dairy Inspector ; 17, Chemist.
* State Officials.

Hyde Park
Edwin C. Farwell.
John A. Morgan, M. D.
William W. Scott. 2
Charles F. Stack, M. D. 1

Hanover
A. L. McMillan, M. D.

Jamaica Plain
Theobald Smith, M. D. 5*

Lancaster
Chester C. Beckley, M. D. 2
Allen G. Butterick. 2
Albert E. Harriman, M. D. 1

Lincoln
Stephen H. Blodgett, M. D. 2
Joseph S. Hart, M. D.

Lexington
George O. Whitney.

Lawrence
William Berger.
Charles E. Birtwell, M. D.
A. D. V. Bourget. 1
John T. Cahill, M. D.
T. J. Daly, M. D.
George S. Fuller, D. V. S.
Stephen de M. Gage. 5 *
F. W. Kennedy, M. D. 2
John A. Magee, M. D.
Victor A. Reed, M. D.
George W. Smith. 6
J. F. Winchester, V. S. 8

Leominster
C. E. Bigelow, M. D. 1
Fredson N. Grey. 2
H. N. Spring. 2, 6.

Lowell
William C. Doherty.
James B. Field, M. D.
J. Arthur Gage, M. D.
Thomas F. Harrington, M. D.
Leonard Huntress, M. D.
William B. Jackson, M. D. 2
H. H. Knapp. 6
W. P. Lawler, M. D.
J. N. Marston, M. D.
Thomas B. Smith, M. D. 5

Lynn
R. E. Hillard. 2
W. E. Holbrook, M. D. 2
W. R. Woodfall, M. D. 1

Malden
C. W. McClearn, M. D. 1

Marshfield
C. W. Stodder, M. D. 2

Melrose
John Timlin, M. D. 2

Melrose Highlands
Clarence P. Holden, M. D.
Paul H. Provandie, M. D. 1

Milton
A. W. Draper, M. D. V. 2
Charles R. Gilchrist, M. D. 1
W. C. Kite, M. D.
Jacob S. Lincoln. 2
Samuel D. Parker.

Nahant
Joseph T. Wilson. 1

Needham
A. E. Miller, M. D.
A. M. Miller, M. D.

New Bedford
J. T. Bullard, M. D. 2
E. H. Gammons.
W. G. Kirschbaum. 1
L. H. Richardson. 7
Manuel V. Sylvia, M. D. 2, 9

Newport, R. I.
Joseph W. Sampson.

Norwood
E. C. Norton, M. D.

Newton
W. F. Harbach. 2
Arthur Hudson. 5, 11.
A. Stanton Hudson, M. D.
Harry A. Stone. 3, 6
E. R. Utley, M. D. 10

New York, N. Y.
Col. W. F. Morse.

No. Brookfield
T. J. Garrigan, M. D.

No. Abington
F. G. Wheatley, M. D.

Palmer
J. P. Schneider, M. D. 1

Plymouth
W. G. Brown, M. D.

Providence, R. I.
C. V. Chapin, M. D. 12
F. P. Gorham.
Gardner T. Swarts, M. D. 13*

Rockland
J. C. Batchelder, M. D.
Gilman Osgood, M. D.

Salem
G. Arthur Bodwell. 1
Wm. H. Colbert. 2
Martin T. Field.
W. H. Gove.
Raymond L. Newcomb. 3, 4
A. N. Sargent, M. D.
Benj. R. Symonds, M. D.

Somerville
A. C. Aldrich. 2
Robert Burns.
Allen F. Carpenter. 1
W. H. Hitchings, V. S.
Wesley R. Lee, M. D.
F. L. Lowell, M. D.
A. E. Merrill, M. D.
Caleb A. Page.
A. R. Perry, M. D.
Edmund F. Sparrow. 2

So. Framingham
L. M. Palmer, M. D.

Springfield
A. L. Brown, M. D. 2
T. J. Collins. 1
H. C. Emerson, M. D. 3
Edward B. Hodskins, M. D.
James Kimball. 6
B. D. Pierce, V. S.

Southbridge
Humphrey C. Moynihan. 1
Joseph G. E. Page, M. D. 13

Three Rivers
Geo. J. Hebert. 2
S. O. Miller, M. D.

Taunton
Charles H. Macomber. 2
Edward J. Shannahan, M. D. 2
Henry H. Wilcox. 7

West Newton
Francis G. Curtis, M. D. 1
Geo. H. Ellis.

Waltham
H. D. Chadwick, M. D.
C. J. McCormick, M. D.
Marshall J. Mosher, M. D. 1
Charles A. Willis, M. D.

Watertown
Sumner Coolidge, M. D.
Vivian Daniel, M. D. 2
Julian A. Mead, M. D.

Waverley
L. B. Clark, M. D.

Westboro
D. P. Cilley, M. D.
Charles S. Knight, M. D. 2

Weston
F. T. Hyde, M. D. 2
F. W. Jackson, M. D.
S. Sanford Orr, M. D.

Whitman
C. E. Lovell, M. D. 2
A. A. MacKeen, M. D. 1

Winchendon
F. W. Russell, M. D. 1

Winthrop
A. B. Dorman, M. D.
H. J. Soule, M. D.

Woburn
George Buchanan. 2
Dennis S. Doherty 2
William H. Kelliher, M. D. 1

Worcester
F. H. Baker, M. D. 5
Geo. W. Batchelder. 2
W. T. Clark, M. D. 1, 10
James C. Coffey. 2
May S. Holmes, M. D.
Prof. L. P. Kinnicutt.
W. W. McKibben, M. D.
L. F. Woodward, M. D.

Minneapolis, Minn.
F. F. Wesbrook, M. D. 5*
(Honorary Member)

Members are requested to send to the Managing Editor corrections or changes desired in the names, addresses or (where members are connected with a Board of Health) in the titles given in this list.

Contributors of Regular Papers.

SAMUEL W. ABBOTT. M. D.,
Sec. Mass. State Bd. of Health.

DAVID D. BROUGH, M.D.
Med. Inspec. Boston Bd. Health.

ALEXANDER BURR, D. V. S.,
Veterinarian, Boston Bd. of Health.

PAUL CARSON, M. D.,
Boston Port Physician.

CHARLES V. CHAPIN, M. D.,
Supt. Health, Providence, R. I.

W. H. CHAPIN, M. D.,
Springfield.

H. LINCOLN CHASE, M. D.,
Agent, Brookline Bd. of Health.

H. W. CLARK,
Chemist, Mass. State Bd. of Health.

JAMES C. COFFEY,
Ex. Officer Worcester Bd. of Health.

FRANCIS G. CURTIS, M. D.,
Newton.

ELBRIDGE G. CUTLER, M. D.,
Boston.

FRANCIS P. DENNY, M. D.,
Brookline Bd. Health Bact. Lab.

SAMUEL H. DURGIN, M. D.,
Chairman, Boston Board of Health.

HARRISON P. EDDY,
Worcester Sewage Disposal Plant.

GEORGE H. ELLIS,
Wauwinet Farm.

PROF. HAROLD C. ERNST,
Harvard Medical School.

W. S. EVERETT, M. D.,
Hyde Park.

JAMES B. FIELD, M. D.,
Lowell.

G. W. FITZ, M. D.,
Cambridge.

X. H. GOODNOUGH, C. E.,
Engineer, Mass. State Bd. of Health.

CHARLES HARRINGTON, M. D.
Milk Inspector, Boston Bd. of Health.

ROBERT W. HASTINGS, M. D.,
Brookline.

H W. HILL, M. D.,
Boston Bd. of Health Bact. Lab.

MAY S. HOLMES, M. D.,
Worcester Isolation Hospital.

S. C. KEITH, S. B.,
Boston.

PROF. L. P. KINNICUTT,
Worcester Polytechnic Institute.

ATHERTON P. MASON, M. D.,
Fitchburg Bd. of Health Bact. Lab.

JOHN H. McCOLLOM, M. D.,
Boston City Hospital.

WILLIAM H. MITCHELL,
Boston.

FRANK L. MORSE, M. D.,
Med. Inspec., Mass. State Bd. of Health.

COL. WILLIAM F. MORSE,
New York.

J. ALBERT C. NYHEN,
Brookline Bd. of Health Bact. Lab.

W. H. PARK, M. D.,
New York Board of Health Lab.

AUSTIN PETERS. M. R. C. V. S.,
Mass. State Cattle Dept.

MRS. ELLEN H. RICHARDS,
Mass. Institute Technology.

MARK W. RICHARDSON, M. D.,
Boston.

B. R. RICKARDS, S. B.,
Boston Bd. of Health Bact. Lab.

PROF. WILLIAM T. SEDGWICK,
Mass. Institute Technology.

T. B. SHEA, M. D.,
Member, Boston Bd. Health.

PROF. THEOBALD SMITH,
Pathologist, Mass. State Bd. Health.

F. HERBERT SNOW, C. E.,
Brockton.

W. LYMAN UNDERWOOD,
Mass. Institute Technology.

JOHANNA VON WAGNER,
Yonkers, N Y.

HENRY P. WALCOTT, M. D.,
Chairman, Mass. State Bd. Health.

EDWARD R. WARREN,
Boston.

ROBERT SPURR WESTON,
Boston.

FRANKLIN W. WHITE, M. D.
Boston.

C. E. A. WINSLOW, M. Sc.,
Mass. Inst. Technology.

List of Members—Continued.

Holliston
N. C. B. Haviland, M. D. 2

Hyde Park
Edwin C. Farwell.
John A. Morgan, M. D.
William W. Scott. 2
Charles F. Stack, M. D. 1

Hanover
A. L. McMillan, M. D.

Jamaica Plain
Theobald Smith, M. D. 5*

Lancaster
Chester C. Beckley, M. D. 2
Allen G. Butterick. 2
Albert E. Harriman, M. D. 1

Lincoln
Stephen H. Blodgett, M. D. 2
Joseph S. Hart, M. D.

Lexington
George O. Whitney.

Lawrence
William Berger.
Charles E. Birtwell, M. D.
A. D. V. Bourget. 1
John T. Cahill, M. D.
T. J. Daly, M. D.
George S. Fuller, D. V. S.
Stephen de M. Gage. 5 *
F. W. Kennedy, M. D. 2
John A. Magee, M. D.
Victor A. Reed, M. D.
George W. Smith. 6
J. F. Winchester, V. S. 8

Leominster
C. E. Bigelow, M. D. 1
Fredson N. Grey. 2
H. N. Spring. 2, 6.

Lowell
William C. Doherty.
James B. Field, M. D.
J. Arthur Gage, M. D.
Thomas F. Harrington, M. D.
Leonard Huntress, M. D.
William B. Jackson, M. D. 2
H. H. Knapp. 6
W. P. Lawler, M. D.
J. N. Marston, M. D.
Thomas B. Smith, M. D. 5

Lynn
R. E. Hillard. 2
W. E. Holbrook, M. D. 2
F. E. Stone, M. D. 2
W. R. Woodfall, M. D. 1

Malden
C. W. McClearn, M. D. 1

Marshfield
C. W. Stodder, M. D. 2

Melrose
E. L. Grundy. 2
Clarence P. Holden, M. D.
Paul H. Provandie, M. D. 1
G. Houston Smith. 2
John Timlin, M. D. 2

Milton
A. W. Draper, M. D. V. 2
Charles R. Gilchrist, M. D. 1
W. C. Kite, M. D.
Jacob S. Lincoln. 2
Samuel D. Parker.

Nahant
Joseph T. Wilson. 1

Needham
A. E. Miller, M. D.
A. M. Miller, M. D.

New Bedford
J. T. Bullard, M. D. 2
E. H. Gammons.
W. G. Kirschbaum. 1
L. H. Richardson. 7
Manuel V. Sylvia, M. D. 2, 9

Newport, R. I.
Joseph W. Sampson.

Norwood
E. C. Norton, M. D.

Newton
W. F. Harbach. 2
Arthur Hudson. 5, 11.
A. Stanton Hudson, M. D.
Harry A. Stone. 3, 6
E. R. Utley, M. D. 10

New York, N. Y.
Col. W. F. Morse.

No. Brookfield
T. J. Garrigan, M. D.

No. Abington
F. G. Wheatley, M. D.

Palmer
J. P. Schneider, M. D. 1

Plymouth
W. G. Brown, M. D.

Providence, R. I.
C. V. Chapin, M. D. 12
F. P. Gorham.
Gardner T. Swarts, M. D. 13*

Rockland
J. C. Batchelder, M. D.
Gilman Osgood, M. D.

Salem
G. Arthur Bodwell. 1
Wm. H. Colbert. 2
Martin T. Field.
W. H. Gove.
Raymond L. Newcomb. 3, 4
A. N. Sargent, M. D.
Benj. R. Symonds, M. D.

Somerville
A. C. Aldrich. 2
Robert Burns.
Allen F. Carpenter. 1
W. H. Hitchings, V. S.
Wesley R. Lee, M. D.
F. L. Lowell, M. D.
A. E. Merrill, M. D.
Caleb A. Page.
A. R. Perry, M. D.
J. E. Richardson. 11
Edmund F. Sparrow. 2

So. Framingham
L. M. Palmer, M. D.

Springfield
A. L. Brown, M. D. 2
T. J. Collins. 1
H. C. Emerson, M. D. 3
Edward B. Hodskins, M. D.
James Kimball. 6
B. D. Pierce, V. S.

Southbridge
Humphrey C. Moynihan. 1
Joseph G. E. Page, M. D. 13

Three Rivers
Geo. J. Hebert. 2
S. O. Miller, M. D.

Taunton
Luke H. Howard. 18
Charles H. Macomber. 2
Edward J. Shannahan, M. D. 2
Henry H. Wilcox. 7

West Newton
Francis G. Curtis, M. D. 1
Geo. H. Ellis.

Waltham
H. D. Chadwick, M. D.
C. J. McCormick, M. D.
Marshall J. Mosher, M. D. 3
Charles A. Willis, M. D.

Watertown
Sumner Coolidge, M. D.
Vivian Daniel, M. D. 2
Julian A. Mead, M. D.

Waverley
L. B. Clark, M. D.

Westboro
D. P. Cilley, M. D.
Charles S. Knight, M. D. 2

Westminster
A. E. Mossman, M. D. 2

Weston
F. T. Hyde, M. D. 2
F. W. Jackson, M. D.
S. Sanford Orr, M. D.

Whitman
F. J. Henly, M. D.
C. E. Lovell, M. D. 2
A. A. MacKeen, M. D. 1

Winchendon
F. W. Russell, M. D. 1

Winthrop
A. B. Dorman, M. D.
H. J. Soule, M. D.

Woburn
George Buchanan. 2
Dennis S. Doherty 2
William H. Kelliher, M. D. 1

Worcester
F. H. Baker, M. D. 5
Geo. W. Batchelder. 2
W. T. Clark, M. D. 1, 10
James C. Coffey. 2
May S. Holmes, M. D.
Prof. L. P. Kinnicutt.
W. W. McKibben, M. D.
L. F. Woodward, M. D.

Minneapolis, Minn.
F. F. Wesbrook, M. D. 5*
(Honorary Member)

Contributors of Regular Papers.

SAMUEL W. ABBOTT, M. D.,
Sec. Mass. State Bd. of Health.

DAVID D. BROUGH, M.D.
Med. Inspec. Boston Bd. Health.

ALEXANDER BURR, D. V. S.,
Veterinarian, Boston Bd. of Health.

PAUL CARSON, M. D.,
Boston Port Physician.

CHARLES V. CHAPIN, M. D.,
Supt. Health, Providence, R. I.

W. H. CHAPIN, M. D.,
Springfield.

H. LINCOLN CHASE, M. D.,
Agent, Brookline Bd. of Health.

H. W. CLARK,
Chemist, Mass. State Bd. of Health.

JAMES C. COFFEY,
Ex. Officer Worcester Bd. of Health.

FRANCIS G. CURTIS, M. D.,
Newton.

ELBRIDGE G. CUTLER, M. D.,
Boston.

FRANCIS P. DENNY, M. D.,
Brookline Bd. Health Bact. Lab.

SAMUEL H. DURGIN, M. D.,
Chairman, Boston Board of Health.

HARRISON P. EDDY,
Worcester Sewage Disposal Plant.

GEORGE H. ELLIS,
Wauwinet Farm.

PROF. HAROLD C. ERNST,
Harvard Medical School.

W. S. EVERETT, M. D.,
Hyde Park.

JAMES B. FIELD, M. D.,
Lowell.

G. W. FITZ, M. D.,
Cambridge.

X. H. GOODNOUGH, C. E.,
Engineer, Mass. State Bd. of Health.

CHARLES HARRINGTON, M. D.
Milk Inspector, Boston Bd. of Health.

ROBERT W. HASTINGS, M. D.,
Brookline.

H. W. HILL, M. D.,
Boston Bd. of Health Bact. Lab.

MAY S. HOLMES, M. D.,
Worcester Isolation Hospital.

S. C. KEITH, S. B.,
Boston.

PROF. L. P. KINNICUTT,
Worcester Polytechnic Institute.

ATHERTON P. MASON, M. D.,
Fitchburg Bd. of Health Bact. Lab.

JOHN H. McCOLLOM, M. D.,
Boston City Hospital.

WILLIAM H. MITCHELL,
Boston.

FRANK L. MORSE, M. D.,
Med. Inspec., Mass. State Bd. of Health.

COL. WILLIAM F. MORSE,
New York.

J. ALBERT C. NYHEN,
Brookline Bd. of Health Bact. Lab.

W. H. PARK, M. D.,
New York Board of Health Lab.

AUSTIN PETERS. M. R. C. V. S.,
Mass. State Cattle Dept.

MRS. ELLEN H. RICHARDS,
Mass. Institute Technology.

MARK W. RICHARDSON, M. D.,
Boston.

B. R. RICKARDS, S. B.,
Boston Bd. of Health Bact. Lab.

PROF. WILLIAM T. SEDGWICK,
Mass. Institute Technology.

T. B. SHEA, M. D.,
Member, Boston Bd. Health.

PROF. THEOBALD SMITH,
Pathologist, Mass. State Bd. Health.

F. HERBERT SNOW, C. E.,
Brockton.

W. LYMAN UNDERWOOD,
Mass. Institute Technology.

JOHANNA VON WAGNER,
Yonkers, N Y.

HENRY P. WALCOTT, M. D.,
Chairman, Mass. State Bd. Health.

EDWARD R. WARREN,
Boston.

ROBERT SPURR WESTON,
Boston.

FRANKLIN W. WHITE, M. D.
Boston.

C. E. A. WINSLOW, M. SC.,
Mass. Inst. Technology.

To the JOURNAL OF THE MASSACHUSETTS
ASSN. OF BOARDS OF HEALTH.

607 *Sudbury Building, Boston, Mass.*

Please send the JOURNAL *to the following address for one year from* ....*190* .

Name ....

Address ....

....

Subscription Price, $1.00 per year.

....*190* .

Lightning Source UK Ltd.
Milton Keynes UK
UKHW02n0801140218
317658UK00007B/901/P

9 780483 608856